Fragments
From a Mobile Life

Margaret Sullivan

© 2019 Margaret Sullivan
Cover photograph and design © 2019 Susan Gardner
© Author's photograph by Jeanne D.D. Tifft, 2017

All rights reserved. No part of this book may be reproduced in any form, by any means, electronic or mechanical, without permission in writing from the author, except for brief quotations for the purpose of reviews.

The author is grateful to the editors of the publications where versions of these essays first appeared.

The Huffington Post as blogs in "The Grandmother ...." series: "Sex and Contraception" Jul. 17, 2013; "Our Many Santas" Dec. 25, 2013; "Tacloban and Multi-layered Memories" Jun. 22, 2014; "Moon Thoughts Forty-five Years Later" Jul. 21, 2014; "Uppity Woman" Aug. 19, 2014; "Curbing the Chicken Little Virus" Oct. 17, 2014; "Watch the Needle and Just Say Ouch," Jan. 30, 2015; "No Sense of Decency" May 17, 2016; "Debts and Trespasses" Sept. 9, 2016

The Foreign Service Journal: "Remembering Another Unforgettable Day" January 2012; "Creepy Critters We Have Known" September 2016

The Washington Post: "How Can I Stop the Coming?" Aug. 21, 1985

ISBN 978-0-9985140-4-8
Printed in the United States of America

RED MOUNTAIN PRESS
Santa Fe, New Mexico
www.redmountainpress.us

For Harriet, Next Sister,
Because she alone still shares most of my China life.

For Dan,
Because of a revolving door.

And for our gaggle,
Just because.

Contents

Preface	7
Eighty Is a Year	9
Where's Home?	13
The China Me	15
Watch the Needle and Just Say Ouch	21
Butter-and-Eggs	24
Soul Food: Course One	27
Celery and Olives	28
An "American Hillbilly"	30
Life with Mother	38
Debts and Trespasses	44
Short Corn	48
Our Panda	50
Soul Food: Course Two	51
A Whistling Girl…	52
No Sense of Decency	59
Becoming Global	61
In Retrospect	75
Memorial Days	77
Blame the Revolving Door	80
Soul Food: Third Course	84
Donning Multiple Identities	85
Soul Food: Fourth Course	90
Pan Am Flight 7	91
Two for the Price of One	96
Lists of Lists	99
"Two-fering"	106
In "Interesting Times"	112
Adding Building Blocks	118
Finding Friends	123
What's in a Word?	129
To Market, To Market	133
My Own Person?	135
Dancing on the Altar	137
Planting Daffodils	141
Who's Native?	146
House Home	149
Raising Rolling Stones	152
Which Kid, Which School?	164
Creepy Critters We Have Known	172
Culture Shocked	178
Once Upon a Yuan Bowl	183

Vietnamese Might-Have-Beens	185
April 4, 1968	190
Moon Thoughts	191
Whose Career?	193
Living with Histories	196
The Consul's Wife	206
Moon Glow	217
No More Two-fers, and Yet…	218
We Hadn't Been There	224
Curbing the Chicken-Little Virus	226
Working Woman	229
Releasing Assumptions	238
The Gift of a Road	243
Soul Food: Fifth Course	254
Passing I, March 1984	255
Rolling Back	257
My First Op-ed	269
Venice Lamb Redux	273
Wearing My Places	281
Passing II, March 1996	283
Aceh—Painting the Sky	285
Yang Bungsu	296
Sex and Contraception	300
Remembering Another Unforgettable Day	302
Soul Food: Sixth Course	304
What Is It about Shoes?	305
Genus americanus	307
Red Bottle, Yellow Rain	314
Tacloban and Multilayered Memories	318
Our Many Santas	320
Down-Sizing	323
Last Move?	327
Walking Sticks by the Door	328
Uppity Women	330
Yellow Dust	333
Afterward	337
Acknowledgments	340

Preface

Rolling stones, they say, gather no moss. Perhaps. Those of us who are human rolling stones gather moss of sorts: memories, objects, stories, lessons, values, meaning, purpose. These provide continuity and context to lives lived as sojourners in many places and times. Our "moss" meets us in odd moments and unexpected locations.

The goal, that years-ago afternoon in a Flemington, New Jersey, antique store, was a piece of cut glass for our daughter's tenth wedding anniversary present.

Something else drew my eyes down: a small, much-walked-on carpet. In traditional Chinese blues and taupes, it depicted trains of camels making their way toward a walled-city gate. The rug had been made in China about the same time in the 1930s that I had been.

Suddenly, I am not yet four. We—my mother, next sister Harriet, and I—are in a rickshaw going out of Peking's walled city toward Yenjing University.

At the city gate, a train of camels, two-humped and shaggy, plods past us from the Gobi desert. Our rickshaw continues along the flat, dusty road lined with poplars.

Many years later, a train carries me from Mongolia toward Beijing, past the familiarly gray, rural north China countryside, for the first time since I was six. Out the window, not the camels but a similar line of trees welcomes me home.

The rug with its camel trains and city gate guards my office—a cherished bit of my "moss"; a talisman of first memories and life lessons.

Eighty Is a Year

I'm past eighty. Having lived so long is a continuing surprise. As the shadows of a serious illness loomed and receded, I couldn't imagine getting here. My last half-century is a most welcome, unearned gift. These eighty-plus years have been a here-and-there, around the world succession of fragments with time marked by place—a disjointed mobile life that has, nonetheless, its own unique continuity. Each fragment is a new invention, living in a separate basket of memory. As the years go by, I am conscious of how simultaneously long and brief eighty-plus years can be, marked as it is by enormous change.

I was born into a world of Western imperialism and financial collapse, was a child in wartime and an adolescent in a time of recovery and revolution. I became an adult amid the flowering of newly independent nations in the hot zone of the Cold War, and a world locked in competition between capitalism and communism.

When I was young, ships took three weeks to cross the Pacific. After World War II, propeller planes took two days to go half way round the world. Today I can fly eighteen hours, non-stop, from Newark to Singapore.

At my birth, it took three months to receive an answer to a letter from China to Mississippi. Today a phone number tapped in Washington rings immediately in Canberra. A face on a screen here talks in real time to a face there.

I remember the death of Franklin Roosevelt, lived through Joseph McCarthy, Kennedy's assassination, and Watergate and Richard Nixon, celebrated the installation of Barack Obama, and voted for the first woman almost elected president. I know precisely where I was when Pearl Harbor, the Tet Offensive, and 9/11 happened.

I first heard news on a round-topped wooden radio, later saw it on a tiny black-and-white TV, and now watch talking heads and British mysteries on a huge, colored flat-screen or on a cell phone in my palm. What once took days and hours is now available twenty-four/seven.

I began writing by hand and continued with a typewriter. Now I compose on a computer, sending the results into cyberspace.

I came of age when most people assumed I would be a homemaker, but I became a two-for-the-price-of-one Foreign Service wife, and had my world expanded by the *Feminine Mystique*. Starting with portable pursuits, I found my own ways to develop skills and change expectations—mine and others'—in order to come into my own and break glass ceilings.

Now I am old. These eighty-plus years have given me much to puzzle over. Yet eighty is simply a number we inch up to then pass. From experience, I know my eighty is not the same "old" as my grandmother's. When I was twenty, eighty-year-old Grandmother Parks seemed ancient. She was the image of American Gothic: gnarled hands, wispy white hair knotted on her head, shirtwaist dresses, low sensible shoes, always a hat for church or shopping. She kept house in what had been her mother's drafty, big Victorian farmhouse but no longer cooked for company. She and the house in Springfield, Missouri, were central parts of my childhood. Then Granddad died. She moved to live with my mother.

Nor is my eighty the same as my mother's. When my mother was in her eighties, I was in my fifties. Daddy had died five years earlier. She lived alone in their long-time home in McLean, Virginia, keeping up the sprawling ranch house, tending her garden, and daily arranging fresh flowers in a crystal bowl on the dining room table Daddy had made. One day, after a dreadful hot summer and a bad case of shingles, she decided she needed to live in a retirement community. She took a year to let go of a lifetime of homemaking and move.

Even for the relatively active, eighty is not the new fifty. Eighty is "antiquey" when it comes to early-morning stiffness or the increasing complication of going up and down stairs or getting out of some chairs. Eighty means huffing up the gentlest hills, sometimes using a favorite Mongolian walking stick. "How are you?" people ask. "Vertical and verbal" is my standing answer.

Other times, eighty is younger than fifty. There's much to be curious about. I delight in shadows, sunsets, and clouds. I don't *always* have to ask one of my children before tackling the learning curve of a new technology.

Eighty is old enough to treasure being "The Grandmother" blogging on *Huffington Post*. Freed by age and experience, I say what I think about politics, life, and the spiraling world around us. I hope to be a voice of been-there-done-that or puzzlement without bombast. I seek words to describe who I am, who we are as a people, and what being an American, a human in the world, is.

Eighty is old enough to be outrageous. I buy the jazziest reading glasses at the drug store (red-rimmed lenses with black-and-white striped earpieces). It's taking home a red felt fedora that spoke to me at a bazaar and cocking it over my eye when I wear it to the dining room. It's sporting wild jackets with my jeans and sneakers and man-cut, long-since-white hair. It's embracing dangly earrings and having a granddaughter laugh when she says, "Gram'ma, that is so *you*."

Eighty is enjoying the comfort of partnering in a long marriage. I've been lucky, falling in love five or six times with the evolving person I see in him.

No one tells young-love couples about the quiet joys of aging. For us, there is the reassurance of each other's presence. The satisfaction we feel, most of the time, with the life we have lived together. We are happy with our children, nearing old themselves, and the children they have given the world, early adults who bring their significant others to meet the Grands. (We hope to see great grandchildren but not yet—I preach safe sex.)

We enjoy oft-told tales, recounted in tandem, as well as our private jokes. ("Think divorce rarely, murder often," we say, mostly teasingly.) Some memories are ours alone: a moonlight night on a beach in Bali, the ocean view from our Freetown bedroom, lovemaking in front of the fireplace in Mclean.

Old bodies have their own beauty even as they sag and crumple. They are exquisitely familiar, well lived in, and show it. In our mind's eye we retain the wonder of the first glimpses of each other's youth.

As curves become softer and backs stiffen, our bodies fail in some ways, not in others. Attraction finds different forms of expression even as old passions run stronger in memory than in possibility. The empty space between what was and what is is filled with other joyous expressions of ever-deepening intimacy: First morning kisses. Deep looks across the table. Coffee brought with the paper. The touch of hands, skin on skin. A tender pat in the middle of the night. His belly, a comforting pillow. There is the reassurance of the gentle breathing and occasional snorts from the pile of covers on the other side of the bed—and the apprehension of no longer hearing those breaths.

Individually and as a couple, we are adjusting to our changing realities. We are each slowing. Getting things done takes longer, but we are still doing them. He sings and watches sports. I write and explore photography. I've become addicted to taking naps and know when I miss one. He wakes early and, before anything else, reads the paper and does Sudoku, to make sure his mind still works.

His pills keep his blood from clotting and strengthen his memory. Mine keep me breathing, not wheezing. He has "hot flashes." I can't keep warm. Who pulls up the comforter? Who kicks it off?

We often walk holding hands, partly for the pleasure of it—we know that our time to walk that way is limited—and partly for added stability.

I keep track of things for both of us. The first thing I say to the man on the other side of the bed is, "Have you put on your ears?" With his hearing aids in, we plot the day. As he goes out the door, I run the oral checklist: "Keys? Cane?" At doctors' visits, I'm the memory and the ears.

We get through some days more smoothly than others. My voice stays calm, not hurtful. We laugh at misplaced things found in odd places or where I said they would be, even though he had "already looked there." Other days, his repeated questions and the accumulation of losts, not founds, is too much. *Come on!* I do not always react well. My speaking louder, more firmly, to be clear hurts him as if I were shouting.

The changes that restrict our lives are harder to make. One of the trials of aging is forcing ourselves to adjust to our limitations, especially when we would rather not. We have entered a time of decreased mobility and increased dependence on others. He no longer drives and feels deprived of his independence and the simple joy of driving. As when the kids were young, I'm the chauffeur, but only in the daytime and only when we're going to nearby locations. Lyft and Uber have entered our lives.

Giving up our condo balcony with its magnificent views of Washington was hard. I found myself asking: Can we let that go? We reluctantly made the decision to move to a continuing care retirement community in Falls Church, Virginia, where we could have our own apartment. We needed to make the move while we still could do it ourselves.

Unlike our other moves, this one is final.

For now, we are aging together, helping each other along this particular bend in our road. We take this passage as a blessing, certain that the end is much closer than the long-ago beginning. One of us will finish walking the road sooner than the other.

For me, eighty has inched by, precious fragment by precious fragment. Yet there is so much more to see. New ideas need digesting and commenting on. There are great-grandchildren to anticipate. I still ask, "What's next?"

Where's Home?

"Where's home?" or its corollary, "Where're you from?," is among the first questions we Americans ask each other. In our mobile country many of us started life elsewhere. We ask to orient ourselves and to discover commonalities that connect us.

For the most part, "Where's home?" means "What street?" "What state?" "What part of this country?" And if we share a place, one of us may ask, "Oh, did you know…?"

"Where's home?" isn't only a question of home as place. In a profound way, it's a question of how a particular sense of home as a location shapes who we are and how we see the world. Yes, we are Americans but we are also Texans, or South Dakotans, or New Yorkers. We are from a small town or a farm, the suburbs or a big city. None of these identifications is more "American" than another, simply different.

In another layer, we are often an amalgam of American and wherever our ancestors (or we ourselves) came from. As generations pass, we are less clearly *from* somewhere.

Perpetually curious about people and their lives, I frequently ask "Where's home?" Many people answer with good stories about how, where, and when they grew up and the values they absorbed. Listening to these stories has allowed me to glimpse the many ways each of us experiences the world.

Asking is tricky. While sometimes I get fascinating answers, other times, people take my curiosity as questioning their Americanness and are deeply affronted. I try to be mindful of how I phrase the question or whether I ask at all, especially if the person "appears" to come from "elsewhere." In asking "Where's home?"—in writing this paragraph—I am wading into the swamp of America's problematic, painful history of skin color, identity, and equality. The swamp is murkier still as immigration roils deeply divided partisan argument.

Never mind that I carry an invisible history of places. I see a familiar face and seek commonalities others, understandably, neither see nor hear. I recognize their indignation. With an uncomfortable history of people's reactions to my answer, I squirm when people ask where I am from.

I was born in China. It's a straightforward answer. Just not Iowa.

More completely I am from Tsinan, Shantung (as it was spelled then) Province, in north China. "What an exciting life," the askers often surmise. In some ways, it had its moments. For me, as for everyone, my early growing up was what it was and all I knew.

13

Other folks ask if that makes me Chinese. To Chinese, I am a "round eye" or a *da bizi* (big nose). By China's definition, a person is Chinese by blood, not place of birth. As a matter of US law my natural-born American parents transmitted citizenship to their children wherever we were born.

Often, when people ask where I am from, I think before I answer, considering if I want the conversation to shift to the whys and wherefores. I sometimes give a bland generic response like, "Here and there" or "Washington, DC." If I choose to be more precise, I might say Northern Virginia, home base for more than sixty years while my husband was in the Foreign Service (I think before I mention my Foreign Service life, too). I might comment that I went to elementary school in Missouri, or that my parents were from Texas and Missouri. These places sound "American," ordinary, not "other."

I have deep roots in many places, on both sides of the Pacific, with no lasting connection to any one piece of land. Although neither side of my family thinks much about it, our forbearers have lived on this continent for nearly four hundred years. They came to Virginia soon after the settlement of Jamestown. In the westward migration, Mother's people moved to North Carolina, Tennessee, and Missouri while Dad's branched off through Arkansas to Texas and ended up in Mississippi.

While we are a long line of storytellers, with Civil War accounts passed down at the dinner table, there are no stories of our predecessors' first arrival. We know the names—Matthews, Ellis, Parks, Preston, Keller, Winfield—are English. One family story is that we are part Cherokee. Given how Southern families spin tales, it may well be just that, a tale. Certainly, the possibility of Native American genes was visible in my father's "wooden nickel" nose and ruddy complexion.

My story, therefore, begins this way: In the '30s, my Texas-born Dad, Jerry Winfield, crossed the Pacific with his Missouri bride, Louise Winfield née Parks, to be a professor of public health and parasitology at Cheeloo University, a Christian institution in what is now spelled Jinan, Shandong, in north China. Jinan is the provincial capital, south and slightly east of Beijing, an ancient city of springs and temples, where the railroad crosses the Yellow River.

Being a China-born American is the bedrock of my complicated answer to "Where's home?"

The China Me

I was born on July 20, 1934, a year or so after my parents arrived in Jinan. Shandong had been blisteringly hot and parched that spring and summer. To usher me in, a storm thundered through, breaking the heat and ending a long drought. The letters announcing the arrival of first grandchild Margaret Ellis Winfield took six weeks to get to Mississippi and Missouri. In another six weeks, rejoicing responses reached Jinan.

One of Daddy's colleagues gave me a *mingzi* (Chinese name), written in the order of family name first: Wen Meilian. Wen, the Chinese family name already given to my parents, similar to the first syllable of Winfield; Meilian, my personal name, means "beautiful lotus blossom." Another colleague welcomed me with an auspiciously red, baby-sized padded silk cape and diminutive cap decorated with silver good-luck charms. Mother kept the cape and cap until they disappeared somehow but saved the charms. I made those into dangly earrings that ring as I move my head.

My baby book has snapshots of a round, dark-haired, big-eyed infant in a screened crib with a lid that closed to keep out bugs. Others photos show that same squirming dumpling being bathed in a small tin tub. In one of life's quirks, as and adult, through a totally non-China connection, I met Joan Green, who, when she was four or five years old, had come with her mother to help with my first bath.

From the time I began talking, I must have been bilingual, though I wasn't aware of it. I just learned to talk. It's funny how language evaporates, yet lingers. I no longer speak Chinese, haven't since I was six. I know some words, daily phrases, and a song or two. If I hear someone talking Chinese I sometimes understand the gist of what's being said. The muscle memory that links tongue and mouth to sound clearly remains. The distinctive *rrrrrh* formed off the back of the tongue comes effortlessly. So do the tones that differentiate meanings. If I ask a Chinese person how to say something and easily repeat it, they say, "You speak Chinese."

When I broke my arm as a twelve year-old and was asked to count as the anesthesia took hold, I scared the doctors by flipping from English, *"one, two…"* to Chinese, *"san, si…"*(three, four). Or so they told me later, as they tried to figure out what had happened.

In the same way I don't remember learning Chinese, I don't recall learning to use a fork and spoon or chopsticks. I just learned to eat—forks for some foods, chopsticks for others. I've since learned to eat appropriately with the fingers of my right hand, another story all together.

15

Unlike most of the other Christian universities in China, where the language of instruction was English, classes in Cheloo were taught in Chinese. Dad's Chinese was so fluent that he created much of the scientific vocabulary for public health and sanitation necessary to educate to a rising generation of Chinese doctors.

Our campus families were Chinese, English, Scottish, Canadian, and, like us, American. Although everyone attended the campus United Church, the missionary faculty and staff, sent by different boards of Foreign Missions, belonged to various denominations. A few were Presbyterians, as we were. Others were Methodists or affiliated with the Church of Scotland. I came to learn in retrospect that, in a mission context, denomination is a more identifying distinction than nationality.

We children weren't concerned with such things. We thought about familiar adults and playmates. The Sargents were in the house on one side of us—two boys, the same age as my next sister, Harriet, and me. The Ferrises were through the hedge on the other side—three boys; the youngest, Dougie, my age, was my first "love," or at least my first kiss. My best girl friend, Sheena Scott, lived across the campus.

My blue eyes and wavy, deep brown hair weren't the same as the straight, bobbed black hair and black eyes of many of my playmates. I never thought about that, then, either. To this day, I feel a familiarity, a natural comfort, and an ease in a group of Asians, especially Chinese. Whether I know these particular people or not, it's like being among "home-folks" from the childhood world I first knew. They may not see me as familiar, but I relax among them.

In those years, our lives centered on the campus. The classroom buildings were two-storied, boxy and charcoal-brown, with gray tile roofs that turned up at the end. (I learned later this was to force spirits, which only travel in straight lines, to fly back up into the air.) Around the rest of the grounds were faculty housing, a chapel, sports fields, and lawns. A camphor tree was near the center of the campus. Its lowest branch, like monkey bars, was perfect to swing from by my knees, my skirt flopping down over my face. Between classes, paths crisscrossing the campus filled with students. Everyone walked, or like Daddy, rode bikes. The main campus was outside Jinan's ancient city wall with its huge gate. The medical school and hospital were just inside the gate. We were regularly in and out the gate and around that part of the old city.

For me, the core of this comfortable universe was our high ceilinged, two-storied, Western-style house and its good climbing tree out front. Mummy had taught me the "rule of three": Always have two feet and one hand, or two hands and one foot, solidly placed as you climb. That rule helped even if it didn't keep branches from breaking. When I fell with a *ker-bump*, she came running.

Our glassed-in playroom was upstairs. Daddy often sat on the floor playing blocks with us. First he would have us organize the blocks by size, making a mini lumberyard. *Then* we could start building. One fall Mummy spilled a whole bottle of cod liver oil on the radiator. The room smelled *awful* all winter. We played with the blocks anyway.

Mummy ran a kindergarten for faculty children in our backyard. Off to one side, there was a hill-like mound of packed earth—how it got there, who knows. We ran up and down it, playing a form of King of the Mountain.

The heart of our life was family: Daddy, Mummy, Harriet, Wang Nainai (Grandmother Wang, the round-faced amah who helped take care of us), Cook (tall and angular, whose name I've long forgotten), and me.

Small kids don't yet know what Daddy does—he's just Daddy. As I grew up, I learned our daddy was a doctor of public health and parasitology (a worm doctor, as I would later say). In China, because sanitation was dreadful and diseases such as cholera, typhoid, and amoebic dysentery were rampant, his research about improving hygiene and public health was vital. The young doctors he taught became China's next generation of public health officials.

Day-to-day living meant absolute ways of keeping safe and healthy. Beyond the ordinary instruction to wash our hands, we were to never drink *anything* from the tap, *ever*, not even for brushing teeth. Bottles of boiled water were kept in the bathroom. Dad and Mummy instructed Cook that the water had to be kept at a rolling boil for twenty minutes before it was bottled in sterile containers.

There were also the instructions about food: Eat only *cooked* food served stove hot, *never* anything raw. There was *no* way to wash raw vegetables so you wouldn't get parasites or diseases from eating them that way. Fruit had peels. The outside had to be washed in boiling water, then peeled—we never simply bit into an unpeeled apple or pear. Daddy was graphic about how Chinese farmers used night soil as fertilizer on the vegetables we ate. If food wasn't cooked or sterilized, the soil could pass on amoebae and other parasites to us. Flies were also disease-carriers. Even so, the sticks of brilliant-red, sugar-roasted crabapples (attracting swarms of flies) sold on the street in the fall looked *so* tempting.

"Wear shoes. Hook worms will dig into your feet and climb into you," Daddy preached. When I got worms—not hookworm but ascaris—Daddy kept the long, grayish-white one that had come out of me in a glass tube. He loved bringing it out and showing it to everyone so we could talk about intestinal parasites, how we got them and why they were bad for us. We never learned that discussing parasites or night soil was *not* appropriate dinner-table talk.

The Japanese invaded our part of China in 1937, when we must have been in the States for a short furlough. After the occupation, every time we went through the gate to the medical school or other parts of the old city, we had to stop at the checkpoint manned by Japanese soldiers. Many of them, most likely missing their own children, talked with us. One always had small gifts for us; Harriet still has a string of stuffed, two-humped camels he gave us.

The checkpoint and the soldiers became as routine as the rest of life: roaming the campus; playing with friends and the students; asking questions and generally exploring; watching Daddy play baseball, always with a wad of gum in his mouth; going with Mummy and Daddy off campus in rickshaws; and, finally, when I was a "big girl," starting at the little school at which some of the other mothers taught.

Fields of *gaoleong* (sorghum) were outside the campus beyond a road that wooden-wheeled carts had cut deep over time-beyond-knowing. The "fingers down the blackboard" squeal of those wooden wheels still shrieks in my ears. My mind's eye sees blue-clad coolies jogging along, their loads, suspended from the poles balanced across their shoulders, swinging with the rhythm of their footsteps. That Chinese faded, everyday-blue, lighter than indigo, is still one of my favorite colors.

Most summers that I was old enough to remember we spent at the beach in Beidahe, splashing in the water and making drip castles. One summer, or maybe it was early fall, when I must have been three or maybe four, we were in Peking. Daddy studied more scientific Chinese while Mummy kept Harriet and me occupied climbing stairs in the building where we were staying. I still hear her warbling: "We are climbing Jacob's ladder..."

My earliest memory is from then. The three of us were in a rickshaw going to Yenjing University. As we approached the city gate, along the other rickshaws, carts, and coolies carrying their loads, we had to stop to let a train of two-humped camels plod in from the Gobi. They passed. We continued out through the gate and down the long, flat plain tree lined road to the university.

Jinan was, still is, known for its lakes and temples. Occasionally, we took rickshaws across town to the big lake, where there were small boats and old pavilions. One pavilion had a long, gentle flight of stone steps flanked by wide stone bannisters, worn slick by centuries of children sliding down them, something children still did.

Oh, how I wanted to join them. But, no, we couldn't do that, Mummy explained explicitly: Small Chinese children wore slit pants and used their urine to keep the banister slick enough to slide on.

One morning during what we didn't yet realize was our last fall in Jinan, the Sargent boys, Dougie Ferris, Sheena Scott, Harriet, and I were playing in the yard.

"*Lai, lai* (come, come)," Cook and Amah called urgently, hurrying us into the house. A dust storm descended with a strong wind and a menacing yellow-gray cloud. They covered our faces, bandit-like, with wet handkerchiefs. Mother lit candles. (We had electricity at night, but I don't remember daytime lights; maybe the campus generator was off in the daytime.) Daylight turned into dust-choking dark as we waited out the storm. How long I couldn't say. It seemed like an extremely long time until it passed and we could see again. In its wake, Amah faced inches-thick dust to sweep out of the house.

All told, our "curiosity bumps," as Daddy called our desire to know about the world around us, were well nurtured. There was always something to see or learn. We sometimes put snails on our arms to watch them crawl, leaving slime trails. Daddy helped us find lovely crawling shells or tiny fish in the tidal pools at Beidahe. He made up stories about a "water dwarfey" that "talked" to the mosquito larvae or dragonflies in a freshwater lake he had worked at in America. Mummy used grown-up words with real meanings, never baby talk; we did too. Thus our curiosity about the world around us was nurtured and valued. *Why? How? What's that?* Those were good questions, with proper answers to be given or found.

Being inventive went with curiosity. Daddy happily told his sister in a letter in August 1940: "...Margaret is in an inventive mood these days. She made a Kodak out of an ink box—holes to look thru—a button to press—a tripod to rest it on while she takes pictures. She goes running around to get good pictures of people or scenes. Then she draws the pictures she has taken."

By December 1940, war was looming. Suddenly Mummy, Harriet, and I were going back "home"—whatever grown-ups meant by *home* to America, wherever that was. I learned later that the State Department had commandeered three ships to evacuate American women, children, and "unnecessary men" around Asia.

Daddy, like so many men who considered themselves "necessary," was staying to continue teaching. The family took the train to the port city of Tsingtao. We blew kisses and waved goodbye to a disappearing Daddy as the tender went further into the harbor. Mother, Harriet, and I climbed aboard the *S.S. Mariposa* to cross the

Pacific. I was six. Except for three months in 1943, we didn't see our father until the war was over. By then, I was twelve, almost a teenager.

I didn't return to China for over half a century, partly because of politics, then lack of opportunity. Later, my husband and I went to Shanghai (where he grew up), then other times to Beijing, Xian, and down the Yangtze. I haven't been back to Jinan, that essential home-place of my heart, where I am literally from. The China-me remains deep-in-the-gut real. Shaped by memory, it has informed what would came later.

Watch the Needle and Just Say Ouch

Getting shots—regularly and often—has been a fact of my life. Today, as I write, it was a flu shot.

In the teaching hospital in north China where I was born, newborns were vaccinated for smallpox before they left the hospital and again every week until there was a "take." When one big "pox" emerged, the doctor knew the body had used the vaccine (an attenuated live virus) to generate its own immunity. That was twenty-six inoculations in my case. Mothers' milk was assumed to provide babies with natural immunity for about six months to diseases like smallpox. But Dr. Scott, our pediatrician, had lost a nursing three-month-old she was caring for to smallpox and wasn't risking such an unnecessary death again. At that time in that part of the world, smallpox was rampant. Only the fortunate few were vaccinated.

Along with those smallpox vaccinations came all the other childhood inoculations of the day—diphtheria, whooping cough, and tetanus. As a five-year-old, I overheard Mother consoling Cook, whose son in the village had died of lockjaw.

"What's lockjaw, Mummy?"

"A disease that made his jaw muscles freeze so he couldn't swallow. He cut himself on something dirty. Germs got into the cut and caused an infection. That's why you had the tetanus shot, so you won't get that disease." Even so I had bad dreams about my jaws locking.

We also had cholera and typhoid shots. Those diseases were rampant, too. The Japanese, who'd overrun our part of China, were concerned about the possibility of epidemics, especially cholera. Everyone was required to carry a certificate showing they'd been vaccinated. Even so, when a single case appeared, the Japanese soldiers set up blockades, vaccinating everyone, certificate or not.

Dad worked in the medical school at the university. He also went regularly to the leprosarium on the edge of the campus to teach health and hygiene. This included the importance of using sterile needles, cleaning up trash, and covering food to minimize disease carried by flies. In the small museum med students had developed for the leprosarium, the model fly, which the lepers assumed was an American one, was a thousand times the size of a real one. "If American flies are that big, we'd be scared, too," they would say.

Knowing that it was essential to be shot by a clean needle, one of the lepers proudly told Dad how, at a Japanese blockade, he had found a way to make sure his cholera injection was given with one. "I counted," he reported. "They were changing the needle after ten people. I let people get in front of me so I would get a clean needle."

21

When Dad repeated the story he always wondered how the nine people who followed the storyteller were affected. With an eye roll, he noted, however, that his lesson about sterile needles had stuck.

Even after we got back to the States, communicable diseases were a concern; classroom exposure and childhood diseases went hand in hand. As an eight-year-old, I spent a week in bed in a darkened room with a high fever and a measly rash. I wasn't allowed to read or color. I just stared at a ceiling covered with silver wiggly-worm paper. Mother and the doctor were afraid that the measles, for which there was no shot then, would damage my vision.

The next year I was covered in itchy chicken pox. I still have a scar on the side of my nose to show for it.

The summer of 1949, swimming pools were closed due to a polio epidemic. We stayed out of large crowds. Pictures of children wearing leg braces or living in iron lungs filled the newspapers, fueling parents' and children's nightmares.

When my own babies came along in the late 1950s and early 1960s, they had the standard childhood shots, including the new polio vaccine. Because we lived out of the country, they (and we) needed to be immunized against tropical diseases. That meant shots for cholera, typhoid, yellow fever, rabies, and, to protect against hepatitis, gamma globulin.

Childhood diseases were a different matter, as we found out when we were living in Kaduna, Nigeria. Soon after the new consul arrived, without his wife, the American ambassador came from Lagos for a visit. In the consul's wife's absence, I was the default hostess/manager for a large reception for the ambassador at the consul's house. I was also responsible for a dinner for the ambassador and the consul (and one or two others), which was to be held after the reception, across town at our house.

I was prepared for day of going back and forth between both places to ensure everything went off without a hitch. But before I had even gotten up, the first, then the second, and finally the third of our gaggle appeared looking like chipmunks with cheeks full of nuts. Mumps. No shots for them yet. Thank goodness for Nanny that day. At least the boys got the disease before puberty, when it threatens to cause sterility.

Two years later, back in the States, our then five-year-old daughter came down with rubella, which she probably contracted from a kindergarten classmate. Shots for those came a couple of years later. In an odd way, we were relieved. If women get rubella during pregnancy, the fetus could be seriously deformed. Now our daughter would have lifelong immunity.

In 1966, the day before all the Sullivan cousins and their parents were to gather at our house for Christmas, one sister-in-law called to tell us her brood had chicken pox. "Should we stay home?"

After a quick consultation, we learned that the other cousins had already had chickenpox. Our kids hadn't. We decided to get it over with and expose them. Everyone came, sick kids and all. Two weeks later, almost to the hour, each of our four kids popped poxes. It was done in one fell swoop, instead of being passed from one child to another over the course of the winter.

When our children, in turn, were parents in the late 1980s and early 1990s, their children had what had become a wide range of routine shots. The chicken pox vaccine didn't come into common use until 1995. Consequently our grandchildren only caught chicken pox, not the rest of the diseases their parents or I got as children.

Lesson learned: Vaccinations work. Dan and I were part of the original trial for the shingles vaccine, which works. A second version is even better. Smallpox has been eradicated. The development of safe, effective vaccines for once common diseases—measles, tetanus, mumps, whooping cough, chicken pox, polio—is one of the major successes of medicine. Ever.

One more lesson: When my sister and I were little and had to have lots of shots, we, like all little kids, didn't like it. To this day, I can hear my dad patiently giving us important advice to help us through the ordeal. I passed it on to my children, who told their kids. Tell yours; it works:

"You need this shot to keep you from getting sick. Watch the needle go in. It stings a little. Just say ouch."

BUTTER-AND-EGGS

Butter-and-eggs—shaggy "weeds" with pale yellow flowers, a splash of orange on their throats, and small tails like miniature snapdragons—appear beside roads in patches of rocky ground in mid-summer.

These flowers evoke a here-there, where's-home moment for Emily Treadup, the main character in Pulitzer Prize–winning author John Hersey's 1985 novel *The Call*. One summer day in the 1920s, Emily, a harried, worn-down missionary wife, is walking near the beach at Beidahe in north China, where she and her children are escaping the heat and a rampaging warlord. Unexpectedly, she spots the hauntingly familiar pale yellow blossoms. For a moment, she is wistfully transported to her tranquil girlhood in upstate New York, where butter-and-eggs were one of summer's regular joys.

Hersey, the China-born son of missionaries, no doubt loosely based the novel on his parents, who were from near Syracuse. A tome, *The Call* places his characters in the often bloody, evolving history of China in the early decades of the twentieth century. The book explores the tensions within the missionary community between those who felt they were "called" to preach the Word to "the heathen" and those who went to teach and introduce modern medicine and science.

Butter-and-eggs and the book are oddly linked to a poster-sized black-and-white photograph of a little girl that hung for years in my parents' powder room. It now hangs on my wall. Her grin is toothy. Her dark, chin-length hair is held to one side with a barrette. Her well-above-the-knobbly-knee-length skirt blows in the breeze as the sturdy child shows off a tiny silvery fish. Just where she's standing is not clear from the photograph, but the crinkle around her eyes says that she's happy.

In my memory's eye, the dress is lettuce-green dotted swiss trimmed with pale pink rickrack. It's one of a pair Grandmother Winfield made in Mississippi and sent to us in China. Harriet was less than happy about the matching dresses in two sizes. She not only wore her own, but then, when she grew into it, my larger hand-me-down twin. On this sunny afternoon in July 1940, my sixth birthday, we were celebrating on top of the flat rocky mound at the end of Baby Beach at Beidahe. Where I got the fish, I have no idea.

As I reconstruct it, 1940 was the third (and last) summer we spent in the cluster of houses on a rise above the curved beach where missionary families gathered to escape the oppressive heat of interior towns. As we had other years, one morning early in that warm summer, we clambered onto the train in Jinan and chugged across the

Shandong peninsula. At one stop, Daddy bargained with someone through the window for tangerines. Since intestinal parasites and other germs made eating away from home risky, Mummy washed the tangerines with hot water from the thermos we always took when we traveled. Harriet and I held the tangerines in our left hands while Daddy, whose hands were also washed, peeled most of the skin from the top, leaving the bottom skin as a base. Mummy carefully rinsed our right hands with more hot water. Using that freshly washed hand we rolled the segments out of the bottom peel and popped them in our mouths. I still feel the sweet tangerine juiciness trickling down my chin.

Late in the day, the train pulled into the final station. We were piled into rickshaws or hoisted onto donkeys. With coolies trotting along, our bags suspended from poles across their shoulders, everyone moved in a long file down several miles of stony road to the house.

Our Beidahe house —several rooms with a tile roof built around an enclosed front courtyard—sat by the path down to the beach. We could easily race down to the water. The days were filled with jumping and splashing in the waves (well, those gentle swells seemed like waves to a small person); building drippy sand castles, then watching them disappear as the tide rolled in; and late afternoon picnics at the beach. I must have had some basic paddle-and-kick swimming lessons, too, because I have always known how to swim. I just don't remember being taught.

The day the Puffed Rice Man came was a highlight of that sixth-birthday summer. Several children who were roughly my age and stayed in the houses around ours gathered in our courtyard. The Puffed Rice Man set up his big machine with a limp cotton bag hanging on the end, lit a fire in the bottom, poured rice inside a pan of sorts hooked to the bag, and pumped a bellows. The fire hissed louder and louder. We waited, dancing in anticipation until— BOOM!—the rice exploded, filling the dangling bag to bulging with our summer's supply of dry breakfast cereal.

My most vivid memory is of the visit of Dr Annie Scott, a tall, dark haired lady who stayed with us for several weeks. Mother and Daddy's close friend and one of several single-lady missionaries we had known forever as a courtesy aunt, Auntie Scott, she who ordered the smallpox vaccinations, taught pediatrics at the Cheeloo medical school and had doctored me, Harriet, and the other children on the campus since we popped into the world.

In the late 1930s, when I was a mother myself, *my* mother wrote to Auntie Scott to tell her that Dan, my US Foreign Service husband, and I were taking our young children to live in Kuala Lumpur, then-

Malaya, where he had been assigned to the American embassy. Auntie Scott had led a team at Duke to research pediatric TB and had become one of the world's experts in the disease. She took time to send me a handwritten letter about the illness. "Don't worry" if the children catch TB, she wrote. Her new research demonstrated that a two-year's course of a low-dose antibiotic would make them well. We were always her "babies," to be medically cared for and guided.

That summer Auntie Scott, who loved botany, introduced us to wildflowers. Many days, a group of us traipsed after our gypsy auntie, tramping around, mostly along paths near the house. She would point out this wildflower or that, showing us how to pick samples. We took them back to the house. Then, carefully, we put them between two sheets of absorbent paper, which we placed in her flower press for several days until they were flat and dry. After that, we mounted them in a book, labeling them with the proper botanical words as well as with the everyday English names.

The flower that sticks in my mind, I know now, was a low-growing member of the pea family. It had small stalks of puffy blossoms; pale yellow, almost white, lower petals; and darker yellow-orange petals curled like a ball in the center with a nearly orange stamen—*Linaria vulgaris*, commonly called "butter-and-eggs." They sprouted everywhere, hugging the rocky ground, and soon became familiar friends: "Look Auntie Scott, butter-and-eggs."

Fast forward to 1986. More than forty-five years earlier we had been evacuated from China, leaving Daddy behind. After he rejoined the family, the six of us moved several places. Finally, Mother and Dad settled in Mclean, Virginia. Dad had died. Mother lived in their house alone. My own Foreign Service family had rolled around the world. When my husband in due course retired, we settled back into our own house down the street from Mother. John Hersey's *The Call* was a best seller the year we moved back. I devoured it before I gave it to Mother.

One afternoon that summer, I was walking along the top of the hill a couple of blocks from our house when, unexpectedly, I saw growing wild by the side of the road, my familiar friend: butter-and-eggs. Suddenly I wasn't a middle-aged woman in Northern Virginia but a six-year-old girl, hiking the paths behind the house in Beidahe. Each summer after that, I happily watched for their reappearance. For the fictional Emily Treadup, for Hersey's mother and for me, in some profound, ingrained way, "home" is where each of us first met those pale yellow flowers.

Soul Food: Course One

"I may not look Chinese but my stomach is."

Definition: jiaozi—*a steamed or boiled dumpling made with meat (*rou, *usually pork), mixed with chopped cabbage, ginger, onion, garlic, soy sauce, and sesame oil, wrapped in thin wheat flour dough, and served with a soy and vinegar dipping sauce.*

Jinan, Shandong, China, February 1940

The *thunk, thunk, thunk* of Cook's cleaver mincing the meat and cabbage alert the household. It's *jiaozi*-making day. He rolls circular wrappers, then, with Amah's help, stuffs and crimps, stuffs and crimps. Before long *jiaozi* fill trays on the screened-in porch off the kitchen. On my tippy-toes, I can just see the neat rows of pinched-edged dumplings, smaller than my six-year-old-fist. The porch is bone-chillingly cold. The dumplings will keep for New Year's happy eating.

I love *doufu* (bean curd) that slips smoothly down the throat with its nutty, "I've known forever" flavor. I also love the neighbor's *mo mo*, meat–filled steamed buns that are usually round. Sometimes her *mo mo* are interesting shapes—fish, or porcupines with spiky quills all over. Then there's *bai cai,* the not-quite-round, pale, crinkly-leafed, almost-sweet cabbage, stored under heaping piles of straw during the winter, when it is a staple vegetable.

Jiaozi are best. Cook brings steamy plates of them to the table. I bite into the slightly chewy wrapper, feeling the *swish* of a burst of juicy, meaty delight. *Yum. More.* Dipping each in vinegar-spiked soy sauce, we eat one two-bite dumpling after another. "*Chi bao le*" (contented full).

Celery and Olives

The Matson Line's *SS Mariposa* was a sleek luxury liner for well-heeled vacationers. Usually plying the Pacific from San Francisco to New Zealand with stops at Hawaii, Samoa, Fiji, and Australia, it had never had passengers like those that boarded in Tsingtao, China, in late November 1940: Evacuees, not vacationers; women, children—lots of children, including Harriet and me—and only a few men. In anticipation of World War II, the State Department had commandeered it to evacuate non-essential Americans, mostly missionaries but also some businesspeople, from north China and Japan.

My six-year-old memory of the ship, and the voyage it took us on, is spotty. The ship was immense (at least to me) with a dining room full of tables covered with white cloths. I still see the great swooping staircase wrapped around an elevator, going from deck to deck.

The elevator was marvelous, at least to children like me who had never seen one before and had always climbed stairs. What fun to ride up and down! The older boys—high-energy ten- or eleven-year-olds who ran in a pack—learned quickly that they could punch the call button, run up the stairs to the next deck, punch it again, and then gallop back down and punch it again, keeping the whole system confused. The crew was not amused.

The ship picked up more passengers in Japan—Kobe, I think. Japanese soldiers boarded to inspect the new-passenger boarding process and to otherwise check out things. We were about to sail when a great commotion erupted. One of the Japanese officers was missing his samurai sword. The ship could not sail until it was found.

Passengers were gathered in the lounge while every inch of the ship was searched. Tension built. Several agitated hours later, the sword was found stuffed into the ship's laundry. The crew was certain one of the missionary kids had stolen it. The missionaries were equally sure it was the crew who had made away with it. In any case, to everyone's relief, the sword was returned, the soldiers left the ship, and we set sail again.

Somewhere in the middle of the Pacific, we hit a storm with seas rolling so hard that rails had to be put up on the edges of the dining tables to keep dishes from crashing onto the floor. At our table, the rails—and our hands—successfully kept the sliding, clattering dishes from spilling.

Not so at a nearby table.

One of the few men on the ship was big, and not just to a six-year-old. He was *big* big, by any definition. The gossip, as I remember, assumed he was embarrassed to be "unnecessary" when most of the men had stayed in China. His wife was not well, so he was returning to the States with her and their children. On the night of the big storm, the ship took a particularly huge roll. A thunderous crash resounded across the dining room. The food on that family's table had broken through the rail, landing, along with one of the children, on the man, whose chair had fallen over, sending him rolling across the floor. He came to a dead stop at the foot of a lady at the next table. I retold the story frequently, always ending "at the foot of a lady." As a six-year-old, the ridiculousness of the image and saying it that way made me laugh. I still snicker thinking back.

Finally we docked in the United States, I guess in San Francisco, and crossed the country to Springfield, Missouri, on the train. I have no memory of that. I just know we wound up there.

The lasting highlight of the trip was the first night at sea. Nothing seemed organized. Everyone—the crew, the passengers, us—was uneasy. The kitchen was slow. Mummy, five months pregnant with the baby who would be our next sister, Nancy, was trying to keep Harriet and me, two fidgety, discombobulated, hungry four- and six-year-olds, calm and quiet.

"Here, why don't you try this," she suggested, handing us sticks of celery from the dish on the table. It was crunchy and…raw—a novel experience as we left a world where everything had to be cooked to be safe. Harriet and I gobbled it up. Then we went through the carrot sticks, also raw. Still no dinner.

"Why don't you try one of these? They have pits in them," Mummy said as she offered us black olives, not sure we would like something that strange. We did, polishing them off, too, before the meal finally arrived.

Mother later admitted she was almost sorry she'd introduced us to olives. After that, she said, she "never got any." As we were growing up and had them as a treat for Thanksgiving and birthdays, the family rule was three pits on the plate. (Mother's effort, I presume, to limit how many we ate so others got some). No one ever mentioned the pits under the table.

When I eat celery or olives, which I love, I'm back on that trip on the *Mariposa* taking my first taste of America.

An "American Hillbilly"

With that voyage, I had crossed the Pacific to a new life. I was no longer a Cheeloo campus child. Abruptly, I was living in America, a remote place where, essentially, I felt out of step. Although I doubt I could—or would—have put words to it, in a way I hadn't before, I "disappeared."

I didn't know then, either, or for a number of years, that I was an American—whoever that was (and is). Labels, more amorphous identities, were added later. I only knew myself as Margaret Ellis Winfield. It was exciting to know my complete name, including my initials MEW, like the sound of a cat.

Harriet and I were plopped in the middle of a huge family: grandparents, great aunts and uncles (many of them until then just names attached to stories or pictures or Christmas packages) as well as neighbors and a church community—all strangers to us, even though they knew who we were. In fact there were two groups of "family strangers," Mother's and Daddy's.

When we got to the States that December 1940, we went directly to Mother's people in Springfield, Missouri. Sister Nancy was born in April. By the following August, we moved to Magnolia, Mississippi, to live with Daddy's parents. In both places, rather than being campus children, we were our grandparents' grandchildren who had returned from some strange place. For the first time in my life I consciously felt different.

This new world smelled somehow bland. Sometimes there was a whiff of the sweetness of rain or cut grass or sharp car fumes or frying onions. But for the most part it was just…flat. There was none of home's comforting, heady mix of cooking fires, food, and sewage. But…we could go barefooted, eat raw vegetables, and drink and brush our teeth with water straight from a tap. *That* took getting accustomed to.

Even though everyone spoke English, it sounded peculiar. We hadn't been in Springfield long when Aunt Gertrude, mother's sister, mimicked my "Mummy," exaggerating the British pronunciation I must have used.

"You sound so funny, Margaret."

Funny? I'd never thought of that.

I felt even more out of place.

In a matter of time "Mummy" was gone, mostly replaced by "Mother." (I never took to using "Mama," commonly used in the South, and we never called her "Mom," either.)

Sometimes I liked the attention I received for being new and different. I welcomed, perhaps even asked for, the opportunity to "say a few words," like Mother sometimes did at church or in meetings, when she told people about our time in China.

I spoke in Sunday school once—I think I was a third grader then, in Springfield, back from Magnolia. Whether I was asked or I offered to "say a few words," I forget. Somewhere between remembering and making it up, I recounted this vivid detail as Truth:

"There was an old Chinese woman whose husband died. She lived in a village. Chinese believe the dead come back to Earth again in a different form. The old woman thought her husband had come back as a huge pink pig. She kept the pig inside her house. Whenever she went out, she took the pig with her everywhere …"

I still hear my child-self all too clearly, but now with chagrin. It didn't take long to learn that telling tales or talking about China was not a good idea. Living in China made me "odd"—particularly to my classmates.

Soon after we arrived in Springfield from China, Mother enrolled me in the first grade in the neighborhood elementary school, Phelps, where several teachers had known my mother before she was married. It was not at all like my Jinan school, which had two rooms and other friends' mothers for teachers. This new school was a dull yellow-orange brick, with long halls and lots of classrooms, upstairs and down. I finished the last half of the first grade in Miss Bennett's class.

Sometime in the summer, we moved to Magnolia, a two-stoplight town in Mississippi, where Granddaddy Winfield was the Methodist pastor. Second grade there, going to a big consolidated elementary and high school, was my first full year in an American school. Classes started in early August. Then we had several weeks off in September when cotton was ready to be picked. Some of the older students must have worked in the fields, but not us little ones.

In those first months in the States, it hadn't taken me long to have a Mizz-urah accent. The next year I developed a slow Mizzippi one, reverting to Mizz-urah when we moved back to Mother's hometown. My talk was quickly full of "yes'em" and "no, sir." Mother and Grandmother Winfield made it abundantly clear we shouldn't say "ain't" or, heaven forbid, "I ain't got nary," although I heard both from my Mississippi classmates. Since then, my English has been chameleon-like, blending with wherever I am (except when I am talking—a bit more distinctly—to non-native English speakers). When I am back in the South or tired, I feel my mouth relaxing, the words coming slower, the vowels extending.

World War II started that December. We learned what that meant: Dad wouldn't be coming home soon. At the end of the school year in Magnolia, we went back to Springfield to be with

Mother's family for the duration. Consequently, as a schoolgirl, I mostly grew up in Springfield, going back to Phelps from the third to the middle of the sixth grade.

Although it took me several years to understand, Magnolia and Springfield were in the *segregated* South. There must have been black people around, but I have no memory of being aware of them then.

In Springfield, we knew some Negros, most notably Mrs. Robinson, to be proper in the way Mother taught us to address *all* adults (not just white ones). At least as old as my grandmother, she first worked for my great grandmother, then for my grandmother, where she took care of my mother and her brother and sister. Then, when we moved back, she worked for mother and took care of us. In the same way Cook and Amah had been, she was family as far as we were concerned. Like all Mother's people did, we called her by her first name, Della. When she came to "help" with Thanksgiving dinner, because a holiday wouldn't be right without her, she sat at the kitchen table, overseeing everything, while Mother, Grandmother, and Aunt Maud cooked and whisked the food to the table. All the uncles, grandmother's brothers, came in the kitchen to pay respects. Whether she or Cook and Amah considered themselves parts of our family, I don't know; as a child, I didn't ever think to ask. Her passing, several years after we moved away from Springfield, left a familial hollow in the heart.

We didn't know Negro children except the Robinson grandchildren, whom we only occasionally met when we went to her house on the other side of town. They were not in our schools.

Mother believed that segregation was wrong, un-Christian, and denied people dignity and equality. She said so when she needed to, acted on her belief, and set an example for us. Grandmother Winfield was even more vocal. Every few weeks, as she had for years, she wrote her Mississippi senator, Theodore Bilbo, a rabid racist, to tell him that his most recent utterance or action was "not Christian." That was a serious charge in the Bible Belt, particularly coming from a preacher's wife. My sisters, brother, and I, indeed, come from a line of strong-minded, outspoken, gentle women.

After the Japanese attacked Pearl Harbor, the "Japs" became a much-caricatured archenemy, bucktheeth, slant eyes, and all. Although I knew the Japanese and the Chinese as real and different people, most people I lived among hadn't traveled far, much less to Asia. They didn't make a distinction between the Chinese and Japanese; all of them were "Asiatics." Some of my classmates, who had heard me talk about where I used to live, linked me with "them," whichever.

At the time, a popular song went "One meatball. You get no bread with *wa-uh-n* meatball." A couple of the fourth grade boys turned it into a taunt and called me "Chinese meatball." It hurt. With such teasing, China and my life there slipped further out of my conversation, to be lodged in my inborn knowledge of the nature of the world.

Day by day over those six years in elementary school, my southern—more accurately, my Missouri Ozarks—small town life became *what was*: ordinary, specific to me, more or less the same as my school friends' daily lives. We walked to school carrying lunch boxes and milk money. Class started with the Lord's Prayer and the Pledge of Allegiance. Between reciting the pledge, heightened wartime patriotism, and learning American history, we were all absorbing a sometimes articulated, shared national identity, of citizenship, as Americans.

For entertainment, we all listened to the same radio programs—*The Lone Ranger*, *The Shadow*, *Jack Benny*. We went to the movie theater on the square to see the same Saturday matinees, such as Walt Disney cartoons, Shirley Temple reruns, and *Meet Me in St. Louis*.

It was the Bible Belt, so most of us went to Sunday school and church. Despite our mothers' attempts to make us wait our turns, at church suppers we learned to race to the head of the line and pile our plates with all sorts of good food.

Just like we had in Jinan, we said the blessing before meals, usually holding hands. In Magnolia, one morning I came to the table late for breakfast, after Granddaddy Winfield was well into his eggs. Ever the preacher, he admonished me to say my own blessing before I ate. "Otherwise you'll have a tummy ache." Our year in the Mississippi parsonage was full of things like that. Grandmother was an expert seamstress—but not on Sundays. "Every stitch you sew on Sunday, you take out with your nose," she told us. We didn't play bridge or canasta (regular playing cards could be used for gambling), just Old Maid.

In Springfield, Uncle Bobby's father, who was a Southern Baptist (not Methodist like we were) seemed to lecture God when he said the blessing, telling God to "*PAAAHdon* and *fohGIVE* our Sins". He usually ended with "Make us mindful of the needs of others." One night his tongue slipped. He blared, "Make us needful of the minds of others." My sisters and I loved to mimic him behind his back.

I first remember Fourth of July—or as many people said, "Independence Day"—in Springfield. We celebrated with picnics, fireworks, and flags flying, all of which further defined us as members of one nation. Early in the morning, Harriet, Gretchen and

33

Kathy (our next door neighbor sisters), and I mischievously crept under Uncle Charlie's window. Stifling our snickers, we set off our loudest firecrackers then ran away whooping, deliberately waking the train engineer just asleep after his late-night run. A white-haired child-at-heart, he was soon out with us, making the neighborhood reverberate with firecracker bangs. Aunt Maud joined the action, demonstrating how to extend the wick to set off a small firecracker under a can so it would shoot up into the air, then egging us on to do it again and again by ourselves.

Like many other families, three generations of us went to the park for a picnic supper. Grandmother and Mother always fried chicken, sliced tomatoes, and chilled watermelon. Aunt Maud was famous for her deviled eggs; Aunt Nancy and Aunt Ruth brought their specialties. One Fourth, Cousin Larry visited Springfield. Born with an egg allergy that he'd finally outgrown, he took one look at the deviled eggs and devoured the whole plate full.

Picnic finished, we went back to Grandmother's and Granddaddy's for fireworks. Granddaddy nailed whirling rockets to the two maple trees in the front yard. To shoot off the roman candles, Uncle Pierce would set up the chicken feed trough at an angle between them. He, Uncle Charlie, and Granddaddy would compete to produce the most elaborate displays and biggest bangs as we danced with sparklers.

For May Day, Mother showed us how to make construction-paper baskets, filling them with flowers from Grandmother's garden: a couple of old-fashioned yellow roses, one tiny red rose, white spirea, a sprig of lilac, a dandelion, a few violets, and a bit of fern. Then we two little girls tippy-toed around the bushes and up onto Aunt Nancy's front porch, rang the bell, left the baskets, and dashed away giggling.

We lived in a nation at war, that much we knew. Daddy wasn't there. Lots of other Daddies, brothers, and uncles weren't there either; they were away in the Service.

As my classmates and I grew from third to fourth to fifth grade, we developed a clearer sense of what was happening through reading the *Weekly Reader* at school, hearing the nightly news at home, reading what we could of the paper, or watching newsreels before the Saturday movies. Most households listened to radio newscaster H. V. Kaltenborn early in the evening. When FDR gave his fireside chats, we, like our parents and grandparents, gathered round. Every Friday, we carefully carried an extra quarter to school to buy saving stamps. Once a person had a full book, it was turned into a war bond. We planted victory gardens and flattened tin cans for the war effort. War also meant that gasoline, sugar, butter, and shoes were rationed.

Things were needed for "our boys." All these shared war efforts further knitted us together with a sense of being patriotic Americans.

In the fifth grade, I started down the road of being a life-long election junkie.

"Quietly," Miss Challis said, shushing our fifth grade class as we filed into the school lobby and sat cross-legged on the floor. The polling booths were lined up near the principal's office on the other side of the room. Voters—our parents and neighbors, dressed for the occasion—arrived and then chatted quietly before receiving ballots and disappearing behind the curtains. We stayed a while, then left as quietly as we came when another class appeared to take our place.

As a ten-year-old, I witnessed the communal act by which Franklin Delano Roosevelt (the only president any of us had ever known) was re-elected to his fourth and final term. This was my introduction to the majesty and responsibility of "We the People" choosing our president.

At about the same time, I also learned civil debate and political disagreement on my grandparents' front porch. Grandmother and Mother were Democrats. Granddaddy and Aunt Gertrude were Republicans. Growing up in that community, sitting on the front porch, I began to absorb the core values of being an American, glimpsing the more complicated notion that America is as much a set of founding ideas as a purely geographical place.

As time passed, the Lake of the Ozarks and "miss 'em if you blink twice" spots in the road, like Joplin and Branson, were added to my mental map. More and more, I loved going barefoot, hearing country music and Sunday morning hymns, and eating corn on the cob—fresh shucked and plopped into the pot of boiling water straight from the garden with "take two and butter 'em hot" buttermilk biscuits. As this became increasingly how the world was, I began to jokingly think of myself as a hillbilly. I'm not sure where the word came from, whether I had heard someone sing it in a song on the radio or say it in conversation. In any case, the sound tickled me. I didn't know it was a derogatory term. To me, it meant a person from the Ozarks.

Over time, I found myself blending with my environment, even though I continued to feel like an outsider. Deep inside I knew another place, another "home," where there were other people with other looks on their faces, where there were other sounds and words and tastes.

We had the last direct encounter with our China life that we would have for many years in late 1944 or early '45, when two tall FBI agents knocked at the door. They wanted to see family pictures of the beach at Beidahe. Mother spread out albums of black-and-white snapshots across the dining room table. We all carefully looked at each picture. Seeing them made our earlier summers and time together there real again. That didn't interest the big visitors, though. They wanted to know:

"How shallow is this?"

"Is there much rough sea?"

"Mrs. Winfield, may we take these away for a while?" they requested about a pile they had set aside. "Thank you for your help."

I didn't understand why our beach should interest them. It was just our beach. Later, I realized the military must have been making plans for a potential landing.

The war ended without a landing in China. On a hot August afternoon, Mother, my sisters, and I were visiting a friend's farm, walking along a dusty road, when, from a distance, we heard church bells ringing. It was finished. We all jumped up and down, whooped and hollered. We kids ran in circles. The United States had won. Daddy would be coming home.

A few months later, he did indeed return to us, full of stories from flying around the world. He recited a list of places he had landed, pointing them out on a map. He told us about how, while he was in Free China as inflation had spiraled out of control there, he had needed a suitcase to carry his money and had spent it quickly before it lost value. He also told us about sneaking behind Japanese lines to help site what, decades later, would be the Yangtze River dam. He had been incurably bitten—much more than Mother—by the international bug. This brought the wider world, in ways other than those we experienced during wartime, back into our daily attention and conversation. Best of all, we were a whole family again.

Because of Daddy's new job with the United Board of Higher Christian Education in China, we moved to New York City. Enormous. Polyglot. Certainly not Southern segregated. People talked fast and loud, lived in apartments, rode subways, and knew which streets and parks were safe to walk down and which weren't. I had a new speech pattern to acquire, a new place in which to feel simultaneously both at home and like a stranger. No hillbillies there, much less made-in-China ones.

My brother, Ted, our family's post-war addition, was born. A year and a half later, we moved to Mamaroneck in New York's Westchester County suburbs, where all the dads commuted, most moms stayed home, and most local businesses were Italian—and where there was a clear divide between the kids who lived near the shore and went to the country club and those of us who didn't.

In Mamaroneck in the fall of 1948, you could hear Harry Truman's flat Missouri twang excoriating the "Do Nothing Congress." The presidential race was in full swing. Aunt Gertrude back in Springfield was rooting for New Yorker Tom Dewey because he looked like the "little groom" decorations on wedding cakes. (I thought that was a silly reason.) And even though he thought like a Democrat, Dad said he would cast his first vote for president, ever, (he hadn't been in the United States at election time before) for Dewey, a Republican. He thought it was a good idea for the president and the Congress to be the same party.

Election night, like our neighbors, our family huddled around the radio following results until the wee hours. We staggered to bed anticipating, as everyone had predicted, that Dewey would win. Everyone woke up—surprise!—to President Truman. We "Missourians" were elated and kidded Dad unmercifully. Our Westchester County neighbors were deflated.

I continued to absorb the central unwritten rules about the essence of our democracy and of being an American: We take sides, argue, disagree, we even throw mud. Then we vote. Whether we expect or like the outcome, the loser concedes. We accept the will of the majority and start politicking for the next time.

That election was only a part of our becoming New Yorkers of a sort. By then I was a teenager in high school, with the sense of dislocation and becoming that is part of that, as well as a tomboy and an independent thinker in a world that didn't approve of smart, outspoken girls. I made friends (though I didn't let them too close to me) and found my way.

Though we rarely mentioned China to others (well Dad did, it was the focus of his work), it hadn't fully disappeared from our lives. Rather, it receded. Eating out usually meant Chinese food, even if it was chop suey, an over-sauced, poorly conceived American variation of a stir-fry that was slopped over rice, or chow mein, an equally ill-conceived dish, with strange packaged fried noodles sprinkled on top.

"Home" continued to be wherever the family lived, not a specific place. Deep down, it remained essentially multiple, a multifaceted experience, built up in numerous accretions of this place and that, these foods and those, this way of speaking and that—one way of understanding who I was and another. Like an onion, home consisted of layers of time, place, and people existing in memory as well as the wherever now.

LIFE WITH MOTHER

During the War, without Dad, life centered on Mother. She was the constant, the continuity from where life had been to where it was.

In mid-pregnancy, she had brought two small girls halfway round the world by herself, had a third child soon after, and managed so life ran smoothly. I didn't think about what any of that must have required and how effortlessly she seemed to achieve it until I had hauled my own children around the world (never by myself, always as a twosome).

From my first recollection of going anywhere on my own, I remember her always stood in the door singing (well, sort of because she couldn't carry a tune even though she loved warbling),"Good bye, good bye, be always kind and true," or saying, "Politeness is to do or say the kindest thing in the kindest way." These were her mantras for how we should live.

When I was no longer a child, I understood that she was, in the best "'tis a gift to be…" sense, a simple, upright, generous woman, who was firm in what she believed was right. She acted on her convictions. No matter what others thought, we were our brothers' keepers with an obligation for the common good. This, she taught us, entailed community action, helping the less fortunate, treating everyone with dignity, and standing up for equality. She modeled all these principles in daily actions, applying them to the small details of life—taking food to a sick neighbor or simply sharing what she had—as well as to major moral issues.

While we were living with Dad's parents in Magnolia, friends of Grandmother Winfield invited us to a lavish Easter egg hunt—a whole new experience for us. Decked out in the Easter finery Grandmother had made, we were smothered with attention. We were the preacher's granddaughters from "somewheah ovah theah." With my large basket and sharp not quite eight-year-old eyes, I made a racing start searching for eggs, including the golden one. Dancing with excitement, I was sure I had won the prize for the most eggs.

"Margaret," Mother said. "You have found so many. Look at that little girl. She only has three. Give her some of yours so she won't be so unhappy."

"Muh-meee."

She bent close. Her voice was gentle: "Margaret, *you're* the big girl."

Whether she or I put some of my eggs in the other girl's basket, I've conveniently forgotten. Eggs were transferred, including the golden one, because, as Mother said, it was "so pretty." Someone else won the prize. I still feel a fleeting twinge that Mother, in her desire to teach me to share and be mindful of others' feelings, didn't recognize my drive to win and joy in having done well. Or if she did, she wanted to temper those feelings with the kind of generosity she believed I should practice.

That summer, we moved back to Missouri to live with Mother's family. We lived with her parents a while and then moved to one and then another rental home. Even though we didn't always live in her parents' house, on Market Street, we were welcomed by a larger community: an extended family of great aunts and uncles who lived on the same block; a group of Mother's friends from when she was young; and the folks at St. Paul's Methodist Church, where the family had gone for years. At St. Paul's we were known as "Love's (my grandmother's name) and Charlie's" grandchildren. Dad wasn't there. Life had a hole. Day by day, we were happily cocooned.

When we weren't living with my grandparents, Mother made our meals, a role that in our other life was usually reserved for Cook. As she returned to cooking, it became clear Mother saw feeding people as the way to shower them with love. "What shall we make when the So-and-Sos come by for supper? Do you think they would like chicken salad? That would go well with the green beans."

Many things were rationed, so meal planning took ingenuity. Following in her mother's footsteps, Mother was a good plain cook—no garlic, no herbs. Such seasonings weren't in their food vocabulary. Granddaddy's garden provided fresh produce in the summer and, thanks to Grandmother Parks' and Aunt Maud's work in the kitchen, canned goods in the winter. Plain cooking, yes, but we ate well.

Della came daily to help in the kitchen and take care of us. Her fried chicken was scrumptious, but she only knew how to cook it with at least a pound of butter—a month's worth of our rationed supply. She wasn't able to work as much as she used to—she was heavy, her legs were bad, and she sat a lot—but the larger family felt it was its obligation to take care of her as she aged. We loved her. Mother kept the house.

One night when the wind was howling our flue caught fire, sending sparks spraying into the sky. Firemen rushed in—it was exciting and scary. Mummy warned us not to tell Della. "We don't want to worry her," she said. The next morning, Della came in the kitchen door looking, well, sheepish, as if something had happened she didn't want to tell Mother. They danced around it, but soon everything came out. Because of the wind, Della's flue had caught fire that night, too. (The firemen must have had a busy night.) She hadn't wanted to tell us because she thought *we* might worry.

Mother found ways to enrich our lives. Despite her frugalness and her own lack of musicality, she bought a used pump organ because it was pretty. Harriet played some. After a while it couldn't be played; still pretty, it lived in Mother's living room until she broke up housekeeping. For me, she bought a three-quarter-sized violin—and lessons. I inherited her tin ear so the lessons didn't last long. The violin stayed on a shelf for years.

Occasionally she bought lovely antique pieces—a cut-glass berry bowl, a glass cruet. She cherished these the rest of her life, particularly if she could put flowers in them or tuck them somewhere to look at and enjoy. She passed on the glass berry bowl one Christmas; it served cranberry jelly on my Thanksgiving table for years. Now it's on my daughter's table.

While she treasured beautiful things, most of all, Mother loved words. She was always talking: "Mile-a-Minute Parks" was her high school nickname—and not because she was a fast runner (although she was). Words poured out of her, a mile a minute, in complete sentences, even with us when we were small.

While she loved to talk, she didn't *play* with words; she was extremely literal. The family joke was that Mother didn't do jokes. She either needed the joke explained in detail or finally got the punch line and laughed unexpectedly the next day.

What Mother may have lacked in a certain kind of humor, she made up for in moral fiber. She was honest to a fault. Take the time Harriet found insect galls on plant stems and put them on the bookshelf in our bedroom. One day the shelf was crawling with what turned out to be thousands of tiny just-hatched praying mantises, no bigger than small ants. After Mother whisked out the vacuum and sucked them up, one of us casually remarked that praying mantises were protected: New York levied a fifty-dollar-per-insect fine for killing them.

Mother was mortified: Who knows how many baby mantises she destroyed? Thousands of dollars worth. Where would she get that? We talked her out of reporting herself, although she was not happy about it. (She shouldn't have worried—I recently googled the fine and learned it was an old wives' tale. Rest peacefully, Mother.)

Her language was fastidious. Something didn't "stink," a word she somehow thought was rude. At worst, it might "smell bad." When someone was being a jerk, you shouldn't say his behavior "stunk," rather it was "anti-social." (She would roundly disapprove of what I call some talking heads on the TV.)

She didn't use slang for bodily functions, either. There were proper words such as "bowel movement" or "urinate." She considered scatological expletives "lazy language," a belief she made clear whenever she heard someone use such words. So we steered clear of that sort of language. Although when I was an adult, I picked up some interesting words from my growing sons.

Near the end of her life, as her mind got stuck in ruts (like old minds can), she repeated the same sentences over and over. One evening, while I was cooking supper at what would prove to be the last family gathering at our McLean house, one of our sons—Jerry, I think—popped into the kitchen. "Mom," he said. "Come out to the porch. You *have* to hear your mother."

One by one, the rest of our four grown children rushed in: "You won't believe it."

I pushed the pan off the heat and went to investigate. Streaming out of her mouth came every imaginable expletive—"f---," "s---," and beyond—interspersed occasionally with the admonition that these words were "lazy language." Mile-a-Minute Parks had a vocabulary none of us knew about.

Along with not using "rude" language, Mother was a Pollyanna who never showed anger. "Being angry is a waste of energy," she would say. Disagreement and passionate discussion made her uncomfortable. She had clear ideas of what she wanted us to do and how we should behave but rarely clearly or openly directed us. We were supposed to *know*. And we did. When she disapproved, it was unspoken. Instead her feelings registered in a subtle look. The pursed mouth informed us that we were expected to talk quietly and pleasantly, not argue or shout. We certainly should not get mad at each other and fight. It was not always an easy atmosphere for a kid, or an adult for that matter, to be in.

On the other hand, our creativity was something she cultivated. One of my first introductions to making art was in church, where Mother gave us paper and pencil to keep us quiet during the sermon. She also helped us put together costumes for plays we wrote.

Mother encouraged us to be observant and inquisitive. The results could be unexpected: Someone gave us a bunch of outdated medicine samples that, presumably, weren't dangerous. It was late summer, when hedge apples were falling in the neighborhood. Without asking or thinking, Harriet and I cut up the crinkly-peel, pale-green balls and put them into a pan with water. Then we added the contents of the medicine bottles and a big dollop of Vaporub, and cooked it all up. Curiosity at work! Our experiment was gaggingly awful. The kitchen had to be vacated. Mother and Della threw open the windows. "Peee-yeww," as we kids would say. Fortunately, Mother thought anger was a waste of time. (Not long ago, Harriet and I, both white-haired, laughed outrageously as we recalled the smelly mess.)

Where Mother's liberal, pacifist bedrock came from, I've never been sure. Whatever its source, it was a defining aspect of her personality, and, no doubt, part of what drew her and Daddy together.

I first became aware of it because Mother belonged to the NAACP. I don't know when she joined, just that she had. As a child, when we were living in distinctly southern, segregated Springfield, I had no idea how unusual that was. Nor did I understand that it might be dangerous, as it was further south. That was Mother. She acted on her beliefs, as we learned when Rosa Page Welsh, a famous Negro mezzo-soprano, came to Springfield to give a concert.

Because she was a Negro, Mother explained, Miss Welsh wasn't allowed to stay or eat in a decent hotel. So Mother invited her to stay in our house as our guest. Mother moved me out of my room and into the other bedroom she shared with my sisters so Miss Welsh could have my room.

Our outraged neighbors threw dirty looks and banged doors. Firmly doing what she knew to be right, Mother paid their behavior no mind and told us we shouldn't either. Maybe we went to the concert; I don't remember. But I do remember that Rosa Page Welsh stayed in our house and ate at our table.

I never thought our paths would cross again. But when Dan and I were living in Kaduna, Nigeria, in 1962, although we didn't know it, Rosa Page Welsh was teaching at the Church of the Brethren mission station in Waka, several hours south of us. She came to Kaduna for Christmas with mutual missionary friends, where we had dinner together. As we talked, somehow, Miss Welsh and I remembered the time she stayed in our house in Springfield.

An evening or two later, some twenty years after our first meeting and half a world away from Springfield, Rosa Page Welsh sat in my Kaduna living room and, at her request, gave an a cappella concert for us and our guests: "…What shall I give him, poor as I am? If I were a shepherd I'd give him a lamb…," she sang the words from a traditional carol.

In my mind I heard: "Be always kind and true."

Mother nurtured. She put family and children's needs and what she perceived as the wishes of others first, always. She ate the piece of burnt toast, claiming she liked it better, and the overripe banana no one else would touch. I never knew what she truly wanted for herself, if anything.

The longer we lived without Dad, the more life with only Mother became "simply the way it was." Running the household and taking care of us must have taken great day-by-day fortitude, even with the extended family for support. She did it, apparently with ease.

When Dad came back at the end of the war, our life shifted gears. Following several years in New York we headed overseas again, to Burma.

After my parents finally had settled in McLean and my two youngest sibs were in middle and high school, Mother began to write. First she scribbled a few articles that were published in *Family Circle*. Then she wrote *Living Overseas,* one of the first books for families living abroad. Written from experience, her book filled a need and was well received. As the discussion of women's roles became more vociferous, she sold an article to the *Saturday Evening Post* called "Let Me Iron the Sheets," defending being a wife and mother.

She described all this writing as "dabbling." Most of it, except for the intensive work of producing a book, was done in bits of spare time she carved out while keeping house, catering to Dad's needs, chauffeuring children, and, later, taking care of her widowed mother, who had moved to Virginia from Missouri. She also willingly agreed to care for our children as needed when I developed what appeared to be a long-term illness.

Her sense that the "right thing" to do was to take care of family first, without much concern for one's own desires, was complicated for me. Because she gave off a judgmental aura (or at least that is how it sometimes seemed), I felt that she thought that my seeking a balance between being my own person and being a wife and mother was "not right."

I didn't realize how ingrained the "others' wishes first" belief was in her, and what that unspoken mantra masked, until I was over fifty and was about to spend six weeks in the Philippines—leaving my husband to fend for himself. The trip was the second one of a series I made to observe elections following the ouster of President Ferdinand Marcos in 1986.

The day before I left, I stopped by Mother's house, as I always did, to say good-bye. As I was leaving, she leaned into the car window. Smiling, she told me something she had never said before to any of us. "You know," she said, "I always wanted to be a journalist."

Wistful, yes. In her own way, approval.

DEBTS AND TRESPASSES

"'Debts'!"
"No! 'Trespasses'!"
In Miss Challis' fifth grade, we absolutist ten-year-olds argued all year about which to use when we recited the Lord's Prayer each morning. The Baptists knew it was "debts"—that was simply what it was. We Methodists were equally adamant that "trespasses" was the way it had to be. That's what *we* were taught. We had all learned in our families and Sunday School that "God is love."

These verbal battles were something else entirely—not about the loving God we had in common but a question of whose *way* was "right." It never occurred to any of us to each say what we knew and not argue. Most of us weren't even aware that Catholics, at that time, said the same prayer in Latin and stopped before "our" ending. Nor did we consider that Henry, our one Jewish classmate, must have felt excluded.

Although such childhood squabbles are just that, discussions roiling the United States today have led me to see our little arguments in a larger context—as precursors of the "my way" religiosity that is being promoted more broadly.

At Phelps Elementary School in Springfield in 1944, classes began with prayer. There was no "under God" in the Pledge of Allegiance—as far as we knew, the words we learned were what the Founders intended. ("Under God" was added to contradict communism during the '50s. My past-eighty-year-old tongue still stumbles to remember the addition. In the early '60s, courts struck down school-sponsored prayer, declaring it an infringement on religious liberty.)

In elementary school American history, we learned that the first settlers risked crossing the Atlantic to escape religious persecution. They came to worship according to their own beliefs, unhindered by an established church's rules. We were not sure what "established church" meant but assumed that being free of it meant something like "no one can boss you around about religion." President Roosevelt, meanwhile, spoke about freedom of worship as well as freedom of speech and freedom from want and fear.

I began to understand that religious freedom, the bedrock of American society, meant that the government could not interfere with religion. For many Americans' the commonly held assumption is broader: No one—not the government, not faith communities, not individuals and, looking at the present time, not corporations—gets to boss anyone around when it comes to religious beliefs.

When I was in school, the emphasis was on Protestant Puritanism, an over-simplified view of our "Christian beginnings" that is still widely held. Important parts of our broader history were missing. We learned little about the intolerance of some beliefs and the imposition of others in many colonies or that Quakers and Baptists were persecuted. Nor did we learn of religion's ties to business in colonies like Virginia, or that a half-century before Jamestown, Spanish Catholics settled in Florida and the southwest. We didn't know that one of the country's oldest Jewish congregations was founded in 1658 in Newport, Rhode Island, We had no idea that many slaves, the dominant population of the colonial south, were Muslim and covertly observed Ramadan, the Islamic fasting month. Later—perhaps in high school civics—I learned that the Constitution's First Amendment ensures the separation of church and state and provides for individuals' free exercise of religion.

In 1940s Springfield, there must have been synagogues and Catholic and Negro churches and schools, but we were isolated from them. Ours was effectively a white Protestant bubble.

When we moved to the suburbs of Washington, DC, over sixty years ago, it was a sleepy, segregated southern town. Now the area reflects our democracy and our many faiths at their most visibly pluralistic. More, or differently, than many places, the nation's capitol area embodies the demographic shifts and social struggles in the United States. While some Americans feel threatened by these changes, this ethnic and religious diversity is one of the things I most appreciate about where I live, and about our country.

In the elementary school our grandson attended, a few miles from us, the students collectively speak sixty three languages. Driving from our former condo to our favorite Chinese restaurant, we would pass the oldest Jewish congregation in Alexandria and an Episcopal seminary, both well predating the Civil War. We also would see a Catholic church and school, a well-established mosque, at least eight different denominations of Protestant churches, from mainstream to Pentecostal—several with notices for services in Korean, Tagalog, Spanish, Vietnamese, or for the deaf—and a house that serves as a Vietnamese Buddhist temple. Plus, we would see signs pointing to Greek and Russian orthodox churches. The condo's Laotian staff would go to their own Buddhist temple. Elsewhere there are other Buddhist, Hindu, and Sikh places of worship. Down Richmond Highway, a Quaker meetinghouse predates Fort Belvoir, where it still stands. On a clear day, we could see from our condo the glint off of Moroni, whose likeness tops the Mormon Temple on the far side of the District. Periodically, various school systems discuss how best to handle absences for Yom Kippur or Idul Fitr in addition to the Christmas holidays.

Our condo community was a microcosm of the same diversity—a place where people of all ages, sexual orientations, ethnicities, languages, and religious beliefs (or lack thereof) converged. Not unlike my fifth-grade "debt" vs. "trespass" argument, the cars in the parking lot sported bumper stickers that reflected a complicated range of beliefs about politics, civil rights, religious freedom, and what it is to act on ones own religious beliefs: "God is Pro-Life." "Pro-Child, Pro-Family, Pro-Choice." "Adam and Eve Not Adam and Steve." "Don't Believe in Gay Marriage? Don't Marry a Gay. Problem Solved."

Despite America's self-definition as a democracy of people who are created equal and are free to worship (or not) as we believe, debates about this religious freedom, civil rights, discrimination, and acts of conscience are not new. Think slavery, segregation, women's lib and LGBT rights. As a nation, we have fought a civil war and many legislative and legal battles over how our country defines personal liberty and equality.

All the issues are rooted in particular religious communities' single-minded certainty about what God intends and, consequently, their "religious freedom" not only to act on their beliefs, but impose them on others. (Whether the Bible or science support their contentions is a valid question but beside the point. They believe it.)

Politics and the retention of power are clearly at stake.

One of the advantages of old bones and long memory is that I have witnessed, and sometimes participated in, the struggles for social change that have occurred over the last two-thirds of a century. Like many Americans, I grew up in a family that believed profoundly in racial equality and interreligious respect and tolerance. We acted on those beliefs. (Like many, we had, still have, family and friends who see the world through different lenses. Some assert they won't vote for a president who is an atheist. Others won't vote for a Mormon.)

As the Civil Rights movement gained momentum, friends with and without religious affiliations joined the African-American–led struggle. A lawyer friend persuaded federal courts to overturn Virginia's "massive resistance" laws. My mother and an interracial delegation from Church Women United lobbied for school integration in Richmond. My husband and I worked on a church-organized drive supporting local Open Housing laws.

We supported the Civil Rights Act of 1964. That act outlawed discrimination based on race, color, religion, sex, or national origin, and sought to end racial segregation. Further, it defined public accommodations and the right of equal access to them, ending "whites only" signs by the water fountains, segregated lunch counters, and other business practices of my Southern childhood. Private owners were bound to abide by the law and could not discriminate against individuals or groups of people, even if their justification was grounded in their understanding of the Bible.

The struggles were not simple or comfortable. Those who felt these changes infringed on their rights and religious beliefs argued: "You can't legislate morality." Certainly you can't, not at a personal level, then or now. Those struggles and the resulting laws established public guarantees of equal rights that focused on race. In my view, equal rights also focuses on religion.

Over time, the Supreme Court carefully balanced individual religious liberty and public action. *Loving v. Virginia* overturned religious scruples and state law to make interracial marriage legal. *Griswold* reversed Connecticut's religiously derived statute prohibiting any person from using drugs or other articles to prevent conception. *Obergefell v. Hodges* established marriage as a fundamental right for everyone, including same sex couples.

In 1968, after a restaurant owner who believed the Bible justified segregation brought suit, the Court ruled he had to desegregate his restaurant chain. Later, a federal appeals court ruled that a Christian school in California could not withhold health benefits from their married female employees despite the school's religious beliefs that married women should stay home.

In 2014, we were at it again. *Burwell v. Hobby Lobby* contested a private company's right to offer employees health insurance that excluded contraception coverage because of the owners' religious convictions that using it was wrong. The Supreme Court ruled for Hobby Lobby. Then in 2018, the Supreme Court decided in favor of the Masterpiece Cakeshop owner who, because of his religious beliefs, refused to make a wedding cake for a same-sex couple. In a narrowly defined ruling, the Court decided that the Civil Rights Commission did not employ religious neutrality, thereby violating Masterpiece Cakeshop owner's rights to free exercise, but also leaving the question open for a later decision on another case.

What an individual or a religious group preaches or practices in these matters is not the issue. That is constitutionally protected.

However, in an open, plural democracy—my understanding of what our Founding Fathers were aiming for and what many of us have struggled to perfect—the issue remains whether an individual or group claiming "religious liberty" may impose their "deeply held" beliefs on others. Or, to use fifth grade language, can they boss the rest of us around about religion? Which takes our fifth grade "debts" "trespass" argument to the existential level. Attention must be paid.

SHORT CORN

The short corn of Iowa's landscape spoke of the tall corn of my Missouri childhood. We were driving toward Iowa City and my first Writers' Workshop that June afternoon in 2009. That corn reminded me of my corn-growing grandfather. My mind's eye suddenly saw him with his hair parted in the middle: A face that surprises me in the mirror some mornings as my own short white hair falls in a middle part.

"Here's how you plant corn," he showed us. We tucked seeds in the well dug earth; he in his big garden, my sisters and I in our small victory patch a few blocks away. What a race we had to see who could harvest and eat July's first corn. The young corn from our garden, still way too tiny and green—but "beating" him to it—tasted *soooo* good!

Raw onions did, too. "We know what's good," he would say as he and I—and no one else at the table—munched on them.

Sunday mornings, his granddaughters on his lap, he read the comics—the *Katzenjammer Kids*, *Mutt and Jeff*, *Popeye*—changing his voice with each character. We all laughed and loved it, he most of all.

Granddaddy sold shoes. He had managed a store that went bust in the Depression. A proudly honest man, he would not declare bankruptcy. He sold their house to pay his creditors what was owed on the store before it closed. Then he and Grandmother moved across the street to live with Aunt Maud in the solid, foursquare farmhouse that had belonged to Grandmother's parents. Granddaddy's large garden was on the side, the outhouse, woodshed, and barn with chickens were out back.

The chickens were for Sunday dinner. Granddaddy grabbed a couple, snapped their necks, let them run around till they dropped, then plucked them. Grandmother fried them up. How he loved her fried chicken. Like me, he particularly loved what I would call the "thigh." He called it "second joint," just as he called the breast "white meat." An old-fashioned gentleman, some words weren't said at the table in front of the ladies.

By the time we moved to Springfield, he was selling Knapp shoes by mail order to a group of regular customers. He was always mailing shoes packed in boxes that had to be wrapped neatly in brown paper and tied with white string. I was his helper. "Fold the corner in like this," he directed, making a crisp point to turn up. I still wrap boxes Granddaddy's way.

He also knew how to calm a crying grandchild. The bee I had disturbed in the flowerbed stung something fierce. I howled. "That pesky varmint," he said, rubbing a baking soda poultice on my arm. "I'll fix it. Gonna tie a knot in his tail."

On summer afternoons, he liked to listen to baseball games on the radio—always the St. Louis Cardinals, never the Browns. Those were the days of Stan Musial and Marty Marion winning the 1944 World Series. Listening with him, I absorbed America's pastime.

Granddaddy also loved to fish. He would take me—his "buddy"—in his pre-war brown Plymouth to the lake on the other side of town, where we caught catfish. Pulling them in was fun. Eating them, even dipped in batter and fried in bacon grease, wasn't so good. Nothing got rid of their muddy, bottom-feeder taste.

Whether dinner was fish or chicken, or vegetables from his garden, his after-dinner ritual was the same: He'd play solitaire on the dining room table, laying out the cards in the pool of light cast by the overhead fixture. Like many men his age in the teetotal Bible Belt, he loved to end the day with his tot of "medicinal" Hadicol (a twelve-percent alcohol "vitamin" tonic).

My eighth Christmas, the third without Dad, there was a little green two-wheeler under the tree. "Com'on, you need to learn to ride this," he said. Up and down the family block of Market Street we went. He, trotting along, held on to the back. I, peddling hard, was not sure when he let loose. "That'a girl, away you go." He was as pleased as I was when I made it down the block on my own steam.

The next Christmas, a homemade wooden toolbox, equipped with a child-size hammer, saw, and other tools, was under the tree. "You're the big girl. You need to know how to use these so you can help your Mama fix things."

All this, sixty years later, as I drove past still-short corn, growing in Iowa in June

Our Panda

New York City, Summer 1943

The Bronx Zoo had a rolly-polly, black-and-white panda. It belonged to Harriet, our youngest sister, Nancy, and me.

After we had been evacuated to the States, Cheeloo University moved from Jinan to Chengdu in Free China, where the university reopened. The students and some faculty members walked across China to get to the new location. Dad got there somehow, "hitchhiking the Chinese way," Harriet suggests. Once there, he shared a house with other faculty members. One of his housemates was raising a baby panda on a big screened-in porch until it was big enough to be transferred to the Bronx Zoo.

Letters from Daddy were infrequent, but each one had some story for "his girls" about the small panda—"the first one I have ever seen." After the academic year in Chengdu, Daddy had moved to Chungking to work for United States Office of War Information (OWI), developing propaganda to undercut the Japanese.

When the panda was old enough, it was, I assume, flown out over the Hump (as the treacherous flight over the Himalayas into India was called) and circuitously on to New York. In any case, by 1943, it was in the Bronx Zoo. That summer, Dad had also Hump-hopped home for a couple of months. It was the first time we'd been together in three years and it would be the last for another three. Two-year-old Nancy had never seen Dad. For her, it was the summer of riding his shoulders. A cherished family picture shows their two smiling faces.

We spent most of that summer in New York City, staying in a furnished Manhattan walk-up while Daddy worked at the OWI headquarters. New York was an adventure for nine- and seven-year-olds who had started life in China and then lived in small-town Mississippi and Missouri. We walked to Central Park with Mother. FAO Swartz's huge toy store was a block or so away and dazzling. Harriet and I took a kiddie singing-and-dancing class at Carnegie Hall: "I'm a little teapot short and stout" (left arm up like a spout, right arm on hip like a handle), "just tip me over," (bend to the left), "and pour me out," (stand back up and curtsey).

Best of all, we visited the Bronx Zoo with Daddy to meet "our" panda. We bounced up and down on an excited ride on the Subway and half-ran through the zoo, passing other animals without paying much attention. Finally, we reached a black-and-white ball of fluff. "Hello, Panda," we three girls said as we hung on the rail watching it. We liked to think he recognized Daddy and in some way knew us and that he was Ours.

Soul Food: Course Two

New York City, January 1947

After the war, New York City is home, not just for a few months, like several years earlier. It doesn't smell or taste like my "crispy-fried chicken, slow-cooked green beans, fresh-from-the-garden beefsteak tomatoes, post-China Missouri" childhood. The stairwell of the West 115th Street walk-up reeks of boiled cabbage and hot grease.

"We're going out to eat tonight," Dad announces. As we walk into the Chinese restaurant, the fragrance floods me with six-year-old-girl memories. Huge photos of the owner's pudgy, perhaps three-and-a-half- or four-year-old grandchild struggling to use chopsticks makes thirteen-year-old me laugh. My hands hold chopsticks in their early muscle memory like my legs do walking.

Dad picks the place because the cook makes *jiaozi*. I had almost forgotten how good the first comfortingly juicy bite tastes. My mouth, like my hands, remembers.

A Whistling Girl...

...and a crowing hen always come to some bad end.

The boys I knew in third grade whistled. (Well, sort of.) So did Mother's Aunt Maud. "Show me," I must have asked. She did. For months I unsuccessfully pursed my lips and puffed. Uncle Pierce joshingly taunted me with the "whistling girl...crowing hen...some bad end" doggerel. He might have brotherly teased his "old maid" sister Maud, too.

After months of *whoofing*, I finally succeeded. In church. In the middle of the silent prayer.

Thinking back, that was the start of my encounters with "boys do, girls don't" and going ahead my own way.

Boys, in the '40s and later, were asked: "What do you want to be when you grow up?" If anyone asked me that, I don't remember. A girl's future was assumed, then re-enforced with the first gift of a doll-baby and, later, with playing house. Boys were given trucks and bats and balls and played catch and, later, baseball.

I loved "Van Doll," as I named my big baby doll; I designed and made her clothes but I didn't play house. It was more fun to climb trees and run around outside; or make up plays for my sister, and Gretchen and Kathy (who lived next door to Grandmother Parks), or play jacks or hopscotch with Aunt Dorothy.

I knew American women in China who had careers: Dr. Annie Scott, our pediatrician, for instance, or Auntie Witham, a professor in the medical school where Dad taught. Auntie Witham was researching tropical sprue. When she had to leave China, she infected herself with it so she could bring it back to America and continue her study. The mission field offered many women, mostly single, access to careers they wouldn't have been considered for in America in the '30s and '40s.

Teaching was mostly "women's work." My role models were Miss Challas and all my elementary school teachers, plus Miss Elliff, our principal. Although mostly men taught in my high school in Mamaroneck, which had a male principal, my excellent high school math and English teachers were Miss McAfee and Miss Bock. In the parlance of the day, they were "maiden ladies," a polite way to say single women. Married women were not allowed to teach as I learned when my first grade teacher, Miss Bennett, got married, and was required to leave the next year. Until much later, the only married working women I knew were black women who cleaned houses and cared for other people's children.

At the same time, we all knew about Eleanor Roosevelt. As well as being the president's wife, she was her own force, writing a daily syndicated column, "My Day," plus making trips around the country, even overseas, to visit the troops on her own or as a representative of the president. Some of us revered her. Others thought she had stepped out of her "place." (The people who thought that probably didn't like FDR, either.)

After Pearl Harbor, Rosie the Riveter posters popped up and women went to work for the war effort. When peace came and the men returned, many women settled back into being happy homemakers, with magazine articles and ads to encourage them. Like Mother, my friends' mothers kept house and took care of their families. If they described themselves, they said they were homemakers or housewives.

Dad's sister—wonderful, over-the-top Aunt Ruth provided the nearest model I had for the partner-wife, mother, creative professional-in-her-own-right route I eventually took. Mother to cousins Larry and David, Aunt Ruth first showed me that eccentricity brought its own freedom.

She and Uncle Joe Brown Love jointly led a succession of Wesley Foundations (Methodist student organizations) at big universities: Louisiana State University, University of Illinois, Vanderbilt, Kent State, and finally Boston University. I didn't learn until years later that she did a great deal of the day-to-day organizing work at the Foundations but received neither money nor much recognition (two for the price of one). As cousin David reports, instead of rewarding her, the powers-that-be disdained and distrusted her; especially if they felt her work threated their conservative roots.

Given her drive and love of theater, she produced professional quality, serious plays as part of Foundation and university life. After the war, Ruth and Joe led European student tours that focused on art and theater. Ultimately she taught speech in the Boston public school system and was actually paid. When they "retired," she and Joe created a book about their Texas childhoods and co-wrote and acted in plays about the evolution of campus student life during their lifetimes. What a role model.

In the late '80s, I mentioned to Mother, to her surprise, how I regretted the lack of career-woman role models around when I was young. When *she* was young, she said, she had lots of them. She wasn't specific about who, what they did, or whether they were married, just that she had them. This fits. As Betty Freidan often asserted, women's magazines in the '20s and '30s published articles about working women. By the late '40s and '50s, they focused on romanticizing women as perfectly fulfilled homemakers and mothers.

The early messages that skimmed past me about what girls should or could do related to a multitude of daily things. I was enough of a tomboy in grade school that I didn't pay much attention.

With Dad gone, I also had "oldest kid" responsibilities (my sisters may see this quite differently—Nancy told me I wouldn't be a good mother, I was too "bossy"). Sometimes I helped shovel coal into the dilapidated furnace. I ran down the block to buy a paper when we heard the cry "extra"—on D-Day when our troops landed in Normandy and when President Roosevelt died. I removed the back of the portable radio when we finally figured out it was the source of a foul smell that seemed to be floating around the house. We'd been taking the radio to different rooms to hear the observances around FDR's death. The "stink"—a decomposing fried mouse—had been tagging along

Looking back, in many families, some of the tasks I did would have been viewed as "boy chores." But we were a family of girls with Mother running the house. The chores had to be done. That was that.

Most of the time, though, I was just a kid, focused on playing, but, then too, in a group of girls. When we played Tarzan with Gretchen (who had a tree house and so got to choose who played what characters) the roles were always the same: Gretchen was Tarzan; Harriet with the long, straight hair was Jane; Kathy was Boy; and I was Cheetah the Chimpanzee. I didn't like running around like a monkey making grunts, but it beat not playing.

In fourth grade, at the height of the war, Peggy and Hannah—my two best girlfriends—and I pretended we were in WACs (Women's Army Corps) or WAVES (Women Accepted for Volunteer Emergency Service, a division of the Naval Reserve). We made "grownup" ladies' purses, complete with pretend lipstick and cigarettes, out of glued-together layers of paper. While most men we knew smoked, no woman did, at least not in front of us. Only movie actresses did that.

What boys and girls did and did not do—whether it was articulated or not—became more real and intrusive in high school.

With the war ended and Dad home, we were in New York, first the city, then the suburbs. The house we settled into in Mamaroneck in Westchester County had a garage. Since we didn't have a car, and Dad liked working with wood, he turned it into a shop. He encouraged us to use it to build things, in the same orderly fashion as we did when we played with blocks: Make detailed plans first, and then organize supplies before actually beginning construction.

He taught us to use real tools to make solid, useful, well-crafted things. "My aunt used to make furniture," he told us girls with pride. "That's how I learned, watching her."

For our family, using tools was not a gendered skill. Dad never met a tool he didn't like or want to use. When the family bought a sewing machine, he watched me to figure out how to use it. One night, when I hadn't quite finished my prom dress and my date was due soon, he sewed in the corded hem while I took my shower. I was dressed and ready when the doorbell rang.

Soapbox Derby racing was Mamaroneck's summer highlight. Boy Next Door was making a soapbox racer—home-made, individually designed vehicles holding a single driver that depend completely on gravity to run downhill—and I wanted to build and race one, too. We had the tools and I would have Dad's guidance.

The rules intervened: No Girls Allowed.

Boy Next Door let me be his mechanic. I enjoyed that, but… His design was big, boxy, and didn't race well. I knew I could have made a leaner, faster car.

The situation goaded me into working around the challenge of being told I couldn't do something because I was a girl. A week or so after the big Soap Box Derby, with Dad's help (maybe even at his suggestion), several of us, including Boy Next Door and other boys in the neighborhood, designed and made miniature wooden racecars from scratch. There weren't kits like the Cub Scouts use now. We carefully carved the cars out of soft pine, then sandpapered and varnished them. Daddy set up a wooden ramp (a four-by-eight–foot sheet of plywood with a sawhorse at one end) in the yard for the races. What a marvelous afternoon.

In the process, we learned that aerodynamics and exactness mattered. If the bodies weren't carefully shaped, with the axels squared on the body and the wheels accurately placed on the center of the axels, even miniature cars wouldn't roll straight or go fast.

Then there was the basketball. Because I owned the ball, the neighborhood boys who used the hoop on our dead-end block made me an honorary boy—for game purposes, anyway. They called me "Mike," a nickname that stuck through high school. (A few friends still call me that. Mother was relieved when Dan came along and called me Margaret.)

Once, those same boys and their troop leader, Boy Next Door's dad, invited me on their Boy Scout hike, mainly, I think because I was in the yard when they were leaving. There was a big whoop-de-do at school the Monday afterward because *girls* didn't do that—what had I been up to?.

As we got older, my relationship with the neighborhood boys shifted, some. Out of curiosity, one summer night before sophomore year, the Boy Next Door and I tried making out on the porch of a nearby empty house. The experiment wasn't terribly daring or exciting. We walked back to our houses and went on being buddies.

I joined the school paper and, junior year, became the editor—the first girl, I believe, to hold that position at Bellows High School. (By then, one of my few non-teacher woman role models was the editor of the town's weekly paper and a family friend.) The printer didn't treat boys and girls differently as he taught us to set text on the linotype machine and handset the type (upside down and backward) for heads. Experiencing a sense of equality (whoever is doing the job needs these skills) and gaining a literal feel for type, were both enormous gifts to a future writer and editor.

At the time however, I dreamed of being an architect. With Dad's guidance, I drew house plans and made a wooden dollhouse and miniature furniture, all to scale. (Our granddaughters were the last to play with that house.) At school, I wanted to take shop; even more, I wanted to take mechanical drawing. Advanced shop, which included electrical wiring, sounded interesting, too. To my disgust, those classes were for boys only.

Girls were required to take Home Ec. Only girls, no boys, took the classes—sewing one year and cooking the next. Both bored me. My grandmother taught me to sew on her treadle machine when I was eight (the dress, made out of a chicken-feed sack, looked odd, but I wore it proudly). I'd made many of my own clothes ever since. As for cooking, I wasn't interested. Mother was the cook; I only made salad.

Like most of the other girls at Bellows, I took college-prep courses, including math and science classes, which usually had more boys than girls. Mostly girls, with a smattering of brave boys, took typing. The implication was that we could support ourselves as secretaries if all else failed (i.e., we found no husband to support us). Actually, typing did end up being useful, although not because I got a job as a secretary.

Girls' sports were different, not sports so much as "gym". We played "girls' rules" basketball, six on a side, three as defense, three as offense, no running past the mid-court line. It was "bad for girls' developing bodies to run too hard or too far," or so we were told. How that logic applied to field hockey or soccer, where we ran up and down a bigger field, was unclear.

Being a bright girl in high school was awkward: I (any girl with brains) was expected to hide my intelligence, especially when it meant showing up a boy. Being outspoken was worse. A girl who spoke up was seen as smart-alecky, unbecomingly bossy, shrill, a "know it all." No one voiced these rules. It was simply the way things were. None of this completely stopped me from being myself. Though, in that environment, the consequences for expressing my intelligence and opinions were not easy to deal with.

Then there was sex. In our family, deciding which parent talked with us or we asked questions of was never based on gender. Dad, the scientist, was often the matter-of-fact family go-to, explaining the physiological basics with anatomically accurate, never colloquial, words. When I later asked Mother some of my more intimate questions, she was also matter-of-fact, showing me pictures as she answered my queries. Physicality and responsible sex were topics of unembarrassed family conversation, as much a matter of religious and moral upbringing as biology. There were two underlying messages: First, sex is pleasurable and satisfying. Second, wait until marriage; waiting makes sex special.

The latter didn't seem like it was going to be a problem since only the "boys who wore glasses" asked me to dances, never the cute guys I had crushes on. While among my class there was certainly some paired off dating, much of our social life sophomore and junior years was group parties at someone's house after a game or the sock hops and other school dances. Some afternoons we hung out at a drugstore with ice cream sodas. My family didn't drink. If some of my classmates drank beer at parties or had a hangout, I was naively unaware of it. (As an adult, listening to friends talk, I know that a drinking culture among teens wasn't unusual in Westchester County or elsewhere.)

Drinking or not, sex was certainly on our minds. In the '40s, adolescents exploring sexuality (which we all did to a degree) lived with a double standard that in may ways still exists: "Boys will be boys." "Nice girls don't." For girls, the fear of pregnancy—both the actual situation and the shame of getting caught—was real and ingrained. We, not the boys, bore the responsibility for preventing pregnancy. Essentially this meant firmly saying no or having the will power to insist on stopping before things went too far. Some of us must have known about contraceptives. Although I learned a bit about them at home (in the context of marriage), there was no mention of them in school. In any case, they were difficult to obtain. We didn't talk about abortions, which were only done in back alleys at that time. If that was ever brought up, it was only whispered about.

Some of my friends were sexually curious, if not active. However, we weren't gossiping about it, at least not the girls I spent time with. Nonetheless, when a popular classmate and her mother simply disappeared junior year, we were agog and whispered with each other, speculating—correctly—that they had gone somewhere else until the baby came. By the time she returned, I was gone so I don't know the end of the story.

With sex—as it seemed with almost everything else—boys had more freedom. Girls were the ones who had to deal with pregnancy; boys did not. Across the board, at school and in the community, girls were expected to be responsible. Boys were taken more seriously about most things and had more opportunities.

Dad and Mother didn't care that I was a girl, not a boy; nor did they expect me to hide my intelligence. I would go to college, as my mother and her mother and grandmother had—and as Dad's mother and his sister also had.

Outside the family, my capacities and interests—girls' capacities and interests generally—were not as valued as those of boys. I often wished I were a boy—not because I wanted to *be* one. Rather, because I wanted to do what boys did, like race in soapbox derbies and take mechanical drawing, or whistle, "crowing hens" and "bad ends"—or not. Where, I wondered, did I fit in?

No Sense of Decency

"Have you no sense of decency, sir? At long last, have you left no sense of decency?"
Joseph N. Welch, Army-McCarthy hearings, June 9, 1954

I still hear Dad's voice that winter night in 1950 as he sat Harriet and me down after dinner to tell us what might happen. I was sixteen.

"If Senator McCarthy has another list, I will be on it," he said, matter-of-factly.

The United States was engulfed in Cold War hysteria, enflamed by Congressional witch-hunts for Communists purported to be infiltrating the government and media. Senator Joseph McCarthy (R-WI) was a bullying, much feared demagogue with a five o'clock shadow and an accusatory voice. Almost daily, he fulminated against people he contended were Communists. "I have a list," he blustered, shaking a sheaf of papers.

Each new list was presented without sources or substantiation. Many of the people he named were, as our father was, China Hands: government employees, journalists, and other specialists who had lived in China and impacted US policy. Experts in the language and culture, they knew both Chiang Kai Shek's nationalist government and, in many cases, the Communists who had taken over in 1949.

During the war, Dad had been in Chungking in Free China, working for the US Office of War Information. Because he was fluent in Chinese and knew China well, he had developed material to support the Chinese and Allied cause against the Japanese. His office had produced a cartoon filmstrip that was widely distributed within China and reprinted in *Life Magazine*. The Americans were portrayed as helmeted eagles; the Chinese were valiant sparrows. Both were swooping to attack the Japanese, depicted as blackbirds. Turtles—a serious insult—fitted in somewhere, perhaps representing Japanese tanks.

When he returned to the States after the war, he wrote what, at the time, was one of the prime books on the country: *China: The Land and the People*. That book, in fact, was my future husband's first contact with our family. Several years before we met, he bought it as an assigned text for a college course.

In addition, Dad had written about China policy for various journals. He knew and worked with many of the people whose lives and careers were in tatters because of McCarthy's accusations. Truth wasn't the point. McCarthy was preying on people, fanning fears of Communism primarily for his own aggrandizement.

Dad wanted us to be forewarned, in case.

Fortunately for us, there wasn't another list.

The Senator didn't get his comeuppance until 1954, four years after that dinner table conversation, when he took on the military during the Army-McCarthy hearings. By the end of the June hearings my husband-to-be and I were courting, spending as much time together as we could. Part of that meant being glued to the black-and-white television in his family's upstairs den. The high point (of the hearings, not the courting) was seeing McCarthy's bullying crumble under Joseph Welch's withering: "Have you no sense of decency, sir?"

Like many other childhood and teenage memories, the night Dad sat us down is rarely in the front of my mind—at least it wasn't until recently. The atmosphere was poisonous, that I remember clearly. It left me with a gut-level aversion to demagogic accusations that have the power to ruin lives and undermine a civil, democratic society. Even if we hadn't been on the fringes of that maelstrom, I would feel the same way.

The atmosphere of our 2016 presidential election campaign and now the presidency itself is similarly poisonous. If anything, it is *more* vitriolic. The country is overwhelmed with anti-democratic, un-American sentiments: "Birther" nonsense demeaning the validity of the previous, popularly elected president. Promises of walls to keep out refugees fleeing violence. Misogynist name-calling. The most overt racism I've seen since my Southern childhood. Bullying threats against Muslims. Nationalist, xenophobic hate-speech. "Fake news." The press as the enemy. Lies heaped upon lies until they become "truth."

As our social media and newscasts are flooded with sound bites that spread this poison, I find myself echoing Joseph Welch: "Have we no sense of decency?"

Becoming Global

We descended the airplane's stairs into Rangoon's thick, velvety, tropical night. Smelling the heady mix of floral sweetness, smoke, and faint whiffs of sewage sent me back, unbidden, to my China little-girlhood eleven years earlier. In an unexpected way, I relaxed. I felt that I had returned "home" after a long absence, yet this place was also wonderfully new and "elsewhere."

Dad had taken a job in Burma as a program officer with what would become the United States Agency for International Development (USAID). In the middle of my junior year, January 1951, we found ourselves headed for this small country tucked in the crevice between the Indian subcontinent and the rest of Southeast Asia. Kipling's "On the road to Mandalay where the flying fishes play" was a familiar song (although who understood then that it spoofed English knowledge of geography?). Otherwise we knew almost nothing about Burma, except that it had recently won its independence from Britain.

The whole family had gotten shots and passports, decided what we would need to take and what we would leave behind. I said goodbye to friends and promised to keep in touch. Going half way round the world—knowing where and why I was going this time rather than abruptly leaving home—was an exciting adventure into the unknown. It was also daunting as I left what had become, with difficulty, accustomed and familiar.

Boarding a propeller airliner (all there was, then) and lifting into the air was an exciting first for all of us, except Dad. After two days hopping from New York to London to Rome to Cairo to Basra, Karachi, and New Delhi, we landed in Rangoon. Someone helped us gather our bags. Meeters-and-greeters from the American embassy whisked us into a car.

We were driven down miles of dark roads, occasionally passing flickering lights, then turned a corner and up a drive. The travellers had arrived at what would be "home." The old British-colonial, two-story house was ablaze with lights. As the car pulled up to the front door, a whole household staff was lined up, waiting our arrival. We met Sundrum, the bearer who would run the household; Nanny, who would mainly follow little brother Ted; and a cook, a sweeper, a gardener, and several others.

The embassy folks showed us around the high-ceilinged barney rooms—empty for much of the war and only recently cleaned and painted so we could move in. There was a "lounge," as the British called it, and a dining room down the center, huge bedrooms and bathrooms off both sides, and a semi-detached kitchen and pantry to the back. Upstairs was laid out the same way, except for the kitchen.

The embassy meeters-and-greeters left, and we were on our own in this vast house. We didn't even know where the light switches were. The household staff served drinks and nibbles, then they too faded away. Since daylight in the tropics is roughly from 6:30 a.m. to 6:30 p.m. year round, it may not even have even been that late. Nonetheless, exhausted, we chose our bedrooms: Mother, Daddy, Ted, and Nancy would sleep downstairs while Harriet and I would each have our own enormous room with its own bath upstairs. We unpacked enough to find something to sleep in, crawled in under the mosquito nets, and with windows open and ceiling fans turning, settled in for the night. Barely.

Bong, bong... bong, bong....

Banging shattered the calm. Before the nearest gong stopped, another started across the road. Then others rang down the way.

The ominous clashing echoed around us in the pitch-black night. *Bong, bong...* Were we being attacked? Was it dacoits? Insurgents? An uprising?

We streamed out of our bedrooms, into the living room.

I had read enough Kipling to have visions of dacoits (as bandits were called in that part of the world) and knew vaguely about an insurgency (a new word to me then) in parts of Burma.

No one had told us we had a night watchman who would spend every night outside the front door hitting a big metal bar to count each hour, every hour, all night long. *Bong, bong...* A watchman at one house who happened to wake up more or less on the hour would hit his bar, waking up the man next door, and so on. That night, our watchman was already awake. He sounded the hour first.

Mystery solved. Assured all was well, we staggered back to our beds. After a few days, we got used to what had became a comforting sound affirming that all was right with the world.

In the daylight, we surveyed the garden and neighborhood beyond. Rather than the dusty gray-green of my childhood north China, Burma was tropical—lush, emerald, and steamy. The house, which sat on the outskirts of the city, was in the middle of an orchard. Tall trees bore small brown fruit that looked like fuzzy potatoes and tasted like creamy cinnamon. We also found guavas, papayas, and, most of all, mangos—so many luscious, addicting new tastes.

Barely recovering from the war and the Japanese occupation, Rangoon was a faded-beauty British colonial-era city. In the humid heat where paint goes smudgy black with mold almost overnight, nothing had been painted since before the war. Although I had no way of knowing then, it was the first of many such former colonial capitals I would live in. By the nineteenth century, Rangoon was already a trading center for the British East India Company. The British had constructed government buildings and laid the city out in a grid along the Rangoon River, which, further on, ran into the Irrawaddy. Despite this British influence, the city was distinctively Burmese, with the gilded Shwedagon Pagoda towering over it and many smaller stupas piercing the skyline.

I began exploring downtown with my simple Brownie camera. Stinky open drains seemed to lay in wait for my unwary feet, but never caught them. I threaded my way down deteriorating sidewalks, passing stalls, shops, and beggars. So much to get used to: women with their faces smeared with thick yellowish-white *thanaka* (a cosmetic paste, made of ground bark, that was worn to protect the complexion). Men in sarongs. Buddhist monks swathed in saffron. Packs of pi-dogs running wild down the roads leading to downtown.

With Mother, we frequented Scott's Market, a sprawling, indoor space full of stalls that sold everything from locally made soap, brooms, and baskets to fish, meat lumps, and amazing fruit and vegetables. Our favorite section brimmed with intricately decorated lacquerware boxes, bowls, and even tables; painted wax-paper umbrellas; and beautifully carved mother-of-pearl.

Imports were still rare; few people could afford them. One day, after a first-ever shipment of clear plastic raincoats arrived, a small boy prancing in the rain and stamping in puddles proudly showed off his new treasure—stark naked underneath.

We lived unpretentiously. Even so, the family was well taken care of thanks to the phalanx of help in the house—many more people than we had in China but not usual for the place and time. Following the British-India caste-based custom, each person had a specifically defined job. One person helped in the kitchen, another cleaned bathrooms.

Poor general sanitation meant taking the same precautions as we had in China—cooking vegetables, carefully washing and peeling fruit, never eating vegetables raw, and boiling water, not just the water we drank and brushed our teeth with but also the water we used to make ice cubes for our drinks. Mother worked with the cook to make food more American and less British. The laundry came back, beautifully starched and ironed, but because it didn't dry completely, smelling faintly sour. Frequently rubbing down shoes and storing them in closets with lights kept them from growing green mold.

When we arrived, the Union of Burma had been independent from Great Britain for three years. The future Nobel Laureate and State Counsellor, Aung San Suu Kyi, was six going on seven and lived across the road from our house. Her father, Bogyoke Aung San, had been Burma's "George Washington," a nationalist leader and hero who had been instrumental in securing the country's independence. He had been assassinated in 1947, six months before Burma had gained its freedom.

When the country held its first national election, I spent a morning watching the Burmese cast their ballots at an outdoor polling place in the square across from the embassy—the first of many elections I would observe around the world.

Looking back, we were there in what was to be a truncated period of budding democracy and developing independent national identity, still filled with a sense of possibility, anticipation, and hope. It was also a time of communal strife. Insurgency had started well before we came and continues to this day. While we lived in Burma, insurgent groups of Shans and Karens, two of the larger of the one hundred or so ethnic groups in the country, were engaged in armed struggle against the central government. Driving out of the city much beyond the airport wasn't predictably safe. We rarely did. Once, travelling in a caravan of cars, we went to Prome, the next big town up the road.

At one point, insurgents blew up the huge pipes carrying water to Rangoon. Whoever did it had been clever about it. They counted the number of spare pipes in the entire country, and blew up one less. That left enough spares so that over time the pipeline could be repaired. Meanwhile, water was trucked into the city. At distribution points, women and children waited with buckets and tins to get what they could carry. (Like the elections, this was the first of many lines of women and children waiting for water I would see around the world.)

One day our driver was taking me into town and drove behind one of these trucks. Two shaved heads bobbed above the top of the open tank—laughing little boys enjoying a cooling dip.

Daddy and Mother were part of the diplomatic community. They also rapidly made friends through the Methodist church and in the wider society. In Mother's usual way, they soon had people over for parties at our house. She quickly observed that the Burmese liked to laugh and have fun while the Indians (about half the city's population) got into serious, sometimes contentious, conversations. It was a generalization, true, but she found it easier to have one group or the other over for dinner, rarely both together.

Besides running the household and the family's social life, Mother also oversaw "school" for my two younger sisters, who were taking American correspondence courses. I believe I had books and assignments, too, although I wasn't keeping at them. Instead, I enjoyed wandering around the area near the embassy, or going up the Shwedagon, or visiting the smaller Sule Pagoda across the open square from the embassy. In the afternoon, Mother, my sisters, my little brother, and I went to the Kokine Swimming Club (another remnant of the British, but by then it had Burmese members, too).

I needed to finish high school. My parents, exploring possibilities, heard from American missionary friends about a school in India located in the Himalayan foothills. In mid-June, three months after the school year had started, Dad and I were on our way to Woodstock, a missionary-run, kindergarten-through-twelfth-grade boarding school with an American curriculum.

At almost seventeen, my feet were headed out the door.

Dad and I flew to Calcutta to take a train north. The city pressed in on our taxi. Vaguely like the center of Rangoon, it was more crowded than any place I had ever been. We pulled up in front of a looming railway station teeming with people. A pushing group of men besieged us.

"Sahib. Sahib. I will lead you to your train," one said.

"Sahib," another pleaded.

"Sahib, I will…." a third yelled.

"You. How much?"

After Dad battled the scrum, chose a guide, and haggled a price, our small procession set off into the station. Together with the guide and the bearers carrying our bags, we edged our way through. The enormous waiting room was crammed with sections of tightly packed, squatting people: Men, women, and children, their faces haunted, tending small cooking fires. Waiting. Bihar, a province in northern India, was in the throes of draught and famine. To get to Calcutta, everyone who could clamber on a train had crushed together in the cars, climbed on the train roof, or hung outside off the windows, enveloping the train. And they were still coming. The station and the platforms were thick with starving people. I'd never seen, nor would I ever see again, such an enormous mass of impoverished humanity.

We had bought a bag of oranges. Oh, how I wanted one. I was hot, thirsty, and shaken. As inexperienced as I felt, I knew that getting out an orange would start a riot. We waited until we were on the train and heading north to eat them.

From Dehra Dun, where the train ended, a rattling taxi wound its way up the miles of hairpin curves on the one-way road to Missourie, one of India's fabled hill stations. We went as far as cars could go. Then, with bearers carrying the bags, we walked through the town, following the road to the school. Dad turned me over to Woodstock before lunch and left.

Nothing was familiar, neither the wider country nor the hillside over which the campus sprawled. We were between six thousand five hundred and seven thousand five hundred feet above sea level on a south-facing slope of the Himalayan foothills, which rose behind us. Donkey trains trotted along the road above the school, their bells ringing. Langur monkeys loped around. The Lyre Tree, the school emblem, grew near the Quad.

Every morning, we climbed from the older girls' dorm, called the College, some seven hundred fifty feet to the main school. Then, half running, we practically slid straight down the path to the dorm in the late afternoon.

Most of my classmates had known each other since kindergarten. Or if they weren't "lifers," they had been together for a long time—seemingly forever to a newcomer like me. Several class members who weren't even there that year were nonetheless so well knit into the group that they were ever-present in conversation and class history. Thirty of us would be there to mount the stage to graduate in November 1951—the others, nonetheless members of the class, were present in spirit.

The faculty and staff were mainly American, Indian, or Anglo-Indian. Like the rest of the student body, the senior class was a polyglot group: About half of us were American, although most had been born in India or lived there much of their lives. There were also half a dozen Indians, several Canadians, and two Burmese, plus Chinese, English, Italian, and Swedish students. For the most part, our families were living in (mostly northern) India. A few, like mine, were in Burma. A couple more lived in Pakistan.

Although we knew which country each of us was from, our nationality was only part of our identity. It never totally defined any one of us. We knew each other's country of origin in the same way we knew who was good at sports or played the piano or whatever.

In another sense, other than the native-born Indians, most of us had roots in two countries—usually India and somewhere else. So we shared a garbled sense of identity and "home." Mainly, we were the Woodstock class of '51, seniors to be looked up to.

If we categorized each other in any way, it was often by what our parents did: Missionary (including denomination), Business, Government. For the most part, even these labels made little difference, except for a few students who thought it was impossible to be in two categories at once: When Harriet went to Woodstock the next year, she mentioned something about being a Methodist. One of her classmates said, "You can't be Methodist, Harriet, you're Embassy." In its own way, Woodstock could be a compartmentalized world. Yet, most of the time, it wasn't.

Still, when I arrived I had lots to adjust to—and so did my classmates. Especially since they were expecting me to be a boy named Mike. I had used my Mamaroneck nickname on some of the school application forms. The administration knew I was a girl and assigned me to the girls' dorm. My classmates, however, had heard my nickname and made assumptions. The boys in particular were looking forward to having another guy to balance out the girl-dominated classes. Even though I wasn't the person they expected, the class welcomed me, the last outsider to join our group.

Looking back, school was, well, *school*. Like my classmates and I had in the States, we took classes and participated in extracurricular activities. I was in the school play and refereed basketball games (the boys games, because I knew the rules). The difference was that this was a *boarding* school. From the time we came up to the campus at the beginning of the year until we "went down" (the term for the end of the year when we literally went down to the plains), we didn't go home to family. Woodstock, the community and the place, was family and "home."

We older girls lived two to a room, each with a bed, dresser, desk and chair, and a shared closet. My first roommate, Charlene, a lifer, was a wonderful musician and outrageously good mimic who still regales us with stories at reunions. She was asked to help me get adjusted and was a great first roomie and guide. Understandably, she wanted to spend part of her last year at school rooming with a particularly dear friend. So after a few weeks I moved in with Georgia, who had joined the class a year earlier.

I settled into the school's routine: waking to a bell; going to breakfast in the College; racing up the road for classes, lunch, and other activities; then heading back down to the dorm for dinner, study hall, and finally, "lights out." We didn't always go to bed when we were supposed to. For the first half hour after lights out (if I remember correctly) no one was allowed to be out of her room. If we got caught by the clock and hadn't already brushed our teeth, we would peek out the door to see if the Housemother were there. (One night, Charlene on her hands and knees, peeking through the keyhole, met her eye-to-eye.) If the Housemother weren't in sight, we would quietly shuffle down the hall in the dark to the bathroom. Sometimes, if one of us had more homework or a good book, we would read with flashlights. Other times we would just chatter and giggle.

I had to get used to new food. And I more than succeeded, hence my addiction to rice, dal, and chapattis. But between the effects of World War II and the political unrest that followed India and Pakistan claiming their independence in 1947, food supplies were sometimes basic. More than one night, Carolyn, the class's leader, stood up in the dining hall, banged on a glass to get attention, and declared the "mystery meat" (probably water buffalo) served for dinner to be "inedible." When Carolyn said something was inedible, it was.

Going to church on Sundays was another part of school life. Woodstock, open by then for almost a hundred years, had been started for the children of missionaries. Although it was international, it clearly labeled itself a Christian school even though not all the students were. Church attendance was required. We were expected to dress appropriately. For girls that meant wearing something dressier than school-day skirts, blouses, bobby socks, and saddle shoes. Sometimes we opted for Indian clothing. One Sunday, a girlfriend helped me put on a sari, a several yards–long piece of silk worn wrapped around the body, with a thick bunch of pleats tucked into the front and the end thrown over the shoulder. My first trip into Missourie, I had purchased a lovely blue sari decorated with silver patterns along its edges and at the end.

As my friends and I hurried up the hillside, I stepped on the bottom edge of the pleats. Every inch of the sari fell to my feet. Fortunately, I also had on a *choli* (a fitted blouse that stops above the waist) and the customary long half-slip so I wasn't in my all-togethers. All of us laughing, my friends reassembled me. After that, when we decided to wear local dress, I put on my Burmese silk *longyi*, a simple silk sarong worn with a sheer top, which was much safer to manage.

The mountains and the seasons shaped school life. A few weeks after I arrived on the hillside, the monsoon season started, and with the rains, ugly green toads appeared. None of us liked them, but they petrified Georgia. One night while we seniors were having a class party in the big room at the back of the College, a couple of the boys slipped into the room Georgia and I shared and short-sheeted her bed, adding several toads to the mix.

With all the party excitement, we weren't ready for bed until after lights out. Georgia climbed in bed in the dark. Her feet met the sheet—and some toads. She shrieked and shrieked.

Our Housemother came, and, displeased, sent all the girls who had flocked to see what was going on back to their rooms. We straightened the bed; she settled us down and turned out the lights. Before Georgia got back in bed, she needed to wash her hands and feet to stop feeling toad slime. Back from the bathroom again, she slipped into her bed again—only for her feet to encounter yet another toad that had somehow escaped and was way down at the bottom. Her screams set off a second ruckus. Needless to say, the Housemother was even more displeased.

In October the rains ended and the toads disappeared. As the air cleared, and the dust on the plains below us settled, views opened up. On clear days, above the school near the Three Sisters bazaar and the community church, we could see the snow-capped peaks of the Himalayas. They bordered Tibet, just over sixty miles to the northeast. Facing southwest from our dorm, we could see across the plains. One magical night, we looked out over hundreds of small villages, their flickering lamps lit for Diwali (the Hindu festival of lights) as far as the eye could see.

In addition to climbing up and down and around campus daily, serious hiking was a school pastime. Toward the end of the year, after the rains but before it got cold, most of the senior class went trekking for a weekend. Since we girls needed to wait until the big pot of Spanish rice for dinner was ready, we left after the boys who had the campsite equipment. Somehow, late in the afternoon, well out on the mountainside, we missed the path and got lost. As evening settled in, we needed to stop somewhere until morning. A small hut looked promising, but we quickly realized herders and their cattle had used it. Clouds of flies and fleas drove us back onto the hillside where we found a reasonably comfortable spot to sit. We had no blankets but we had food. That Spanish rice was the best thing we had ever eaten. Under the stars close and bright, some of us slept some of the time.

In the morning, we discovered we were directly above the path we should have been on. Bounding down toward the boys' riverside campsite, we got there in time for breakfast. Replenished, all of us set out to climb a mountain, its bald, round top well above the tree line. Making it to the summit was exhilarating, especially for someone who had never climbed anything, much less a mountain. The view was spectacular. Lunch was good.

As most of the gang galloped down, like the mountain goats they had always been, I looked out into what felt like infinite space and froze. A few classmates clustered around me encouragingly while I turned around and went down backward, looking into the mountainside until we got to the visual safety of the trees. I made it.

With a backdrop of mountains, a surrounding hillside, and the plains below, the campus had an impressive setting. As the weather changed, the unheated dorms and classrooms that were designed for the semi-tropics were less alluring. The school year started in March, as the plains heated up and the mountain coolness was a relief. It ended in late November, before the heavy snows enveloped Missourie—but not before the air got *cold*.

By the time we took our final exams, it was so frigid we wrote with our coats buttoned tight and a glove on the hand we weren't writing with. When we finished one exam, we rushed outside, took off our coats, and sat in the sun to warm up before taking the next one. In my dorm room, in addition to snuggling under a wonderful wool blanket, I slept in several layers of clothing (including sox) and used my coat as an extra blanket. The dorms had only cold running water, which meant that, although I didn't learn much Hindi, I did master the phrase *garam pani lao* (bring the hot water), critical for Saturday baths.

In many ways, the school was an isolated community unto itself, yet India was always part of our lives. From time to time, we girls would go into neighboring Landour (a cantonment area nearer the school) or down the road into the town of Mussourie. Prowling the shops for goodies, we loved treating ourselves to *jelabi*, pretzel-shaped dough cooked in boiling cardamom-spiced sugar syrup or *gulab jamun*, small balls of sweet milk-solids. On one of our trips, I bought a small brass container for kohl (the black powder Indian women used as eye makeup.) It has sat on my dresser ever since.

Besides going on these casual town outings in small groups, the class also went on a class trip, to Haridwar—one of the seven sacred cities on the most sacred river in India, the Ganges. While the purpose of the trip was to visit an ashram to get a formal introduction to Hinduism, my overwhelming memory—like at the train station in Calcutta—is being engulfed by humanity: Multitudes packing the streets leading down to the river; throngs of believers praying and bathing; crowds huddling around food stalls and cooking fires, or just milling around; sacred white-humped cows wandering aimlessly. That weekend was my most intense experience of actually *being* in India.

Many aspects of India—from sounds and smells to food and pastimes—were constants at Woodstock. The school's culture (like all international schools, as I would learn) was not Indian or American. It was a third culture: a unique amalgam of place, time, and location, plus the cultures of the students and staff.

In Woodstock's case, one of the influences was a relatively conservative social ethos—or so it seemed to me. My earlier experience with teenage life in the States shaped how I saw things. At Bellows we danced and dated. At Woodstock we had parties; we didn't have school dances. I heard that when some parents were on the Hill, they would hold dance parties at their houses, though I was not on campus for them. Students didn't date, in the American sense, either or so it seemed to me. A few couples paired off, sort of, walking back to the dorms together and finding a quiet place along the way, as teenagers will. My classmates no doubt knew more about this than I did.

Although Presbyterians played a big role in starting and supporting the school, the mission boards that jointly ran Woodstock represented a range of denominations. There was more preaching and literalism than I was used to, even though I came from a mainline Protestant family with a missionary background. This specific aspect of the school culture sometimes made me uncomfortable. Yet the foundation of the school was inclusive, respectful, and harmonious. It was a community based on living, not shouting, deep faith.

Eventually November came and with it graduation. I made a long, white dress, and my parents treated me to a white rabbit-hair capelet. Mother came for the ceremony. Afterward, like breathing out, the students "went down," making their annual migration to the plains and home.

My five months at Woodstock were a short term bubble. Even though when I first "went up" I felt like a complete outsider, I was securely woven into the community by the time we graduated. I had learned how to fit in and enjoyed being a part of the senior class and the school itself. This unique cultural immersion was a happy way to begin experiencing new places and communities—on my own.

I went on to college with five of my classmates and found others there who had graduated from Woodstock. I wrote regularly to a few classmates and still keep in touch, thanks to email and Facebook. Judie, our tireless class secretary keeps us together with her letters. Many of us still gather for reunions when we can.

For our fiftieth class reunion, in 2001 soon after 9/11, Dan and I joined many in the class in going back to Woodstock. For me, it was the only time I've returned since we graduated. As the group travelled, I saw a great deal more of India for the first time, gaining a deeper appreciation of a vast, complicated, modernizing country.

Both the school and I had changed. I was seeing a familiar, yet unfamiliar, place with new eyes. My classmates and I laughed at the same stories and memories—they, more than I. Their experiences of Woodstock were deeper and richer. I remembered enough, though, to rejoice in reconnection and our shared love of spicy food.

More important than memories, we shared and still share a particular sense of the world we don't have to hide from, or explain to, each other. We were there at a decisive point in our lives. "I learned early," one classmate observed recently, "that things aren't just black and white." We—certainly I—had left Woodstock with tools to live in several worlds at once.

Back in Rangoon, with college still nearly a year off, I settled into an interim space and time, living at home, with a foot already out the door. Being a seventeen- going on eighteen-year-old single female, I was in a different nether-land: I was not generally included in the events the young diplomats organized. But I was too old to be in the group of younger teens who had arrived while I was gone and would go to Woodstock in March.

Sometimes I was invited to embassy social events on my own. More than likely, however, the "Miss Winfields" (Harriet and me) were invited with our parents. We went to the American National Day reception—held on Washington's birthday because July Fourth was in the middle of the monsoon and not good for a garden party. The Marine Ball, a gala to celebrate the anniversary of the US Marine Corps' founding, proved to be the first of many I would attend. Occasionally, I went to the ambassador's residence with our parents. More often, I helped in a range of ways at the USAID director's house.

To keep me busy, Dad gave me my first job: accompanying American development workers as they went to the field, usually in nearby villages. I interviewed them about what they were doing and why, then wrote profiles for their hometown newspapers. One man was introducing bored-hole latrines and squat plates to improve community sanitation. Another, Mr. Green, was surveying milk production.

Mr. Green showed me one way to get real answers, especially when asking about questionable practices. Inquiring whether water was added to the milk, he asked "How much water do you put in the milk?" Not: "Do you water the milk?" Adding water to milk was a practice that not only weakened the milk's nutritional value but also, because the water was contaminated, made it unsafe to drink. In many cases, Mr. Green showed me, that by assuming something was happening, I was more likely to get an accurate answer.

I learned too, that if you are interviewing, you must take notes, if for no other reason than to earn the trust of the interviewee. My memory was good and I trusted it, at least for the small pieces I was writing. But one person I was tagging along with didn't trust me to keep the facts straight, and he told me so. Thereafter, I took notes.

Altogether, the experience was my first taste of being (almost) grown up, doing real work.

The family travelled to the degree we could. The last trip the six of us took together, we flew to Maymyo, a hill station in the northern Shan states, for a week of relaxation where it was cool. We spent one day on Inlay Lake. The fishermen stood to row their boats with a leg. The old women puffed on cheroots. Other women wove interesting cloth on back-strap looms on the porches of their stilt houses.

I began taking serious photographs on that expedition. Dad encouraged me to use his good reflex camera to take thoughtful shots, not just a quick snap here and there. We were both pleased with my results. He chose five or six of the black-and-white photos (no color film then), cropped them slightly, and had them blown up. Then he sent my photographs to Congress as part of a report on this early development aid mission and what Burma was like. This experience started a lifetime of serious looking and image-making.

Several months before the trip to Maymyo, Harriet and I went with Dad to Mandalay, the last royal capital of Burma. Mandalay is well into the center of the country; nothing like Kipling's spoofy song about flying fishes or dawn coming "up like thunder out of China 'cross the bay." Dad and a movie team went to film the Burmese water festival, Thingyan. Held in mid-April, the five-day festival ushers in the Buddhist New Year. The rituals bring welcome relief from the sweltering days at the end of the dry season. At its most genteel, people lightly sprinkle jasmine-scented water on each other as a blessing. But for the most part it is an endless, raucous water fight with crowds sloshing buckets of water onto each other—a delight for young boys as well as the young men who up the ante with water hoses.

The first day in Mandalay we drove down the main street. Dad and his crew were in a van with a cameraman and big camera on a tripod standing on the roof. Harriet and I followed in an open jeep, getting deluged. Later we learned that, using his loud speaker, one of Dad's crew was exhorting the crowd in Burmese: "Don't throw water on the camera. Save it for the girls behind us." Picture two laughing, completely drowned rats.

A month later, the Indian ambassador to Burma, a family friend with a daughter my age, called our house. "Margaret," he said, "Eleanor Roosevelt has been paying a visit to India. Her plane has a stopover here in a few hours. I am going to greet her. Would you like to meet me there?" Would I! I grabbed my small camera. Mother arranged a car and driver. Off I went to the airport.

I found them in the guest waiting room. For about an hour, I sat cross-legged on the floor at her feet, listening, and taking a few snapshots. She focused on each of us intently, asking me about my plans and hopes for the future. When our grandson, Sam, started first grade at the Eleanor Roosevelt Elementary School in Morrisville, Pennsylvania, I sent the slightly-faded-to-sepia close-ups of her I took that day to her namesake school.

The trips and meeting Mrs. Roosevelt were some of the highlights of that interim year. At an everyday level, though, I became hooked on markets and the lovely practical things people make and how and why they make them. This began a lifelong curiosity that served as one way I would get to know a place and its people on their terms, at least as well as an outsider can. Describing the things people make and the people that make them became a life-long tool I have used for helping others appreciate a new place and different way of living.

As the time to go to college got nearer, I geared up to fly off into the world while my parents readied themselves for my departure. Mother was not entirely sure I would be safe, especially flying on my own. Some days it felt as if she were going to make me wear a sign that said: "Please don't feed the baby." As I experienced later, something much more unsettling was going on: The first fledgling was literally flying the nest.

In July I boarded a plane alone to cross the Pacific to the United States and the College of Wooster. On my way there, I paused for pre-arranged visits with my folks' friends. At the first stop, Hong Kong, I stayed with the doctor who delivered me in Jinan. After that, I went to Tokyo, followed by Guam and then Midway, where the plane stopped for refueling. Both places, the stewardesses took me in tow to navigate the military bases, which were also commercial airports, so I wouldn't be harassed.

Honolulu was the next to last hop. Dad's Johns Hopkins classmate, Dr. Chaing, a Chinese-American doctor, met me as I came though customs. That night, the Chaings took me to a Chinese restaurant to celebrate my eighteenth birthday. I'd already had three quarters of a birthday in Tokyo on the other side of the date line. That didn't make me nineteen—perhaps thirty-six?

Habitually, I picked up chopsticks to dig into dinner. The two young Chaings, about my age, picked up forks. Everyone laughed at the optics. The younger Chaings were American-born. Beneath the skin—certainly in the stomach—I was Chinese.

When I finished circumnavigating the world and landed back "home," this time on my own, I returned to the States changed. I was not totally transformed. Perhaps it's better to say I was "modified." I didn't know yet how that had already shaped my life.

In Retrospect

During our first weeks of classes, freshmen at Wooster wore dinks, as we called beanies, and hung cutout maps of our home states around our necks.

Figuring out my "home state" was a puzzle. New York never felt that way; it was more temporary. Missouri? Too long ago. I didn't consider China. I hadn't spent enough time in India. Wearing all of the states and countries I had lived in was impossible. Family equaled home equaled… Burma?

I drew an accurate, elongated, lumpy map with a squiggly tail dangling off its eastern edge. Cutting it out of cardboard, I colored it green, put a string on it, and hung it round my neck.

It was partly true that Burma, if not a state, was in a sense my home. In another way, I was trying to fit in by standing out, much like I did when I told the odd tale about a Chinese woman and her pig in Sunday school years before. I also chose Burma because I wanted to identify myself with our small gang of Wooster freshmen who had parents in India or Burma and who had been in classmates at Woodstock. As I saw lots of maps of Ohio, Illinois, Pennsylvania, Tennessee, or even New York hanging from students' necks, I realized that my experience didn't equate with those of my new classmates. I didn't have a "going-back-to-place" anywhere.

As a way of getting to know each other, my dorm-mates—perhaps feeling as fish-out-of-waterish as I did—talked endlessly about their senior years. Comparing notes, they laughed at stories about football games, sock hops, senior proms, class trips, movies, summer jobs, making out in cars, getting braces locked together one night while making out. Even though their high schools and hometowns were different they had lots in common.

To a degree, my memories from sophomore and junior year paralleled theirs, but those didn't have a senior year cache. My senior year—an important year I enjoyed and shared with my Woodstock friends—certainly didn't parallel theirs. I didn't go to a prom. I went mountain climbing, took a trip to Haridwar, went to a Marine Ball, and got doused in Mandalay. Then I flew half way around the world by myself instead of driving to school with my parents.

So I said less and less about before-Wooster, as I had learned to say less and less about China. I stopped wearing *phanat,* my lovely blue velvet thong-through-the-big-toe-gap slippers (unusual then in the States; rubber flip flops came much later). I wrote letters home and waited for answers. I spent Thanksgiving with a Wooster family and planned to celebrate Christmas with my Missouri grandparents.

Like my fellow freshmen I made new friends, began dating, and found my academic feet. The day-to-day life of being a college student kept everyone busy and increasingly linked to each other and this shared place and time as we established our new, emerging adult selves.

That spring, my world history professor invited me to talk on his weekly radio program about what the United States was doing to aid Burma. "What sort of development projects did you see?" he asked on the air that Sunday afternoon. I began to describe a project on community health and hygiene. I was halfway into a sentence that I knew should have ended with "bored hole latrine and squat plates" when my mind told me that wasn't what you said in Ohio on family radio, particularly on a Sunday afternoon. I don't remember what euphemism I pulled from nowhere. I said something.

Laughter greeted me when I went on to have dinner that evening with a missionary family I'd known in Burma. They knew what I hadn't said. Their reaction further brought home how out of sync part of me was with most of my age-mates, as well as with small town American life and ways of doing things—with America altogether.

In retrospect, spending two years in Burma and India, then returning to the States for college on my own when I was nearly an adult, profoundly influenced the person I grew to be. It has taken a lifetime and many moves to understand and articulate the essence of that person and of what I have come to understand: To use my shorthand, in my gut I know that the world is what I would call "multiple," not "singular"; different, not better or worse. Although we have humanity in common, and in that sense, we are "singular," within that there are many ways of being and doing, therefore we are "multiple." In its own way, for its own people, each society works; thus each is different, neither better nor worse, valuable for itself.

In such a world, I have been molded irrevocably into what felt then, and feels now, like a perpetual outsider—visible in some places, invisible in others, with heart and mind always in at least two places at once.

Clearly, I am an American in my own way. Figuring out what that has meant has been a confusing process. As I have aged, internalizing basic American values, representing them to others and speaking out to defend them, I have become increasingly relaxed in my American skin. Yet I remain irreversibly a global person—or as I would say now, culturally dexterous. I am a curious participant-observer, comfortable simply to see people as people rather than as stereotypes. Because I am at home in the world—in many worlds— I am stronger, more joyful, more "myself."

Memorial Days

When we still lived in Springfield, we helped Grandmother Parks and Aunt Maud fix flowers on Decoration Day (as Memorial Day was called then) to take to the cemetery. We used whatever flowers were blooming: White spirea that grew by the side of the house. Early roses—yellow, I think, with spikey little thorns. Maybe purple iris or deep pink peonies. We made three bouquets, each in its own glass jar, with water to keep them fresh.

The family piled in Granddaddy's old brown Chevy, and, like our neighbors, we went to clear the family plot of winter's debris and leave a bouquet. We drove through the cemetery, past white headstones and gently rolling green lawns dotted with maple trees. After we went to the family plot, we stopped to leave flowers at the tall monument on the side of the cemetery with Union graves. Then we went to the monument on the Confederate side, where we laid the last bouquet. Missouri was a border state. Folks had not so distant kin who fought on both sides

With World War II at its height, there were new graves to pass and be sad about. Great Uncle Hershel—still alive and living on Market Street near the rest of the clan—had been gassed in World War I. He survived, but he had buddies buried in the cemetery. The losses we were honoring during those small-town Memorial Days had faces and stories.

Today I live surrounded by many of America's historical ghosts, as well as its present. When we still lived in the condo the Capitol and Washington Monument with the City of Washington splayed around them was our daily vista. The Potomac River, threading through that view, got its name from the first Americans who used it as a trade route. Nearer us on the Virginia side, dominating the view, the Alexandria Masonic Temple, where George Washington was once a member, was attractive when it was lit at night. Mount Vernon, our first president's stately home, was above the Potomac a few miles south and slightly west of our condo. Quander Road, south of us, was named for the family of freedmen who had once been George Washington's slaves. Robert E. Lee's mansion, now host to the National Cemetery and honored dead from all of our nation's wars, was not far up the road the other way. The Episcopal High School, on the ridge to our northwest, lost more students in the Army of the Confederacy than Harvard College lost in the Union Army. We had a ringside seat for much of this panorama in our condo, which sat atop a ridge covered with the battlements the Union Army built to defend the nation's Capitol. From that ridge, it would have been possible to watch Washington burn in the War of 1812.

Every year on Memorial Day, phalanxes of motorcycle riders (mostly Vietnam veterans) collectively called Rolling Thunder leave the National Cemetery, cross Memorial Bridge, and ride to the Vietnam Memorial Wall to salute their comrades. The memorial's V-shaped stark black walls of polished stone reflect the life around them even as they honor the fallen. Fifty-seven thousand nine hundred thirty-nine names are etched there. The names of the first soldiers lost are listed in the center while those who perished last are on the memorial's outer edges. These too, had faces and stories.

At the Korean War Memorial on the other side of the Mall, life-sized bronze statues of an infantry platoon slog their way up a hill—a particularly moving site in the rain or snow. That wall is etched with faces, not names.

At unexpected moments, not just when we go to that Memorial, I remember Dennis Lofgren. His name and a small piece of his story I know. His face I no longer see.

Dennis and I met when we went to the same New York City church youth group. I was in seventh grade, he was in eighth. Our birthdays were two days and a year apart. I don't believe I knew if he had family beyond parents. I think not.

After my family moved to Mamaroneck, Dennis and I saw each other for what would be the last time, at a weeklong church camp on Long Island. After the camp, we became occasional pen pals. I was never sure why, but we were. Later, when I moved to Rangoon and then on to Woodstock, he thought I needed to know the music he was listening to and sent me a record. Halfway round the world, I was tickled that he wanted to keep me in the Stateside loop.

In July 1952, I was eighteen and had returned to the States for college. He had already joined the army and been sent to Korea. We continued to exchange letters. They were infrequent, buddy-to-buddy, friendly, full of his everyday life.

"Joe Gook's pretty active today…"
"…like to see almost anything in skirts…"
"…be home in July sometime, I guess."

Easter of my freshman year, 1953, I received a card with white lilies on it. It was signed, "Lovingly yours, the Lofgrens" on the front. Inside, below the printed greeting: "…the heartbreaking news that our son was killed March 23 in Korea." Dennis would have been twenty had he come home in July.

I haven't taken flowers to a cemetery in a long time. When we go to the State Department for whatever reason, I pause in front of the memorial plaques at both ends of the lobby and read the names of diplomats and consular officers who gave their lives in the nation's service. Some I knew. Some I had only heard of. My father-in-law's name should be there, but isn't yet.

Evenings, we watch the NewsHour. As it has for years, the program shows pictures of the fallen from Afghanistan, Iraq, and now Syria, "as their deaths are confirmed and their pictures become available." We sit in silence. We honor lost young lives. As the Afghanistan fighting began, they were the same age as our grandson. As the years have gone on, as he has reached his thirties, they have gotten much younger.

Each day, not just Memorial Day, has its own rhythm, its cycles of light and shadow, its own small wonders, its own reminders of people, times, and places. Paying attention: Another form of honoring.

BLAME THE REVOLVING DOOR

Dan Sullivan and I have been married over sixty-four years. Blame his parents. They were caught in a revolving door. Blame my parents. They heard the story. Like that door, "our story" goes round and round.

"Dear Margaret and Harriet," Mother's letter said. "I have met just the nicest family." Sisterly sophomore and freshman eyes rolled. Such letters had been coming to Wooster all fall. Harriet and I were both there my second year. Mother and Dad had recently moved back from Burma to McLean, Virginia; in her own way, Mother wanted us to look forward to coming "home." Instead of the usual next sentence—"They have a college-aged son"—this letter had a twist: "They have two sailors." Howls of laughter. The first whiff of Dan in my life.

Apparently, the Greens were visiting. They were long-time friends and colleagues of Mother's and Daddy's, first in China and again in Burma. Their daughter Joan had helped give me my first bath; in Rangoon I gained insight from him in asking questions and getting answers. One evening, Mother, Daddy, and the Greens went to a Rock Spring Congregational Church potluck and were sitting with the pastor's wife.

How the story came to be told, who knows? One of the Greens recounted something about their friends the Sullivans: Bess and the children were evacuated from Shanghai on one of the ships sent to bring Americans home in anticipation of war. Phil stayed to continue heading the economics department at St. John's University and was trapped in Shanghai after Pearl Harbor. When the United States government interned the Japanese living on the west coast, the Japanese retaliated by interning Americans still in Shanghai. Phil was in a prisoner-of-war camp for the better part of a year. Ultimately, prisoner exchanges repatriated Japanese nationals held in the United States to Japan and American and Canadian civilians in Asia to North America.

Phil Sullivan was among the men arriving in New York on the second exchange on the *SS Gripsholm*. The men's wives, separated both from their husbands and their China friends for much of the war, were gathered in a hotel lobby in New York. Waiting. Suddenly someone spotted a taxi. "Oh Bess! There's Phil."

To the cheers of "thousands," she hit the revolving door going out. He hit it coming in. They chased round and round and caught each other on the sidewalk.

"Bess and Phil Sullivan?" the pastor's wife asked. "They live near here. I work with Bess on Church Women United." Mother invited the Sullivans to have dinner with her, Dad, and the Greens. As mothers will, they compared children. Hence, the letter.

On December 22, 1953, the Sullivans' sons, the "two sailors," were brought to dinner to meet the Winfields' older daughters. Dan came in last: A lieutenant, junior grade, not a college boy. Ruggedly handsome. Wavy black hair. Craggy face. Blue eyes. His slightly jug ears the only feature that kept his face from perfection. He was taller than me by five or six inches.

He asked me out a few days later. One date. A spark. Not love at first sight. All that winter and spring, letters traveled from ship to dorm and dorm to ship. In June, I returned from Wooster by train and was looking for Dad as I came out of Union Station. A voice behind me said, "Margaret." Surprise. Dan, not Dad, had come to pick me up.

He had completed his hitch in the Navy, was newly home, and planning on grad school in the fall. That whirlwind summer the mothers competed for "best cook" honors, or so it seemed. For Dan and me, the daily question was which family—his or mine—was serving the most interesting dinner. We'd go there.

One dinnertime, he won my heart further and made my siblings jealous. Everyone in my family loved chicken gizzards. To avoid fighting over who got the gizzard whenever Mother fried chicken, we kept meticulous track of whose turn it was to have it. The Sullivans didn't eat gizzards. That night his Mother must have fixed chicken. Dan arrived for dinner at our house, bearing a gizzard, perfectly cooked and beautifully wrapped in aluminum foil.

As we got to know each other, Dan and I discovered how much we had in common. Dan was born in Shanghai five years before and five hundred twenty-six miles southeast of my birth in Jinan. Even more coincidentally, he'd been tossed around on a small inter coastal ship off of Shandong during the same devastating storm that broke the night I was born. He lived on the St. John's University campus until he was eleven. Like me, a college campus, as much as the city itself, was part of his home. Also like me, he had a gut-level sense of "place" he could taste and smell.

The Sullivans were Episcopalian missionaries, mine were Presbyterian. Like my parents, Dan's mother had been raised Southern Methodist. In 1922, just out of college, Mama Bess, as I came to call her, had come to Shanghai with her mother, the secretary for Women's Missions for the Southern Methodist Church. That year, Dan's grandmother, known as Hauboo, the Chinese term for grandmother, carried out her work traveling to various mission stations around China. They had also come to visit Oie, Hauboo's older daughter who was married to Sid Anderson, a Methodist missionary and the pastor of a church in Shanghai. While Hauboo traveled, Mama Bess stayed with her sister. Already trained as a medical lab tech, she taught at Margaret Williamson Memorial Hospital for Women and Children. The attractive Bess Lipscomb soon met Phil Sullivan, an eligible bachelor. When her mother, her work done, was returning to the States, Mama Bess decided to stay in Shanghai. Soon after, Bess and Phil married. Given the Mission that Phil, Dad Sullivan, worked for, she became an Episcopalian.

Unlike Mama Bess, my Southern Methodist parents had been "sold" to the Presbyterians. When they were ready to go to China at the height of the Depression, the Southern Methodists were broke and couldn't afford to fund missionaries. The Presbyterians had money and needed someone to teach public health at Cheeloo. Membership in the denomination came with the job. So my parents became Presbyterians. When they moved to McLean, Rock Spring Congregational Church spoke to them and they joined it. After Dan and I married, I followed the Sullivan "family pattern" and became at least a nominal Episcopalian. To me, since the mainline Protestant denominations share similar beliefs, the distinctions are mainly liturgical.

In the mass departure of families from China in 1940, Mama Bess, Dan, and his sister and brother left Shanghai on the *SS Washington* five days before Mother, Harriet, and I sailed to the States from north China on the *Mariposa*. Dan and I have memories of the same storm at sea.

To compound matters, and make ours an even more shaggy-dog *suhthern* tale (with a China spin on it), before she joined the Southern Methodist Mission Board, Hauboo, more formally known as Bessie Lipscomb, had been Dean of Women at a small Methodist women's college in Mississippi. My grandfather Winfield had been the president. The Winfields were also somehow connected to the Andersons, Dan's aunt's husband's family. We stopped asking after that, and make jokes about our "idjit" children's "pointy heads."

Dan and I had similar experiences and common values. We didn't have to explain to each other how we knew and understood the world and intended to live in it.

On my twentieth birthday, five weeks after I got home from Wooster, Dan and I were engaged. My parents blessed the idea provided I promised to transfer and finish college in Washington, where Dan was going to grad school. We planned the wedding for December.

Kitty, the Sullivans big yellow tabby, must have had other ideas. The summer we courted, if I opened the kitchen door, Kitty wouldn't come in. If I opened the can of cat food, Kitty wouldn't eat it. Then two nights before the wedding, we were sitting in the living room. Kitty marched in, tail in the air. She looked around the room with a disdainful air, stalked across the rug, and climbed in my lap. The wedding could proceed.

On the frigid afternoon of Thursday, December 23, 1954, a year and a day after we first laid eyes on each other, we were married in the same church where the story about the revolving door had been told. The reception was in the room where we met. The bridesmaids wore fire-engine red and carried holly. My mother made the wedding cake.

"Arranged Chinese marriage," we say, laughing.

My sister did not marry his brother.

Some stories have sequels worth telling. Within the first week at the continuing care retirement community where we now live, we had dinner in the community dining room with a couple we had known in our younger lives. "You should meet the Termans who live here," they told us. "They were both born in China, too,".

I found Sigrid and Ric Terman in our directory. Both a few years older than Dan, the Termans came to our apartment for drinks, followed by dinner in the downstairs dining room. Our stories were full of unique commonalities. Sigrid immediately became my *Jiejie*, Big Sister, and I her *Mei Mei*, Little Sister.

"What did you do when you left China?" Dan asked Sigrid.

"Went to Wellesley."

"What class?"

"Nineteen forty-seven."

As Dan started to sing the class song, her eyes got big.

"My sister was in that class," he said. "Liba Sullivan."

"Liba? My best friend."

The two women had lost contact when Liba began her life as a second generation missionary and went to Japan with her husband.

Besides the story about Liba, there was another twist to our shared history. Since the *Gripsholm* arrived in the States, the Sullivans have had a family picture that had appeared in *Life Magazine*: Three men in their shirtsleeves on a ship's deck. All were being repatriated after spending time in a Japanese prisoner camp. All were fathers of Wellesley freshmen.

We knew who two of the men were: Dad Sullivan and Dr. Mills, also from Shanghai. We never knew who the third man was, until dinner that night. He was Dr. Robinson, my new Big Sister's father.

SOUL FOOD: THIRD COURSE

College of Wooster, Wooster Ohio, February 1954
   The small group of undergrads with China in our American bones needs comfort from "home." "Let's make *jiaozi*," someone suggests. None of us has ever made them. Intrepid, we decide to try, letting our memory of how they taste be our guide.
   Finding the ingredients in the middle of '50s good-plain-American-food Ohio is tricky. A faculty wife who is also China-born produces powdered ginger (a poor substitute for fresh, but it works) and soy sauce. Ground pork is no problem. Round American cabbage, instead of *bai cai* (Chinese cabbage) will have to do.
   Some brave souls knead the dough and roll out the little circle-shaped wrappers, some of which are thinner, more together than the others—they will do. We sit around the table assembling the dumplings. Place a spoonful of ground meat and cabbage in the center; fold over the dough and wet the edges; crimp tight. Repeat. Drop the dumplings into boiling water. Skim out the cooked ones when they float to the top. Success—they taste more than enough like childhood and home to satisfy.
   As we make and eat them, my mind is elsewhere. Dan and I are in the tender first stage of a letter-writing romance. Wouldn't *he* love these *jiaozi*? "You can send him some," my inner six-year-old says. "Cook made them in the winter. They keep"
   I take six dumplings—beautifully crimped, not yet cooked—back to the dorm. I find the perfect container—the Dromedary fruitcake tin—and place a piece of folded Kleenex at the bottom of it.
   "Dampen it to keep the *jiaozi* moist," prompts my inner six-year-old.
   The *jiaozi* fit perfectly. I add another damp Kleenex on top.
   Down with the tin lid. Wrap. Address. Mail.
   "Dear Dan," that night's letter starts. "The China gang made *jiaozi*. I knew you would like some, and I have mailed them to you. They should get to Philadelphia in a day or two."
   The next morning, visions of red and green penicillin-mold prevail.
   "Dear Dan, Don't open the *jiaozi*. It's a penicillin factory."
   "Dear Margaret," the crossing letter says. "We are moving the ship to Newport," the big naval base on the Narragansett Bay.
   Letter three: "<u>Never</u> open the jiaozi!!!!"
   Letter four: "Throw them overboard IMMEDIATELY."
   He looked first, then ditched them overboard. No fish kill was reported in Narragansett Bay.
   He married me anyway.

Donning Multiple Identities

To get our marriage license in December 1954, Dan and I confronted Virginia's laws regarding women. For a woman to be issued a marriage license on her own, she was required to be twenty-one. I was several months short, therefore one of my parents was required to accompany me to the Courthouse to sign the license, thereby giving me their permission to marry and giving me to Dan. Had I been male and eighteen, I could have signed for myself. This was one of many paternalistic laws—designed to "protect" women—that were still in place across the country. The law presumed women were fragile, clueless to the wider world. In a deeply feudal sense, we were property, first of our fathers, then of our husbands.

I came to breakfast dressed with extra care, wearing stockings (which I usually avoided) and a good skirt.

"You look awfully dressed up," Mother remarked.

"Of course she does, Louise. She should," Dad hastened to say, not quite implying "silly woman." "She's going to get her marriage license." Mother was going with us to sign for me.

As a matter of law, I was becoming an adult woman. As a matter of personhood and identity, I was embarking on a much more complicated journey—a lifetime of evolving with Dan.

One box of the crisply engraved note cards read, "Mr. and Mrs. Daniel P. Sullivan," the other, "Mrs. Daniel P. Sullivan." They were ready for me to write thank-you notes for our wedding gifts: China. Dozens of pairs of silver salt-and-pepper shakers. Thick bath towels, carefully initialed *dSp* Twelve place settings of antique silver, their original monogram elegantly changed to *S*.

"Sullivan, Margaret," the art history professor called in the first class after Christmas break.

"Sullivan, Margaret," he called again, looking at me.

I stared back blankly. It was too soon in the alphabet for Winfield. Then it dawned on me! "Here," I said. Everyone laughed.

I had much to learn, starting with my new name and its variations.

Sometime in the early spring, Dan took me to Virginia Theological Seminary in Alexandria. "The Seminary," as it was referred to in certain Virginian parlance, was on "the Holy Hill," next door to the Episcopal High School, where Dan had been a boarding student for three years. "The High School," as it was called, was founded in 1839 to provide well-prepared students to "The

University" so there would be qualified candidates for "The Seminary."

That Saturday afternoon, Dan donned a coat and tie, as one does to be properly courteous. I wore my red wool "leaving the wedding" dress and a hat. Suitably dressed, the newlyweds went to call on Mrs. Virginia Bell, the retired seminary librarian.

When Dan was at the high school, Mrs. Bell had "adopted" him as an honorary Craighill. (Yes, this is another shaggy *suhthern* tale with a China spin.) Dan had known the Craighills since he was a boy in Shanghai. Mrs. Bell was a Craighill or somehow connected to that family. On Sundays after church, she would invite Dan, Peyton Craighill (one of Dan's classmates both in Shanghai and at the high school), and several other schoolboys who were somehow Craighill-related to her house to read the funnies and drink coffee.

Dan felt obliged to take his new wife to meet the formidable Mrs. Bell. White-haired, erect, and elegant, she greeted us at the door of her house on the seminary grounds. "Oh, Dan, how nice to see you. Do bring your bride in."

She turned to me and, in the most patrician southern voice I believe I have ever heard, asked: "Mrs. Sullivan, who *wer-uh* you?"

Realizing she was a well-connected First Family Virginian who needed to place people in their ancestry, I grasped what she was asking. I have an old Virginia maiden name: Winfield. All was well.

I knew *the people* I had come from, for all the difference it made, except evidently to her. I was only beginning to know where I was going, or what my sense of place (places) or my many identifications would be.

One new identity, "Dan's wife," meant being introduced into Dan's mother's sprawling Jackson, Mississippi, family. Unlike my grandparents, Dan's grandmother (aka Hauboo) hadn't come to the wedding. She was frail. Virginia was cold. Soon after the wedding, pictures were being mailed south.

"I don't think we should include that one," Mama Bess said, removing a receiving line shot of Dad's handsome, dignified, and black colleague from Rangoon-days kissing the bride. "They wouldn't understand," she said. By "they" she meant her uncles, aunts, and cousins, not her mother and oldest sister. The other pictures of that Negro family didn't get sent either. This was my introduction to the "what everyone knows but doesn't talk about" custom that glues many Southern families together. "No need to make an issue of it"— at least not over wedding guests.

Our first married summer, 1955, Dan and I drove south to Jackson to visit his grandmother and the Watkins and Lipscomb clans. In anticipation of our trip, Mama Bess taught me the "begats"—the names of her mother's seven Watkins brothers and sisters, her father's twelve Lipscomb siblings, and all their children and children's children.

In good Mississippi fashion, Hauboo's extended family hosted a reception for the bride and groom in Jackson. Though everyone was not related to each other, they were related to Dan, and by extension, they were now related to me, "Bess's daughter-in-law." Knowing vaguely who was who helped in facing a room full of new kin.

A few days later, we drove Hauboo back to Lexington. She lived there with her middle daughter, Tiddly (properly Tallulah) and her son-in-law, Ben, the local pharmacist and drugstore owner, Dan's aunt and uncle. Lexington, known as the "little tinder box in the hills," was the last Mississippi town to have had a lynching—until Emmett Till was murdered in Money later that summer.

The next morning, Dan and I strolled to the drugstore. While we enjoyed drinks at the soda fountain, Aunt Tiddly or Uncle Ben introduced us to all their customers as "Sistah Bess's son, Dan, and his bride."

"Where did you go to school, son?" one of the men asked.

"Princeton."

"Oh, I hear they just hired an African."

"I didn't know they had an African studies department."

"You *know* what I mean, son."

Incited by the year-old *Brown vs. Board of Education* decision, the man went off on the most racist diatribe Dan or I had ever heard. We were flabbergasted, infuriated and, as Aunt Tiddly's guests, speechless. We knew we shouldn't answer back. Dan looked one way. I looked another, waiting for the first possible chance to escape. At his next pause for air, and with a "Nice to meet you, Sir," we hastily excused ourselves.

Irately spewing about what we had just experienced, we burst into the house to find Hauboo. "How can you possibly live with that?"

"Everyone knows how I feel," she said, soothing us. "We just don't talk about it. We're family and have to live together."

Her funeral service two years later revealed that she had clearly found a way to speak up when it was necessary: The church in that small, usually segregated town was overflowing with an integrated congregation.

Nine months before that trip, in the fall before our wedding, I kept my promise to my parents and transferred to American University (AU) in Washington, DC. As a junior, also a bride-to-be then a newlywed, I continued my college-student life. Dan enrolled in

Johns Hopkins School of Advanced International Studies (SAIS), also in Washington. He planned to specialize in Asian studies in preparation for joining the Foreign Service (presuming he passed the exam).

Thus we started married life as students, living on the GI Bill in a small apartment in downtown Washington. Another couple and a six-pack of beer was a party.

As was the case at many colleges and universities in the early '50s, for the first time SAIS had a population of married students—mainly, like Dan, Korean War vets plus a few World War II vets who were going back to school. In our tightknit graduate school community, no one quite knew what to do with wives. Most of us were getting our PhTs (Putting Hubby Through), working to support our families while our husbands studied. Only one other wife and I were still undergrads.

The upshot was that we, like our grad-student husbands, had the run of SAIS, using the library or sitting in on courses if we wanted. (We also cooked for student parties; that, too, came with the territory.) Between popping in on courses and special lectures at SAIS, taking one course in Asian history at American University, and typing Dan's papers (he hunted and pecked some of mine in exchange), I got a reasonably firm grounding in Asian studies without a credential. It served the purpose.

Life was full. I was learning to become a wife, without knowing what a wife was, or even if I wanted to *be* whatever a wife was. I was beginning to learn, too, who I was as an adult, if I were, indeed an adult. If I were an adult, was I becoming the person I wanted to be?

There was sex to explore. That, too, took learning and practice. I found myself wondering, *Is this what it's cracked up to be?* Yes? No? Yes. Maybe... I've had a lifetime exploring and enjoying that one.

Having not yet begun to take homemaking seriously, in many ways, I was only "playing house." I had a GI Bill budget to stick to, cooking to learn, groceries to buy, meals to fix, and laundry to do. Plus I was still a student with textbooks to read and term papers to write. Senior year, to bring in some income, I was a teaching assistant with papers to grade and classes to plan.

On the bus to and from AU that first spring, I puzzled over niggling doubts: What have I gotten myself into? Who is this person I've married anyway? The commitment I had made quickly and joyfully I was solidifying by fits and starts.

Before we met, Dan had decided to sit the Foreign Service exam in hopes of being a diplomat. I'd happily, casually, seconded the plan. The notion wasn't totally foreign. I'd lived on the fringes of an American embassy in Rangoon. Dan's coursework and the papers

I typed for him included diplomatic history. I knew the fundamentals: Diplomats and Foreign Service officers represent the United States and advance American interests abroad. And, as I came to learn, diplomacy is the front line of American security. Being part of that had its attractions.

Little did I know that these two commitments—to each other and his career—would shape the long haul. He jokes that if he hadn't been planning to live internationally I wouldn't have married him. We laugh. He was (still is) extremely attractive. The prospect of living around the world, especially returning to Asia, and doing it with Dan was enticing.

When I graduated from AU in June 1956 with a major in English and minors in French and economics, I was within weeks of delivering our first child. We had consciously decided to become parents. That commitment—which, like marriage, was a leap into the dark—gave us *irrevocable* identities and responsibilities as parents.

Dan took the exam and passed. In September, two months after his master's degree was conferred and three weeks after Jerry was born, Dan—essentially all three of us—joined the Foreign Service. We donned yet more identities.

Soul Food: Fourth Course

Washington, D.C., February 1956

Most expectant mothers crave ice cream or dill pickles. I crave *ling ling tang* (zero-zero soup) and *jiaozi*. On a GI Bill income, we eek out the occasional cure for my cravings at the Peking Palace, a restaurant far out on Connecticut Avenue, which serves home-cooked–smelling, authentic-tasting comfort.

Ling ling tang is hot-and-sour soup without the hot, red pepper, or the sour, black vinegar. It's made of *doufu* (bean curd) and a few vegetables. Their *doufu* is good. But it doesn't pass the recollection test of the fresh-made nuttiness from my childhood. The *jiaozi*, however, make this expectant mother six again.

Pan Am Flight 7

November 9, 1957

Not yet morning. Soft darkness. Comfortable bed. An insistent phone jars us awake.

"Daniel Sullivan? This is Pan American Airlines. Has your newspaper come?"

No it hadn't. Or, if it had, we hadn't opened the apartment door to get it. Pre-dawn quiet and more time dozing—particularly on a Saturday—is a treasure when there's a still-sleeping toddler in the house.

"Are you the son of Phillip and Bess Sullivan?"

"Yes."

"We need to tell you that Flight 7 is overdue in Hawaii. The pilot checked in at the Point of No Return. Nothing has been heard since. We want you to know before you see it in the paper."

The hollowed-out waiting began.

Dan's parents, along with thirty-four other passengers and eight crewmembers, were on that plane. The round-the-world flight was scheduled to end in in the same place it started, San Francisco. The plane had taken off at noon West Coast time (three in the afternoon in the Virginia suburbs) on a ten-hour first leg to Honolulu. Some five hours later, when it could no longer turn back to San Francisco, it disappeared.

As the Labor Officer for the State Department's Far East Bureau, Dad Sullivan had returned occasionally to Asia since the war. This time he was leading the US delegation to the International Labor Organization's regional meeting in India.

Mama Bess hadn't been back to that part of the world since the family was evacuated from Shanghai in late 1940. She was going as far as Hong Kong to visit her sister, Olive Anderson. Oie, as everyone called her, had moved there from Shanghai when her husband became the colony's Methodist district superintendent. After his meeting in Delhi and her visit with Oie and Sid, Mama Bess and Dad Sullivan were planning to spend Christmas with their daughter, Liba, and her family in Kyoto, Japan.

Dad Sullivan had meetings in San Francisco before heading across the Pacific. Dan had seen him off at the airport several days earlier. The night before Mama Bess was going to join him, Wednesday, if I remember, she came by to have supper with our then fifteen-month old son, Jerry, and me. Dan was at Naval Reserve training. Thinking of her dietary restrictions and health, I made a simple supper seasoned with lemon, not salt.

91

Mama Bess had warm black eyes, graying hair, and an addiction to feathered hats. Ever since I had met her nearly four years earlier, she had struck me as loving and firmly principled. An upright woman who never lost her Mississippi accent, she preferred to say she was from Tennessee because she had graduated from Vanderbilt. She was embarrassed by Mississippi attitudes toward race. She and my mother—who met Mama Bess before I did—shared a Church Women United connection and participated in interracial activism well before the civil rights movement.

Mama Bess had clear ideas about raising children: "Don't ask if he wants to wear a sweater. Ask if he wants to wear his blue or his red one." She and her sons—Dan and his younger brother, Don—played cutthroat triple solitaire with a single rule: One foot on the floor. Dad Sullivan, a sweet, round, teddy bear of a man with a dry wit and a twinkly eye kept out of their way. (So did I.)

Dan's mother wasn't always an easy woman. I occasionally hear remnants of extremely firm childhood "training" in her son and his expectations of himself. I experienced her disciplined way of doing things from time to time, too. She loved him, me, and us. I was grateful for that.

As strong as she was on the outside, she was fragile on the inside. A great many pieces of her—breasts, part of her stomach, other organs—had been removed over the years. Each time she said: "Well, that's one less thing to die of."

When she came for dinner that night, we talked some about how her digestion was not working well again; how occasional dizziness had returned (hence, no salt.); and how further tests would need to be run when she got back from her much-anticipated trip to Asia to see her sister and daughter.

I did not tell her that I was newly pregnant—maybe three or four weeks, in that early queasy stage. We were barely certain, not quite ready to tell even family. She and Dad Sullivan did not know about the prospect of Gay.

That Saturday remains a blur. We called my parents and must have called Dan's brother, Don, in Massachusetts and Hauboo, in Mississippi. Somehow we—or maybe Pan Am—contacted Oie and Uncle Sid in Hong Kong and Liba and Ed in Japan. Ordinary folk didn't make international phone calls in those days. We tried and failed to reach Dad Sullivan's brother, Uncle Walter, in Detroit. He heard about the missing plane on his car radio. The announcer had said that "Phillip Sullivan, formerly of Detroit" was on the flight.

Our phone kept ringing. Reporters called with awful, intrusive questions that they seemed compelled to ask and believed we, even in our shock, were obliged to answer: "What are your thoughts?" "How do you feel?" "Did you have a premonition?" I still boil at those questions, particularly the one about the premonitions.

Maybe it would have been better to take the phone off the hook. Except that there was no caller ID. We needed, wanted, to answer some of the calls. We were waiting to hear from family and friends. We hoped for more information from Pan Am.

Only there wasn't more information.

Not on Sunday.

We went to the church at the nearby seminary, where the congregation knew us and was getting to know Mama Bess and Dad Sullivan. They tried to comfort us. I felt I was actually comforting the comforters, who struggled to say something helpful. We knew they were holding us in concern and that we were not alone. That helped.

Not on Monday.

Not on Tuesday.

There was a request for dental records. Otherwise, the news was our main source of information. All we heard was that nothing had been found. Pan Am 7 was lost without a trace. Ships and planes were scanning the Pacific in the largest peacetime search since Amelia Earhart.

Not on Wednesday.

Not on Thursday. Nor Friday.

For two months, we'd been planning to go to Princeton for the Yale game and a gathering of Dan's classmates. Somehow that week, getting away seemed, well, like a chance to take a break and go back to being normal. Mother kept Jerry. We left contact numbers and drove up early Saturday morning.

The weather was lousy. One team won (we were there in body, not in enough attention to remember which). Friends were concerned and comforting. Late afternoon, somehow (the details are blurred) we got a message to call Mother and Dad.

Debris had been found. And a few bodies. A US naval ship was bringing what they had been able to recover to Los Angeles. Pan Am needed Dan and representatives of the other families to fly there, at the airline's expense, to possibly identify bodies. The flight would leave Washington late Sunday evening and arrive in California Monday morning.

We left Princeton immediately and headed home. Apprehensive. Relieved. Still hollow.

The night was foggy, so thick we couldn't see. Just beyond the Delaware Memorial Bridge, when we couldn't even glimpse the taillights immediately in front of us, we decided to stop at the first motel we could find. Inching along, we hoped a lighted sign would appear in the gloom.

The kid who checked us in and led us to our room smirked as he offered ice to us—a young, baggage-less couple. We still laugh at the memory of the two of us, physically and emotionally exhausted, falling immediately asleep under the flimsy blanket, still in our clothes—a far cry from the image of us the leering kid had in his wishful-thinking mind.

Don came from Massachusetts to fly to the West Coast with Dan and me. No one of us was willing to let the others go on a plane alone, even if it meant buying two tickets. Flying still wasn't something folks did at the drop of a hat. While I had flown internationally, this would be Dan's first commercial cross-country flight.

With each change in pitch in the propellers or jolt as the plane hit an up or down draft, we *knew* we would crash. We flew all night. How many long hours, I don't recall. It was endless. We didn't sleep. Dan remembers seeing the lights of Las Vegas. I recollect tension and yet another alteration in engine sound and bump in the air—and then another and another—feeling certain we would crash. Then we landed.

Pan Am gathered the family members in a hotel ballroom, each individual or family group lost in their own fears and silence. There must have been food and some conversation. Finally a Pan Am representative took us aside. They had identified Dad Sullivan's body. His passport was in his pocket, not too waterlogged so they hadn't needed the dental records. Mama Bess hadn't been found.

We flew home. The plane changed pitch and jolted. Somehow, like getting back on a horse after you've been thrown, Dan and I were completely relaxed with flying.

As bereft as we were, we were also, in a way, relieved for them that they were together. They were still young, neither yet sixty. One long wartime separation had been enough. A lifetime for the person left behind would have been too much. But, for us, double the loss.

Two Episcopalian priests, longtime family friends, came to lead the funeral service in the Bethlehem Chapel at the National Cathedral in Washington. As they duly prayed for "Thy servants Philip and ... Elizabeth," I looked at Dan and he looked at me. It was hard not to giggle. Her name was, had always been, Bess. Not short for anything. Bess. We could see her, up on a cloud watching, nudging Dad Sullivan and saying: "Phil, who's that woman they're burying you with?"

Ultimately, there was an inconclusive report. To this day, nearly sixty years later, what happened is a mystery. The passengers probably knew they were going to crash. Some bodies had on life-vests. Their shoes were off. There may have been fire. Why it went down—electrical difficulties? lightening strike? a thrown propeller? something else?—was a question that was never definitely answered.

Gay arrived in July. So did Eric, Liba's fourth child, followed later by a daughter. Mama Bess and Dad Sullivan didn't know about them. Nor did they meet Don's wife or their children. Even the older grandchildren never had the chance to know their grandparents except as faded snapshots and characters in family tales.

Our lives went on, full, yet missing something. The daily moments without them were joyous and sad. Thanksgivings and Christmases were celebrated. Milestones were passed. Great-grandchildren, then great-great-grandchildren were born.

Dan and I have flown the Pacific more times than I can count, no longer worried. Somewhere along each trip we think of Mama Bess in her resting place. The words in the telegram from Oic that arrived the day after the crash remain true: "Still we are together in Our Father's House."

When we wake in the early morning to radio reports that a plane has disappeared, lost somewhere in some ocean, that earlier Saturday morning echoes. Pain reawakens. Empathy of the "takes one to know one" kind goes out. Our empathy is not so much for the eventual loss, hard as that is, but about the waiting. The not knowing. The never knowing it all.

Two for the Price of One

When Dan was sworn into the Foreign Service in 1956, we set off on a multifaceted, life-defining adventure. He took the same oath to protect, defend, and uphold the Constitution of the United States of America that he had when he joined the Naval Reserve Officers Training Corps as a college freshman. I was along for the ride, unsworn. Nonetheless, I was bound to represent and defend.

I felt as if I were returning to something familiar, going "home" in a way. To a degree I was. This time, however, I wasn't the teenage daughter in the embassy community in Rangoon. I was a Foreign Service Wife (FSW). Often said as if it were a proper name, this was a profession and an identity for many women. For me it became a partial identity and a springboard to what became a career of my own. As I was to learn, being an FSW was a time-consuming role. The longer one did it, the more of a full-time job it became, albeit without a paycheck. Even so, it came with its own rewards: a ringside seat with walk-on roles in a fast changing world.

In 1959, after an initial tour at the State Department, Dan was assigned as the third secretary of embassy in the consular section of the Embassy of the United States of America in Kuala Lumpur, Malaya. This marked a major change in our lives.

I had been home with our two small people being a mama and housekeeper while Dan went off to his office at the State Department every morning—the typical '50s pattern. With this assignment, we started on common yet parallel journeys. While his assignments determined the road we traveled as a couple and family, where he was posted and the particular job he had gave him his own Foreign Service Officer's (FSO) story to tell. It gave me, a Foreign Service Wife, my own story, too.

In anticipation of going overseas, I attended the Wives Course with other young wives of incoming FSOs. Several ambassadors' wives, each a formidable "grande dame" (or so they seemed), instructed us on what would be expected of us at post, as wives, and in purely social terms, as couples. In their way, they initiated us into what at the time was an arbitrarily defined "two for the price of one" occupation.

It was also a kind of sorority. Our husbands may have been hired, but we, too, had duties expected of us. In essence, each of us assumed her place in a hierarchy headed by the ambassador, who was the personal representative of the president of the United Sates. The ambassador's wife led the wives. Position, title, years in service, and time at post determined the husband's diplomatic rank, which was automatically grafted onto his wife. Just as the officers had a combination of substantive and representational obligations, there were expectations—stated and unstated—of what a wife would do to support the embassy and to foster her husband's career.

Technically the officer, not the wife, is the official American diplomat. In other ways, though, the wife is a diplomat, too. (For instance, she travels on a diplomatic passport, as do her children.) Consequently, wives are extended the courtesies that go with that status, including immunity from taxation and prosecution under local law. Willy-nilly, the wife—actually, the whole family—is seen as a formal face of America. She must mind how she behaves and what she says about the people and country where her husband is assigned. She must also think about how she speaks about the United States and the current Administration, no matter her personal views—leave those thoughts and words in the bedroom. (And, at many posts, be careful even there; the house may be bugged.)

Within days of arriving at post, the grand dames instructed, wives made formal calls or were called upon. There was an intricate protocol, which we learned in detail, for making diplomatic calls. How the officers' and wives' cards were worded, how many were left when one called, and which corner of the cards were turned down under what circumstances was all prescribed. Who called on whom depended on the husbands' ranks, e.g. juniors called on seniors. Since Dan was at the bottom of the diplomatic list, that first post was simple: I called on everyone.

As a member of the embassy family, we were further told, when we were invited to senior officers homes—especially the ambassador's residence—we were to arrive fifteen minutes before the appointed hour. The instructions continued: Recognize you are not a guest but there to help entertain. Leave after the last guest. At other events where the ambassador and his wife are present, greet them promptly. Be available if they need something. Don't hover; be in eye-catching view. Do not leave before they do.

Dressing appropriately was important: For tea, cocktails, or a black- or white-tie occasion, it was presumed we would always appear in a suitable outfit chosen from a wardrobe sufficiently expansive for the constant social round. We also needed to own white four-button and eight-button gloves and know when to wear which (these specifics I've conveniently forgotten).

In our first two posts, we lived in the fading remnants of the British Empire and its unique sense of propriety. Even on the equator, the British wives wore hats, gloves, and hose with a seam up the back that needed to be kept straight. From my experience in Rangoon, I already knew stockings made sweat drip down my legs. After the cockroaches ate my nylons I'd thrown them out. I didn't bother after that. Long gloves were far too hot on the equator, so I nixed those, too. However, my big, deep-green Italian straw hat was the perfect walking umbrella for the Queen's Birthday garden party in Kaduna, Nigeria.

Dan fared better. For men tropical dress was a white dinner jacket, white shirt, and a black bow tie. He purchased two jackets from a specialty haberdasher in Baltimore that sold clothes for the tropics all year round. They lasted (and fit) his entire career, all of which was spent on the equator. His seersucker suits had to be replaced occasionally. That was it.

What I remember most clearly from the Wives Course, however, was the hierarchy of sitting on the sofa. The basic rule: Don't sit on the sofa—no matter how long it is or how few chairs there are in the room. The sofa is for the guest of honor. Period. The hostess invites one person at a time to sit and talk with the special guest. No one else joined them without invitation. In my experience, this rule applied mostly to ladies' teas or coffee mornings, although it was also observed at the end of the meal when the ladies left the dining table to have coffee elsewhere. (The men stayed at the table for their coffee, brandy, and cigars.) I had assumed that the Sofa Rule was only for the wives. Many years later, a retired male Foreign Service officer told me he had to follow the rule at his first post, too. We had a good laugh.

There was much more: appropriate diplomatic and consular titles and forms of address; how to word formal invitations and responses; how to give a formal dinner and seat people according to protocol; how to set a table, with its different forks and wine glasses; whether to send flowers before a dinner or after. On and on.

These dictums and practices had been set when diplomacy was a tight little island that focused on Europe and prescribed European manners. For a new Foreign Service Wife embarking on her first tour abroad, the gist was this: At post, wives were expected to do whatever the position of the husband, his boss's wife, and, above all, the ambassador's wife required. This could feel like, and sometimes indeed was, an imposition. For all the ways it struck me as pompous and stiff, protocol, as a commonly held set of social rules, worked (though only partially in some places, as we were to learn), ensuring that much of the social work of diplomacy was carried out smoothly. In their own way, they also reinforced a sense of belonging.

As I learned what was required of me, it became clear that, though the Department hired Dan, they *expected* to have both of us: "Two for the Price of One." I was instructed and forewarned. We embarked.

LISTS OF LISTS

As Dan's tag-along and a Foreign Service Wife—a "two-for one-er" or "two-fer"—I made nine international moves in twenty-nine years—roughly half my adult life. First adding children, then peeling them off, we circled the equator, always landing in post-colonial, independent nations with strong Muslim components: End-of-the-emergency Malaya. Newly independent, last of the Brits Nigeria. Suharto's New Order Indonesia. Martial-law Philippines. Pre-bloody civil war Sierra Leone. Late Lee Kwan Yew Singapore. And four stints in Washington, where we started, mixed in.

Life in the Foreign Service was richer and more complicated than the formal diplomatic protocol laid out in the Wives Course. Foreign Service culture had been mainly East Coast Ivy League elite and Eurocentric prior to World War II. The Service we entered in the late '50s was changing, as was American society more broadly. With the GI Bill and its options for higher education, incoming officers came from more diverse backgrounds, educationally and regionally. Likewise, before the war, there had been few women officers. Afterward, more women and non-whites joined.

When single officers met and married, the woman, *not the man*, was expected to resign and follow him as a Wife, not as a fellow FSO. A friend who resigned without regret said, "You can always get another job. Good husbands are hard to find." Regulations changed eventually so that both spouses could keep their positions. Wives who had been required to leave, like my friend, were given the opportunity to rejoin as officers. Some, like her, did.

Tandem couples (both spouses serving as FSOs) are now more common, although finding a post together or two posts near each other is its own complication. By the late '90s, gays and lesbians were no longer denied security clearances and began to feel comfortable being "out." Now same-sex couples, including ambassadors with young families, are openly part of the Service.

With the end of World War II and the explosion of post-colonial newly independent countries in the '40s and '50s, the United States was opening scores of new embassies and consulates, many in Asia and Africa. This, too, enriched and complicated Foreign Service life. Dan and I were excited to be a part of what we sometimes called the "other" non-European Foreign Service. I had already dipped my toes in that world in Rangoon and India, but even so, each time we moved, there was so much more to absorb.

Much of the practical dailyness of non-European diplomatic living was not covered in the Wives' Course. Reading the post report, which covered everything from weather to schools and shopping, helped. Mostly, we figured things out on our own or learned by word of mouth. At most posts, another couple—the wife, usually—would meet us newcomers and help us settle. Beyond that, we found colleagues who were deeply involved in local life to show us the ropes. And we in turn took others under our wing as we assumed our roles in the meet-and-greet, mentoring network that furthered the sense of community and belonging in the Foreign Service.

Dan's assignments shaped our lives. When he joined the Service, junior officers' first two overseas tours, usually two years each, were in two different parts of the world. Once at post, the junior officer rotated through various positions. The point was to help an officer find his niche, and, more critically, for the Service to learn where he would be most useful.

During our first tour, at the recently opened small embassy in Kuala Lumpur, Malaya, in Southeast Asia, Dan started as a consular officer, issuing visas to foreigners going to the States and providing a range of services for American citizens. After a year, he worked in the political section, a position that required him to follow internal politics and the host country's foreign relations and write reports about what he learned.

His next tour was at a new two-officer consulate in Kaduna, Nigeria, in West Africa. It was the constituent post for our embassy in Lagos, the capital. As the vice consul, he had across-the-spectrum responsibilities, including consular work and political and economic reporting as well as serving as the acting principal officer when the consul was gone—the works.

After the first two posts, officers usually opted to focus on a single geographic area. Generally the officer also specialized in a specific area of work, "cones" as they were called: political, economic, consular, and administrative.

Dan's career primarily involved political work related to Southeast Asia. His specialization provided both of us the opportunity to develop a deep base of knowledge about the history, politics, and culture of that specific area of the world. We also established networks of personal relationships, both in countries in the region and, when he was stationed at the State Department, with officers working on those countries. Such expertise and relationships were (and are) the bedrock of diplomacy.

For Dan, his specialization also meant being "owned" by a geographic bureau, in his case FE (Far East) and when the name changed, EA (East Asia). Which bureau owned you, who you knew or worked for, made a difference in terms of hearing early about new position openings or having a good word put in up the line.

Every two to four years, as he neared the end of a tour, Dan checked out posts and positions that would be available at the right time for the next transfer. We would discuss the possibilities, then he could "bid" on a position that he hoped would be the next assignment. The bidding was competitive; everyone wanted a "good" post. In the end, the needs of the Service determined where and when he, we, would be assigned. Travel orders arrived. We moved. Never mind how the timing might suit the family's preferences or needs. Our transfers, like most, happened in the summer when American schools were not in session. This timing didn't always coincide with school calendars at the new post.

Dan continued his old position until it was time to travel. After we left, we might spend a few days somewhere on the way, to see someplace new or visit family. If we could, we arrived at a post on a Friday so we had the weekend to deal with jet lag and settling in. (The rule of thumb for recovering fully is a day per time zone. Traveling half-way around the world, we usually shifted twelve hours, so it took twelve days to recover—more as we aged.)

Dan was off to the office a day or two after we landed. Though his specific position, title, rank, colleagues, and boss changed, his basic responsibilities stayed largely the same. For him, this meant considerable continuity between one post and the next.

Not so for me. First I had to organize getting us there, then I began from scratch—reinvented myself—in each place.

When the travel orders came, with anything from several months to several weeks notice, I started making lists.

My job was organizing and packing up the household, which necessitated that I walk away from whatever I was doing outside the home. Whether I had community obligations or, later, a job, I rushed to hand over my responsibilities to someone else, or I left things unfinished.

The basic organization started with the entire family being required to pass physicals—Dan and I at the Department health unit, the kids with our pediatrician. We also needed to get the appropriate shots. We set travel dates, and then, working from an approved list of movers provided by the government, organized times for them to come pack us out. The government covered shipping costs within weight limits, and paid storage costs for what we left behind.

After the basic timeline was set and I had read the post report, I then began figuring out what we would need to take and what to leave in storage. Additionally, because we were usually going to places with limited shopping options, I had to decide what I had to purchase to be sure we had what we needed and couldn't get there.

I knew, for instance, we would need a range of small transformers to use one-ten equipment on two-twenty current. Or not take my hand mixer at all. General Electronics in downtown Washington was on my "go to" list.

Clothes were an issue. Ordering from Sears from overseas was by guess and by gosh, depending on whether packages came to the post through a pouch or open mail. Buying ahead also had its downside. I had to try to guess what size clothes each kid would need for at least the next year. The bought-before-we-left, peculiar-colored pants (an odd orange if I remember) that one son simply didn't outgrow and had to keep wearing (unhappily) for two years, were a disaster. Buying shoes was tricky. Who knew how fast small feet would grow?

In addition to figuring out what to buy ahead, I organized how everything was managed—more lists! Airfreight would arrive at our destination about the same time we did. Each member of the family got a two-hundred–pound allowance. The sea freight got to the post when it got there—often at least three months, sometimes more, after we did. That allowance depended on whether we were going into furnished or unfurnished housing. So I figured out what went in the airfreight (immediate necessities, bedding, the kitchen, kids toys), what went by sea (books, art, furnishings, more kids things), what stayed in storage (anything that didn't go but we wanted to keep), and what we disposed of (the remains). Every few years we literally handled everything we owned.

The Singer Featherweight portable sewing machine—my weapon against government or local owner interior decorating—was at the top of the "must be in the air-freight" list. Imagine walking into your new living room, as we did at our first post, to rattan furniture covered in pale blue fabric splashed with tropical huts and palm trees. Slipcovers were my savior; white duck conceals a multitude of decorating sins.

By chance, we were always sent places with furnished housing. Therefore we had a limited sea shipment. For the most part, therefore, our furniture was stored—except our bed. After four years of pushing two single beds into one big bed with a crack in the middle (a State Department form of birth control? If so, it didn't work), we decided never again.

As the organizing and sorting progressed, I kept making lists of lists. I checked things off knowing that at some point, done or not, the packers would come as scheduled. At the date and hour on the tickets, we would board the plane, having sat on the last suitcase to make sure it locked. Some things wouldn't get done. The letting-go point came as a relief.

I didn't move us alone. Dan dealt with the Department regarding tickets and other official arrangements. On weeknights and weekends, he ran all sorts of errands. He dealt with the family business matters: arranging insurance as well as figuring out how to manage a bank account long distance and pay bills from two places at once. Once we were on our way, he performed the herculean task of carrying multitudinous hand luggage on and off trains or planes. In Kyoto, where we were visiting his sister, we had a minute and a half to move our baggage off the high-speed train. While I hustled three little kids off, he, pushing against Japanese travellers, extracted eighteen small bags in two dashing trips. That ordeal resulted in a painful case of bursitis.

Every Foreign Service family has its own "What the...?" shipping stories. While we never unpacked the proverbial "well-wrapped last bag of garbage," we had friends who did. Our story involved a case of Tampax. Dan had picked it up at the grocery store, pushing the whole thing around while he looked for a pound of sugar. By the time the sea freight arrived with the case (minus the three-month supply that went in the airfreight), I was pregnant. The remains of that case went on to the next post and, two years later, back to the States, by which time I was pregnant again. After that, I had my relevant plumbing fixed and never needed to buy another box of Tampax, much less a case, again.

Then there was the Freetown mess. Late at night, when our sea freight had finally arrived from the Philippines, the truck carrying it up the steep road to our apartment made a sharp turn into our driveway that tipped the wooden shipping container off the low-loader, breaking it open. Floodlights were set up. Boxes of belongings had to be collected from where they had scattered down the hillside. A case of champagne, carefully packed in the Philippines, ended up gracing other parties. We never found one of the croquet balls.

Once we arrived at post, just as I managed packing us out, I settled us in. In no particular order, I checked off the basics: Suitcases and airfreight unpacked. House-help hired. The house as organized as possible. Processes for boiling drinking water and safe food-handling established. Children settled in school. Curtains measured. Drugstore found.

I also needed to get the "two-fer" newly-arrived-at-post activities underway: Make and receive formal calls. Set up our social calendar. Attend or host wives' gatherings. Make or receive more calls as newcomers arrived.

In addition to taking care of the basics, I started looking for things that fed my own needs. By our second tour, I had learned that

103

portable pursuits, efforts I undertook seriously although not necessarily remuneratively, were critical to my wellbeing. At each post, I would reinvent myself based on the local opportunities. Although it usually took a couple of months, I would find things that fed me: Exploring markets. Studying language. Discovering local crafts. Getting out my paints and brushes. Making art. Joining the PTA. Getting involved in school reorganization. Starting a research project. Doing whatever else that said, "Here I am, explore me."

Before we left or at post I would buy and read everything I could lay my hands on concerning the history, culture, and art of where we were, paying special attention to locally written English-language fiction. In Kuala Lumpur, I read W. Somerset Maugham, a British author who, while he was in Malaya in the late '20s, had been taken in by the rubber planters. Based on those experiences, he skewered their idiosyncrasies and revealed their scandals in several of his books. (When I got to know some pre-war rubber plantation managers and asked about him, they were still furious.) In Nigeria, Chinua Achebe, Amos Tutuola, and Wole Soyinka were newly published authors who recounted stories about the impact of colonialism on traditional communities. The new translations of José Rizal's seminal books, which propelled Philippine identity, nationalism, and drive for independence, were great reads. From F. Sionil José's *Rosales Saga* series, I gained insights into issues of colonialism and class in the Philippines. In Singapore, Catherine Lim and Goh Poh Seng, who became acquaintances in book form and in person, were examining both the city's past and future.

Other books were perfect companions for traveling in a country. Alfred Russel Wallace's *The Malay Archipelago* was neither fiction nor new. His account of traveling through outer island Indonesia in the 1860s on an exploration of flora and fauna led him to a theory of evolution that actually predated Darwin, but was published later. Filled with descriptions of cities like Menado, we read the relevant chapters before we landed in each town during Dan's and my foray into that part of Indonesia, a century after he was there.

Besides reading culturally relevant books, I also paid attention to local politics, learning who was who, listening to gossip to find out the back-stories. For me, this was part of the point of being there. Being well clued in deepened my understanding of what we were living through. And it helped keep me from putting my foot in my mouth. Dan and I could also compare notes about what we had observed and the gossip we had picked up. We knew overlapping circles and paid attention in different ways, he much more constantly than I did.

We were due six or so weeks of home-leave every two years—once in the middle of a four-year tour and usually between other tours. Home-leave was a welcome time. We saw family, reconnected with the United States, and checked in with the medical unit at State to be sure we hadn't picked up some tropical bug.

We also restocked. I made lists of what I presumed we needed to purchase to take back, including a dozen sets of bras and underpants for me (the tropics does in elastic)—actually, underwear for everyone—and new shoes. (I hoped sandals would be in stock and that the kids' feet wouldn't grow too fast.) Buying for the tropics was never easy unless we happened to hit the end-of-summer sales. We also bought "tastes of home," such as American chili powder or cranberry sauce. Then there were much needed, hard to get out-of-season purchases: One July, an extremely kind clerk at the drugstore climbed into the attic to dig out three strings of Christmas lights and extra bulbs.

I took care of details like changing our address for charge accounts. That was never simple. Imagine trying to help a clerk on the other end of the phone understand that we were moving from the American Embassy Kuala Lumpur—"K-U-A-L-A L-U-M-P-U-R"—to American Consulate Kaduna—"Where?" "K-A-D-U-N-A N-I-G-E-R-I-A." I was devoutly glad it wasn't to O-U-A-G-A-D-U-G-U U-P-P-E-R V-O-L-T-A.

For twenty-nine years I juggled this entire act: Get travel orders. Make lists, then lists of lists. Reinvent. Repeat. Start over. Six overseas posts, six reinventions. Plus three Stateside tours between overseas postings—three times relearning to live back here.

105

"Two-fering"

The "two-fering" part of being a wife connected to the embassy meant involvement in events on the diplomatic circuit: Receptions, national day celebrations, dinners, cocktail parties, state visits, even military parades.

Until Dan was the principal officer, the ambassador's wife set the pace and tone. Pleasant and interesting as it often was, representational life—a wife being the face of America—was time consuming. How much time was spent varied from post to post. My first post required enough energy to be stimulating and fun. But at the second post, in a small, isolated town where we were labeled and visible wherever we went, my "representational" duties became practically full time. As Dan increased in rank and position, we were attending or hosting an event (sometimes two) almost every night.

These duties were on top of our individual everyday responsibilities, his at the office, mine filled with other activities, compulsory, family, or otherwise. My daytime calendar included ladies' coffee-mornings, teas, and meetings. Some I attended because I had been bidden while others I went to because I wanted to. I joined a group of Indonesian and American ladies who met regularly to talk—the first hour in English, the second in Indonesian—because I wanted to. But I was bidden to join all of the wives in the political section when they made a formal call on a newly arrived senior officer. It was always compulsory to participate in an event when the ambassador's wife requested the wives' attendance.

The ambassador's or section chief's (Dan's boss's) wife could be unrealistically demanding. Even when they weren't (and in my experience they mostly weren't), they could request unpredictable "command performances": helping with a bazaar, taking a visitor shopping or sightseeing, filling out a dinner table at the last minute, or making an emergency fourth for bridge. As much as I might enjoy lots of it, many of these could suddenly fill hours when I had planned to do something else.

After a couple of posts, I found that if I could be counted on for truly obligatory occasions and was willing to volunteer to do things I wanted to do anyway (serve as the moderator for a fashion show, for example), other times I could pick and choose my activities. I didn't want to work a table at an international bazaar. However, our household made delicious watermelon pickles. Donating six jars of them for the American embassy wives' table filled the bill. They sold quickly. I was asked to produce more the next year.

Throughout the Service, stories were rampant about ambassadorial wife "Dragon Ladies." One, so we heard, decreed the colors of dresses "her" wives should wear to parties at her residence. Others "ordered" wives to make and bring dozens of hors d'oeurves ahead of a reception, or set the table the morning before a formal dinner and return afterward to clean up. I never knew how accurate these tales were. We, fortunately, were never at a post with one of those *truly* formidable dragons.

The ambassadors' wives I "served under" took their position and the status that went with it seriously, filling their roles with "by the book" professionalism and dignity. They defined themselves by their efforts to both support their husbands' careers and be stellar representatives of the United States. Since all the ambassadors we served under were career FSOs, their wives, too, were by then lifetime "two-fers." If my calendar was full, theirs overflowed.

One wife with a reputation for being difficult (admittedly deserved) was, underneath it all, extremely shy. We kept in touch with her until she died. Another, at the end of an evening and several gimlets, would say, "Call me Jane"—but it was always "Mrs....." when you next saw her. Still another was particularly warm and only stood on ceremony when it was important. I would have metaphorically walked up a hill on my hands had she asked. Her graciousness inspired that kind of support and respect. So did that of another ambassador's wife, who, when she left the post, gave our son her golf clubs—his first full set. At her request, I happily called her by her first name—Hoov—and thought of her as a friend.

Throughout these representational responsibilities and resulting social obligations, I was raising children. Arriving at our first post with a baby and a toddler meant that promptly making formal calls on senior wives was a juggling act. I had to leave the children with *amahs* they didn't know, organize a car, and do what was expected.

Of all the calls I made in the Foreign Service, my call on that first post's Deputy Chief of Mission's wife was particularly memorable. I phoned to ask her what time it would be convenient for me to come. Her first comment was, "Don't you have a little boy? Please bring him because I know it's not easy for him to be left with people he doesn't know." This was an unusually thoughtful gesture, especially from someone who had no children herself. Jerry, not quite three, and I called together. She had cookies and juice and a small collection of toys to amuse him while she and I had iced tea and a pleasant getting-to-know-you, here's-how-things-work chat.

From the beginning, we not only went to events, we hosted them. Even when Dan was a junior officer, we gave dinners or small cocktail parties for his contacts and colleagues as well as our new friends in the host government, other embassies, and the wider community. These events were often for fun because we enjoyed being with delightful friends.

While Dan might *say* he wanted to entertain so and so, I was the one who did the planning. We had a cook at each post, some better than others, who usually prepared the food. Even with help, these parties took a fair amount of my time. Before we went overseas, Dad had given me *Betty Crocker's Picture Cook Book* so I would have a visual aid for teaching even non-English speaking cooks how to make American food. For many dishes, however, the question was not whether the cook could understand how to make it but whether the critical ingredients or workable substitutes were available.

The first big "how do we entertain in our house?" discussion Dan and I had was whether to serve alcohol. Hard liquor was sold duty free to diplomats and widely served at most events (although not by some Muslim and Buddhist diplomats). I hadn't drunk alcohol until after I met Dan and then not much, although I was enjoying exploring and drank some when we went to parties. My parents had not served alcohol at "diplomatic" parties in their house in Burma and I thought that was a perfectly good example to follow in ours. "But, Margaret, you drink when you're out, you can't not serve it here." His logic won the day. We learned more about what to serve and how and always made a point of having good non-alcoholic drinks for guests who didn't drink.

As Dan's rank and responsibility increased we got an allowance that covered *some*, not all, of the costs of our *official* entertaining. The purely-for-fun parties were always on us. When he was a junior officer, he didn't have an allowance (or much of a salary), so we had to cover the expenses ourselves. Even so, we were expected—and wanted—to be generous hosts.

When the ambassador and his wife or other senior officers entertained, we weren't really guests, even if we received an invitation. We were assistants, assuming our assigned parts in what were often carefully choreographed affairs. At large formal receptions or big dinners at an ambassador's residence, Dan frequently stood at the door to announce the guests' names to the receiving line. Several officers and wives would be at the other end to step in to further welcome guests and take them to get drinks, which kept the line moving. When the evening was over, Dan would go back to the door to call cars for the departing guests. Meanwhile, I acted as a "sweeper," ensuring that guests weren't still chatting on the back porch or in the ladies room and escorted them to the front door.

At receptions, I enjoyed passing trays of hors d'oeuvres. I could move from group to group, chat briefly, and then move on, rather than get stuck in a conversation I couldn't gracefully leave. The task also gave me the opportunity to seek out fascinating people I might not otherwise have had the chance to meet. In Kuala Lumpur, that included the Dutch ambassador, a renowned Sinologist who was also the author of the wonderful Judge Dee mysteries set in eighteenth-century China. In Jakarta, we met a young German colleague, Baron Von Richthofen, grandson of the flying ace. (We laughed, as did he, when we brought a "curse you Red Baron" Snoopy tee shirt for him from home leave.)

These evening events, and the "ladies mornings," were pleasant, boring, or interesting, depending on the occasion and the people I spent time with. Nonetheless, the expectation that I would attend certain ones was absolute. If one of the children wasn't well, I thought twice before I asked if I could beg off. Still—like the morning the kids popped mumps and I had to act as major domo for a reception for the visiting American ambassador—there were times I simply had no choice.

At our first post, the ambassador's wife was an avid bridge player and golfer. She assumed "her" younger wives would drop everything to serve as a fourth when one of her guests didn't show. Even though Dan and I enjoyed playing bridge in college, I consciously stayed off of her "fill-list" by never playing bridge—not even a friendly hand with neighbors.

As for golf, my lack of skill protected me. Having played since childhood, Dan was a good golfer with a high handicap that he often shot well below. She was counting on him to be her partner in a mixed-doubles tournament the morning he called her to say our third child was on the way. He would be at the hospital. She was less than pleased. Yet the next morning the ambassador sent a bunch of long-stemmed red roses, hard to come by in the tropics, and a hand-written note to welcome Walter.

Abroad, diplomatic social obligations and representational entertaining writ large were among the mainstays of our lives. At home, diplomats were often called "striped-pants cookie-pushers." The derisive cartoons that portrayed us as such featured a rotund bald man with a walrus mustache attired in a formal frock coat and striped pants. A martini glass in his hand, a dishy young thing on his arm or near by, he was the presumed image of a constantly doing-nothing-except-partying diplomat. Congress, particularly members from the teetotal Bible Belt, was always threatening to cut the State Department's "whisky money." When CODELS (congressional delegations) arrived at post, they assumed they would be wined and dined and dined and wined—at events organized and managed by us "two-fer" wives.

How much of this entertaining was truly necessary was, and is, an open question. Yet, the constant round offered opportunities to share views with colleagues or take care of business "out of sight in plain view." For many of us, entertaining also enhanced a sense of community and belonging.

Being a "two-fer," for me at least, involved more than diplomatic social obligations. As my skills and interests became more apparent, the director of the Bi-national Center in Jakarta began asking me to work on events for him: Organizing readings of plays by American authors. Helping explain American elections. Displaying my art. I began participating in the more formal aspects of public diplomacy and, in a different way, became a less tangential face of America. That, I really enjoyed.

The Women's International Club (WIC) asked me to moderate a fashion show at our ambassador's residence. Appropriately attired, including hairdo and makeup, I described the clothing as it appeared on the runway: a section of designer-made Western clothing fashioned from Indonesian fabric followed an array of traditional Indonesian (mainly Javanese) dress. The most unexpected was Javanese girl's attire for female circumcision—*kain batik* (a batik body wrap) worn with a hoop in front to keep cloth away from the location. How to discuss that? I needed to know more, as would the non-Indonesian audience. Still startled by the idea, straight from the rehearsal, I dashed to the home of an Indonesian anthropologist friend for guidance. Although seven- to twelve-year-old boys were actually circumcised and wore similar hoops, excision was not performed on females, he explained. Rather a symbolic nick was made, either on the woman or on a cucumber.

Because I explored the back corners of the cities where we lived, I was regularly asked to take visiting dignitaries or their wives sightseeing and shopping. George Romney, then governor of Michigan, was considering a run for president when he and his entourage came through Jakarta. The plan had been for me to take them through one of the big city markets so they could see everyday activity. But at the last minute, someone shifted the program. Instead, I took them to a unique shop on a quiet back street that sold high-quality local art. As we drove there I talked about the fluctuating price of rice and the problems that created, and other aspects of Jakarta that would have been visible in a market. While they shopped, I fended off the local and foreign press who wanted to ask "just one question."

The following year, after Apollo 12 landed on the moon, the astronauts visited Jakarta as part of a worldwide tour and were paraded through the city. Alan Bean, the fourth person to walk on the moon, wanted to see local life. On the spur of the moment, he and I went to Sarinah, Jakarta's big department store, which catered to the local, not the foreign, market. We rode the escalator with a clear view of each of the five floors we were going up. Of all the people I escorted, he was both the most curious and the most observant. What a pleasure.

My "two-fer" role—showing people around, "working" at social events, and performing other representational activities—was not simply wifely obligation. Our unpaid roles were an evaluated part of diplomacy in action. The system and senior wives made it clear that how I fulfilled my duties mattered, to the Foreign Service and for Dan's career. Until 1972, a wife's "job" performance was written up in her husband's annual efficiency report.

It remains a mystery how Dan managed to be promoted. Despite my appreciated capacity to entertain and otherwise be active in the embassy community, I was always "too outspoken." Nevertheless, he was. Although I chaffed under some of the obligations, Dan and I found our diplomatic life a stimulating, rewarding adventure. We always welcomed the next round.

In "Interesting Times"

The Foreign Service we entered was expanding rapidly as post-colonial nations gained independence and diplomatic relations were established. New embassies and consulates opened, not in major European capitols but in sprawling cities and insignificant outposts in the developing world. Each had its own history, culture, colonial background, and struggle for nationalism, and each was in its own stage of becoming uniquely independent, more modern and self-governing.

Consequently, we served in fascinating places at not entirely peaceful but interesting times in each country's own development, in a wider world that was mired in the tensions and realities of the Cold War.

In 1959, Malaya was at the tag end of the Emergency. The guerilla war the Malayan National Liberation Army of the Malayan Communist Party was waging against the British Commonwealth forces had started in 1948. Insurgents had targeted tin-mines and rubber plantations, burning and killing. The goal of the counter insurgency, begun by the colonial government, was to starve the primarily Chinese "communist terrorists" (CTs) out of the jungle and depths of rubber plantations, denying them a base. Scattered farmers were moved into fenced New Villages. Strangers were not allowed to enter or stay overnight. No one was allowed to take food or water outside a village or town. (We couldn't even carry water or cookies in the car when we drove twenty miles to take the children to the beach.)

I volunteered in a well-baby clinic in a New Village near Kuala Lumpur where we came in through the gated entrance and passed the extremely crowded everyday activity in these enclosed communities. We dealt with mothers and children; the men must have been elsewhere. Over the ten years of the Emergency, the "starve them out" plan slowly worked. We only experienced the final few months. After we had been there a year, the CT resistance ended. The Emergency was lifted.

Just as we met planters who had known Somerset Maugham, over time we became acquainted with many more planters who had lived under the threat of CT attacks and had close friends and colleagues who were killed. For us, the Emergency was real even if we were distanced from the worst of it.

We arrived in Kaduna, Nigeria, in 1961, eighteen months after Independence. The Biafran War would not begin until four years after we left in 1963. Our daily interactions, however, made clear some of the tribal tensions that led to it. The consulate was in Nigeria's Northern Region, the seat of political power for the new nation. Northerners were mainly Hausa, a proud, dignified and predominately Muslim people.

When Nigeria was a colony, the British had established a cadre of low-level civil servants, postal and government office clerks (said "clArk"), and nurses, to be assigned throughout the country. Most of them were Igbo (erroneously but commonly, Ibo) who were from the Eastern Region of the country. Smaller, generally more literate than the Hausa, they practiced Christianity, or their traditional religion, or some meld of both.

If I, or an Igbo, went into the post office with a shilling and wanted a six-pence stamp, the Igbo clerk would give me my stamp and change. A Hausa or other northerner doing the same thing would be sent away to come back with correct change. A similar dynamic, so I was told, played out in hospitals: Igbo nurses extracted tips for bedpans, especially from Hausa patients.

This constant, demeaning behavior contributed to the explosive environment that upended the blossoming democracy after we left. The Igbo resented their lack of political power in the newly independent country. Others resented the Igbo's power over their daily lives. In January 1966, Igbo military officers carried out a coup, killing the Sardauna of Sokoto (the Premier of the Northern Region) in his bed. His murder triggered mass killings of Igbo in the North and ultimately the Biafran War.

In 1965, a few months before the coup in Nigeria and two years after we had returned to the States, Dan was assigned to the Indonesia Desk in the State Department. Desk officers are on the receiving end of reporting from the field and help generate policy guidance back to the post. Dan was following President Sukarno's efforts to balance increasing tensions among the army, the communists, and the conservative religious factions—a situation spinning out of control. In particular, he was paying attention to the Indonesian economy, which was deteriorating badly.

About 6 on the morning of October 1, he was shaving before going into the Department to screen and prepare overnight telegrams for the Assistant Secretary and others in the front office. I had the radio on in the bedroom. The news included trouble in Jakarta.

"Dan," I called. "You'd better hurry. There's been a coup."

"Nah. Probably just a new cabinet—we've been expecting that. The newscaster got it out of proportion."

I marched into the bathroom with the portable radio. He heard that, indeed, there had been a coup and nearly cut his throat with his razor as his head jerked. Dan threw on clothes and dashed off to the Department. We hardly saw him for several days.

Sorting out the basic facts took time. Six generals, the young daughter of a seventh, and a staff lieutenant had been assassinated in Jakarta in an attempted coup on the night of September 30. Junior officers who had been connected to President Sukarno and perhaps also to the Communist Party had carried out this coordinated attack on the military high command. Political upheaval followed, leading to mass killings over the next year, and to Sukarno's fall.

After we were transferred to Jakarta in 1967, General Suharto, who, *de facto*, had already been the acting president, formally replaced Sukarno. In 1968, he was elected president.

Suharto was establishing his New Order government. With the help of an impressive team of Berkeley-trained Indonesian economists, the focus was on much needed economic recovery. We got to know many Indonesians, the economists and others, who were deeply invested in reframing their country to be more democratic. The changes were welcome. Those early New Order days appeared to be hopeful and exciting, a time of new beginnings.

The period was also tense, with undercurrents and rumblings. Really knowing what was going on and what had happened was murky. One heard. One *knew*. Not the details, or the scale. Activists, intellectuals, and writers were being imprisoned. Stories reverberated around the capitol about mass killings that had taken place in 1966, the year before we arrived: Purported communist sympathizers, ethnic Chinese, and alleged leftists were killed, apparently in large numbers. Thousands of others were sent into internal exile.

In Jakarta, particularly in our first year, students demonstrated around town against any number of things, including Sukarno as well as the increasing price of rice, gasoline, and kerosene, and outside the American embassy, for who knew what reason. Truckloads of soldiers, their guns pointing in the air, careened along the main streets and circled roundabouts. I was driving behind one of those trucks one morning when it hit a bump. A soldier's gun went off. No one was hurt. Even so, it was jarring.

Despite the tension, most of the time things were quiet, at least where we lived. We went about getting acquainted with a fascinating country at a complicated time. Over the next thirty-three years, the New Order would degenerate into military dictatorship, with Suharto at the helm. Elections would become less an exercise in democracy than state theater, designed to return Suharto's party, and the military, to power.

In the past few years, parts of the fuller, thorny story of that period have come out with the release of documents from the late '60s. Additionally, old people who were part of the bloodbath are telling stories they were unwilling to discuss earlier. Based on this accumulation of new, more detailed information, historians are able to demonstrate that, at the instigation of the army and the New Order government, at least half a million people were massacred.

Because we have returned periodically, we are in our own way knit into the country. We now have fifty years invested in friendships with Indonesians and with Americans from that time and later. We continue to keep trying to delve beneath the surface of the country and the events that shaped it. Looking back, it is difficult, certainly uncomfortable, to place our lived experience in the context of information emerging about the early Suharto era.

In August 1971, we were transferred directly from Jakarta to the two-officer consulate in Cebu in the central Philippines. Our first stop was Bagiuo, to see our oldest son, who was already there at boarding school. The country was gearing up for a nationwide senatorial election. On August 21, while we were in Bagiuo, the opposition Liberal party was holding a campaign rally at Plaza Miranda in Manila. A bomb exploded. Nine were killed. Ninety-five others were injured. One of the key political survivors, fighting for his life, was Senator Sergio Osmena. The head of the opposition, he was from a political family in Cebu. Dan was scheduled to call on him two days later. The Plaza Miranda bombing was our introduction to the Philippines.

We had been in Cebu a few weeks when the vice consul left on a well-deserved vacation. Other than the small local staff, Dan, the brand new consul, was in the office alone, a fact that, in a community where news travelled fast, everyone knew.

One day Dan was extremely late coming home for lunch. When he *did* get home, he headed straight for the bottle of Scotch, something I have never seen him do before or since. After a big slug, he told me that a visa fixer had held him at gunpoint. The man had come to apply for a visa assuming Dan, on his first solo day, didn't know who he was or anything about his business. Because of the fixer's reputation and information left by the absent vice consul, Dan had rejected the man's application. He was about to make a notation to that effect in the fixer's passport (an agreed-upon signal between the consulate and the embassy so that one couldn't be played against the other) when the fixer whipped out his gun. Brandishing it wildly, he grabbed his passport. Dan shouted to Carlos, the consulate driver, who was still waiting in the front office: "Call the police!" Carlos almost ran into the gun as the visa fixer sped out of Dan's office, collected his wife and mother in the waiting area, and left. Mercifully, everyone was unscathed, only shaken.

About a year later, on Saturday morning September 23, 1972, we turned on the Voice of America, as we regularly did when we woke up. That morning, the news wasn't usual. Late the night before, President Ferdinand Marcos had declared martial law. The stated reason was that, to stop escalating political strife, it was necessary to impose direct military control on normal civilian life and curb civil rights. The common assumption, not a part of the broadcast, was that, nearing the constitutional limit of his two four-year terms as an elected president, he wanted to stay in power.

Dan needed to know what this meant, for political reporting and because there were American citizens all over the consular district under his responsibility. He walked from the consulate to see his friend the General who headed the constabulary. The General had the text of the proclamation of martial law, 1081. While they talked, he left it on the desk in such a way that Dan could read it. Dan memorized it like mad. He then managed to phone the embassy in Manila. None of them had seen 1081. Dan dictated it. Score one for Dan and the consulate.

By midday, transportation between islands was stopped: no airplanes or boats. Inter-island and international telephone communication was shut down. Dan, our youngest son, and I were in Cebu. We couldn't reach our middle son, who was in boarding school on Luzon. And we couldn't let our two older children in the United States or my parents know we were safe.

On the third day, telephone connections were finally reestablished. I grabbed the phone to call my mother in Virginia, something we only did in emergencies. I was anxious to be connected to the world again, to prove I could make a call even under martial law, and to relieve my family's fears for us—in that order. "Oh," Mother said, "I knew you were all right. I thought that martial law was only in Manila."

For the rest of our three-year tour, we lived under heightened security and many other ramifications of martial law, including growing crony capitalism. For the Philippines and Filipinos, it was another decade of arrests, torturing, and killings.

All this made for sometimes exciting, sometimes concerning, and always interesting times. Despite living with political tension, for us life was not particularly risky—or at least we didn't feel it was. We were much more fortunate than friends: those who were held hostage in Tehran for four hundred and forty-four days; others who faced long family separations as the husbands were assigned to places like Vietnam, where families could not accompany them; and still others who were at posts where embassies were bombed or colleagues were assassinated in their driveways. We were luckier than even families who had been in Jakarta two years before we arrived. Women and children had been evacuated for a number of months when the tensions surrounding the aborted coup were at their worst. During that period, Dan had spent innumerable extra hours at the office and came home late to dinner.

All of us knew, still know, that our Foreign Service lives involved risks. Yet, we lived as we lived because we loved the life and believed that representing our country was an honor. We understood that diplomacy—then and now—is the front line of American security, and therefore worth the risk.

Adding Building Blocks

We never knew until we arrived at a new post what would seem familiar and what would hit us in the face. With each move we added layers of building blocks for approaching other ways of being.

Getting off the plane in Kuala Lumpur—another former British colonial capital in the Southeast Asian tropics—didn't give me the same surprising jolt I had had eight years earlier in the dark Burmese night. "KL" (shorthand for Kuala Lumpur) was welcoming; neither an unexpected reminder of the past nor totally new and strange. The people were a different mix of Southeast Asia.

Unlike KL, arriving in Kaduna, Nigeria, in West Africa, two years later, meant starting from scratch. Kaduna was a hot, dusty, low tin-roofed small town surrounded by the scrubby bush of the sub-Saharan savannah. As the capital of the country's mainly Muslim Northern Region, it was traditional and tribal. The nearest international airport, Kano, was a four-hour ride on bad dirt roads. The local airport had a grass strip where the occasional two-prop plane landed. Kaduna was on the nether end of the communications chain. Letters from home took two to three weeks. Although we heard headlines on BBC's World Service when the reception was good, we didn't learn details of major events like the Cuban missile crisis until the *International Herald Tribune* arrived four or five days late. By then, we knew the world had escaped nuclear apocalypse.

If our previous two posts had been in small cities, Metro Jakarta—where we arrived from Washington, four years after Kaduna—had a population of close to nine million. City though it was, it seemed like the world's largest sprawling village, partly moldy colonial decay, partly basic Southeast Asian rural *kampong* (village): Barely lit at night, with only one tall building boasting a neon sign, vast areas of the city were filled with red-tile roofed houses. The air was redolent of cooking fires, spices, and tropical sweetness with undertones of canals used for all manner of human purposes. The five calls to prayer marked the days. And shadow plays about good and evil indirectly shaped life, allowing clowns to comment on politics in ways mere mortals couldn't. Different and complex though Jakarta was, as part of the wider Malay world we had already begun to understand, in its own way it welcomed us back.

In "KL," recognizing the difference between the Malays, with their brown skin and Southeast Asian features and Chinese by the looks of their faces came easily. The Chinese, from South China, were mostly fine-boned rice eaters, not the bigger, more square-faced wheat-eating Northerners of my childhood. The Indian community was composed of mostly smaller, boney-faced Tamils rather than the taller northern Indians from my Woodstock memory. Nonetheless, I'd met these peoples before.

West Africans were a new experience. Arriving in Kaduna meant acquiring a new set of visual identification skills to recognize the various peoples we were living among: chocolaty tall Hausa; rangy, coppery Fula; sturdy sometimes nearly eggplant-hued Yoruba with specific scarifications on their faces; and the even shorter, rounder ebony-faced Igbo.

Various groups, we also observed, had their own resonances. In multiracial KL, the Chinese wet market, populated mainly by Cantonese and Hokkien speakers, sounded like a perpetual fight. The Malay night market was a quiet hum. West African crowds reverberated in a dancing rhythm. In the Malay world, the more important the topic, the lower the voice. Passive, indirect constructions were used rather than direct ones.

Even though the countries were newly independent, some of their government institutions were easy to recognize. In the former British colonies, parliaments opened with a dignitary processing with a mace. In courts, lawyers and judges wore black robes and white wigs (despite being in the tropics). In the Philippines, a former American colony, the presidential government and the school system were based on the US model (with stories in textbooks about snow).

Establishing a new federal government and meshing it with earlier customary rulers had produced a unique variation on a constitutional monarchy as we quickly learned in KL. The Federation of Malaya (the new nation's proper name) had a Prime Minister and parliament based on a British model. The monarchy, however, rotated. Every five years there was a new Yang di-Pertuan Agong (literally "He Who Is Made Lord," or as I put it, less accurately but more to the point, the "Than Whom There Is No Whomer"). Historically, the peninsula had been divided into two British Straits Settlements (Malacca and Penang) as well as nine separate Regencies, each governed by its own sultan or raja. At independence in 1957 (two years before we arrived), a system was devised by which these sultans rotated as national monarch, with the succession based on the traditional hierarchy among them.

During our two-year tour, two monarchs died within a few months (with a royal installation in between). Dan's naval-officer black ties got a workout. As required for all diplomats, he wore one daily during each forty-day mourning period. He loaned his other to a colleague who didn't have a black one. After the second forty days, tattered beyond reuse, we ditched them.

With their British heritage, the Malayan military bands had been trained by British-Indian troops. Imagine incredibly erect bass drummers with tiger skins draped down their chests cushioning their drums. As the funeral cortege of each of those Muslim kings paraded through the city, the main dirge was the Christian hymn, "Nearer My God to Thee," played at a half-step-at-a-strut pace.

Of all the former British colonies we were assigned, we were plunged most directly into colonial customs in Northern Nigeria, although with a distinctly West Africa spin. We arrived near the end of the change over from British senior civil servants to Nigerians. Until the Brits left, this meant dressing formally for dinner as they always had, even in the bush. The British etiquette of the ladies retiring from the dining room after dinner, leaving the men to their port and cigars, took on new meaning.

Dan and I had been invited to our first dinner party at the home of the most senior British civil servant in Northern Nigeria. "Margaret, when you are asked by your hostess if you would like to 'go through,' *always* go," our consul pointedly warned me. Going through—usually both before and after dinner—meant joining the other ladies in the upstairs bedroom. In the old colonial barn-like houses, that was the *only* room with access to a toilet. "When the women 'go through,'" the consul continued, "the men 'see Africa.'" His 'go through' admonition applied not only that night, but for every British dinner party we went to in Kaduna.

Dan, resplendent in his white dinner jacket and black bow tie, first 'saw Africa' near a bush in the garden. The senior British civil servant (Sir OBE) was on his left, the Anglican Bishop of Northern Nigeria (the Right Reverend) on his right.

"Oh, and Margaret, remember your host isn't called Sir Sexy Rexy for nothing," the consul added. "His hands tend to wander under the dining table."

Beyond "seeing Africa," and despite the lessons from the Wives Course, which had not then caught up with the non-European world, living and entertaining in these newly independent countries meant adapting to many locally different patterns of how things were.

Take the sofa. In Indonesia, lots of women, not just one or two, sat on the sofa. There was always space for one more than we Americans saw. That's how Indonesians see space and experience relationships. I learned to squeeze in. I also learned to walk across a room somewhat ducked so my head would not tower above those who were seated. That was a matter of deference.

At several posts, acceptances meant: "Thank you, I received the invitation," not necessarily "I'm coming." Often there were no acceptances. Sometimes everyone came. Sometimes, despite having accepted, guests didn't appear. Sometimes, before a guest had left home, a family member had arrived unexpectedly and was brought along to the party. Although we knew how to seat a dinner according to protocol, we quickly learned that formal seating wasn't necessarily the best way to proceed. Buffet dinners with guests sitting at round tables worked better. That way, places could be added or removed and seating reorganized after everyone had walked in the door—or another seat could be squeezed in if someone arrived after dinner started.

Time was often flexible. Indonesians called it *jam karet* (rubber time) although flexibility without the graphic words was not uniquely Indonesian. Instead of arriving at the exact time given in the invitation, guests could come early or late. If being exact about time was critical, we made a point of firmly saying *jam tepat* (exact time). We also knew that when a particular ambassador's wife was our guest, she expected she would be served one drink when she walked in the door and then would sit down to dinner in exactly half an hour.

Food is its own form of diplomacy. Depending on where we were, menu planning had to take into account that Muslims didn't eat pork, Hindus didn't eat beef and that perhaps both were coming to the same dinner. Chicken or seafood usually worked. Except when, unexpectedly, there was also a Buddhist vegetarian. That night a single, quickly whipped-up omelet served the purpose.

Our guests liked our "exotic" American food. They generally preferred it not as large hunks of meat but in spicy stew-like dishes served with rice, not potatoes. Jambalaya or Texas chili was popular. So was fried chicken.

Food was a two-way street: We served ours and enjoyed theirs. Kuala Lumpur (and later Singapore) was a great what-will-we-eat-today mix of Chinese, Malay, and Indian, plus the distinctly Straits Chinese amalgam of Chinese-Malay, all of which propelled the whole family on a life-long eating and cooking experience.

The world over, grilled meat is a favorite. In Kaduna, skewers of thinly sliced tough beef were thickly covered with ground-up peanuts, chopped hot peppers, and ginger, brushed with oil, and cooked over fire (done small, excellent cocktail party fare). Across our area of Southeast Asia, we found many variations of *sate* (spelled elsewhere *satay*), meat soaked in a marinade of soy and spices. Whole pig, *lechon*, is the Philippine meat spitted over a fire pit.

Indonesia is a whole archipelago of food flavored in spicy combinations—"Go-to comfort food," as our daughter puts it. In the Philippines we ate both Spanish cuisine with a local twist and uniquely Filipino dishes, often inflected with Chinese influences. Sierra Leone was a whole new range of flavorful stews, sometimes served with rice or fufu, a thick white paste of cassava and plantain flour.

We explored tastes, textures, and fragrances. I accumulated various names for the same vegetable in different languages. Experimenting with the totally odd and unfamiliar meant I knew that cooked banana flowers taste like artichoke; green mango substitutes well for peach in a pie. We learned how to express the difference between hot, spicy (*pedas*) and hot, stove (*panas*) in Indonesian. We knew which food was eaten with a fork and spoon, fingers, knife and fork, or chopsticks. We understood when to linger over coffee after dinner (European hosts) and when to leave immediately after the meal was finished (Chinese hosts).

By becoming familiar with the food as well as the food-ways that went with it, we walked deeper into the lives of our host countries and felt more at home. All told, be it sounds or sofas or tastes, so many building blocks, so much to learn.

Finding Friends

The best reward for moving from place to place was the variety of people we got to know. To the extent we could, we lived outside the foreigner bubble (even though we were, willy-nilly, of that bubble) enmeshing ourselves in the wider place and time.

We knew we weren't there forever. We could leave if things got too rough or would be evacuated if the government decided families must leave. We knew we *would* eventually leave, in any case. In some ways, we were skittish about putting down roots too deeply, only to have them abruptly jerked up again when it was least expected or wanted.

Nonetheless, Dan and I invested ourselves in developing relationships. Sometimes, they grew into lasting friendships. In many of the countries where we were, friendship is built on long-term reciprocity rather than being casually in the moment. We are fortunate. Some of our close friendships have lasted half a world away over half a century.

Because we lived in countries that were newly independent, many of our peers would end up being future leaders in their own governments. We also met a few charming rogues (in government and out) who ultimately went to jail. Not to mention the time I shook hands with a cannibal (another story, for another time.)

In KL, we ran with a crowd of young civil servants and their wives. We were guests in their homes as often as they were in ours. Successively, twenty-some years later, several were named as ambassadors to Washington, where we saw each other over friendly meals again with the special gift of having known each other when we were young.

When we arrived in Kaduna, we were told we wouldn't meet Nigerian civil servants' wives. Ministers in the regional government were extremely traditional Muslim men. Indeed, we never laid eyes on their wives. The exception was the Minister of Health and his wife, both Christians, who became good friends.

The "perm secs" (as everyone shortened the title permanent secretaries, the professional heads of various departments of the regional government) were men our age. Many of their children went to the same school our son Jerry did. After they learned that when we invited them to dinner all our guests would be, like them, perm secs, and maybe another of the few young foreign couples, they often brought a wife. One evening Ahmed Talib, a man we especially enjoyed, called just before he was expected to arrive to say his wife wouldn't be coming after all. She had delivered a baby that morning. He was coming.

The perm sec's wives in turn invited me to coffee mornings, usually as the only foreigner, even though our common language was minimal. The particularly outgoing wife of a mid-level military officer and I went places around Kaduna, with me driving our car. One morning we suddenly heard the distinctive horn indicating that the regional prime minister's green sedan was approaching from behind. Like everyone, I pulled to the side of the road to let him pass. My friend jumped off her seat crouching below the window. She was glad to be out on her own with me in a way the others weren't but being seen by the prime minister was something else all together.

Perhaps my most touching friendship was with Aisha Joda, the mother of one of Jerry's classmates, whose husband was the perm sec in the regional Ministry of Information. A tiny woman who spoke a little English, she had perhaps a third-grade education. Our second Christmas, she invited me to cut branches from her casuarina tree to use for a make-do Christmas tree. In another kind gesture, when President Kennedy was assassinated after we returned to the States, the mail brought a short, sweet note of sorrow, hand printed on lined paper, signed Aisha. Friendship.

We'd been in Kaduna about a year and were used to having perm secs bringing their wives to dinner. Nothing, therefore, prepared us for the time the new aide to the still-British governor of Northern Nigeria (the first Nigerian to hold that position after his British predecessor left) regretted a dinner invitation for him and his wife: "Because I have two." Some of the others had four (the Muslim maximum), but we never got that response. Those men would bring the youngest, most outgoing, and best-educated one, or would alternate between wives.

We sent the next invitation to the aide and his *wives*. Both came, dressed in matching pink satin wrappers and head ties, and sat next to each other all evening. (Two months later they both left him at the same time, too; I never knew why.)

We were even less prepared when the Emir of Zaria, the ruler of a small emirate a short distance from Kaduna, informed us on about three hours notice that he would come to our house that afternoon for tea. When our ambassador and his wife had come up from Lagos earlier, Dan and I had escorted them to call on the Emir in his elaborate, traditional mud-brick palace.

After the men's call ended, the Emir had taken the ambassador's wife and me to his harem, where his wives and many concubines stayed. We met his four wives. Each had her set of rooms on one of the four corners of the compound. The ceilings were covered in brightly enameled tin platters. A customary warning system as well as decoration, they would clatter to the floor if the mud-brick roof were about to collapse. The senior wife was clearly a love match. He had kept her for many years even though they had no children. The youngest wife had a newborn that the Emir happily showed off. "See, he's mine," the proud father asserted as he placed the tiny hand next to his large one, pointing out that they both had a sixth finger.

The next time he came down to Kaduna, the Emir chose to call on us. We didn't do British tea. Given the short notice, Micinyawa, the cook, and I decided to serve homemade ice cream, which he could churn quickly, along with home-baked cookies, which we always had on hand. (I had hepatitis, so was only up for short periods of time. After organizing things, I collapsed back in bed. I missed the actual event.)

When the entourage arrived, the Emir, a regal man in flowing white robes (think Othello), and his primary aides joined Dan in the walled patio. The accompanying truckload of red and green clad retainers sprawled around the back of the house in the shade, happy for the two cases of Coke that we happened to have.

Micinyawa, a tall man with his own stately bearing, brought the bowls of ice cream and the cookies out on a tray. He stepped into the patio, dropped to his knees, held the tray above his head and moved on his knees across the patio with grace and pride to serve the Emir. He knew what was appropriate.

When I heard about it later, what seemed like respect to him and servility to me was hard on my egalitarian American sensibility. If I'd been there, I'm not sure what I might have done. Just as well I wasn't. Even so, I learned a valuable lesson about showing deference properly on someone else's turf.

The American way of doing things is *not* universal, as we learned again in Jakarta. The Political Counselor, Dan's boss, enjoyed inviting guests on various sides of political issues to small dinners, then probing their often-conflicting points of view. Americans use this approach frequently and, in our terms, learn a lot from it. Nonetheless, it has repercussions.

At the time, I was teaching at the University of Indonesia. An Indonesian colleague invited me to stop by her home on the campus for tea late one morning. Her husband, who later became the Minister of Education, happened to be there. He made a point of commenting, almost as an aside to our conversation, that the Political Counselor's dinner parties made their guests extremely uncomfortable. Further, he continued, it often took months, and many intercessions on various people's parts, to restore comfortable relationships among the dinner guests.

In other words—in the indirect Indonesian way I had already recognized, particularly regarding delivering delicate, uncomfortable messages—he was telling me so I would tell Dan. So Dan could, perhaps, tell his boss. Indonesians want harmonious personal relations, at least on the surface. They go out of their way to maintain them. I told Dan. Whether he told the Boss, or whether the Boss understood, I wouldn't hazard a guess. For us, lesson learned. American directness and willingness to engage in face-to-face disagreements doesn't always work for others.

In Indonesia (and elsewhere) I particularly enjoyed making friends with impressive women—impressive in their own right and because of the officials they had married. One senior economist's wife was a psychologist who taught at the university and had her own private practice. She has gone on to teach several generations of her professional successors. The head of the English Department at the University of Indonesia, my friend and boss (and daughter-in-law of the prime mover in developing Bahasa Indonesia, the national language), founded a company to publish new women's magazines, which are a long-standing Indonesian tradition. Her magazines would roughly parallel *Good Housekeeping, Seventeen*, and ultimately, *Ms*. Her daughter, a baby when I met them, now runs the publishing company.

A member of parliament I knew well was at the heart of the negotiations to write and enact the family marriage act, and was, like her husband, a dentist. Like all these women, she was also a homemaker. One day, I popped in to see her about something because the phones were on their usual fritz. Yetty was in the back of the house, seated on a stool near a faucet, scrubbing the family laundry on a washboard.

A Balinese woman educator and parliamentarian, also working on the marriage act, enjoyed dinner at our house often. We had brought a tall carving of spirits topped by Lord Krishna back from a driving trip to Bali. When she saw it, she suggested we should, in traditional Balinese manner, make a small offering to it each week so it would protect the house. She was silent a minute and quickly corrected her self: "No, you better not. If you forget once, bad things might happen." We took her advice and lived happily with the carving, never feeding it.

The women in our block of Jalan (street) Hang Tuah 7 in Kebayoran (suburban Jakarta), where we were the only foreigners, were married to mid-level civil servants who earned extremely limited government salaries. These women belonged to an *arisan,* a traditional women's group that, every few weeks, met in a different member's home. After Dan made the expected call on the *lura* (neighborhood head), which made us residents in local terms, my neighbors invited me to join the group. At every meeting each of us put a specific small amount of money into a pot. In rotation, each member took the total amount—a communal way to help pay for a wedding or another major life event. Each woman (except me) also had her own buy-sell business, as many Indonesian women did. While we drank tea and ate sweets, we looked at each other's wares.

These were all educated women who felt no apparent conflicts about being professional in their own right as well as being traditional wives and mothers. For educated Indonesian women (an opportunity many women did not have) the combination was assumed. To me, they were startlingly more liberated than similar American women at the time, despite our country's emerging women's lib movement. It made sense: In the '50s and '60s Indonesian women had the largest women's movement in the world. Dan's colleague, one of the few female FSOs of her day, aptly called them Iron Butterflies.

Until we got to Singapore, we were in countries that, even though we lived in their cities and knew educated women, were basically rural with barely above subsistence economies. This meant that most women I saw and a few I got to know worked at that level. Markets are full of women who buy and sell. One seafood vendor in the wet market in Kuala Lumpur always had a small crab to tie on four-year-old Jerry's finger when we stopped at her stall for fish. We drove through the Onitsha market (the largest in Nigeria), which was the purview of truly redoubtable women who both ran the market and major truck companies. Throughout wet rice Southeast Asia, women—bent over, knee deep in water, their heads sheltered in conical hats—planted new shoots, did much of the harvesting, tossed the grains in the air to thresh them, and did the cooking. In Sierra Leone, men slashed and burnt fields; the women I talked with planted and tended the crops.

Highly valued for their skill, fleets of Chinese women in Kuala Lumpur—faces sheltered in pointed pastel bonnets all of which were pale green for a few weeks then suddenly all pink, or all yellow—peddled to construction sites. The women in the Gara tribe of Northern Nigeria, wrapped from waist to knees in indigo cloth, were beasts of burden, plodding along, piles of firewood on their backs, nursing their babies as they walked. The Fula women, erect and handsome, calabash bowls of milk from their cows balanced on their heads, moved gracefully through the bush.

These people we got to know and others we moved among in different societies expanded and reshaped our understanding of the world. We were ringside as new countries struggled to define themselves. From observation and through friends, we learned to navigate how others lived, showed deference and shared hospitality. Above all, we were privileged that we, and our children, participated in this process of nation building while representing our own country and its values the best we could.

Nonetheless, we lived on the peripheries of any particular society. We could "get in" only so far. We were highly visible, both in our status and our appearance. At core, we were forever outsiders—welcomed outsiders, insider-outsiders, but always outsiders. What we gained in the wider practice of bridging cultures and in inhabiting the spaces between them was a priceless education in how to thrive in an increasingly interconnected world. The experience was well worth being the "two-for-the-price-of-one" in Dan's and my Foreign Service partnership.

What's in a Word?

Walter, our middle son, was born in 1960 in the then Federation of Malaya, where, at the time, mothers and babies stayed in the hospital for ten days after delivery. After two summer babies, I'd sworn not to have another one in humid heat. Surprise! The third one was due in January—"winter," yes, but we were on the equator. So much for "not another hot weather" baby.

Bangsar, the long, wooden, colonial hospital on a hill above Kuala Lumpur, had a long porch that ran outside the rooms. When the breeze swept through the tall casuarina trees shading it, new mothers sitting in deck chairs outside their rooms could imagine themselves on a ship's deck. Tea was brought in the afternoon. Our babies slept in white canvas cots beside us. In this setting, I read Somerset Maugham.

Dan stayed with me in the delivery room that Friday. The doctor had predetermined the date to induce the just-due baby if it hadn't already put in an appearance naturally. He wanted to get as many new mothers and their babies in and out of the hospital before the city and all but emergency medical services shut down for the Chinese New Year.

An overhead fan in the delivery room kept the air moving. The British doctor, wearing khaki half-pants (as the flaring British-style shorts were called), a white sleeveless singlet, a big rubber apron, and rubber boots, broke my water in the morning. He returned in the late afternoon to catch the small, squirming, lusty baby boy. It had been a long day with nothing to eat and only sips of water. Once Walter popped into the world, the Chinese midwife who had been helping the labor along all day treated me to a strong cup of black tea laced with condensed milk. Wonderful.

When Walter was several days old, Matron (as the head nurse, who was Chinese, was called) asked me to fill out the Registration of Birth—a government form written in both Malay and English. The first basics were simple enough: Date of Birth. Name. Sex. Weight.

Then the kicker: Bangsa/Race. Within the linguistic nuances of these two terms were an extremely complicated collision between history, cultures, purposes, and meaning—British, Malayan, American, and mine.

Bangsa is a Malay word that is best literally translated as "people." More deeply, it connotes something between ethnicity—heavily located in language, place, and race—and community or nationality. Consequently, to an American, who doesn't know its complexity, it carries a strong implication of nationality. At the same time, for

129

Americans, the English term "race" is no less complicated, with its own nuanced meanings to navigate.

What threw us even more than the Bangsa/Race category itself were the five particular boxes that could be checked, each its own once-British, now-Malayan category: Malay, Chinese, Indian, European, and Other (the latter solely used for Eurasians or mixed race)—nothing more.

None of the permitted options fit this baby. Or us. That was my concern. Because both Dan and I had been born in China, I knew birth registration started the process of documenting not only the birth of a child, but also its citizenship or nationality. I wanted Walter's clear from the beginning.

The intent of this form was not remotely related to declaring citizenship. The categories, as I learned much later, were a legacy of colonial census taking. They had been created during a time when not only the British, but also the colonial Dutch and Americans were pre-occupied with getting the "racial" categories right and with being scientifically precise, as they defined scientific precision and race at the time. Above all they were concerned with fitting everyone into a countable box. The issue was not one of individual identity, but of meeting the requirements for creating social statistics: documenting the relative political power of racial groupings, then fitting individuals into that pre-defined system from birth.

British pre-World War II censuses for the colony had included a much larger, more detailed set of categories across a much wider geographic and linguistic spectrum than what appeared on this Registration of Birth form. There had been a separate category on those censuses for non-British whites referred to as "foreign Europeans," which meant Dutch and Austrians. There had been another category for "white races," including Americans. These categories had been compressed into five major "races" when the Federated States of Malaya was formed. We were required to choose from among those five.

Clearly, Matron expected us to declare that our hamburger-pink, blue-eyed baby was European. But no one in our family had been "European" in many generations. With a single exception, all of Dan's and my forbearers had been in the United States since before it was the United States. We aren't European. We don't think of ourselves that way and have no oral memory of ever having been, except remotely, European. We are American—with all the complexity that term carries.

So I didn't want to check "European." But writing in "American" was not acceptable to Matron. I suggested "Other." She didn't see us that way at all. She, and, for their purposes, the Malayan government, saw us as European, by which they meant not so much a continent of origin, but "white"—a category that would appear on an American document with a skin-color definition of race or ethnicity.

The entire experience brought up my own beliefs and issues about race, skin color, and equality as it was linked to being American. As a child of the South, I had been brought up with the Sunday school song "red and yellow, black and white, they are equal in His sight," and I could still hear those words in my mind in both English and Chinese. Despite my beliefs about how God saw us, I was all too aware that life in America didn't treat everyone equally. Among some Americans at that time, there was an effort to *not* even use skin-color designators on forms. Rather, we wanted to substitute "human," in an effort to promote the notion of overarching equality. I was idealistic, bull-headed, and no doubt naïve. As much as I was concerned about being clear about his citizenship, I also didn't want to label this new baby "European" given what, on this form, it implied.

Yet, on American birth notification forms, as on this one, the issue wasn't citizenship. The American forms, as I found out with the older two babies, required race, denoting the kind of "better worse" dichotomy I found offensive. By our Constitution, children born in the United States are American, no matter their parents' citizenship. They, in turn, can transmit American citizenship to their children. I knew that Walter as the child of two American parents —especially a child with diplomatic parents—was American even though he was born in Malaya.

My urgent feelings about needing to clarify all this were inchoate and complicated. Other than the issue of nationality, I wasn't trying to articulate them then as I am now. Some of those feelings had to do with my own mobile history and puzzlement about what it meant to me to be an American, as an individual as well as someone who represented the country in a global community. However, I wasn't thinking about any of that. I just wanted to complete the form to say "American."

Matron and I went back and forth. When she asked me to check the form "European," I'd shake my head no. She'd do the same when I said "American." It was almost a joke between us. For her, it was a matter of fulfilling her responsibility to get the form that put this child into its proper, government-defined box signed. For me, it was a matter of that word, that identity, and my child.

Finally, my ten-day hospital stay nearly over, she reluctantly let me write "Caucasian," then "American Citizen" after the "European" box, which more or less satisfied both of our needs.

I knew the word "Caucasian" was equally problematic. At the time it was more acceptable to me than "European." A contentious, weasel-word substitute for "white," the term literally means people from a specific area, the Caucasus Mountains. Caucasoid had been adopted, along with Mongoloid and Negroid, as a classification of people well before we knew as much as we now do about all people evolving originally out of Africa.

"American" is also an interesting word. As our Canadian and Mexican colleagues would remind us, they, too, are Americans writ large—they live in the Americas. While "United Statesers" isn't a term, our using the term "American" implies, in a sense, that we "own" both continents.

In any case, the completed Malayan government birth registration, plus a US consular report of birth and an American passport, resolved the legal citizenship issue before we took Walter to the United States for the first time when he was a year old. For him and everyone in our rolling-stone family, sorting out what it means to be an American—a United Stateser—has been the work of a lifetime.

To Market, To Market

Kaduna Nigeria, 1962

The open market sprawled endlessly, a shimmering pall of dust. Heavy, sun-baked air. Cooking-smoke. The rich smell of ever-present peanuts. Whiffs of rotting vegetables and open drains.

Vendors displayed their wares in neat heaps on the ground: Rice that had to be checked again and again for small stones. Dried black-eyed peas. Peanuts—"ground nuts" as they were called—by the heap and the gunnysack. Gnarly, small red peppers that made you sweat and your eyes water. Golf-ball sized, sharp onions. Dust-brown potatoes. Stubby carrots. Seasonal vegetables: okra, green beans, and cabbage—plus a slew of different greens that appeared in the few months it rained.

Unidentifiable lumps of fly-encrusted meat hung in the shade of the few big trees. Lopped from the skinny white cattle that had ambled miles across the Savannah (and sometimes into our backyard from the surrounding bush) on their way to be slaughtered, the meat was often so tough it had to be ground twice, then pressure-cooked.

Micinyawa, the proud Hausa who ran our kitchen, usually went to market on his own, bringing the day's purchases home on his head. Occasionally, I went too, following at a discreet distance so my presence didn't raise prices. But I always kept his erect back, crisp white gown, embroidered cap, and Hershey-chocolate head in view.

Late in the second October we lived in Kaduna, he and I went together to get a pumpkin for Halloween, carefully examining the big, fat ones perfect for carving. I chose. He haggled. A deal was made. He refused to let me carry it as we wound our way back through the maze of vendors to our car. Looking back, I realize this must have cost him self-respect: pumpkin was the food of poor men. The *bature*, the foreign, white people he worked for—his household—should not eat pumpkin. His dignity also would not let me, the woman he worked for, carry it. He moved majestically through the crowd ahead of me, bearing the pumpkin.

Eggs came to the kitchen door—rather than from the market— the seller balancing her full basket on her head. Micinyawa tested them in a bucket of water. Rotten ones, full of gas, floated.

When we needed European staples, Micinyawa dictated a list for me to get at the Cold Store. The tin-roofed, single story structure was overshadowed by towering trees, a roost for vultures drawn to the fetid smells of the meat counter. The shelves in the main room were scantily stocked: sugar, yeast, milk (powdered, condensed, or evaporated—nothing fresh), and often, but not always, flour. There were tins of baked beans, a staple of English breakfast; Lea & Perrins

Worcestershire sauce; bottled gherkins; tins of vegetables (usually Crosse and Blackwell, sometimes Fortnum Mason) and biscuits (we would call them cookies); marmite (a salty brown paste to spread on bread or eat by the spoonful); chutney; Christmas pudding in season; and a few dejected, supposedly fresh, vegetables. The freezer burned meat, unlike the lumps we bought from the market, was more or less identifiable: chops, bacon, mince, or Brit-beloved bangers.

Micinyawa was a magician in the kitchen, no matter how unrecognizable the blob of meat he brought from the market and turned into lunch or dinner. We ate well even if for much of the year we had boiled cabbage and carrots, with the odd side trip to green beans or marble-like tomatoes.

Vienna, Virginia, June 1963

Newly returned to the overwhelmingly green Virginia suburbs, we needed to fill the larder. The Safeway door swung itself open, revealing air-conditioned cool and an enormous, dazzlingly lit space filled with aisles and aisles and aisles of shelves—and food: shiny, sweet green peppers; Red Delicious apples; fragrantly ripe peaches. As we turned into other aisles we saw a rainbow of Jell-O; Ritz crackers; red-and-white cans of Campbell's soup; yellow bags of Domino sugar. Then there was an entire refrigerator section of whole milk, chocolate milk, and eggs—boxed by the dozen and dated. The freezer section yielded Birdseye peas, frozen lemonade, and—

"Oh, Mommy, ice cream. L-o-o-o-k. *Lots* of ice cream."

There was no place for the eye or the mind to rest.

Across the back of the store there was a mile-long meat counter overflowing with yellowy chickens, rosy hams, streaky bacon, sirloins, standing rib roasts, and Porterhouse steaks—all precisely cut, weighed, and packaged.

"I want to see the other side," the man next to me grumbled loudly, having repeatedly picked out and replaced his selection. "You may have hidden all the fat underneath."

Surveying the luscious, well-marbled, *recognizable* sirloins, I heard myself say: "I don't know what you're fussing about. The last meat I bought had walked a thousand miles before we ate it."

Both the butcher and the man stared at me as if I were mad.

I fled, the grocery cart still empty.

My Own Person?

The early storm surrounding Betty Friedan's *The Feminine Mystique* blew past me. In February 1963, when it was published, we were living in Kaduna, Nigeria, nearing the end of Dan's second overseas tour in the Foreign Service. I was twenty-eight, married eight years, a college graduate, and mother to three children: six, four, and just-turned three. Being young and adventurous, and having help in the house for our gaggle, I was finding living in the newly independent Third World a demanding, exciting, satisfying education.

That June we moved back to the States. Dan was assigned to the State Department as an Assistant Staff Assistant to the Assistant Secretary of State for United Nations Affairs. Mainly he was a paper pusher, no diplomatic striped-pants about it.

We bought a house in Virginia and began to settle into what was then the outer fringe of suburban Washington. There was much to adjust to and catch up on: well-stocked grocery stores with innumerable unfamiliar brands; water from the tap we could drink; dependable electricity; television; driving on the right side of the road instead of the left.

Friends we hadn't seen in two years asked: "What was Africa like?" Almost immediately, without even listening to the start of a response—such questions were more "make nice" than real interest in the totally foreign—they went on to ask us if we had seen, say, *West Side Story*. We, however, hadn't seen a new American movie in years. Nor had we read books or articles that addressed ideas that, in our absence, were being embedded in the American consciousness.

This included *The Feminine Mystique*. Freidan's book laid out the problem that "[had] no name": bored suburban housewives who were unhappy with their lives and needed, just like men, to find fulfilling, meaningful work.

When we got back I had no time to read it or any book, for that matter. I was relearning how to manage a household on my own. There were children to keep up with, a house to clean, groceries to shop for, meals to cook, and laundry to do. I had a husband who worked sixty-hour weeks, not including the time he put in some Saturdays and the occasional Sunday.

By the time John Kennedy was assassinated that November, I was pregnant again. With a new baby plus three active, inquisitive older children, the next winter was horrible. Strep throat bounced from child to child so often I could smell it. There were days when I didn't talk to another adult. The children ate early, we read stories, and they went to bed. To figure out when to have Dan's and my dinner ready, I listened to the six o'clock news. Had there been a

135

political disaster—say, Tonkin Gulf or Cyprus? Such incidents often required an emergency late night Security Council meeting in New York, which meant that all the UN Affairs support staff in DC would have to pull another late-nighter. This happened often enough that the kids were saying, "Good night, Dad" when Dan left for work, if, indeed, they were up when he needed to be out the door.

Even so, in odd moments I found time to paint. (I'd begun painting seriously in Kaduna after a British woman asked me to join a small group that worked together regularly.) I contemplated writing a book; about what, I can't remember. I was learning, that for me, planning such projects, even with no time for them, was an aid to sanity. That dreadful winter gives me great sympathy for mothers who, overwhelmed, go mad.

A feminist head of steam was building among my friends. We talked about fairness, our own possibilities, our own dreams. Hillary Clinton, thirteen years my junior, recalls it was a heady time. For college women it no doubt was. For those of us already engaged in the all-encompassing job of raising young children, the blossoming ideas expanded horizons and opened windows, but they didn't so easily change our everyday lives. We were negotiating a different, maybe rockier path.

Because Dan and I expected to be reassigned overseas, I didn't quite fit into the unhappy, trapped, unfulfilled suburban housewives Freidan was writing about. While I was getting the hang of the "trapped" part fast, I also knew that before too long I was going back into an international life I found stimulating. However, it was a life where I was also clearly defined as "wife of." As Dan progressed up his ladder, there would be even more "required" duties to entertain, appear and, above all, to give priority to in supporting his career.

What I heard about *The Feminine Mystique* resonated with my growing need to be not only a mother and Foreign Service Wife, but also my own person. Even though I loved him and was mostly a happy wife, I was skittish about being *only* "Mrs. Daniel P. Sullivan." I welcomed "Ms." when it became popular. For most purposes, I started to simply use "Margaret Sullivan,"—*my* name, at least the name that I had chosen to take when I married. Me, basic and straightforward.

Dan's views were never the issue. We were a partnership. He changed diapers, often got up at night when a baby cried, played ball, taught the kids cribbage, and encouraged my projects. The issue was how to be my own person as we faced the fallout of our earlier decisions. It would take another decade before the Foreign Service would begin to shift gears. In individual women, in me, the seed was planted.

Dancing on the Altar

There is something ridiculous about being pregnant—not the anticipation and wonder of a new life coming, but the pure bumptiousness of the ballooning body and other pregnant escapades.

When I was pregnant with Whoozits-the-First, Dan and I were teaching a Sunday school class of boys in the seventh grade—an interesting stage. "Full of beans," as my grandmother said. We routinely frisked them at the door; they liked to sneak in straightened wire coat hangers and hook each other under the table. They also liked to target each other with spitballs when they thought we were looking elsewhere. As I got nearer to showing, we decided it was a good idea to tell them I was expecting a baby. The next Sunday morning Dan made the announcement before I came in the room. As I entered, these wonderful rascals all shot to their feet, each offering me his chair. I was expected to take all ten seats at once. Our baby was theirs. The only problem was that it was due in August. The class was out for the year in May. So before class ended, they hosted a baby shower. We were given ten pairs of infant-sized rubber pants.

That year, I was in my last semester at American University, minoring in economics—not exactly a "girl's" subject in 1956. The only woman in a course on international economics, most of my classmates were, like me, barely out of their teens. More boys than men, they were uncomfortable with being near a pregnant woman and sat as far away from me as they could. I sat near the few Korean War vets whose wives were expecting or already had small babies. Pregnancy was natural, not embarrassing, to them. They even asked well-informed questions about how things were progressing.

One late spring day, the baby was particularly energetic, bouncing from hipbone to hipbone, setting my clothing to dancing the hokey-pokey. First-pregnancy-me was self-conscious. While the unmarried students looked away, the professor, who had three nearly grown kids, couldn't help smiling.

In June I lumbered across the stage to receive my diploma. Then, toward the end of that sweltering sub-tropical Washington summer, Jerry squalled into the world—"Bright and shiny like a new penny," as the elevator operator in our building said.

That fall, the six of our former seventh-grade Sunday school students who were altar boys all insisted on serving at the christening of "their baby," Gerald Winfield Sullivan.

Two years later, Whoozits-the-Second was on the way, expected again in a hot and humid Washington summer. By early July, almost due, I was bulbous and waddling. Dan's brother Don, newly graduated from college, had accepted a teaching position in Japan. He absolutely had to sell his Volkswagen Beetle and he had other things to do, or so he claimed.

Bugs, with their then-unusual gear-system, had just burst onto the late-'50s car scene. Since none of the prospective buyers were familiar enough with a Bug to test-drive one, I had to drive them around. This meant putting a not-quite two-year-old, who may or may not have been napping, into the back seat, and squeezing my ballooning belly behind the steering wheel. As I drove around several blocks, I tried to explain to bemused potential purchasers how the thing worked. I sold the car but didn't get a commission. Gay Beach Sullivan arrived soon after.

A few months later, we were in Kuala Lumpur. Something must have been in the water that first year since almost all the young wives we knew, both in the American embassy and the larger expat community, got pregnant. I hadn't been there long before our third Whoozits was on the way, much sooner and closer to the second than we had planned.

By the time I met Venice Lamb she was also pregnant. The Lambs had come to Malaya from England so Venice's husband could do his doctoral research. She and I were on the same young-expat social and play-date circuits. We got even better acquainted as partners on the altar guild at St. Mary the Virgin, the old Anglican cathedral in the heart of the British colonial city.

Our duties involved following strict guidelines on caring for the altar linen. The Guild's dear but imposing Chinese and Indian ladies—cut from the same imperious "grande dame" cloth as some of the old guard British members—instructed us that we were to always wash the altar linen ourselves. Our non-Christian house staff (read: heathen) should never handle it. The water in which the linen was washed should always be poured directly onto the ground.

I didn't think God cared how we handled the linen. Just the good ladies did. So I didn't pay attention to their rules: The amah washed and ironed the linen with better care than I was capable of. Since we lived in a second-floor flat, the water went down the drainpipe to the ground. The linen went back to St. Mary's crisp, clean, and lovely just the same.

Venice and I were responsible for cleaning the altar each Saturday morning, then vesting it for Sunday services. The inside of St. Mary's was absolutely English Victorian Gothic: dark, old carved wood (perhaps imported English oak) with the altar pushed back against the elaborate reredos. This was the tropics, so unless such wood was regularly, vigorously wiped down, it grew a thick coat of white mold. Because of the altar, there was no possible way to get a ladder close enough to the reredos to do the job.

Rather than let it grow mold, we got there early each Saturday morning and took matters into our own hands. After closing the doors and taking off our shoes, we—two young, increasingly bulbous foreign women—climbed cumbersomely up onto the altar to give the reredos a good wipe down. We devoutly hoped none of the pious ladies would arrive early to fix the flowers or that no parishioner would come in for quiet contemplation. They would have been beyond shocked at two pregnant ladies dancing on the altar. God, we figured, is practical, with a well-honed sense of the ridiculous, and wouldn't mind at all.

In February, Walter Peyton Sullivan was christened in front of that well cared for, danced-upon altar.

Four years later, soon after we settled into our first house in the States, bingo, Whoozits-the-Fourth was determined to put in an appearance. Maybe it was because of the ostrich egg. Oh, I knew. Literally it wasn't. Still…

As we were leaving Kaduna a few months earlier, our landlord, an important minister in the regional government, came bearing gifts: a pair of huge ostrich feather fans and an ostrich egg decorated with a red-and-green leather casing. For a while I thought I would have to do a fan dance to get on the airplane because the fans barely fit in the biggest suitcase. In a fishbowl community where news traveled, we couldn't be known to have left them behind. The decorated egg—thick-shelled, maybe six inches in diameter, and emptied of contents that equaled about two dozen hens' eggs—tucked easily into the corner of a bag. When we got to our new house in the States, without thinking, I hung it in the family room in the basement, forgetting why people gave those eggs as gifts and hung them up in their homes: blessings for fertility. In another few weeks, totally unplanned but happily wanted, Whoozits-the-Fourth was on the way.

Eight months later, it was a warm spring day. Gay and Walter were playing in the woods across the road. I was working in the half-basement where, perhaps eight months along, I could also, sort of, keep an eye on things. Suddenly, Gay flew into the basement, yelling, "Mother, Mother. Come quick. Walter's in the tree house. He can't get down." The communal tree house was easily twenty feet up one of the big oaks. No other adults were around—anywhere. Moving as quickly as my bulging figure allowed, I went to investigate, assuming I could talk him down.

Awwwwwk. There was Walter in the tree house looking down on the first of several ladder boards nailed to the tree's trunk. Clearly, it was too far away for his barely four-year-old stubby legs to reach. Somehow he had gotten himself up unaided. No way, no how, was he getting down.

Toes on the bottom board, fingers on one several higher, belly rubbing on the tree in between, I inched my way up, step by step, speaking quietly to Walter: "I'm here, it's okay. Turn around. Get down on your tummy. Now, stick your feet out. I'll help you get your feet onto the top rung... There, you're on it. I am going to move down one step. The other rungs are closer together. You can reach. Come down just like you went up. Let's go carefully."

We made it. Charles Parks Sullivan bounced into the world less than a month later.

Planting Daffodils

The lump was definitely there. Goose-egg sized, it was tucked between the top of my leg and pelvis. It wasn't painful. Just noticeable, insistently calling "here I am" as I got out of bed that Saturday morning of Memorial Day weekend, 1965.

"Dan, feel this. I know this lump wasn't there last night."

He felt it, firm, palpable under my skin—definitely not my imagination.

The lump certainly hadn't been in my groin on Thursday when we were getting the first part of our physicals at the State Department. We were preparing for Dan's assignment to the consulate in Surabaya, Indonesia, and the doctor had checked me over carefully. There'd been nothing out of the ordinary. Puzzling.

"Mom," I heard. "What's for breakfast?"

"Coming."

Raising four kids under nine, the youngest not yet one, meant the household never stopped. All that day and the next, I kept feeling the lump both with my fingers and in its simply "being there" as I moved around, changing a diaper, listening to the gaggle chatter, fixing breakfast—the usual.

When I had a minute, I called our family physician. "What should I do?"

"Come in Monday. I'll take a look."

"Probably just a lymph node doing what they are designed for," he told me when I went in. "Usually we would watch it for several months and see what happens. Since you're about to leave the country, let's just have it out."

Tuesday, I saw State's doctor again to finish the physical. "No, it wasn't there last week," she confirmed, feeling it, making notes. "Your doctor is right, it's probably just a hard node. Good you're having it removed to confirm that. I'm so sure it's nothing I'll go ahead and sign your travel clearance. If there's a change, let us know." Cleared to go.

Three weeks later, the lump was removed.

The morning after the procedure, I was dressed, waiting to leave the hospital and get the household ready for the movers. Dan came in, followed by Dad, then my doctor. Solemn faces all.

What they actually said remains fragmented, hazy. Dan, clearly shaken, held my hand. He already knew. "So sorry, Margaret," the doctor began. "Didn't look right when the surgeon removed it…Edges fuzzy…Minimal biopsy suggests a malignancy…. Sending to other labs…takes a week or so…need to do other blood work…. Stay in the hospital another day."

I guess I asked questions. I always do. Dad and the doctor hugged me and left. Dan stayed. We just sat there, holding hands and each other. Then he was gone.

Malignant. How? Why? What? Why me? The children were still so young. So was I, barely thirty.

I bargained with God. "Gay needs me to see her grown and married. I need that too…" I did a lot of that. Not sure why I focused on Gay, the boys needed me, too—and I them. Dan and I needed each other.

The next days were a blur of "hurry up and wait." I stayed busy in the day because I no choice. At night, petrified by uncertainty, I imagined all sorts of horrors.

"Hodgkin's Lymphoma." There was no question. The Armed Forces Institute of Pathology result was definitive. The prognosis was not good in 1965. Life expectancy was maybe two years. My fear was no longer an abstract mass of worries. It was a specific disease to understand, to adjust to living with—and dying from.

My doctor referred me to an oncologist in the city. He sent me to George Washington Hospital for a lymphangiogram, then a relatively new technology, to see if the node was isolated or the disease had spread. (There were no MRI or CAT scans then.) I spent five hours flat on my back with no pillow, not allowed to move. Drip bags tubed to small needles plugged in each foot ran radioactive dye through the whole lymph system. (Think something akin to the capillary action demonstration we did in third grade with colored water and celery.) I was x-rayed from head to toe.

"There are fuzzy-edged nodes up into your lungs," the oncologist reported. "Lots of involvement. None actively fulminating now. We have new drugs that seem to work. They are as difficult as the disease. We can only use them once or twice. Let's wait until the Hodgkin's acts up again. You will know—another node will pop up. You will run a fever and feel flu-ish. Then we will treat it. Until then, when you have other x-rays, particularly of your chest, tell them about this. The dye will show for several years and scare the radiologist. Call me if you have questions. Come see me in a month."

We waited. I felt myself all over every day at first. Is that a lump? Oh, there's a pea. "Dr. S, what do we do?" I would ask anxiously on the phone.

"Does it hurt?"

"Yes, it's sore."

"We won't do anything. That's just what lymph nodes do when they're working properly and ridding your body of infection. Only worry if the node gets bigger but doesn't hurt."

The world didn't stop, no matter how empty, bewildered, and numb I felt. Our travel orders were rescinded. Dan was assigned to a job on the Indonesia Desk at State. The baby began to walk, then to run, his babbling becoming words. Meanwhile, the older ones were always up to something. We got up, ate; I grocery shopped, filled the day. During the quiet times, at night, the "what ifs" hit.

"I can help with the children," Mother offered. "But you need to live in our school district so they can come to my house on the school bus if we need them to." She left the rest—what might happen—unsaid. Grandmother Parks, her mother, well into her eighties, was living with them. Mother couldn't easily come to us six miles away, particularly if it needed to be daily.

My family has always been good about dispassionately solving problems during emergencies. We don't deny feelings, just set them aside when it's important to do so. We keep on keeping on, doing the needful, finding strength and comfort in that. When we were little, Dad taught each of us to detach, focus on the process, and ask questions. "Keep your eye on the needle as it goes in to inject the shot. Say ouch when it hurts." So I said "ouch," not for something that "hurt." Just "ouch."

We hunted for houses close to my parents'. Doing something, anything, constructive made the unknown…easier. Yet not really.

"I think we found your house," Mother said on the phone. "A neighbor down the street is building on his back lot. Your dad and I saw it last night. Mr. Ezzel's not quite finished with it yet, but it's ready to sell."

The six of us went to see it. Yes. It was larger than we had thought we wanted. Still, it was just right—surrounded by woods, smelling new, available before school started, and a block down the road from Mother and Daddy's. The kids could use the same school bus, whichever house they were traveling to. Yes. Our new house.

That October I planted daffodils behind the top of the retaining wall along the lower driveway. Two rows of sixty bulbs promised golden trumpets in the spring.

In part, planting them was an ordinary thing to do in the fall, particularly in a new garden. But it also wasn't. Planting that fall was a deliberate act of faith that spring would come even if—even though—I would not there to see it. The daffodils would bloom, cheerful and lively for the family.

They were lovely the next spring, bobbing in the breeze—and the spring after that, too, augmented by more I planted the second fall to naturalize in the backyard.

Slowly, as the weeks and months passed, I felt for lumps less often. I never stopped, though. I switched to seeing the oncologist every three months. My "what ifs" haunted me as I got up in the morning, fixed meals, laughed with the children, chased the toddler. The children tell me I was difficult during those months. I yelled a lot. They didn't know what was going on. We only said I might get "sick," and let it go at that. When they were older, we told them the whole story. Dan tells me he was terrified—of losing me, of being a father on his own. We didn't talk about it much, just lived.

As time passed, I came to terms with dying and stopped being afraid of it. I was scared more of the process and of the effect on Dan and the children. While dying remained an unwanted, unasked for tangible possible, slowly each day became a gift. In an odd way, so, too, was the Hodgkin's, with its unexpected blessing of forcing me to face mortality, life's fragility, while I was still young.

In that second year, I remained well. Nothing fulminated. We began talking with the oncologist about going overseas again. State agreed. We were assigned to Jakarta. There was a good vacancy for Dan. More importantly, the post had a clinic with an American doctor, actually two, and a nurse. In addition, hospitals in Singapore and at Clark Field in the Philippines were easy flights away. In August 1967, we packed up, said good-bye to the family, the rented-out house, and the daffodils and flew half way round the world. We stayed away for nine years, living in three countries, with only three short home-leaves.

Hodgkin's continued to hover over me like a black cloud, although I felt for lumps less and less often. I saw the oncologist each home leave. While he and I both marveled at what appeared to be a spontaneous, unexplainable remission, we never labeled me "cured." Still don't. "I tell new Hodgkin's patients about you to give them a sense of what is possible," my oncologist told me.

I occasionally told people too. I still tell people, if I think it might give them hope. I speak cautiously. I was and am well and alive. Many of them might not be doing well. Increasingly I lived with an enormous "Why me?"—not about being sick but about being alive and apparently healthy. I must have special work to do beyond raising a family. What? I still can't answer that.

The daffodils had finished blooming when we moved home again nine years later. That fall, I planted more bulbs, filling the back hill with blossoms that would delight us in the spring and blend with wild flowers in the summer.

The following June, Gay was married in the front garden on a perfect, leafy-green, birdsong-filled afternoon. Time passed. I planted more bulbs each fall. Dan and I went overseas for a last tour and returned to the house and the daffodils.

Gradually, I went months, even years, not thinking about the Hodgkin's. I was simply grateful for what I learned about life, for each day and for interesting, occasionally valuable, work.

Twenty years ago, as the house got too big for just us, the gutters too high to clean, the driveway too long to shovel, we moved. Our over-the-back-fence neighbors had fallen in love with the house because of its spring daffodils. They bought it.

Memorial Day weekend 2015, fifty years had passed since that lumpy Saturday. There hasn't been another. Dan and I have enjoyed long, rewarding lives together. We continue to look forward to what is to come. Our small people have matured into unique productive adults. Their babies have grown, becoming wonderful adults in their turn. I, we, have been here to be part of it all.

This half-century has been an enormous, inexplicable, undeserved, happily accepted gift. I still plant bulbs each fall, around Thanksgiving. Instead of daffodils, I grow Paper Whites in my mother's low, soft-green Rookwood bowl. They bloom for Christmas, filling the apartment with smells of spring, of promise.

Who's Native?

Times were tense when we moved back to the States from Nigeria in June 1963. The struggle for civil rights was going full throttle: "Ole Miss" had rioted. Bull Connor had used fire hoses and police dogs on black demonstrators in Birmingham, Alabama. Medgar Evers had been murdered outside his home. The March on Washington for Jobs and Freedom would fill the Mall that August. "I have a dream…" has resonated ever since. The month after that, a bomb set off in the Sixteenth Street Baptist Church in Birmingham killed four little girls. The Civil Rights Act of 1964 and the Voting Rights Act of 1965 were yet to be passed. "Black Is Beautiful" was growing into a cultural movement.

Americans, then, knew little about Africa. Most weren't particularly interested. Americans of African decent were identifying with the continent, but not yet so much with specific countries, seventeen of which, including Nigeria, had gained independence in 1960 alone.

In Kaduna, young black Americans were among those who came to work for the Peace Corps and USAID to help the newly independent country. They were also intentionally returning to the continent of their ancestors. Many, I think, expected to be welcomed with open arms as homecoming kin. What initially jarred them—as we observed and from what they said—was discovering they were truly, at their cores, *Americans*. Although they blended more easily into crowds, they were almost as visibly outsiders as we were. The differences were subtler no doubt. Nonetheless, their walks, haircuts, clothes, mannerisms, and voices made them visible. Yes, they were long-ago descendants of Africa. But they were not African. Nor were they *seen* as African.

Take our friend, a remarkable young lawyer from the University of Syracuse's Maxwell School of Citizenship and Public Affairs. He was in Kaduna developing laws for the Northern Region of Nigeria, and while he was here, had become fluent in Hausa. Good humoredly, he told about sitting in a meeting of civil servants in Zaria, the town north of Kaduna. The main speaker, the Sardauna of Sokoto, the prime minister of the Northern Region and the primary political force of the country, was addressing the group in Hausa.

In the middle of his speech, the Sardauna singled out our friend, unaware (or perhaps not), that he understood what was being said. "He may look like us," the Sardauna intoned. "Beware, he's not. He's *bature*." (*Bature*, vernacular for "white person," more broadly referred to an outsider.)

I'm not sure what the Sardauna meant when he said "beware." Maybe this: Nigerians, like other Africans establishing post-colonial nationhood, were engaged in the existential work of defining who they were, as citizens of their own independent country as well as of the twentieth century's increasingly interconnected global community. Nigeria the country was both a new and a colonial entity.

Historically, Nigerians from different tribes, speaking different languages, were often at odds with each other. These peoples were now in the early stages of forming a unified nation within boundaries drawn, not by them nor in consideration of their tribal régimes, but by their colonizers. The proud Hausa had a clear sense of identity, built on being Muslim, with their own history and power structures that predated colonial intrusion. In different parts of the country, other tribes were also proud of their cultures, histories and identities. Members of those tribes living in Kaduna were, with few exceptions, only slightly less "outsider" than we were. Often more distrusted, they lived in the part of town called *sabongari,* or "strangers' town."

Being Nigerian in Nigeria as a whole was a completely new deal. In many ways—particularly in terms of legal structures, levels of education, and which groups had been chosen as civil servants—the country was the product of British colonialism.

That may be why outsiders, even black ones who spoke Hausa, were people to "beware of"—not so much in the sense of "to be fearful of," although that was no doubt a part of it, but rather in the sense of "to be wary of, to keep an eye on." Advisors like our friend were welcome to assist, but that was as far as it was to go. He was, we outsiders were, to step with respectful care. Perhaps the Sardauna was also saying that Nigerians should not overly defer to or depend on outsiders.

Adjusting to living in a new environment and different culture is never simple no matter how often one does it. Perhaps arriving knowing it would not be an ancient home made that process easier. I don't know. Like the newly independent Nigerians we lived among, we were figuring it all out for ourselves.

Living in different parts of the world gave Foreign Service Wives stories to tell and knowledge to share. Stateside, the Association of American Foreign Service Wives (AAFSW) had established the Windows on the World program as an avenue for us to share what we had learned with District of Columbia public school sixth graders, the grade when the curriculum focused on the world.

After I was diagnosed with Hodgkin's and staying in the States longer than we had anticipated, I became a co-chair of the project. Although the DC public schools were technically integrated, District demographics meant that most of the classes, teachers, and students we met with were black—one of the reasons why those of us who had lived in Africa were in great demand.

Going into those schools at a time of burgeoning change and racial tension was a different form of cultural immersion for me. As someone who had lived in and wanted to talk about Africa, I was welcome. The situation was also—how to put it?—edgy. The students and teachers were wary of me. Like my "*bature*" friend, I was a resource and a window but also an outsider.

For my classroom stints, I had a big bag of props: Maps of Africa and of Nigeria; men's, women's, and children's clothes; pots and baskets for daily use; a python skin; and a few small pieces of African art. I enjoyed helping the children dress themselves in Nigerian clothes and seeing them smile and strut. It was a particular pleasure to watch students and teachers alike feel a direct connection to Africa as they excitedly handled real African things and saw how well made and beautiful they were.

Before I brought out my bag of treasures, I always started with the same question. "When you hear 'Africa,' what do you think of?" Invariably, I got three answers, not always in the same order: jungles, animals, and natives. In reply to the latter, I would ask, "Do you know you are a native?"

The room would get tense, the teacher more than the students. Clearly, they were imagining dancing people with bones in their noses in the way that the movies *Tarzan* and *Ramar of the Jungle*. They weren't alone in making those associations. Hollywood movies were largely responsible for a shared American vision of Africa. At that moment, however, the classroom was feeling as if that vision was being applied to them.

"Yes. You are natives," I would say. Another collective intake of breath, an air of held-in resentment. *Who is she to say that?*

Then I would say, "So am I. 'Natives' literally means 'people born in a place.' You and I are natives of the United States." The entire classroom would exhale. We were equals with something in common.

I knew that in the literal sense of the word *native*, I wasn't from the United States because I wasn't born there. In a different way, as I identified myself and as they saw me, I was.

Then, as it is now, the concept of what it was to be a native of a place was far more complex and fraught than I led my students to believe. For that role and that time, the most basic definition was all that was needed. The air would begin to clear.

House Home

"House...House...House..." my perceptive fellow writer commented. He was tallying the number of times I used the word in an essay to refer to one of our dwellings. "You never say *home*."

His observation hit (yes) *home*.

Yet the choice of *house* not *home*, while unconscious, was spot on. That house in suburban Washington, which we owned for nearly thirty years and lived in off and on for sixteen, was not "home." At least not in the sense that the word is often used: a place where you come from, where you always can return and be welcomed.

We loved the house—an oversized Cape Cod surrounded by towering oak woods. We also loved how we had modified it: a glassed-in dining room that was light-filled on all but the darkest days; skylights above the bed where we saw moonlight on a winter night when the leaves were gone; and a back deck that made a comfortable "tree house" to sleep on when the nights were steamy.

For the children, it was home. They were young when we moved in and returned to the house periodically until they finished college. Some even bounced back after that. When we sold it, our daughter said that, while she understood our decision, she found it harder to let go than we did. We kept leaving it and coming back. Because my time there was intermittent, I never felt completely "at home" there.

If home means anything to me, it is the large stucco house on a campus in north China where I was born and lived my first six years. But before I had had time to truly internalize my sense of home in that house, in *any* house, Mother, my sister, and I suddenly had moved to the United States, never to return.

After we left China, keeping track of our houses, homes, was confusing. We lived in four houses over the six years Daddy was away: Mother's parents' house on Market Street in Springfield, which, perhaps, is as near to a childhood home (other than the house in China) that I have; Daddy's parents' parsonage in Magnolia, Mississippi; and two more houses in Springfield—a two-story house on Normal Street and a one-story house on Page Street.

After Daddy returned, the following six years we lived in a walk-up on 115th Street in New York City; a bungalow in Mamaroneck, New York, and then a barny house in Burma.

Several months after we got to Rangoon, I left my parents' home to go to Woodstock School in India. While I returned to the Rangoon house for nine months, I knew that was temporary. Then, I flew around the world to live for two years in dorm rooms at the

149

College of Wooster in Ohio, with summers and holidays spent with various relatives. I was rootless, belonging no place.

After my parents returned to the States, I stayed briefly with them in their house in suburban Virginia. Then I married Dan. He joined the Foreign Service and we began moving: three places in the DC area in five years. Then there were two posts of two years each, in furnished government housing. First we stayed in an apartment in Kuala Lumpur, Malaya. Then we moved to Kaduna, Nigeria, where we lived in a walk-up flat over a grocery store until our house, the only house I have ever had a hand in building, was finished.

Back in the States again, we bought our first house in Vienna, Virginia. Two years later, we moved to The House, in McLean. Then Dan was assigned to posts overseas so we lived in three more countries over nine years. There were houses in Indonesia and the Philippines and an apartment overlooking the sea in Sierra Leone. We went back to The House before heading to our last assignment, Singapore and a high-rise apartment on the twenty-third floor. After that we moved back into The House, where we resided for nearly eleven years. Ultimately, when I was sixty, we moved to Alexandria where we lived in a condo overlooking the city for twenty years—the longest continuous period of time I have ever lived in any dwelling, ever. From there, we made our final move, into a continuing care retirement community in Falls Church, not far from Alexandria. In other words, I started life as an international "rolling stone" and have remained so. This is not to say that I have no home. For me, home is the people, the things, and the creative attitude I carry with me from place to place.

Which leads me, oddly, to carrier shells. When we lived in the Philippines, our shell-collecting middle son was given a particularly lovely *xenophoridae*, or a carrier shell. Wonderfully delicate, this mollusk, about the size of a silver dollar, cements other shells, stones, and whitened coral to its back.

It is a perfect metaphor for my definition of home. It, like us, carries its home with it, adding bits and pieces along the way as remnants of where it has been. Only, for us, instead of shells and stones, it's the people we meet, the things we collect, the experiences we remember that make up the "shell" we always carry with us from one place to the next and call our home.

When we started, we didn't have much: books, children's toys, family pictures—familiar things that, when put in a new-to-us place, made it ours. Each move we collected more. From Malaya, we brought several good prints by a famous Chinese artist, a pewter coffee pot, and two big wooden bowls used for panning tin. From Nigeria we brought African carvings, textiles, and my own early paintings. From Indonesia, we added antique Asian ceramics, including the flat Ch'ing Dynasty bowls we use for dinner parties, a few pieces of Chinese-inspired Indonesian furniture, and an old Dutch wall clock that filled wherever we were with a gentle tick. Still more came from the Philippines, Sierra Leone, and Singapore.

While some of the items we only looked at and enjoyed as art, I deliberately found ways of practically using many things and making them parts of our life. People asked to borrow the tin-panning bowls so often they went to more parties than we did. The bottom of an old lacquered box became the repository for recycled paper. African and Asian hand-weavings still cover chair seats or are used for snuggling on the couch. And I cook with a wide range of handmade utensils.

Over time, because I was curious and then for research, I watched and wrote about craftspeople. As I wrote about them, their work joined our portable home. "When you see these, you see me," said the old man who made wooden swords for Chinese martial arts on a street in Singapore as he handed me two swords. They hang in my office. Another old man, about to close his sign-making shop, removed his small, elegantly gilded shop sign from its place by the door. It lives on a living room shelf—his shop still open in spirit. When mother broke up housekeeping, a few pieces from my childhood migrated to me: her cloisonné bowl, her mother's cut-glass berry bowl, and a Chinese carved wooden stool I sat on as a child.

These are more than decorations and memories. They carry the spirit of the people who created them and whom, in some cases, I was privileged to get to know. As we made our last move, some pieces migrated to our children's homes, taking those spirits with them. The essential bits stayed with us, for now. "This looks like where you have always lived," guests frequently comment when they walk into our apartment here at the Home. They are pleased to feel the familiar comfort of what came with us.

Although we create home with these things that travel with us, the true meaning of home is people. Without the friends and colleagues we have added to our shell, we would have neither community nor base.

Above all, there is the shell itself—family, however many we may be at a particular time: just Dan and me or the whole clan. The place bubbles with life when everyone—for now eleven in three generations—gathers. Spirits of absent friends hover as vigorous discussions, laughter, old tensions, and the smell of lots of communal cooking fill the air. Then everyone goes back to the places where they are creating homes of their own in whatever houses they now inhabit. We return to being us: Shared time, shared space, shared laughter, shared huffles in the darkness. Home.

Raising Rolling Stones

"Did you take your children with you overseas?"
"Wasn't it hard to move them from place to place like that?"
The simple answers to these chronic questions are:
"Yes, they went with us until there wasn't a school for their grade where we were and they had to go away to boarding school," to which I usually add the answer to the second question: "I have no idea what it would be like to raise children in just one place. Or what it's like to grow up in one place either."

Dan and I were rolling stones raising a second, even more nomadic generation. Being mobile was the family normal.

I don't know if having grown up internationally made being parents raising kids all over the world easier. No matter where you do it, being a parent—day-by-day, often minute-by-minute and, in our case, in four directions at once—is challenging and mostly rewarding. Certainly, there is a lot of learning by doing.

Wherever they were, our gaggle were kids, doing what kids do. We were parents, doing the best we knew how, raising four individuals with their own personalities and needs while living the itinerant life of diplomats.

Family dynamics were—dynamic. The family changed with the arrival of each new member and each place we lived, morphing again as members in turn rolled away. No two of us experienced the family in the same way. We share "belonging," a communal structure, a cast of characters, and many mutual, though differently shaded, memories.

I clearly remember my first flight. Our children don't. They started flying before they could remember. We flew to Kuala Lumpur as a foursome, with two-and-a-half-year-old Jerry and six-month-old Gay. Then came Walter. Two years later, we went on to Kaduna as five. Jerry started first grade our second year there. We flew back to Washington. Charley joined us the first year in the house in suburban Vienna. When found the "move-back-to" house in McLean, we were the "forever and ever" six, with the three older children in kindergarten and elementary school.

Two years later, we moved to Jakarta, arriving with sixth-, fourth-, and third-graders and a three-year-old. In its own way, Indonesia was "home." Not only was it where we lived the longest overseas, it was also the last place we lived as a family of six in the same house. By the time we moved to Cebu, in the Philippines, Jerry was in the tenth grade and away at boarding school, only home for vacations. Thereafter, each year was a different combination of schools and resident and non-resident children. The middle two also started their boarding school lives from Cebu, which left Charley alone for a year. The first year in Freetown, Sierra Leone, the three younger kids were residents again. The second Freetown year, the older three were all away in boarding schools. Charley was home alone. After nine years abroad, we were assigned back to the States. By then, young adults began stepping forth, then moving back, then striding out again.

Rolling stone parenting was its own education. We stumbled on our first lesson before we had begun. Jerry was four months old, that lovely stage when new babies interact and laugh. Dan was working in the Department's Bureau of Intelligence and Research in an office that followed events in South Korea; Yi Ki-bung was vice president. As we kept repeating it, the mere sound of Yi Ki-bung's name rolling off the tongue—a giggle in its self—became a game that made Jerry laugh. Particularly if he was on the bed and we made him bounce every time one of us said: "*Yi* (bounce) *Ki* (bounce) *bung* (bounce)." Several weeks into this game, we realized we might be assigned to Seoul. Having our son programmed to laugh heartily every time he heard the vice president's name was a truly bad idea. We stopped. The memory is a good snicker.

We embarked half way round the world the first time—to Malaya, not Korea—on a prop plane for what seemed like endless refueling stops and flying time. With a toddler and a baby, we were burdened with mounds of cloth diapers (the only kind available then) packed in two carry-ons. We also carried plastic bags for storing diapers in their objectionable stages until the end of the trip.

Although I had stopped nursing Gay, she was still only drank evaporated milk formula. To feed her we carried twenty-some four-ounce baby bottles filled with a measured amount of sterilized water, an equal number of small tins of evaporated milk, and a church key to open the tins with. (This all required another two carry-on bags, as I remember.) If Gay was hungry, I opened a can, mixed the correct amount of milk from it into the warmed-on-the-plane water, and disposed of the opened can and its remaining contents. I kept the empty bottle after she finished. When she needed to be fed again, we repeated the process.

Walter was fourteen months old, in that hold-on-to-the-finger not-quite walking stage, when we left Kuala Lumpur. While we were waiting in the open stretches of the Tokyo airport, he suddenly realized he could cut loose and run. Nothing would stop him. Up and down the aisle, he and I walked, effectively, clear across the Pacific.

As returning rolling stones, we had our moments, particularly early in the first US stint. Newly back from Nigeria, we were living in northern Virginia—yet another different, unfamiliar place for the kids.

We took them, by then seven, five, and three and a half, into Baskin-Robbins. They knew about ice cream: We had a hand-crank ice cream maker that the cook, sometimes with the help of the children, had churned. They ate that ice cream, usually vanilla, with a spoon, out of a bowl. They'd never been to an ice cream parlor, much less chosen a flavor or eaten a scoop from a cone. We had to teach them: "Lick the ice cream piled above the cone to keep it from dripping, and then start on the cone, top first. No, don't bite the bottom point." Something most American kids learn at, what, two? The other patrons looked at us as if we were demented, miserable parents.

Besides welcoming new experiences, coming back also meant clinging to, then letting go of, old habits. In Northern Nigeria most men and boys wore multicolored, embroidered caps. Walter was affixed to his, unwilling to go anywhere without wearing it, like any boy should. That October, with his two older sibs in school, I took him to the Foreign Service Wives book sale.

Suddenly, I realized he wasn't clinging to my skirt. Nearby, a Hausa-capped, almost four-year-old Walter was engaged in serious conversation with the extremely recognizable wife of the Secretary of State. "I saw his Nigerian hat," she said, turning toward me. "We were given one when we visited there." She put out her hand: "I'm Virginia Rusk." That winter, as Walter was more settled in a place where boys didn't wear embroidered hats, he put his away. He kept talking seriously to people, though.

While Dan was assigned to the State Department, we came "home." Thus, the kids were knit tightly into their larger family in the ways that profoundly grounds and shape us. Their Winfield grandparents' house, where a great grandmother and a young aunt and uncle also lived, was up the road. Our kids could be in and out by just running up there. Thanksgivings and Christmases were memorable multigenerational gatherings. Other aunts, uncles, and cousins lived in New York and Wisconsin, easy places to visit.

At the same time, home tours also gave our gaggle several successive years of in-depth growing up as suburban Americans: public schools, neighbor kids, Cub Scouts, Brownies, Little League, Sunday school, TV, a pediatrician, chicken pox, swim team, allowances, chores, homework, museums, and Fourth of July fireworks.

The second home tour, when they were teenagers, it was driving lessons, driver's licenses, and nights not going to sleep until a door slammed and a voice called "I'm home." I presided as stay-at-home, some-volunteer-activity mom until college costs loomed. Then we refinanced the house and I went to work.

After a while, a travel order arrived and with it another family transition. Going back overseas meant both missing "home" and family and returning do a different familiar way of living. The American and expat communities—large or small—functioned like both an extended family and a village, with school serving as a center of activity. Even so, community didn't just happen. We needed to invest time and energy into *creating* it.

Celebrating holidays were particularly important. Partly long-distance acculturation, partly a passing on of familiar ways to mark the year, they strengthened a sense of belonging to both where we were and where we came from. In Kaduna, the majority of the small group of expat kids were Brits who celebrated Guy Fawkes instead of Halloween. Our kids joined them. The festivities included roasting potatoes in a bonfire and setting off fireworks, the latter a reenactment of an attempt to blow up Parliament in 1605. With the others, our kids sang: *"Remember, remember, the fifth of November. Gunpowder and Guy Fawkes."*

Jerry and Gay enjoyed it so much that the next year, back in Virginia, they were more interested in having a bonfire than in Halloween. They hadn't yet experienced getting dressed up in costumes and going trick-or-treating door to door, neighborhood style. At the beginning of the next Stateside tour, after nine years abroad, Charley was a seventh grader. Too old for trick-or-treating in our community, he insisted on doing it anyway: "Because I never have."

In Jakarta, Halloween "makings" didn't appear on store shelves months in advance like they would have in the States. So the American mothers organized everything from scratch. One way or another, we created costumes for our kids. Once, using wire and orange cloth from the market, I turned Gay into a jack-o-lantern. Another time she was a butterfly. The boys were cowboys and pirates, costumes that were easier to assemble from whatever was around.

One year we set up a trick-or treat route and drove groups of kids around so they could knock on pre-determined doors. That was a hassle. Most Halloweens, we organized a community party at the American Club. Imagine trying to keep a horde of roaring, costumed, sugar-high kids out the pool on a steamy tropical afternoon.

As distinctly American celebrations, Thanksgiving and July Fourth were special. They bound the American community together while reinforcing our national identity.

Just as my parents' Thanksgiving tables had been welcoming to those who were missing family, so was ours. In the Philippines, shortly after the imposition of martial law, we produced the traditional meal of turkey (two birds as I remember) with all the fixings for fifty-four of us. We moved every table in the house, along with some borrowed folding ones, into a big horseshoe. Joining us around it were the other consulate families, the Borromeos (an extended Filipino family who had "adopted" us), five or six Peace Corps volunteers, and Eddie.

A well-known American businessman, Eddie was in the stockade (the political jail established after martial law) for some reason no one could pin down. The commander of the Third Constabulary District, his good friend in earlier and later life, had given him time away to celebrate with us. After the meal was finished, Eddie went home for a "family" visit. At the end of the evening, he turned himself back in to the stockade.

Depending on where we were, the Fourth of July was often a double celebration: a diplomatic National Day event, sometimes large and sometimes small, and for the entire American community, a family picnic. Where we were, this was sometimes at the American Club, other times at the ambassador's residence. Once, when Dan was the American consul in Cebu, the picnic was in our garden. Any year, hamburgers were easy. Some places there were also hot dogs. If they weren't available locally, with some advance planning, we could import them for the occasion.

As a residue of British and Dutch colonialism, Christmas was a national holiday in all the countries we lived, even though the majority of the populations weren't Christian (except in the Philippines). In the tropics, we could only dream of a white Christmas. Hot seemed normal; the day often ended with a welcome late afternoon swim.

Our way of keeping Christmas traveled with us, evolving as we went. We carried lights and ornaments, including a few from Dan's China childhood trees. As we needed more decorations, the children, their friends, and I made them. Our Christmas "trees" were improvised: In Malaya, we put bamboo branches in a big jar. In Kaduna, the first year we went out to the bush to cut a branch of a thorn tree. There were lots of spikey thorns and no green leaves, but dangling lights and decorations from the thorns was perfect. We used casuarina branches from a friend's garden the next year. Like at Thanksgiving, we gathered people who needed "family."

Christmas in the Philippines lasted from mid-December until Twelfth Night, January 6, with Christmas Eve midnight Mass at its heart. Our Filipino friends teased that it actually started in September when jeepneys full of carolers using loudspeakers began cruising from house to house. "*Maligayang Pasko* (Merry Christmas) Consul and Mrs. Sullivan," came the call from the road. They sang and sang until we sent out a small financial "thank you."

Parol, traditional star shaped Christmas lanterns made of bamboo covered with rice paper, appeared in the market around then, too. Beautifully lit, they hung outside every house, from large villas to simple thatch-roofed homes made of matting. We decorated the consul's residence, our home, with them too. One year, the kids even learned how to make them in school.

A small antique *belen* (a crèche) became a cherished part of our portable Christmas collection. Whether the figures—who-knows-how-old images of Mary, Joseph, and the Christ Child—were carved in Mexico and brought to the Philippines or made there by Chinese artisans, I don't know. I found Mary and Joseph at an antique shop in Cebu; a friend gave us the baby Jesus. Miguel, the gardener, made the manger of split bamboo that was tied together and filled with bamboo shavings. Each year we were in Cebu, he devotedly repaired the manger if need be. Then, kneeling near the chest by the front door where we put the *belen*, he placed it in front of Mary and Joseph and gently laid the baby in it. Now, as I get out the *belen* and, press the manger back into shape, I feel Miguel's devotion.

We also celebrated local holidays with friends. In Malaya, the kids enjoyed going on Chinese New Year's calls with us. They received traditional red packets with a bill and coin inside. We, in turn, gave five oranges, symbols of good luck and wealth, to each family and red packets to their children.

In Indonesia during Lebaran (Eid al Fitr), the feasting days at the end of the Muslim fasting month of Ramadan, calling on friends was also customary. As we went from house to house, we joined in eating all sorts of delicious sweets and exchanged the traditional greeting: *Ma'af lahir dan batin*, a request for forgiveness for any offenses of word or deed, known or unknown, over the last year.

We traveled as often as we could in each country, sometimes by car, other times by train or by air. Jerry went with us around east coast Malaya (the other two were still babies and stayed home with the house help, a neighbor checking in on them).

When we traveled on bumpy dirt roads through Nigeria, the three children (no fourth yet) turned pink with the laterite dust our car kicked up. The bathtub was full of mud as we bathed that night and one set of each person's underwear was everlastingly pink.

I thought twice, however, about when we took Gay places there. She was three and four, with fair skin and bleach-blond hair and thus a particular curiosity for local people who loved to touch her straight almost white hair and feel her skin. Understandably, she hated that and reacted—crying and kicking. We didn't want to put her through that or have her be rude and for a while rarely took her in large crowds. Being visible—as we always were—had a price.

In Indonesia, more than once, we piled into our Jeep Wagoneer to drive from Jakarta around Java. On those trips we climbed Borobudur, one of the world's most impressive Buddhist monuments, and watched dance performances of the Ramayana in front of Prambanan, a Hindu temple outside Jogjakarta. On the trip that included Charley's sixth birthday, we had driven the length of Java and crossed over on the ferry to Bali. Dressed in traditional Balinese clothing, the family ate Balinese food, sitting at low tables in the small hotel courtyard, a gamelan tinkling in the background.

Each year Dan was the American consul in Cebu, he and I flew to the next island for the annual ceremony to commemorate the Leyte Landing, when General McArthur led American troops ashore to liberate the Philippines at the end of World War II. One year we took the children. After the ceremony, we crossed to Samar, the next island over. All of us rode a small boat up a jungle-draped river, through a spooky defile that had been the site of a massacre nearly three-quarters of a century earlier during the Philippine-American War. In a *sotto voce*, as only a nine-year-old could, Charley asked, "Mother, are the natives friendly?" His question reflected how eerie the place was, especially for a boy with an overactive imagination—and a tongue that didn't always say what was appropriate.

In Sierra Leone, on one of several family road trips out of town, we drove to a nearby village for the dedication of a Peace Corps volunteer's project. While we were there, our children joined the village children in their daily chore, carrying full buckets of water up a hill from the river. After that, they had a greater appreciation of simply turning on the tap.

Another time while we were in Sierra Leone, we took Charley, the only one home at the time, to Mali. From Kulikuro, near the Malian capital Bamako, we took a several-day boat trip on the Niger River, stopping for a short dive into Timbuktu, around the Niger bend where the river literally cuts through sand dunes, to Gao.

For rolling stones, traveling when we got back to the States—as "foreign" a place as wherever we were calling home at the moment—was equally important. At the end of our home leave in 1969, we drove across the United States to catch a ship back to Indonesia. The kids still remember that we stopped in Kansas to visit cousins; sat four hours in a Navajo trading post waiting for the station wagon to be repaired; and took the requisite picture of one child in each state in Four Corners, New Mexico. We also met a film crew in a motel in Colorado, drove through Bryce and Zion, locked the keys in the car in Yosemite, and visited the aquarium in San Francisco. On that great trip we experienced the vastness and variety of our own country.

Above all, we were fortunate to simply live in places. To the degree an outsider can, we made ourselves part of the community, absorbing the rhythms and customs of everyday life. In Southeast Asia, taking shoes off to enter someone's house became habit. So did giving and receiving with the right hand, and greeting the older people in the room as we entered and left. Like many local boys, Walter and Iwan, his Indonesian buddy who lived next door, fought paper kites with strings waxed and rolled in ground glass so they worked like knives. When one's kite cut the other's down they scrambled on the tile roof to retrieve the fallen kite. (In the process they shifted tiles, how many we discovered when the rains started and we had to put buckets around the living room to catch leaks—nine one year.)

In Indonesia, the five Muslim calls to prayer that sounded from the mosque around the corner marked our days. The first call, *fajar*, came when it was still dark. For us, it meant another hour of sleep. The *maghrib* call just before dusk summoned the kids home for supper. To meet their obligation for *zakat* (giving of alms to the needy—like the five daily prayers, one of the five pillars of Islam), our neighbors gave food, mostly small bundles of cooked rice, to the poor people who knocked on our gates on Fridays. We followed suit. Later, in Freetown, when we went to the market on Fridays, we carried coins in our pockets to put in open palms, again an observance of *zakat*.

Food was an important part of "living there," wherever we were. In Kuala Lumpur, as the two smaller children were weaned we made their baby food because we couldn't buy it in the grocery store. A variation on Chinese congee, it was soft-boiled rice with bits of vegetable and meat. That beginning turned the children into life-long rice eaters.

Street food and hole-in-the-wall eating-places made life tasty, particularly in Indonesia (as long as it was fresh cooked and hot). We listened for the distinctive call of the *bakso* vendor as he came down the street, then slurped up his spicy soup. Charley relished eating *trasi* (pungent dried shrimp paste) and rice with the help in their rooms in the back of the house. After his snack, he would still scarf a "regular American" meal with us at the dining table.

Health precautions were necessary everywhere until we got to Singapore. Following in my father's footsteps, I taught our kids which street foods were safe; that they *must* brush their teeth with the boiled water, never water from the tap, and that being mindful of what they drank anywhere was an absolute necessity.

We also had regular shots. Additionally, in Nigeria, we regularly took a malaria prophylactic. At the reception to welcome us to

Kaduna a few days after we arrived in 1961, the British doctor rushed over to me. Not bothering to saying hello and barely introducing himself beyond saying he was the doctor, he asked, "What malarial suppressive do you take?"

"Chloroquine phosphate, every Sunday."

"Perfect. If your children run a fever over 101, give them a dose. *Then* call me. We have cerebral malaria here. It can kill in eight hours. Welcome to Kaduna."

By being invariably strict about the critical things, we were all able to stay healthy and the kids were still able to follow their "curiosity bumps," exploring food and other aspects of life in the places we lived.

Within the household there were other challenges: chores. At each post, like most of our expat and local friends, we had help in the house. Since each of them had specific responsibilities, it was difficult to assign our kids a chore, such a washing dishes, that they would have had in the States. We did expect our children to pick up after themselves and make their beds. If they "forgot," they rapidly learned that it would be done for them by the time they got home. The helpers didn't want to leave the kids' messes. In their minds cleaning up was their job—and they did it proudly. Moving back to the States meant reestablishing who did what chores. That wasn't easy—old habits die hard.

We paid our house staff well, by local standards. Additionally, in Jakarta, since prices for rice were volatile, we paid them a rice allowance based on how much a certain amount of rice cost that month. All told, they received more than a living wage. Even so, one of their salaries amounted to a bit over a child's generous monthly allowance in the States. Consequently, giving our children the same amount of money as our helpers earned would have given them a false sense of the value of money. Our solution was to give them no allowances. Instead, when a child wanted something we would talk to them about the money required to buy it. The situation made teaching financial management difficult. But it also encouraged reading, since—as the children quickly learned—we never turned down a request for a book.

Like chores, family dinners were another American ritual that frequently eluded us. Although we tried to have meals together as often as we could, the diplomatic social circuit meant we were out many evenings. "Where are you going tonight?," Walter was always the one to ask. "What time will you be back?" Dan and I had a longstanding agreement that, unless an invitation was a command performance, we saved Sundays for family outings.

On that score, in the Philippines, we were immensely fortunate. Cebu's Borromeo clan took us in and made us family—an ongoing relationship of now forty-five years and four generations' standing. Dan's secretary opened the door. Her mother, Lola (meaning grandmother) Pilar, the matriarch, insisted we join the Sunday Beach bunch of several families.

Beach Sundays meant potluck lunches, snorkeling, and shell hunting in the Bohol Strait. One memorable full moon we spent the night in a *banka* (a traditional outrigger). At low tide, with the clearest of clear water lapping around our knees, we walked on a sandbar exploring nocturnal shell life.

When Lola asked her adopted "children" and "grandchildren," to come, we did, happily. Like her actual children and grandchildren, when we arrived and left, we kissed her cheek and then the cheeks of the other Titas (aunts) and Titos (uncles)—a custom that introduced us to Filipinos' respect for family. The Borromeos enveloping warmth and friendship was a welcome chance to not only be with them, but to get out of our fishbowl and simply *be* for a while.

Wherever you are, parenting teens is a rollercoaster at best. By 1970, Jerry and his classmates were fourteen, needing more independence and "teenage" life. He sometimes went around Jakarta on his own or with his buddies. Two years younger, Gay chaffed because she couldn't: "Unfair!"

"Sorry, girls don't go out alone here, they always go in groups," I said.

While Gay had a point—it was unfair—so did I. Local custom carried the day. These kinds of decisions required frequent family conversations exploring when and where we followed local custom (in general, when we were out and about) and when we followed ours (within the family). We also had talks about what was appropriate because they were visibly part of the American embassy or consulate. Charley had a tee shirt he loved that proclaimed "Everyone Has Rights." The day after martial law was decreed in the Philippines, we put it away; not a good idea for the American Consul's son to wear when the government had just clamped down on those rights.

With teenagers, keeping up with what was hip in the States became more urgent. While tweens and teens there socialized at school dances, the school in Jakarta didn't sponsor them. Several families took turns hosting parties that could include dancing if the kids wanted to. A living room was cleared. Someone's coolest records played. We hostesses smiled together at how the boys stayed on one side of the room and the girls on the other—until it was about time for the party to break up. Then suddenly everyone danced with gusto.

Newly arrived classmates wore more current, hippie fashions. Our kids and their friends who had been in Jakarta a while immediately wanted to have a local seamstress copy them. Or they wanted us to order something similar from Sears.

Marijuana was another concern. *Ganja*, as it was called in Indonesian, was everywhere—for sale on street corners and commonly used to season food. Other international schools across the region (Bangkok in particular, as I remember) had serious drug problems. The fear of widespread student usage in Jakarta took hold like a fever. The community held meetings for parents and, separately, for the older kids. Whether, beyond experimentation, there was much actual ganja usage, we never knew. Jerry says his classmates felt unduly blamed for what they might and might not have been doing.

The Vietnam War was at its height when we were in Jakarta. With no TV, we weren't seeing footage of anti-war demonstrations or of the fighting. *Time* and other news outlets came by mail and were full of reports on, and photos of, both. In a sense those magazines were the primary way our teenagers were learning how to be American teens.

Within the American community, many fathers were US government employees. And, correctly or not, kids often assumed that they were *for* the war. Dan was silent on the subject; we talked little about it. Across the board—and not just in Jakarta—American sons—certainly Jerry—daughters, and some wives, were against the war. As for other officers, I don't know. As we heard over time, conversations within families were difficult and painful, if they happened at all. For me even now, nearly a half-century later, that time and its tensions are still troubling.

The Cold War provided a larger context and created its own friction. Jerry told us that one of his American classmates, no doubt repeating what he had heard at home, was going on and on in class about how terrible Communists were. Before long, one of their Yugoslav classmates interjected: "My Dad's a communist." Silence.

All of them had been to their classmate's house. They knew and liked his dad, who wasn't different from their dads. As with so much in mobile living, they learned hands-on how complex it is when generalities and specifics collide.

Just as with each move the children were introduced to different customs, they were also exposed to new languages. Some of them found it easier to learn a new language than others. By our fourth year in Jakarta, we were used to having the phone ring on a Saturday or Sunday morning with a call from a friend who wanted to borrow Walter for a shopping expedition. He knew the ins and outs of bargaining, and he sounded as if he were *anak betawi*, a child of Jakarta. Given he was a small *bule* (foreigner), he got good prices.

Soon after we got to Cebu, much of the children's Indonesian lapsed. The younger two learned some Cebuano. When we were in Sierra Leone, Charley added Krio, to communicate with his friends, and French, for school. The children didn't retain much of these languages either, although some did more than others. Yet, as with my memory of Chinese, their tongues didn't forget entirely and words lingered. When Dan, Charley, and I went back to Java from Singapore, in the early '80s, Charley hadn't been around Indonesian, much less Javanese, for a decade. Yet as we rode around Jogjakarta in a *betjak* (a pedi-cab), he kept asking: "Does that mean…?" to confirm his understanding. He was usually right. Learning new languages was just one more example of the many ways mobile living was an education—for all of us.

Many years later, someone asked Charley why he'd been to so many places. The same question could be asked of any of our four and would get the same answer: "Dad was a diplomat."

Which Kid, Which School?

Making sure our children got solid schooling overseas was an ongoing concern. With each child at a different stage and each post with unpredictable options, it required planning, with much more hands-on involvement than if they just walked out the door to the public school bus. For what seemed like forever, I choreographed a "who is going to what school, where, this year?" dance.

When the children were all elementary- and middle-school–aged, we were fortunate: Each post had an English-language option that met our needs. High school proved a different matter.

Jerry started first grade in Kaduna, Nigeria. His school had been established during the colonial period for young children of British senior civil servants. By the time Jerry went there, a year after independence, the transition in government leadership was well under way. His classmates were mainly Nigerian. I don't remember the nationality of the teachers. The British curriculum was taught in English, in the literal sense.

This highlighted the differences between British and American English usage at one point. Jerry had a foreign teacher (American, if he recalls properly) for part of the year. At morning roll call, using the British English they had been taught, the students responded with "present." Expecting "here" (American English), she apparently thought they were asking for gifts and was miffed.

In 1967, after four years in Virginia's Fairfax County public schools, we enrolled our three oldest children in the Joint Embassy School (JES), in Jakarta, the main school for the expat community. JES taught an American, English language curriculum, went through the eighth grade, and was managed by representatives of the American, British, Australian, and Yugoslav embassies. When they started, our third, fourth, and sixth graders were three percent of the student body. After the political upheavals in 1965 to 1966, the expat community was growing exponentially. So was the student body. When we left four years later, there would be over a thousand students enrolled.

A wide-spreading waringin tree (commonly called a flame tree) shaded the T-shaped, single-story, wooden buildings. The string of classrooms that had louvered windows for the breeze to go through, a small library and an office all opened onto long covered walkways that protected students from the monsoon rains. Playing fields were out back. The campus was called Patimura, for the road it was on in suburban Kebayoran.

JES needed a major upgrade, including current textbooks, a larger library, and science labs. It also needed to become an internationally accredited twelve-year school so older children could stay with their families rather than having to go to boarding schools elsewhere. With the backing of the managing embassies and the American business community, a group of us, mainly mothers, set about making these improvements. Significant funding would be required.

I began to cut my teeth in school development as the PTA vice president. The president was a businessman who was rarely in Jakarta, but a man, as the president "should be"—it was the '60s. After over two years, and countless meetings and politicking, the Joint Embassy School morphed into the Jakarta International School (JIS). The State Department's Office of Overseas Schools facilitated the transformation. They helped the school upgrade its curriculum and hire an American principal and teachers to complement the Indonesian and local-hire foreign teachers already there. To cover the increased costs, the board significantly raised tuition, and required organizations with students in the school to invest in it as well. This left smaller embassies from poorer Asian countries and some mission groups in financial difficulties. While the board made bursaries available for those children's tuitions the first year, I was tasked with helping them work with their home offices to understand that sending their children to the school would cost more after that and that they would need to find those funds.

Expansion began. Ninth (Jerry's class) and tenth grades were added to the Patimura campus. The board found land further out to build a new high school. The last thing we did in 1971 before leaving Jakarta for our next post was tour the nearly completed new campus. The following month, JIS opened with twelve grades plus kindergarten. Several years later, after a rigorous multi-year application process it was internationally accredited.

When I was working in Indonesia many years later, I visited JIS, renamed the Jakarta Intercultural School, now one of the best international schools in the region. A high school, middle school, and elementary school are on the new campus. The original Patimura site has a newer elementary school: two stories high and modern, sheltered, still, by the waringin tree.

JIS clearly marked our children and their classmates. Much like my Woodstock schoolmates, they have re-connected with email, text, and, mainly, Facebook. Now in their late '50s and early '60s, they, too, have the special gift of sharing memories and not having to explain who they are or how they understand the world.

From Jakarta we moved to the Philippines, where our three youngest went to the Cebu American School (CAS), which had only seven grades. Founded in 1924 during the American colonial period, it was out of date, underfunded, and undersupplied. Like JIS, it needed to shift gears, become more international, and ultimately to add a high school. Along with other parents, Dan (both as a parent and officially as the American consul) and I were much involved in making school improvements. The connections with the Office of Overseas Schools I had made during the JIS transformation helped simplify the process.

Beyond updating the building and curriculum, the school and the community faced the complicated set of cultural and pedagogical differences between Filipina teachers and their expatriate, mainly American, students. American parents encouraged children to ask "why?" as well as to participate in active give and take and expected teachers to teach in ways that challenged students to think on their own. However, the Filipina teachers had been brought up to respect their elders without questioning. As they had experienced in their own school days, they taught specific facts they expected to be accepted as given. To them, the students' questions seemed challenging and rude.

Jointly, teachers and parents explored—sometimes painfully and certainly slowly—how to better appreciate each other and facilitate change. Key to their efforts' success was a young Filipina teacher who grasped the need for transformation and served as a bridge between teachers, parents, and students. After we left, she became principal. What became the Cebu International School (CIS) moved and grew. Long after our departure, it expanded through the twelfth grade. Over forty years later, our children's Filipino friends' children attend CIS. It, too, has become what we had envisioned.

When we were assigned to Cebu we knew that Jerry, being a tenth grader, couldn't go to CAS and that the local schools for boys seemed inappropriate. We hadn't anticipated sending our teens away to school but didn't see a viable alternative. One of the advantages of the Department paying school tuitions when we were abroad was that, if we could not find an appropriate school at post, they paid so we could send our children elsewhere. With mixed feelings, we sent not yet sixteen-year-old Jerry ahead of us from Jakarta to the Philippines to an American boarding school in Baguio. Although the school was in the mountains of Luzon, a different island from Cebu, we could visit him, and he could come home easily for short vacations. However, over the year, the school proved to be a terrible fit for him.

Another advantage of having tuition paid is that it was easier to send a child to a school in the States that better suited their needs. The next year, we decided he should finish his last two years in a small Friend's school outside Washington, DC, not too far from his grandparents. The distance was greater, and visits were fewer but the school itself worked well. Although he came back home for summer holidays and for a year while we were living in the States and he was in college in DC, he never lived with us in the same way again. I was a little older when I left for Woodstock, but looking back, when I remember that adolescent experience, I understand how he must have felt cut loose and distanced from the rest of us. At the time, I also gained a greater appreciation of what my parents must have felt when they said goodbye to me.

Before we left Cebu, the two middle children had also outgrown CAS. So they, too, went away to school. Walter stayed in the Philippines, going to the school in Baguio where Jerry had been. It suited him better than it had his brother. Gay went to school in the States, living with my sister a year and then attending a small boarding school.

Charley, used to being part of a gang, became an only child—but only up to a point: He was absorbed like another son into the second generation of the Borromeo family. I was empty-nest-ish, letting my children go in stages. Parents, certainly mothers, know a great deal about children through observation, but long-distance parents know only what their children want to share. Letters were slow and irregular. International phone calls were used for emergencies, not simply keeping in touch. My heart still breaks when I remember hearing Walter on the phone from Baguio, sick, almost delirious. I knew his kind school housemother was taking good care of him. I also knew I couldn't get there right away and that by the time I did, he would be well. Even so...

The State Department paid for one round trip to a post per year per child, until the children were twenty-one. My biggest regret is that we didn't have, or thought we didn't have, enough money to bring the Stateside boarders home for a second trip at Christmas. They went to my parents. When they finally did return after nine months away, they were different people we had to get to know.

The school adventure continued in Freetown, Sierra Leone. We gave the boarders in the States the option to stay where they were or go with us. Jerry stayed where he was and then began college. He came to Freetown for summer vacation, working for the Peace Corps, which hired him for grunt work. Gay and Walter opted to come with us, as did Frankie, a girlfriend of Gay's. The three of them—the girls in the eleventh grade, Walter in the tenth—would do correspondence work using the University of Nebraska's homeschool curriculum.

Weekly lessons arrived in the embassy pouch. School was the family room of our apartment on Signal Hill on the outer edge of the city. In a fit of snickers, they named it the Signal Hill Institute of

Technology. They designed rings, which they couldn't get made, alas, emblazoned with the school's initials. In a way those initials meshed with the lesson from Walter's biology workbook that we recall gleefully. "Go to your sewage treatment plant," it directed, "and describe how it works." He puzzled a while, then wrote: "In Freetown, we have open ditches and vultures." The teacher in Nebraska gave him an A-plus: "We can't hold you responsible for what you don't have."

In the morning the three did schoolwork under my loose supervision. Most afternoons, after Charley got home and we had lunch, I drove us to the beach. Walter hung out with the Sierra Leonean caddies at the golf course across the road. We dropped his buddies off at their village on our way home. Every time our car went past, whether he was in it or not, someone would call out "Walta."

The beach was lovely. Far too often, the girls had to endure being propositioned by young Lebanese men, who all assumed they were God's gift to women. Every Saturday, Gay and Frankie volunteered in a home for disabled Sierra Leonean girls about their age, helping with games and crafts and making local friends. Once again, Gay's hair was an object of curiosity. The girls wanted to braid it into cornrows like theirs—but it was straight and fine; after two or three twists, it would slip out, to the laughing delight of all concerned.

The gift of homeschooling was that the kids discovered they could learn on their own. However, since the expats their age were in Britain at school, it was also its own form of isolation. (Frankie left us when she needed an emergency appendectomy and as soon as it healed and she could travel, returned to her family.) So, after a year, we decided our middle two should to go to high school in the States.

We opted to send Walter to a Washington, DC, boy's school. He could start as a boarder, and then, after we moved back to the States, live at home and become a day student. Finding the right school for Gay was not as simple. So she and I came home briefly to check out possibilities and found a good fit for her senior year.

Freetown was a different story for Charley. We enrolled him in local schools where he was one of the few non-Sierra Leoneans, highly visible and known to be connected to the American Embassy. The first year, for what would have been fifth grade in the States but was the last elementary year there, he went to the teacher-training school at Fourah Bay University. When that year ended, he and his classmates took the West African School Certificate, a school-leaving exam given all over English-speaking West Africa. Based on the results, he was admitted to Prince of Wales, one of Freetown's best-known boys' prep schools. Many of his classmates there were the sons of the government officials Dan worked with. As we invited his friends and their parents to screenings of American movies in our apartment, official friendships became more personal. Colleagues also appreciated seeing Charley in his Prince of Wales uniform—a white suit, school tie and straw boater—marching in the All Schools parade: "Never thought we'd see someone from the American Embassy in the parade."

Through all this, we had countless conversations with Charley about what, as the son of an American diplomat and a guest in the country, he should simply accept. Much of it revolved around school discipline. Caning was customary. When he was at Fourah Bay, he came home one day with two red welts. I wasn't happy, neither was he. Apparently he and two other boys had been rude to the teacher, at least in her eyes. I asked enough questions to confirm that he hadn't been singled out and they had all been treated equally. Even though I was unhappy about caning, I told him to be more careful about his behavior: "This is their way, even though we don't like it."

The next year he told me that the Senegalese French teacher made a student who answered a question correctly hit the hand of a student who answered incorrectly with a ruler. I was ready to object—this went well past my sense of what made educational sense or I wanted Charley doing. "Don't, Mother," he responded. "This is their way. I don't often make mistakes, and I don't hit hard."

In a relatively small city, he was known and easy to spot. He sometimes used public transportation. So when we were informed there was danger of a purported Lebanese group that might attack Israelis and Americans, we had to talk with him about the possibility of being kidnapped. No one should have to talk about that to a twelve-year-old, but that too came with the territory.

When the Freetown assignment ended we returned to Washington after nine years abroad. Charley, then a seventh grader, entered public school for the first time; he was well prepared, except for American history. Late one afternoon, he roared into the kitchen. "I had to go tell the counselor what she should do," he raged, explaining why he was on the late bus, not the early one.

"Those kids," he blasted on, about a gang of boys roaming the school corridor, "were calling the Japanese boys names and taunting them. I told her she had to stop them from doing that. The Japanese are diplomats' sons and *can't* talk back." His explosion was beyond heartfelt. I realized then how much he had internalized, simply swallowing his feelings because, as a diplomat's son, he had had to bite his tongue and accept what he sometimes saw as unfairness.

By the time he finished middle school in McLean, we faced a last "which school" dilemma. We believed in public schools and had good ones in Virginia. At the same time, we anticipated moving again to who-knew-where in his last year or so of school and felt that continuity in high school was also important. Therefore, we sent him to the same private high school Walter had attended to start as a day student and, if need be, continue as a boarder.

Our move back from Freetown proved to be the last with children. Five years later, when Dan was assigned to Singapore, Charley became a boarder for his senior year. Walter was in college. Gay was a college graduate and already married. Jerry had also graduated and was working. I had completed my life as a day-to-day, hands-on parent choreographing who went to what school.

One of the advantages of being raised as a rolling stone is exposure to various countries and cultures and acquiring the adjustment skills that go with that. However, children who grow up that way also need a period of what is nominally home-place stability. Sorting out where they belong requires time "at home" when they are old enough to absorb what that means and how it fits with their emerging adult mobile personas.

Reentry shock—adjusting to what is supposed to be "home," yet in important ways is not—is difficult. Coming to the United States as a not-quite adult, essentially on your own without the family unit you have always been a part of, compounds things. "In many ways, I was alone in the world," is how Jerry puts it.

Back in the States, he quickly learned, as I had, not to talk about where and how he had lived. His dorm head asked what he had done over summer break. "I told the truth," he said, telling me about his experiences much later. "I said I had been to West Africa. The dorm head's face fell. He'd been to Pennsylvania. Americans don't like feeling lesser." Jerry continued: "Another time, earlier, I was asked where my parents lived. 'The Philippines.' 'Oh, where is that?' 'About a thousand miles this side of Vietnam.' That last they knew." He also fielded other questions, like whether "folks there" wore clothes. His conclusion: "Better to keep one's mouth shut, or become an anthropologist."

Ruth Useem and other academics who studied families like ours used the term "Third Culture Kid" (TCK), to refer to children who were raised in a culture outside of their parents' for a significant part of their developing years. These children have internalized some combination of their parent's culture and the cultures of the places where they have grown up. Or, as I heard once, being: "Too foreign for home, too foreign for there."

Our children fit that description of a TCK. So do we. I'm not sure, though, that the term completely applies to second-generation rolling stone families like ours. Dan and I each started with our own unique move-around-the-world identities. As a result, our children were both their own unique brands of TCKs and an extension of ours, living in what was the family identity. I prefer to identify us as American intercultural migrants at home in the world.

Watching your children evolve into productive adults is a gift, at least when you are not holding your breath for them. While Dan and I were in the middle of it, we thought—and *know* now—that we all benefitted from the mobile life the family led. The priority we tried to give to talking with our children about their experiences as we went along was well worth the effort.

The outcome? A son who, rather than "keeping one's mouth shut," became a professor of anthropology who is an expert on the work of Margaret Mead and Gregory Bateson particularly in Bali; a medical biller with her own business; a Quaker educator and social activist; an historian specializing in Southeast Asia who also coaches crew (or the reverse, a crew coach who is also an historian specializing in Southeast Asia)—and a pair of extremely proud parents.

Creepy Critters We Have Known

You can't live in the tropics without intimate contact with creepy critters. Us old-tropical hands delight in swapping sagas about these encounters.

Little house lizards were ubiquitous. Given their gentle *tik tik tik* "conversation," they had different onomatopoeic names each place we lived. The most commonly used was *gecko*, a Malay word that has morphed into ordinary enough English usage that we now see funny American TV ads for the GEICO Gecko. They were *tjitjak* (or *cicak* in the new spelling) in Indonesia, *tiki* in the Philippine Visayas.

With sensuously sprawled clay-pink bodies, huge round eyes, and four seemingly Velcro-padded toes splayed out at the end of each widespread leg, they clung to the walls and ceilings or scuttled around to snap up insects. It was good luck to have them in the house.

I first met geckos (and their bigger, louder, more dragon-like cousins, *toktu*) in 1951. Dad took an assignment in Rangoon. My parents, sibs, and I moved into a barn-like, pre-war house. Geckos roamed the nearly twenty-foot ceilings with impunity, ultimately playing a leading role in a favorite family tale.

Sometime in our second year, two American ladies of a certain age, friends of friends of friends of Mother's, came to Rangoon on an ambitious "good-works–driven" trip. They had no idea what to expect, but assumed they were going to a vast wilderness. Wearing stout shoes and sensible dresses, they were traveling with their own primus stove, some basic dry food, pith helmets, and an endless supply of water-purification pills. To us kids, they were, to put it bluntly, weird.

Mother took them up the Shwedagon, Rangoon's towering Buddhist pagoda that had been sacred throughout Burma for several thousand years. The dazzling stupa, covered in layers of gold leaf, which was built to house eight of the Lord Buddha's hairs, is visible all over the rambling city. Daily, thousands climb steep flights of cool, roofed-over stairs lined with stalls selling all sorts of religious accouterments and other crafts. (I still serve dinner with a pair of brass spoons Mother bought there and gave us when we married.) Along the way, worshipers buy flowers, incense, candles, and maybe gold leaf as offerings.

At the top, everyone removes their shoes to show respect before stepping out onto the sizzling white-marble plaza around the pagoda. The main stupa is ringed with small ones, some gold, some whitewashed, each dedicated to a particular day of the week and segment of that day. At the personally appropriate one (related to birth day and hour), each worshiper kneels, puts the candle in a holder, lights it, and, bowing several times, offers the flowers, incense, and prays.

Mother must have taken the ladies up late that afternoon when the sun was less direct and not so likely to blister their bare feet. At dinner, they were bubbling on and on about their day, particularly about their visit to the "exotic gold temple."

"How sweet," one of the women opined firmly. "They must have gotten lighting candles from Catholicism."

With exquisite timing, to the delight of us kids, a tiny, pinky-sized gecko let go of the ceiling and plopped into the woman's soup, splashing dollops of the liquid onto the tablecloth.

Years later, as Dan, our children, and I moved from tropical post to tropical post, geckos became our house familiars—and grist for my artist's mill: I painted them across ceilings, down walls, or around a corner. The high-ceilinged, board and batten downstairs reception room in the American consul's residence in Cebu was the best "canvass." Soon after we moved in, I climbed a ladder, drew curving gecko outlines with a fat black crayon, chose several colors of paints—blue, orange brown, or deep rose (maybe red, too)—and filled in the shapes. When I finished, five three- or four-foot long geckos, twisting together on different planes, dominated one corner of the room.

Several nights after I painted the lizards, we hosted our first official party. All of Cebu came, curious about "their" new American consul and his wife. The guests arrived, were served drinks and *pika-piku* (nibbles), and, as they milled about and gossiped, began looking around to see how we had changed things. Soon, the creatures on the ceiling caught a guest's eye. Another snuck a puzzled look. Others suppressed a smile. The party gained volume. No one, to my knowledge, knew quite what to make of the exaggerated geckos. Nothing was said to me. Years later, as I kept returning to visit, the first thing friends and even new acquaintances said was, "You had those great geckos on your ceiling."

In addition to those painted ones, we had *real* huge lizards around the house. The *toktu* (or *tokay* or other similarly sounding names, depending on the language) were more likely to live on the outside wall by a security light. Maybe a foot long with rough, gray-green and blue polka-dotted skin and yellow eyes, they had none of the cuteness of their little cousins. Their startlingly loud call commenced with a rumbling *tok tok tok*, gaining volume until it built up to the distinctive *toktuuuuu*. In the Philippines, we were told to count the number of times the call repeated: seven and thirteen calls were good luck; three calls, bad. Once you knew luck was involved, you always counted.

Toktu didn't just like to hang out by lights. They also loved to dive into toilets. I discovered that soon after we arrived in Rangoon. I got up in the middle of the night to do the needful without turning on a light. I pulled up my nightie and was about to sit when—*whoosh*—something ran out from under me. I jumped, having met my first *toktu*, up close and far too personal.

Snakes, thankfully, didn't make their homes in the toilet, at least not in our experience. They didn't make a distinctive sound, either. They just slithered. Some spit. As the daughter of a doctor of worms and parasites, not to mention bugs, I never thought I would ever teach kids to be afraid of such critters. After all, I grew up watching snails leave slime trails up my arms and being shown my own intestinal worms preserved in glass tubes.

In northern Nigeria, with a five-, three-, and an almost two-year-old who were much too curious for their own good, we had to scare the bejeezus out of them when it came to snakes. Especially since our newly built house on the edge of the bush was surrounded by *doka* (deep-rooted scrub bush), which would be dug out so we could plant a garden. Snakes came with that still bushy yard; the name of one, roughly translated from Hausa, was "there is no tomorrow."

We drummed into the kids that when they saw a snake, they should turn and run, shrieking "*Maciji!* (snake)." We instructed the staff, particularly the gardener, to kill every one they found and to show me the bodies. I lost count of how many dead snakes I saw.

One Sunday morning in the dry season we invited another American family with children to lunch after church. The older boys were shooting basketball against the garage when Peter, the houseboy, appeared around the corner.

"Masta. I get one snake for *quata*," meaning down at the servants quarters.

He certainly did. A headless python, at least twelve-feet long and maybe eighteen inches in diameter, was stretched out in the dirt behind the house help's rooms.

A few weeks into the dry season, northern Nigerians burned the bush to force a second growth of grass to feed cattle. The night before, we had seen fires across the river, way into the distance. The smoke stunned various critters, making it a good time to hunt. Peter and a friend had found the python's hole. Peter stuck his leg down, let the smoke-drugged python coil around his leg several times, then pulled it out. They whacked off its head with a machete and carried it back to the compound.

"What will you do with it?"

"Good to eat."

Peter and his friend carefully removed the skin, scraped it, and then staked it out on the ground to dry. They hacked the body into cross sections about eight inches long and slowly smoked them over a smoldering fire behind the quarters. Vultures sat on the roof eying the goings-on hungrily.

We bought the skin. (Over the years it went to innumerable "show and tells" in our kids' and God-kids' classes in the States until finally, stiff and badly cracked, we trashed it.) We also bought two pieces of the smoked meat. Our family ate one, tastefully prepared by the cook—the meat had about the same texture and taste as smoked pork chop. The other piece remained in the freezer. When the State Department inspectors came from Washington (they visited all Foreign Service posts about once every two years), I planned to serve it for dinner: "We live on the local economy. Do enjoy the python." Alas, we were reassigned before they came.

If we scared the children about snakes, we made them extremely cautious of scorpions. They looked like miniature lobsters except that their tails, which ended in a nasty stinger, usually curled up over their backs, ready to strike. The stings could be extremely painful, even dangerous for small children.

I first encountered them as a teenager in Rangoon. Our house had been unoccupied for several years since the war and so had become home to the critters. For the first six months we were there, it was not unusual for a scorpion to appear suddenly from who knew where, tail up and waving, in the middle of the lounge's red-concrete floor. They appeared so frequently we developed a fool proof, or *Fortune* proof, disposal system. Take a newspaper, plop it on top of the scorpion. Then take one or two copies of *Fortune* magazine (best because they were big, thick, and heavy) and drop them on top of the paper. Jump up and down on the magazines to smash the invader. Remove the magazines and put aside for the next time. Carefully wrap the squished scorpion in the paper and trash it. Repeat exercise as needed.

We got so blasé that even my five-year-old brother dispatched scorpions with great aplomb.

When my own family moved to northern Nigeria, we re-encountered scorpions. Most were in the yard, usually under rocks. These were bigger and blacker than the Burmese variety—perhaps more dangerous. The gardener got stung when he was clearing a flowerbed. His badly swollen hand and arm were an object lesson for the kids, who developed a healthy skittishness about turning over rocks. They learned how to do it without putting their fingers underneath.

We did find one or two scorpions in the house—nowhere near the experience of some Peace Corps volunteers who were teachers in a smaller town further north. One evening, they were playing bridge in the walled courtyard of their house when a scorpion climbed over the wall and down toward the ground. The person who was playing dummy whacked it. Soon another came over the wall. Then another. Over the course of the evening perhaps fifty appeared. Whoever was playing dummy was the designated scorpion-whacker.

I was more than ready to leave snakes and scorpions behind when our two-year tour in Nigeria ended. With no movers there, I packed everything to be shipped to Washington, putting the necessities in two trunks of airfreight. This included the china, which I put back in its original packing box that I had saved in a closet off the car park.

We bought our first house; somewhere in the woods in a town called Vienna in suburban Virginia. I knew the address but had no idea, yet, where it was or how to get there. Dan and I began moving in while the kids stayed with my mother. The airfreight trunks were in the kitchen. A moving van was scheduled to bring the minimal furniture we had left in storage. Through the kitchen window, we saw the van go past the house and down the road. Dan jumped into the car to guide it back to our cul-de-sac.

Meanwhile, I continued unpacking the airfreight, removing the cups from the top layer of the dish box. Then I took up the dividers and the bigger piece of cardboard under them.

And...

On the top of the stack of dinner plates lay a thoroughly comatose scorpion. I don't even pick up dead ones with my fingers. Grabbing a pair of tongs, I reached for it—up popped the tail. *Uuuuuh!* Away it skittered across the plate and down into the box.

Watching the box from a distance, all aplomb lost, I kept trying to think where to call to treat scorpion stings. We were in the middle of who-knows-where. Did we have a phone book yet? Did the phone even work?

"Dan," I shouted, relieved he was back. "There's a live scorpion in the dish box. Let's get the box out into the carport to finish unpacking it. Here are the tongs. Get the plates out—carefully."

Dan lifted the plates piece by piece, cautiously looking under each one until he found the scorpion hidden under the last plate.

"You could sell something like that to the zoo," suggested the van driver.

"No, we need to kill it." I declared. "And burn the box. Now. Who knows how many eggs might be in there. We don't need scorpions in our Virginia garden."

Dan immolated the whole thing at the bottom of the driveway. The scorpion scare was over.

Mercifully, however, no cockroaches—horrible, pervasive critters—had hitched a ride in the box. My stomach still churns remembering the kitchen drawers in our second-floor walk up in Kaduna that had swollen shut during the rainy season. When we could finally open them after they shrunk in the dry season, they were overflowing with *thousand*s of cockroaches, cascading down onto the floor and scrabbling under the cabinets.

The top critter-story of them all harks back to 1960 and our first post in Kuala Lumpur. The British Deputy High Commissioner and his wife, with whom I had worked at a well-baby clinic, were hosting their own farewell reception. Dan and I were invited.

That night we were far and away the most junior of the otherwise senior diplomats and government officials who attended. I could sense the puzzled disapproval of our "by the book, rank conscious" ambassador's wife when we paid our courtesy greetings to her. After speaking with the ambassador's wife, we made our way across the room to the ambassador, who was talking with the jovial Brit who was still head of the Malayan navy.

Several months pregnant, I was wearing an elegant, natural linen, loose-from-the-shoulder dress. As we stood in the middle of the crowded reception talking with them, I felt something crawling up what I thought was the outside of the back of my dress.

"Dan," I whispered, "please brush the back of my dress." He did unobtrusively. The sense of something crawling up my back continued. "Please reach inside the neckline and find whatever it is."

He did. It was a huge cockroach—the flying kind.

While he rushed it to the open veranda door, I continued chatting calmly (at least I was calm on the surface). The ambassador was less than amused. The head of the Malay navy, however, smiled broadly, fished a coin out of his pocket, and presented it to me: a Royal Medal for Not Screaming: Bravery Above and Beyond.

177

Culture Shocked

I had only seven items on my shopping list and twenty minutes to pop in and out of *my* Safeway before picking up the kids.

Awwwwk!

Why isn't the tomato juice in the middle of the third aisle? Why aren't there any juices here at all?

Overnight, the store had been totally reorganized. Nothing, except the vegetables on the right and the meat counter across the back, was where it should be.

Bewildered, blank-faced shoppers wandered around the store, annoyed—very annoyed.

What happened to o-u-r store?

Some people stomped out immediately. Some searched a bit and gave up. Others, like me, eventually found the things we came for. *Except,* for me, the tomato juice.

Frustrated, chuckling, and knowing I would be late to pick up the kids, I checked out.

Over the next several weeks, the tomato juice and other familiar items "suddenly" reappeared in new places. With the store's reorganization, I discovered some things Safeway no doubt had always carried that I'd never seen before. The store once more seemed familiar. I could pop in and out.

For me, that day has become a small-scale example of culture shock. I use it as shorthand for explaining how culture shock works, and as a demonstration of how it hits us anywhere, when we least expect it.

A grocery store is ordinarily stocked so regular patrons (a mini-culture, as it were) shop without having to consider which shelf holds what. Members of a society grow up in a culture so they operate instinctively. Things get moved, as in the grocery store, or a person, to a new place. Fruit basket upset.

Just as most grocery stores carry the same things, most cultures have the same basic building blocks, which are organized and emphasized differently—on a different shelf as it were—from culture to culture. Thus, my gut wrench when my store was newly reorganized was parallel in many ways to my feelings when I moved to a new country and culture where everything felt strange. Similarly the varying levels of shock lasted until I found the new shelf for the tomato juice or understood more about how those people behave, what they assume.

When you move someplace new, with a different language, a different smell, a different appearance, you *expect* to feel like a lost fish for a while. That can be exciting, stimulating, scary, and disconcerting all at once—with its real but in a way anticipated surprises of culture shock. If you move to England or Australia expecting to find it familiar, and, starting with how English is spoken, it isn't, that's an unanticipated jolt. We're the "same." But not.

Wherever you go, it's the totally unexpected, something little and ordinary, that upends own assumptions about how things *are* that crunches the gut.

When you hear people speaking a loud, guttural language you don't understand, you might be sure they're arguing. In reality they just may be talking about the weather or where to move the bricks. After a while, you learn some vocabulary or at least get used to the sounds, and you are more at ease—you've developed a customary sound-level appreciation. You know, perhaps, to be more concerned when it is too quiet.

Or maybe what jolts you is seeing something for the first time that's their normal but contrary to yours. In Freetown (and many other places), men or boys walk down the street holding hands or with their arms draped over each other. Seeing this rocked the sensibilities of a teenaged guest from western Connecticut we once hosted. "Look at those boys. They're *holding hands*," she shrieked as we drove from the airport. In her world boys holding was something that was *just not done*. She got used to it over time.

Which hand you use—right or left—makes a difference in some countries, particularly in the Muslim world, but not in others. We Americans don't think much about it. Some people are lefties, most of us are right-handed, a few are ambidextrous. If you are to my left, I will likely give you the change or the pencil or the cookie with my left hand, even if I am hard-core right-handed. Handedness is not attached to any kind of social custom; we don't think of which hand we use in terms of being polite. That's how our world is.

Not so in Muslim countries, where one of the first things newbies learn is: Always, always, always give and receive with the right hand, *never* the left, which is rude. If people are being blunt they will make the reason clear: The left hand is reserved for personal cleanliness.

When we arrived in Kuala Lumpur, this "do not give or receive with your left hand" injunction topped the list of cultural dos and don'ts. Knowing that and doing it naturally were different matters. The two years we were there, I kept my left hand in my pocket to stymie my inborn impulse to use whichever hand was easier.

Over time, I learned to present money with my right hand, left palm down on the right wrist; to serve food with both hands, with the right hand a bit ahead of the left; and to eat only with the right hand at a traditional meal where food is eaten with the fingers. (I always eat with my right hand so that part was easy.) Even so, I caught myself after dinner at the home of Malay friends inadvertently putting the fingers of both hands in the fingerbowl. Oops.

In Kuala Lumpur, the Chinese amah would stop our children from using their left hands to take things or put food in their mouths, just as she trained her own small people how to be polite and respectful. While the practice, I understood, was Muslim in origin, it had long since become ingrained among the Chinese, who made up half the population.

After KL our next two years were in Nigeria, in the region where most people were Muslim and had the same basic customs for using hands. I continued keeping my hand in my pocket and reinforced the amah's guidance for the children. Over time, I thought less and less about it. I automatically gave and received with my right hand, politeness increasingly ingrained in my muscle memory.

One day soon after we moved back to Virginia, I drove into the gas station to fill up. In those days, someone pumped your gas. Customers paid cash. The fellow filled the tank, looked in the window and told me how much to pay. I got the bills out of the purse in my lap, using my left hand because that was easier. Instinctively, to pay him, I put the bills in my right hand even though it involved twisting my body and reaching across the steering wheel to give him the money. He quickly made change and handed it to me with his nearer left hand. Crunch in the gut. I was insulted. Hadn't his mother brought him up to know better? Culture shock (especially in reverse) happens when you least expect it.

Besides learning about appropriate handedness, we also experienced differences in people's sense of personal space. In KL, our downstairs neighbor was a lovely woman from Mexico. As we got to know her, we realized she left about eighteen inches between herself and the person she was talking with—nearly a foot inside the personal envelope for most Norteamericanos. As Dan recounts, at first he was always backing up so he didn't feel like he was too close and therefore being too intimate with her. She would step in. He would step back and so on, dancing a dance, with him circling backward. Finally, he realized that was her comfort zone. As he said: "I let myself relax and enjoy it."

Some years later, soon after we moved to Jakarta, I found Pak Hadji, a handy man who would come take care of odds and ends. He was an unfailingly deferential, older Javanese man. Short with a grinning brown face, he sported bristly gray hair, chin stubble, and work-worn hands. He wore a *petji* (the traditional brimless black velvet hat), and, following custom, always left his sandals at the door.

When we needed bamboo blinds made for our bedroom windows, he came over, measured carefully, and went off to make them. Several mornings later he returned to install them. Normally one of the house-helpers accompanied him on his tasks. That was customary and made him comfortable—he wouldn't be held responsible for anything other than what he was doing. But that morning all the helpers were busy. I went with him to our bedroom. He stood on the only chair and installed the blind; I sat on the foot of the bed hemming a curtain for one of the kid's rooms. We chatted.

The task finished, he wanted to discuss the next one. He grabbed the chair he'd been standing on, pulled it next to me, turned it backward and sat down, perhaps ten inches away.

Chunk. My stomach clinched: strange man sitting way too close to me in my bedroom! I leapt up and sped out of the room, talking about what to do next as I went, with him trotting after me.

It took me a while to process what had happened. In my ingrained world order, someone working for me, particularly a man, would have remained standing at a certain distance while we talked, unless I invited him to sit in a chair that was not particularly close to me. In his world—where we lived—not only was the speaking distance between people closer than what I was used to, but also people spoke quietly, especially about important topics. In addition, to show deference, because he worked for me and I was a foreigner, he needed to have his head lower than mine. Hence the low chair and the uninvited, close sitting. We had two different deeply ingrained sets of expectations regarding space, politeness, and relationship.

Personal space didn't just affect in-person interaction. It was evident in driving culture, too. To get around Jakarta, a sprawling city with narrow streets and heavy traffic where people drove on the left, we had a personal driver. He drove our Jeep most of the time, ferrying Dan to work, the kids to school, and me to the university or to run errands. This was particularly helpful because parking was virtually impossible. The embassy also had a small fleet of official cars with drivers.

When our driver was off, I drove. One afternoon, I was leaving the school with a car full of kids, in a part of the suburbs designed on a spoke-and-wheel system. I was approaching a circle on what in my mind was a side street. The major street to my right had the right of way, again in *my* mind. I idled up to the circle and stopped to let the approaching vehicle (which happened to be an official embassy car) go first. The driver came to a screeching halt, never mind the car behind him. The Jeep belonged to a "Tuan's" wife (literally a title somewhere between sir and master—how he would have considered the wife of an embassy officer). He was giving me right of way, expressing space and deference, as he understood it. I gulped and pulled out ahead of him with a wave, grateful there hadn't been an accident.

Moving from our Virginia condo into the new-to-us monoculture of the Home provided its own culture shocks well beyond the fact that everyone is "old" and describing yourself as the one with white hair, a good ploy when you're forty, no longer works. Learning how to navigate through swarms of walkers, rollators, a few self-propelled wheelchairs and one or two small electronic scooters, particularly just before meals or when everyone is leaving the auditorium, was like figuring out how to get through Jakarta's traffic. Clearly there were unspoken "rules of the road." What or who has the right of way? Who gets into the elevator first—a walker, a wheelchair, or someone who holds the door open? How do we arrange ourselves?

Gradually, I got the hang of it: For the most part, the walkers and rollators go straight across a room, without their operators necessarily looking up and at full tilt. Step out of their way and be prepared for them to stop unexpectedly. As for elevators, although a walking person nearer the door may sneak in first and get in a corner, wheelchairs or rollators often have right of way, if there is enough space for them to maneuver. Canes are good for holding the elevator door open to keep it from closing on someone moving more slowly.

Those of us who are more upright and mobile fit ourselves into a back corner or wait for the next elevator. But that "rule" can flip: A person with a rollator who gets to an elevator that is almost full may decide there isn't space and back out., no moving or leaving of the upright necessary. Whoever is nearest the floor buttons asks, "Which floor?". People away from the buttons will ask for a floor number to be pushed. I've learned that the casual "How are you today?" has many black-humor answers: "Vertical and ventilating." "Walking and talking." "Able to get to pasture and take water." I've also learned when not to ask.

More to the point, neither the use of rollators, wheelchairs, or canes or walking unaided is an indicator of age. Some people who are upright actually look and move as if they are old. Others, equally white haired, wrinkled, or even bent and hovering over their walker, still sparkle with youth. That lively sparkle, not years lived or rollator use, becomes the definition of age. Hobbling somewhat, cane-less, I'm recognized by my orange shoes.

Knowing some of the rules of the road in my new home, I no longer feel culture shocked. I have, in effect, found the tomato juice.

Once Upon a Yuan Bowl

The Yuan bowl lives on our kitchen counter. Grayish celadon, its body flaring broadly from its dainty round foot, the bowl is usually filled with garlic, red chilies, and sometimes drying sage or thyme. Incised scrolling leaves and flowers decorate its inside. Like Humpty Dumpty, it had a great fall forty years back. Unlike that cracked egg, it was put together again—not seamlessly. It more resembles a three-dimensional jigsaw puzzle. While its perfection is missing, its elegance remains, like the good bones of a faded beauty.

A *tukong*, one of many itinerant merchants peddling antiques, brought it to our Jakarta house late one afternoon.

"*Nonja, Nonja*—Madam, Madam" a *tukong* would call, knocking on the gate. "*Antik*?" If I were in the mood and asked him into the driveway, he would unbundle a market of Asian ceramics—Ming, Ch'ing, and sometimes Yuan Dynasty Chinese; Swankalok or Soukathai from Thailand; and Cambodian, Vietnamese and Japanese. Most were real, some were fake. All were part of a centuries' old trade. I would perch on the porch step, and we would talk while I examined the objects, turning them over, thumping for cracks, dancing the delicate back-and-forth of bargaining, putting down one object, inspecting another. I might not ask for a price unless I wanted to actually buy but perhaps not for the one I really eyed. I would laugh at his offer, joking with him, before eventually making a counter offer. Or I might shift gears, picking up a pot of little interest, then suggesting a different price. We'd laugh more, chatting about something else entirely, and then return, at last, to the original negotiation.

Finally, we would reach a price he would accept and I thought affordable. I sometimes wondered later if I had paid way too much. In any case, these afternoons provided a crash course in evaluating Asian ceramics of many periods, including Indonesian-made fakes or pieces overly repaired with fingernail polish instead of red and green glaze. Better yet, they provided extremely practical Indonesian-language lessons. The prices paid for the pieces themselves were cheap tuition.

Neither porcelain-thin nor stoneware-thick, the graceful bowl "spoke" when I saw it. I've always thought it to be Yuan dynasty because of the tiny foot and wide flair of the bowl. I could be wrong. In any case, I gave it a place of pride among my growing collection on display shelves in the dining room. It was easily seen, but not placed high enough, as it turned out.

When Charley was almost four, we took him and his siblings to a late night *wayang orang* (a traditional form of Indonesian dance drama enacting stories from the Ramayana and Mahabharata). The next morning, Charley, who had an uncanny ability to mimic movements, reenacted the entire story. He enthralled the household staff with a succession of demure court maidens fluttering downcast eyes, brave warriors strutting and posing, and fearsome giants taking huge, menacing steps, toes upturned. "When I grow up, I am going to be Bima," he announced that morning, referring to the biggest and strongest of the five Pandawa brothers, heroes of these adventures. "I will have a big fingernail like Bima and win." (At forty, he danced that role. That's another story.)

I should have thought more about where I had put the bowl.

A year later and somewhere else, Charley saw a Sumatran candle dance. Lissome girls had swayed and stepped delicately from side to side, holding small saucers with lit candles in each hand, twisting them in intricate figure eights, as they do today. Our small dancer must have decided to try it at home. He needed a saucer. The Yuan bowl, candle-less, was handy. Well beyond saucer-sized, it outspanned a dinner plate. Certainly it was too big for Charley's hand that still matched his sturdy, small boy frame—by no means long-fingered and supple like the Sumatran girls'.

I don't know for sure when, because I was in the next room. But at some point, as hand and bowl tried to trace a figure eight, the bowl slid to its inevitable disastrous rendezvous with the terrazzo floor. I heard the crash and went to investigate.

He stood puzzled and abashed.

I was annoyed, sad, and bemused. It was impossible to be angry. "Oh, Charley!" was all I could say.

As I picked up the pieces, in my mind's eye the bowl remained too beautiful to dump. I ruefully saved the shards for a rainy afternoon of puzzle piecing.

Thus the Yuan bowl migrated from a display shelf in the dining room to a succession of kitchens. Always in easy reach, it's a tangible reminder of long-ago language lessons and a small boy who had to dance.

Vietnamese Might-Have-Beens

The Tet Offensive started in our bedroom in Jakarta.

Jakarta is roughly a thousand miles due south of Saigon. On good nights, after dark—when radio waves shot farther, traveling in a straight line, bouncing off the ionosphere, and caroming from Saigon beyond the Earth's curve to Jakarta—we could pick up Armed Forces Radio. On January 30, 1968, we went up to bed at ten or so. As we often did, we flipped on the radio to catch up with the American world before we turned out the lights. Usually we heard Stateside news and sports commentary designed to make those far from home feel less remote.

Not that night. "Something seems to be up," a man's voice said urgently. "We're getting reports of action…. Keep alert."

We'd never been to Saigon and didn't know the streets we were being told to keep away from. Clearly whatever was happening was widespread, serious, real—and in our bedroom. Alert followed alert, each one more specific—and urgent—than the last, warning listeners to avoid certain areas and ordering units to return to post.

Transfixed for a while, plunged into the middle of the chaos, we listened from the distanced comfort of our bed. Relieved for the calm of our night, but nonetheless rattled and worried, we turned it off. We went to sleep because we could. We were a thousand miles away.

Vietnam was one of those enormous "might-have-beens" for everyone in the family.

In 1950, my Dad had taken a position with the precursor of USAID. He was to be part of a small team that went to what was still French Indochina to lay the groundwork for a rural development program. The team would be working in tandem with the military advisors President Truman had sent to assist the French in the First Indochina War. In the early fall, Dad had flown to Saigon to start the project. He was coming back to take us there in January 1951.

His letters were filled with descriptions of L'Ecole Francaise, the French school we would be attending; Cercle Sportif, a French athletic club with a wonderful swimming pool; and all sorts of other bits and pieces about this new city that was to become our home.

At sixteen, I was reluctant to leave my friends. Even though I had taken high school French, the idea of studying *in* French was challenging. At the same time, I was curious about this new place. As the time to leave drew nearer, I was increasingly excited to go there. Adventure beckoned.

Dad flew home to get us. For Christmas, we went to Nashville with his mother, Aunt Ruth, and Uncle Joe. We returned to

Mamaroneck, where we roared into high gear preparing for a rapidly approaching departure date.

On January 13, General Giap and a large contingent of Viet Minh troops assaulted the French positions in the Red River Delta. Overnight, French Indochina became more dangerous. The US government wanted Dad to go back. The family, however, would not be allowed to accompany him. We might or might not be permitted to join him later.

The family had already had one long wartime separation. Mother and Daddy weren't accepting another one. Dad told the government he wouldn't return to Saigon. A new aid program was opening in Burma with a good job for him. Within a week we were off to Burma, instead.

Ever since, I have wondered what it would have been like to have gone to a French high school and lived in Vietnam, or as it showed on my map then, French Indochina.

After our first two Foreign Service assignments, Dan and I had returned to Washington in 1963. As the Vietnam War intensified, national tensions grew. On the news and other places, we began to hear the taunt: "Heh, heh, LBJ, how many kids did you kill today?" One morning, when Charley was about two and talking, he and I went grocery shopping. We were chitter-chatting through the aisles: "Charley, should we get some carrots?"

A man nearby must have heard me: "Why did you give that nice little boy that *awful* name?" He nearly jumped down my throat.

"It was his grandfather's," I shot back.

I was shocked. How dare he. Then I realized he associated it with "Victor Charlie," American soldiers' name for the Viet Cong.

The TV news had been showing disturbing footage of Buddhist priests self-immolating in Saigon. One evening in early November 1965, the news led with the story that a man had set himself on fire outside the Pentagon. His name, the reporter said, was Norman Morrison. My heart stopped. I went to college with Norm. Freshman year, we went out a time or two. After that, we drifted in different directions. Nonetheless, he was a friend from my past. With the news of his death, the war became personal in an odd way, even more difficult to deal with.

The US Foreign Service as well as the military presence in Vietnam grew. Many of Dan's colleagues served there. He didn't. What difference that made in his career and promotions, we'll never know. He had studied Indonesian and worked on the Indonesia desk, which is why we were in Jakarta. We shared a formative family life together rather than the separation many of our friends' families had to endure—for example, an officer in Saigon and the family in Bangkok, Manila, or back in the States. Certainly we did not experience the anxiety of our military friends and their families, or take the risks they did.

Dan, working on other things, said little about the war. Later he stated it was painful to feel personally demonized by anti-war demonstrators taunting government employees, particularly those who worked at the State Department. Especially when he was doing his best to serve his country with integrity.

Because we were living overseas again in 1967, we missed direct involvement in an experience that became a critical part of the collective American psyche. Although Tet "happened" in our Jakarta bedroom, we did not own a TV and so did not "see" the Vietnam War nightly at our dinner tables the way most Americans did. Nor did we experience the larger anti-war protests that filled college classrooms and American streets. We knew what was happening thanks to *Time* magazine. And we found discussing the war—when we did over the years—as divisive as other families did. Yet we were distanced from the collective impact.

We glimpsed the reality of the war's effects, however. On our way back to the States for home leave in the summer of 1969, Vietnam was the next Pan Am stop after Jakarta. As the plane landed at Tan Son Nhut, from a great altitude, it dove almost straight down. Landings were like that because the Viet Cong sometimes fired rockets at incoming and outgoing planes. We disembarked onto an airbase that was more military than commercial, although it was in fact both. Military planes lined the runway, sandbags barricading each.

We Pan Am passengers were herded into the far corner of a mammoth Quonset hut, light filtering down through a haze of cigarette smoke. Outside the big windows, transport planes arrived. Their back ends opened, and troops marched out. Inside, the space buzzed with voices and the movement of hundreds of battle-fatigued people simply waiting until they had to move somewhere else. Orders were shouted. Another group moved or stopped. From time to time a voice called over a loudspeaker, "Welcome to Veeet Naaaam," which met mocking jeers from hardened troops on their way out.

I was sitting on a bench with the four children—the oldest thirteen and the youngest five—nearby, when I heard a voice beside me: "Excuse me, Ma'am. Are you American?"

"Yes."

"Where are you going?"

"To Virginia, on home leave, from Jakarta."

A young man—a *terribly* young man—sat down next to me. He was wearing fatigues I believe. His face was leathered from the tropical sun. His light brown hair was freshly sheered in some sort of a buzz cut. Perhaps he was fortified with "Dutch courage." In any case, he was tense and intense.

Words spilled out. He was ending a year traveling on swift boats on the Mekong River, in and out of the tributaries deep into the jungle, living on a constant rush of adrenaline and fear. He was convinced he would never get out.

But there he was at Tan Son Nhut, alive, flying home in less than an hour. He didn't quite believe it and was more petrified than ever. Perhaps two weeks earlier, a rocket had landed on a plane headed Stateside, moments before it was to take off, blowing up everyone on it. He was convinced that would happen to him.

He was going home to Detroit and was planning to join the police force. He intended to break up with his girl, although she didn't yet know it; that terrified him as well. Surrounded by kids, I must have looked somehow "normal," a neighbor or an older sister maybe—someone it was safe to pour everything out to.

Our flight was called. I wished him well. With the rest of the passengers Dan, our gang, and I got back onto our plane. It took off, shooting almost straight up into the air, safely away. We went on to visit grandparents, enjoying a break before we returned to our ordinary life in Jakarta.

While the war disintegrated and the anti-war movement grew at home, Vietnam continued to merely brush our overseas lives. By 1973, when the fighting officially ended—at least for the Americans, not the Vietnamese—we were in the Philippines. Dan went with the ambassador to welcome a group of released POWs as they stepped off the plane onto Clark Field. In late April 1975, driving from Virginia to Connecticut, Gay and I, home from Sierra Leone for two weeks to visit possible boarding schools, listened to radio reports of the helicopters evacuating the last Americans off the roof of the embassy in Saigon, leaving behind the frantic Vietnamese who had worked with and for us.

Our most direct connection with the war, at least with its residue, came in the early '80s. Dan's last Foreign Service assignment was as US refugee coordinator in Singapore and Indonesia. As boat people flooded out of Vietnam in search of better, safer lives, he oversaw the program that resettled some in the United States. A hand-traced, oil-splattered map showing the route one of those boats took still hangs on our wall. It's signed in the corner with a name, a departure place, and a date: "*Bui Man Lac. Ho-Van Hoi. 20.03.1982.*"

This piece of their journey lives on with us. We still wonder where it continued and who they became.

Thirty-five years after our first touchdown in Tan Son Nhut, Dan and I finally traveled in Vietnam, indeed through all of what had once been French Indochina, and before that, ancient kingdoms. We flew into Hanoi from Laos and took the train north to Sapa on the Chinese border. We arrived back in Hanoi on that uncomfortable, déjà vu day of "shock and awe," when the United States started bombing Baghdad. The people around us, glued to TV images, knew about being bombed by Americans.

Over a couple of weeks, our small tourist van stopped in places with war-familiar names: Halong Bay, Hue, Danang, Hoi An, Dalat, and, of course, Saigon, renamed for Ho Chi Minh. The fecund tropical environment had returned once defoliated, bombed-out countryside to verdant green. We declined our guide's offer to stop at My Lai and the tunnels where the Viet Cong hid. Pictures taken during the war had been enough. While we couldn't avoid reminders of the war, it wasn't why we'd come. We were in Vietnam to finally visit "the place *I* might have been." The guide, a former medic for the South Vietnamese army, was relieved. He didn't want to revisit those devastating days, at least not with us. He much preferred sharing the beauty and rich history of his country.

When we reached the Mekong Delta, we took a small craft through jungle-lined tributaries once inhabited by swift boats—and for months, the young man I had met at Tan Son Nhut. Our destination those many years later was a friendly village with a pleasant open-air restaurant where we would eat a lunch of deep-fried river fish spiced with a sharp, sweet, gingery sauce. The next day, on a passenger boat, we sailed up the broad brown Mekong, past floating markets and houses on stilts, into Cambodia. Relishing the wooden boats with painted eyes, we watched the countryside slip by.

I assume my young swift-boater must have gotten back to Detroit. Did he join the police force? Did he break up with the girl? How did Vietnam change him? What had changed in the States while he was gone? How had his life turned out?

I wish I knew.

He never told me his name—just shared part of an hour and a small piece of his story. He was as close as we got to war in Vietnam. In our family history, Vietnam, writ large, remains a might-have-been.

April 4, 1968

Martin Luther King had been shot.

News didn't travel with the speed of a tweet or text then. Still somehow, half a world away, we had heard.

It had happened a bit after 6 in the evening in Memphis. Jakarta was twelve hours ahead, so it was morning.

The news, the fact of it, was a punch to the gut. I was horrified—sad, for the man and for us all.

There was a pall in the lobby of central Jakarta's American Embassy, not my everyday haunt, when I walked in mid-morning on some errand. Maybe the flag out front was already at half-staff, I'm not sure.

What I do remember, far too viscerally, was one of the crisply uniformed Marine guards standing duty at the front desk. He was ranting gleefully and loudly about how "that man" had gotten what was coming to him.

Incensed, I raced upstairs before the other guard could stop me (wives had to be escorted to the second floor). I hurtled into Dan's office, full blow.

Dan, in turn, strode down the hall to his boss, who called the Marine sergeant.

In no uncertain terms, the sergeant reprimanded the young Marine—not long out of the States for the first time—and immediately sent him back to their quarters: His conduct was totally unacceptable. He could privately express his opinions on his own time. Not in public. Not in a military uniform. Not on duty, representing his country on what was official American soil. He *could not* spew forth like that.

Elsewhere, a different anger overflowed. Washington burned that night.

On so many levels—national, local, personal—the pain of that loss and of the hatred that killed Martin Luther King remains. Nearly fifty years after that young Marine spewed hatred, those who think like him showed up on the streets of Charlottesville, Virginia. We continue to have work to do.

Moon Thoughts

We were in Washington in 1957 when the Russians launched Sputnik. A first child and Dan's new job were our focus more than the start of the space race.

We were in Virginia on leave on May 25, 1961, when John Kennedy—new, young, charismatic—spoke in a special joint session of Congress, challenging Americans to land a man on the moon by the end of the decade.

It was a particularly cool spring. Since we had spent two years in the tropics of Malaya and had only warm-weather clothes for our growing young children, we had to scrounge sweaters, overalls, and footed jammies from friends.

On the first hot day, June 4, we left again, headed to the American consulate in Kaduna, Nigeria, fifteen degrees above the equator. Kaduna was a four-hour bumpy ride south of both the Kano airport and the NASA talking station. One of several stations that Mission Control used to monitor satellites and talk to the astronauts, it was located in Kano because the arid environment meant little chance of atmospheric interference.

John Glenn's circumnavigation of the Earth was scheduled for January 1962. A week or so before the launch date, Dan had business in Kano. We piled the kids into our car and bumped through the dust to visit the big city. Dan needed to check in with the NASA station on consulate business. With all its dials, screens, and buttons, the big monitoring room was fascinating, particularly to our six-year-old: "Jerry, keep your hands in your pockets."

Although we hadn't asked to come back for the big day, the station manager volunteered apologetically: "Sorry I can't invite you to be here for the launch."

Too many people wanted to be in on the action. Even friends and official colleagues had been banned. That was just as well, as it turned out. Bad weather in Florida, then more bad weather at the landing site, led to postponement after postponement. Finally, on February 20, Friendship 7 blasted off.

When the mail arrived three weeks later, my mother had written from Virginia: "Today, I had time to iron two pairs of pants and five shirts and John Glenn was passing above your house."

Over the next eighteen months, other satellites, manned and unmanned, were launched from Florida. Like Glenn's flight, their orbit was literally over our house. On clear nights, we could sit in the courtyard in Kaduna under a blue-black sky dotted with stars and, if we timed it right, awe dinner guests with a view of a slowly moving "star" overhead.

Charley was born when we got home from Kaduna. As he grew into talking toddlerhood, one televised launch after another kept him, and all Americans, enthralled with space. When, at about eighteen months, he first learned to count, it was: "Ten, nine, eight, seven, six, five, four, three, two, one, blast off!"

On July 20, 1969, we were again on home leave, from Jakarta this time, staying with my parents in the Virginia suburbs. Apollo 11, along with astronauts Neil Armstrong, Michael Collins, and Buzz Aldrin, was landing on the moon, ending the space race. I was thirty-five that day, four years younger than the astronauts, all three of whom were born in 1930.

That night was balmy, almost steamy, as Washington summer nights can be. It was not truly dark until nearly 9:30 p.m. Mosquitoes buzzed and fireflies, chased by over-stimulated children, flitted. We had devoured one of Mother's birthday dinners. Oven fried chicken was her usual specialty. I am sure she had cake and ice cream—what's a birthday party without it? There was watermelon, too. She knew I loved it.

Excitement reigned, not so much about my birthday as about the Apollo landing. We'd all watched the fuzzy grayish images of the space capsule easing down onto the moon at 4:10 in the afternoon. After a day of running, their tummies stuffed, the kids conked in the evening. They weren't at all curious about this momentous occasion.

At about 10:30 p.m. EDT we forced the loudly protesting children up again. Our family joined people around the world breathlessly watching as Neil Armstrong's foot appeared on the ladder, then on the moon: "One small step…"

Time is tied to the spot where we experience it as well as the passage of the sun, not to the movement of the moon or to humans circulating the Earth in space. In the historic accounts, the moonwalk started on July 21, 1969, at 2:56 UTC (Universal Coordinated Time, the standard timing centers around the world use). But, in my memory, with the quirkiness of time and attention, for me in McLean, Virginia it was 10:56 on July 20, in the depth of night on my thirty-fifth birthday, when I was no longer young but not yet middle-aged.

At that single moment, it was also July 21 at 5:56 a.m. in Addis Abba, where it was about dawn and 11:56 a.m. in Jakarta, with the sun full blast. At all those times, on both those days, in all those places, Man cavorted on the moon.

Whose Career?

"Margaret," she said, her voice over the phone turning to ice. "Whose career do you care about, your husband's or your own?"

Gulp. Forty-two years later, I still mentally hear N's (as I'll call her) question with a combination of disbelief and affront—and a rueful laugh. It seemed wrongheaded at the time. It's even more unbelievable today.

My caller that morning in late 1970 was Dan's boss's wife. She was a woman who had been a friend—not a close one, a friend nonetheless—for nearly twenty years. Our husbands were serving simultaneously in the American embassy in Jakarta, marking the third iteration of our relationship.

N and I first met in Rangoon in early 1952. I was on a nine-month break between high school and college. She and her husband, L, as I'll call him, had arrived at the embassy with their dumpling of a toddler daughter. He was a junior Foreign Service officer on his first posting. As a not-quite adult, I was on the outer fringes of their lively young social circle. They knew my parents better than they knew me.

Though my memories are vague, I recall that they were fun-loving and active. Tall, with her long hair swirled in a loop on the top of her head, she wore flat shoes, stooping slightly so as not to tower over her otherwise larger-than-life husband. A bit of a free spirit, her earrings were long and dangly instead of small and "proper."

When Dan and I arrived at our first Foreign Service post in Kuala Lumpur, Malaya, in 1959, N was on the tarmac at the bottom of the airplane stairs to meet us—carrying out a Foreign Service tradition of caring for new arrivals and old friends. (I counted as both, even though she had not yet met Dan.) Their daughter was a not-quite teenager with long braids. Our two children were under three. L was a middle-ranking officer serving in the political section. Dan, assigned to the consular section, was a Third Secretary and the most junior officer at the recently opened embassy. For much of our tour, Dan didn't work directly for her husband. As was usual for first assignments, he rotated into the political section before we left. Regardless, we were in the same small circuit so our paths crossed regularly.

We'd been in Jakarta for nearly two years when L was assigned as head of the Political Section and Dan's boss. Someone else from the section was designated to meet them at the airport. I went by their house the next morning to welcome them in a neighborly, old friend way, carrying food and volunteering help as they settled in.

N looked basically the same, graying a bit, still slender, slightly stooped, wearing her trademark dangling earrings. When the USAID

199

family planning program got a shipment of faulty IUDs, she liberated a handful and bunched them into striking earrings. Since most people had never seen IUDs they weren't generally recognized, but she would point it out with great glee. From time to time, I invited N to a ladies lunch, always making a point of serving an onion tart. She loved onions, but her husband was seriously allergic to them. She didn't have an opportunity to eat them often.

Even though she was full of gusto, she was also a "by the book" Foreign Service Wife. The morning of the phone call, N was going down the list of "her" wives to tell us that the Political Section wives would be paying a formal call on the new Deputy Chief of Mission's wife the following Tuesday at 10:30 a.m. I should be there. Command performance.

"I am so sorry, I can't. I teach at the university that morning," I replied. "I'll make an appointment to call on her early next week."

I was a rarity in a world where Foreign Service Wives were adjuncts to their husbands and expected to give priority to helping support their husbands' careers. The prevailing ethos—imposed by the State Department, senior wives, and the limitations of diplomatic status—normally precluded the possibility of a wife working for pay. She could be a teacher at the international school or have some job in the embassy, if there was one. Otherwise…

I fell outside those parameters. Though I supported my husband's career, I also had a local paying job. It was only one day a week, hardly full time and by no means a career. But I was formally employed and receiving a salary. I took my teaching responsibility seriously.

Shortly after we arrived in Jakarta (well before L and N arrived), I had been asked to replace another embassy wife who had been volunteering as a native speaker and writing instructor in the English Department of the University of Indonesia. At the end of my first semester teaching as a volunteer, the department head invited me to become a visiting lecturer, to teach two required courses each semester. The university wanted me. They also wanted the paid position on their books when I left. I would be paid at the same annual rate as my Indonesian colleagues—the rupiah equivalent of $24.76. A year.

My colleagues couldn't live on that pay even though most of them received housing and rice in addition to their salary. Because they were fluent in English, they could get better-paying jobs translating for foreign companies in the afternoons, after morning classes.

Because I traveled on a diplomatic passport, I couldn't be issued an Indonesian work permit without losing my diplomatic status. To accept the university's offer, I had to obtain special permission from both the Indonesian government and the embassy. The former gave its permission immediately. At the embassy, there was trepidation, at least on the part of the administrative officer. My local job would set a precedent. Working for the Indonesian government, as the university lectureship entailed, would normally raise issues regarding diplomatic exemption from local taxation and legal prosecution. I had Indonesian government approval, so these concerns did not apply to my particular case.

More to the point, the administrative officer expected me to be the traditional "Lady Bountiful" and continue teaching as a volunteer. If I weren't paid, then I could (and would, he presumed) forego my teaching responsibilities whenever Wife duties called. He hummed and hawed. I asked what the decision was. Dan asked. He kept humming and hawing. Ultimately, he kicked the decision upstairs to the ambassador, who promptly approved: "She does her share and shows up when we need her."

By this third posting, I did do a lot and showed up when it was important. I had learned to say "yes" to, or volunteer for, something I wanted to do anyway. In my own mind at least, this allowed me to selectively say "no" when I couldn't or didn't want to do something. I also kept my sense of independence and more control of my time.

Ironically, teaching at the university during a time of ongoing student unrest meant I knew people who were not always involved with people from the embassy. I naturally heard things that they might not otherwise have heard. In any case, I was nearing the end of my third year teaching at the university. Dan and I would be moving to a new post in a few months.

There was deep silence. "Whose career do you care about? Your husband's or your own?" N repeated.

I was flabbergasted. It took some doing, but I managed to say with equanimity, "Neither. It's the end of the semester and my students need to pass the course."

N hung up, clearly annoyed.

My students finished the year well. The next week after the phone call with N, I paid a formal call on the new Deputy Chief of Mission's wife. I learned later that N felt compelled to call off an important obligation of her own in order to do what she had been bidden to do. We were all trapped one way or another. The Foreign Service hadn't yet caught up with the major shifts beginning to happen in American women's lives.

Change, however, was not far off.

LIVING WITH HISTORIES

In August 1971, Dan became the principal officer at the American consulate in Cebu in the Philippines, home for us for three years. Until we got there, I had no firm idea where it was or why the United States had a consulate there. Nor could I have begun to write these essential snippets sorting out *Cebu*: the word, the island, the province, and the city.

Cebu, the word, derives from the Cebuano *sibu,* meaning trade. The early settlement was the center of the Rajahnate of Cebu (or in Cebuano, *Gingharian sa Sugbu*), a kingdom founded in the thirteenth century by a prince of India's Chola Dynasty. From that entrepôt, Cebuanos traded with China, exchanging fabric from the fiber of the cotton tree for Ming Dynasty ceramics.

Cebu, the island, which lies ten degrees north of the equator, is the vertical "buckle" in the Visayas, the cluster of islands belted between the Philippines' two largest land masses: Luzon to the north and Mindanao to the south. All told, some seven thousand islands comprise the Philippine archipelago. In the Austronesian seaways, the archipelago is at the crossroads of the Pacific. Boats of all sizes moving people and goods have plied those waters for millennia.

Cebu the province includes the main island bearing its name plus some hundred fifty surrounding smaller islands and islets.

Cebu City, a prosperous port and the "second city" after Manila, is the capital of Cebu Province.

I arrived knowing what I *thought* were the basics: The Philippine Islands were annexed as an American colony in 1898. The islands had been a Spanish Catholic colony for roughly three hundred fifty years prior to that, and as a result the Philippines is the only majority Christian country in Asia. The United States granted the Republic of the Philippines (*Republika ng Pilipinas*) independence in 1946. (Filipinos joke: "Three hundred years in a convent, fifty years in Hollywood.") Most Americans, certainly schoolchildren, weren't taught pre-colonial Philippine history, or even that it existed.

As a child of World War II, I knew that the Japanese had invaded the Philippines immediately after Pearl Harbor. I was familiar, too, with the Battle of Corregidor, the Bataan Death March, and General Douglas MacArthur's famous assertion: "I shall return." I had heard about Santo Tomas, the old university in Manila that became an infamous prisoner of war camp under the Japanese. (My parents knew people interned there.) I had seen amazing pictures of the Banaue rice terraces. But what I knew revolved around Luzon, not the Visayas—certainly not Cebu.

What I learned is that Cebu, which was a substantial, well-organized, independent, pre-colonial trading center, is at the heart of the modern country's history and the anchor of Spanish Catholicism. In 1521, Cebu is where Magellan and the Spanish conquistadors first set foot in what would become the Philippines. (At least this is what Cebuanos claim; other Filipinos argue his initial landfall was on Limasawa, a small island south of Leyte.) From Spain, he and his crew and five ships had sailed south and westward, rounding the Horn of Africa and across the Pacific. Their mandate was to explore and Christianize. When Magellan landed, he planted a large wooden cross, claiming the territory for the Church and for Spain. Soon after, the priests traveling with him baptized Humabon, the local *rajah*, and his wife, giving them the Christian names Carlos and Juana. To mark their conversion and to demonstrate Spain's peaceful intentions, Magellan presented to them a wooden statue, about a foot tall, of Christ the Child, Santo Niño.

Humabon convinced Magellan and his men to join him in fighting Lapu-Lapu, the ruler of Mactan (an island across a narrow straight from Cebu). Early in the attack, Lapu-Lapu killed Magellan (or so went the story we heard when we got to Cebu). Without their leader, the Spaniards hastily departed. One of Magellan's five ships, under the command of Sebastian Elcano, completed the journey to Spain. Mactan and Cebu are as far as Magellan got on *his* circumnavigation of the globe.

Near the mangrove swamp on Mactan where the battle purportedly took place, three monuments mark Magellan's voyage. The first, a stepped obelisk—shabby with grass growing out of the cracks in its sides by the time we saw it—was built in the late nineteenth century by the Spanish colonial rulers. It reads, in Spanish: "To the Glory of God, Spain, and in honor of Queen Isabella." Near the bottom, as almost an afterthought, is "Magallanes" (as the Spanish spelled the explorer's name).

The second, a large plaque erected by the Philippine Historical Society in 1940 under the American colonial government, recounts the circumnavigation "by the facts," much as I have. It starts with Magellan's death "on this location" and ends with Elcano's completion of the first circumnavigation.

The third was erected in 1952, again by the Philippine Historical Society, by then under independent Filipinos. It reads: "In honor of Lapu-Lapu, who killed Magellan, thus becoming the first Filipino to fight Western aggression."

Three different monuments recount three different versions of the same event—the person telling it frames the story. Or, as historian son Charley reminds me: "One man's pirate is another man's freedom fighter." Time, too, makes a difference. Recent research indicates Lapu-Lapu was seventy-five; the popular images of him as the stalwart young fighter are a Filipino myth. His men did the killing.

Ironically, Elcano and his men were *not* the first to circumnavigate the Earth. Before he made his westward journey, Magellan, a Portuguese explorer who defected to Spain, had sailed eastward, around the Cape of Good Hope, across the Indian Ocean to Malacca, a trading center on the Malay coast of the Strait of Malacca. There, he captured a slave, presumably a Malay man from Sumatra familiar with many of the languages of the region. Magellan named him Enrique (his real name has been lost to history) and took him back to Spain.

Enrique accompanied Magellan on the westward voyage. After the explorers left Cebu, somewhere near his home-place, Enrique apparently jumped ship. Thus, Enrique, not Elcano and his men, completed the first circumnavigation. He certainly got farther than Magellan, who, if you start from Malacca, *almost* made it clear around.

Like everyone, I learned in grade school that Magellan was the first circumnavigator (never mind that he couldn't have done it alone). I wouldn't have been curious about this more complicated history if we hadn't been assigned to Cebu or lived among that journey's monuments.

Two years after we arrived, Samuel Eliot Morison (the eminent historian who wrote definitively about the voyages of discovery across the Atlantic and Pacific) was taking a trip following Magellan's route. He and his wife were being flown through the Philippines in a small private plane. For their map, Morison was using the geographical descriptions Antonio Pigafetta, a Venetian explorer and scholar on the voyage, kept in his journal.

We went to the airport to meet Morison, who was to speak that night in Cebu. When they arrived (late enough that we were all beginning to hold our breath), he wanted to see where Magellan was killed. After looking at the monuments, he wondered where Magellan had actually died. I pointed toward the nearby mangrove swamp, adding, as he strode in that direction, that it was extremely wet.

"Samuel," his wife called. "You heard what she said."

"You can't write history without getting your feet wet," replied the patrician Morison, by then in his early eighties. He kept going.

"Samuel," she, also in her eighties, called again, a bit louder. "You don't come in my bedroom if you do." Morison turned around.

Four decades after Magellan's voyage, Spain began its conquest, conversion, and "civilization" of the islands in Cebu. In 1565, Miguel

Legazpi led an expedition from New Spain (Mexico) across the Pacific, establishing a permanent settlement in Cebu. When Legazpi became the Governor-General of the Spanish East Indies, he spread the patterns of conquest throughout most of the islands. His expedition's initial settlement in Cebu made it the colonial Philippines' oldest city and its first capital.

In due course he sailed north to another major trading center, now Manila, on Luzon. The twice-yearly round trip voyages of the Manila Galleons between Acapulco and, first, Cebu, then later Manila became key to that trade. For nearly two hundred years, they carried spices and Chinese porcelain and silks to the new world. The crews were largely Filipinos, "Indios Luzones." During an exploration of the California coast one of the galleons made in October 1571, the first Filipinos landed on what would become the continental United States before continuing to Acapulco. (While there were small settlements of Filipinos in the States in the early eighteenth century, the mass migration began in the early 1900s after the islands became an American colony.)

For the Spanish, Christianizing and civilizing the islands was as important as establishing a major trading route. "Civilization" to the conquistadors meant concentrated settlements built around a church and a government center. They forcibly moved upland farmers to new lowland settlements within the "sound of the bells," meaning around a church. Consequently, the bells and hours of Christian prayer—rather than natural cycles of sun-up and sundown; rainy season and dry season; and planting, harvesting, and lying fallow—marked time. Building "civilization" also meant imposing Spanish Christian names on Filipinos. Although the Spanish didn't see it that way, their bringing "civilization" obliterated older, sophisticated patterns of communal order and ways of naming and bestowing honorifics that had served as social glue.

Soon after they landed, Legazpi's friars discovered that Cebuanos were still worshiping Magellan's statue of the Santo Niño. To enshrine the image, they built the first Catholic Church in the islands, Cebu's Basilica Minore del Santo Niño. Greatly revered, the oldest Catholic relic in the Philippines has miraculously survived fires, earthquakes, several re-buildings of the Basilica, and World War II unscathed. Daily, throngs of devotees, believing that Santo Niño performs miracles, light candles and pray for blessings and mercies.

Each January 21, at the Feast of Santo Niño or *Sinulug*, women who are the current generation of families who have followed this long-standing tradition dress the statue in elaborate new clothes. Believers come for miles to accompany Santo Niño, dancing and carrying their own small images of the child as the *carosa* bearing him is processed through the city's narrow streets.

Along with the Santo Niño, Magellan's cross was preserved and continues to be revered. Encased in an outer wooden shell to keep believers from chipping bits of it away, the cross stands in its own small, candle-filled shrine beside the Basilica.

The history of Cebu's Fort San Pedro, initially a triangular wooden stockade on the shore across the plaza from the Basilica, reflects the Philippines' colonial occupation. A century after Legazpi's men built it as the stronghold for the Spanish settlement, the fort was reconstructed in stone and fortified with cannons. The modifications were made to repel "Muslim pirates"—sailors from the Sulu Sultanate, a Muslim state of multilingual, literate people. The hub of a well-established trade network, the Sultanate stretched across the Indian Ocean to Africa and the Arabian peninsula, and up into China and Japan. Long before the Spanish, it ruled the Sulu Archipelago and parts of Mindanao as well as portions of Palawan and northeastern Borneo. Consequently, although the country is the only Christian nation in Asia, Islam was the first monotheistic religion to reach the present-day Philippines.

Cebuanos feared attacks from the pirates. The series of substantial stone churches they built along the coast also served as watchtowers. The Spanish, now Filipino, saying "*Los Moros en la costa*" ("there are Moros [Muslims] off the coast") harks back to that time. The warning stems from Spain's earlier struggle to fend off the "Moors" from Africa. But today, at least for Filipinos, it means something akin to "little pitchers have big ears."

At the end of the nineteenth century, Cebuano revolutionaries took over Fort San Pedro after the Spanish were defeated. During the American regime, it became Warwick Barracks, headquarters for the new occupiers. At the end of World War II, when Cebu was liberated from the Japanese, the renamed Fort San Pedro served as a military hospital.

Filipinos are proud their country had the first independence movement in Asia. In 1896 the Katipunan, a secret anti-colonial organization, started an armed revolt against Spanish rule. They had effectively defeated the Spanish before the Americans ships appeared for the Battle of Manila Bay, the first major engagement of the Spanish-American War. During the battle, the American Asiatic Squadron under Commodore George Dewey destroyed the Spanish Pacific Squadron. Five weeks later, on June 12, 1898, Emilio Aguinaldo and other revolutionaries declared the first Philippine Republic's independence.

The 1898 Treaty of Paris, which ended the Spanish-American War, didn't recognize that the revolutionaries had defeated Spain and that the Philippine Islands were an independent nation. Instead, it ceded the islands to the United States. President McKinley justified colonizing the islands by saying Americans needed "to educate the Filipinos, and uplift and civilize and Christianize them." In other words: Manifest Destiny and Little Brown Brothers. He sounded remarkably like the Spanish *conquistadores* who had invaded the islands three centuries earlier. Never mind that most Filipinos had been Catholic for generations and were civilized well before the Spanish arrived.

The extremely bloody Philippine-American War—still called the Philippine Insurrection in many American textbooks, if it is included at all—was the consequence. Although the United States "won," the war is a woeful history of battles, torture, massacres, ruthless US troops, and the deaths of thousands of Americans—and hundreds of thousands of Filipinos.

With American colonial rule, English became the common second language. American forms of law and education were introduced. As colonizers, the Americans established limited self-government with the intention that full independence would be granted "when Filipinos were ready." American business found the new colony fertile ground.

While we lived there, Filipinos' immediate memory was that we had fought together during World War II. The Philippine Scouts, a Filipino unit of the American army that fought as American nationals (since the islands were a US territory), was the backbone of the battle of Bataan. In addition to being part of the American army, the Filipinos had their own resistance movement (*Kilusan ng Paglaban sa Pilipinas*). This increasingly active underground, which included Scouts collaborating with small groups of American guerillas, engaged in constant hit-and-run tactics and risky intelligence gathering against the Japanese. Filipinos joined the American troops, who landed in 1944, to defeat the enemy. Philippine independence followed in 1946. By agreement, the United States kept a strong military presence, maintaining some of its pre-war facilities there. During our time there in the '70s, two major US bases remained on Luzon—Subic Bay and Clark Field.

On July 4, 1946, the stars and stripes came down and the Philippine flag went up. However, Filipinos still celebrate June 12, the date they declared independence from Spain in 1898, as their National Day. July 4 is Filipino-American Friendship Day.

Appreciating this long colonial history—especially America's fraught role, which continued after the Philippines became an independent nation—is critical to understanding the formal relationship between our two countries.

It was also crucial to our personal interactions. Above all, we were living among proud Filipinos. Some quickly assured us they were members of what they called the "fifty-first state party." (Dan and I didn't think admitting the Philippines as an American state was realistic or a desirable possibility; the people who brought up the subject did and assumed we concurred.)

Other Filipinos viewed the United States, our colonial history, and our continued military presence as responsible for many of the country's troubles. They demonstrated outside the embassy to make it clear they wanted our troops and military establishments gone. At the same time, it seemed many Filipinos we met wanted to at least visit the United States, if not move there. (A standing witticism was "USA go home; take me with you.")

However Filipinos framed it, they considered the Philippine relationship with the United States to be "special." (In fact, it is. We share a particular history.) Most assumed it had to be *as* special—in an almost familial sense—to Americans as it was to them. The notion of a special relationship, that we see a country as exclusively important as they see us, between the United States and many countries was not unusual, more diplomatic shorthand in a way, although the basis for each was unique. By then, we'd learned that most countries pay more attention to the United States and know more about us—or presume they do, even if it only comes from watching our movies—than most of us do about them. Part of it, no doubt, hinges on the "when elephants fight, its the ants that get trampled" view of how the world works. In our unique way, perhaps we are the elephant.

For most newly arrived Americans, what resonates about the Philippines is the outer layer of American culture. Think: language, music, beauty pageants, consumer products, suburban communities that look like they are straight from California—all encrusted over centuries of Spanish Catholicism. Yet at their core, Filipinos are Malay. What many Americans don't see or understand at first is those inner, deeply ingrained layers. Then they are thrown when the commonality of thought or behavior they expect from that surface layer doesn't play the way they anticipate.

Coming as we had from the other direction—the encompassing Malay world, which also included Malaysia and Indonesia—it was the Americanized, Catholic aspect of the Philippines that was new to us. The Malay-ness was the familiar. The importance Filipinos place on relationship and respect we had already experienced in other parts of the Malay world. We also recognized the oblique, indirect way of speaking, sometimes through a third person, when the issue is important or a request may be declined. This ambiguity and indirectness most disconcerted American newcomers to the region. In many ways, we felt fortunate having come to the Philippines from the direction we came.

As a child of America's deeply Protestant South encountering Spanish-derived Catholicism for the first time, I struggled with mixed feelings. I respected our fundamental shared faith writ large, our commonly held essential beliefs and our mutual self-identification as Christians (even if I was not terribly observant). As an Episcopalian, the services were largely familiar and comforting. My discomfort stemmed from often-conflicting practices and specific doctrines, rooted in convictions and tensions going back to the Reformation. The longer we were there, the more comfortable we became—a welcome and enlarging experience.

Language was equally complicated. We had a good handle on Indonesian and anticipated we'd learn Cebuano, the local language. They are in the same language family although not mutually comprehensible. Common words in Philippine and Indonesian languages can mean the same thing or have different but related meanings. In Cebuano, stress on syllables is phonemic. Emphasis changes meaning; saying a word the wrong way could sometimes transform something ordinary into something incredibly rude. For me venturing to use it was daunting. English was widely spoken, which made learning Cebuano less imperative. Ultimately, I spoke some Cebuano as well as a few Spanish-derived words and phrases and understand more than I spoke. And that was as far as it went.

Each language, like other aspects of culture, carries its own load, illuminating historical and political differences. Some three hundred different languages are spoken in Indonesia, with more than one hundred seventy in the Philippines. One of the first steps early nationalists took to meld multiple islands and language speakers into a single nation was to create a national language.

When Indonesians began to develop theirs, Bahasa Indonesia, in the 1920s, they deliberately chose a version of Malay from a small part of the country, the Riau islands, that was also widely used as a *secondary* trade language. Indonesians could have imposed Javanese, the language of the largest population, on minority populaces. But that would have been viewed as an internal "colonialism," so they didn't. Bahasa Indonesia was widely accepted.

In the 1930s Philippine nationalists decided to create a national language, Pilipino. They opted to use the most common words from the various semi-related regional languages, with some Spanish thrown in. The grammatical rules and much of the vocabulary were

Tagalog, the major language of Luzon. Roughly as many people spoke Tagalog as they did Cebuano (though there is debate about that). While Bahasa Indonesia effectively integrated widely diverse communities, conversely, primarily Tagalog-influenced Pilipino did not. Over time, I sat in on heated discussions among Cebuano writers who were disdainful of how Tagalog "colonized" Pilipino. That must be less true now, as younger generations have grown up with Pilipino.

The longer we were in Cebu, travelling in Dan's consular district in the Southern Philippines, the more we experienced events linked to the country's history. For the most part, we lived among town squares, city halls, and centuries-old Spanish churches and participated in commemorating key historic events. "Within the sound of the bells," as it were, of the colonial era.

Remnants of the pre-colonial world were less obvious, but were there, nonetheless. Mostly, they were parts of deep culture. Saying *"puera buyag"* (shoo, evil eye), for instance, if someone complimented your child. Ancient ritual had been repurposed. The Santo Niño devotees' shuffling dance probably predated Magellan. With the statue's arrival, the shuffle had been attached to venerating it.

The Ati Atihan held in Aklan Province where everyone dances a similar sliding step through the street was partly a modern Catholic fiesta. In essence, however, it acknowledges ancient times when Malays arrived in boats and drove the original inhabitants into the mountains. In the Philippines, the term *barangay* (small village) derives from both the Malay word, *balangay* (sailboat) and the word for the community the people who came in those boats created.

While dances and word usages have endured, buildings and other wooden structures have not lasted in the Philippine world of termites and rot. Thus places of worship—be they churches like the Basilica or mosques in parts of Mindanao—have had a succession of structures. Many of those sites have long been hallowed, predating Islam and Christianity.

A decade after our tour in the Philippines I visited upland communities in Banaue on Luzon that even now have only changed minimally since the arrival of the Spanish and Americans. Animism and an active belief in spirits prevail, sometimes syncretized to Christianity. For hundreds of years, these tribal people have constructed remarkable rice terraces to control the flow of water down steep mountainsides. In order to manage rice production, they understand their own microclimates in great detail. Because weather changes from one side of a mountain or valley to another, with any particular weather pattern varying in length of days, each small group has developed its own weather-cycle-based calendar with rituals timed to mark it.

And so it was: We lived our otherwise present-world lives enmeshed in this pre-colonial and colonial Philippine history that was uniquely linked to the United States. Americans had been both adversaries and allies. This awareness enriched our understanding and appreciation of the Philippines and Filipinos. It also forced us to examine from a different viewpoint who Americans were—and, as I write, who Americans *are*. As the monuments to Magellan demonstrate, history has many ways of being seen.

Perhaps because the Philippines was—and in meaningful ways, truly wasn't—closer to being a mirror of the United States than any other place we had or would live, I learned more there about seeing multi-culturally: my culture in some ways (or what sometimes felt like a parody of it); mostly uniquely, wonderfully, multiply Filipino. Living in the Philippines gave me the gift of appreciating that complex history for what it was and what I learned from it. I also gained a greater understanding of the legacy of being American, both the parts of our history that make me uncomfortable as well as those that make me proud.

As I moved from country to country and related to different peoples, I became increasingly aware that I was ultimately learning more about myself than about "them." (I find myself repeatedly making that observation, not only about myself but about everyone who lives this way.) The more I discovered, the more I knew there was so much I would never find out—would never know. Wherever I lived, I was only seeing pieces of another place in the kaleidoscope of the world.

The Consul's Wife

The American consulate in Cebu, a small suite of offices on the third floor of the Phil-Am Life Building, was the branch office of the embassy in Manila. The consulate issued visitors' visas (not immigrant ones, that was done in Manila), was responsible for American citizens throughout the district, and reported to the embassy on political and economic matters. Above all, it was the formal American presence in the Visayas, Mindanao, and Sulu—effectively the southern half of the Philippines.

The consul—the senior American official in the district—and the vice consul were both Foreign Service officers. The director of the United States Information Service Library (further in town), and the regional representatives of USAID and the Peace Corps (each with offices elsewhere) and their families were the other resident official Americans. A succession of us had come, stayed a while, and been transferred elsewhere, to be succeeded by others.

The local staff provided continuity. Marisol Borromeo Putong, the long-time consulate secretary, effectively *was* the consulate. Marisol knew, in many cases was related to, anyone who mattered in Cebu. Without her, nothing would have functioned.

From 1971 to 1974, Dan was the American Consul.
I was the Consul's Wife.
For both of us, these titles—although not official, my title was just as real—conferred a complicated mix of position, highly visible status, depersonalization, responsibility, and unique opportunity.

We quickly learned that Cebuanos, southern Filipinos in general, viewed the American consul in Cebu (and the consul's wife) as *theirs*. We were their link with the American government, their signifier that they were as important as the Tagalogs in Manila. We were known by title if not in person. Although many people got to know us as individuals, we were unavoidably the Consul and the Consul's Wife, written with capitals.

When we traveled in the region, only the American ambassador was treated with more deference. Once we were escorting a group from the embassy and were staying at a hotel in Zamboanga. The ambassador and his wife checked in first and were given one of two air-conditioned rooms. The political counselor, senior to Dan in rank, checked in next and was assigned the other air-conditioned room. Dan checked us in last. When the man at the desk saw "American Consul, Cebu" on the form, he blanched, informed the political counselor that a mistake had been made and assigned him somewhere else. We were given the second air-conditioned room—to our embarrassment—and could not get the matter rectified.

Everyone we met expected us to know the whereabouts of previous consuls and vice consuls. They assumed we kept in close contact because we were all "Cebuanos."

Even before we were formally in residence, we were welcomed in our official capacity as new "Cebuanos" and, personally, as family. Anticipating the move, I hitched a ride on a military flight from Indonesia to the Philippines in order to check out schools, housing, and furniture. My first night in Cebu, Diege and Barbara Borromeo, Marisol's youngest brother and his wife, were hosting a large party. Of course, I was to join them. That warm tropical night was a wonderful introduction to Filipino hospitality, many-soon-to-be friends, and delicious food—and to the three generations of Borromeos, who would "adopt" us, as we would them.

I had so much to learn.

The Consul's family lived in a fishbowl, which eliminated a great deal of family privacy. Soon after we arrived, with a beach Sunday in the offing, we needed snorkeling equipment. Our car hadn't arrived—I couldn't have found my way around at that point, anyway—so the consulate car and driver took me shopping. When my order was assembled, I didn't have enough cash and asked the shopkeeper to hold things until I came back with the right amount.

"Never mind, Mrs. Sullivan," he said, wrapping them up. "You take them. Your driver can bring the money later." Fishbowl name-recognition, it turned out, came with instant credit.

Nine months later, we were going on a home leave that had been delayed. I'd parked my car outside a shop. A young man I vaguely recognized as a collateral member of a well-known family stopped me. "Mrs. Sullivan, I hear you're leaving. Are you selling the car?" (Although we hadn't planned it that way, it was a model of Toyota that was not normally available in the country.) The young man was disappointed; we weren't selling our car. Apparently, the second piece of "leaving Cebu"—"coming back after two month's leave"—hadn't travelled the bamboo telegraph as fast as the first.

It didn't take long to realize that Cebu (all of the Philippines) comprises thickly webbed layers of relationships based on family—clans rather than immediate nuclear units, multiplied by the extended families of those who had married into them. Other carefully cultivated relationships—schoolmates or godparents (chosen not just for babies, but also for marriages)—thicken the mix. Reciprocity in large matters and small as well as constantly sharing the detailed minutia, the *chismis* (gossip) of daily lives, glues it together.

Knowing these familial connections was critical to knowing "who was who" and "what was what," in terms of politics and the broader community. So a few weeks after we arrived, we hosted a small, carefully assembled dinner in order to pick the brains of our guests, particularly a local gossip columnist who knew everyone—and everything about them. Soon we were all down on the floor. On huge pieces of paper, he drew genealogies of the major families on Cebu and across the Visayas. Since our guests loved *chismis*, we heard amazing tales about multiple generations.

Before long, we were happily enmeshed in this web of enduring connections. Since Lola Pilar, the Borromeo matriarch, had been a young woman, the family's women had been the custodians of the main *carosa* honoring Our Mother of Perpetual Help for the Redemptorist Church's fiesta. (A carosa is a carriage decorated with flowers that processes a religious icon through the city). During the war, the family had hidden the image of the Holy Mother so the Japanese wouldn't destroy it. Our third year there, Lola asked Charley and three Irish boys his age, all part of the Borromeo beach group, to serve as candle bearers around the carosa. Dressed in red cassocks and white surplices, they walked at the corners of the carosa with four of the five Borromeo sisters dressed as angels riding on it. To this day, with the help of Facebook, the close family relationship continues.

We had to learn to navigate widely held, unspoken Filipino cultural expectations and their personal and official implications. Beyond generously hosting us, Cebuanos were quick to give us gifts. Returning their hospitality was easy. We gave parties. However, by American law, we couldn't accept the gifts. By cultural practice, had we accepted them, we would have been obligated to return the favor in some form or other. We faced the socially difficult task of returning most gifts with as much grace as we could. Food was an exception. Occasionally, before a reception or big garden party, a contribution to the evening's fare arrived at the door—most memorably enough fresh heart-of-palm salad to feed three hundred. Even that meant treading carefully when the donor later asked Dan to issue a visa for a friend.

Requests were often indirect. If a friend needed to go to the consulate on business, she called me first to let me know she was going and for what, assuming I would then tell Dan before she got there and grease the skids.

In addition to the natural desire to entertain friends and colleagues who entertained us, Dan's being the consul required more official representational responsibilities for both of us than his earlier assignments. We frequently hosted dinners or receptions for visiting

American government officials, musicians and academics, and US naval ships that called in the harbor as well as local officials from Cebu or elsewhere.

Such events did not always go as anticipated. We had extended invitations for a July Fourth *vin d'honeur* (a noon gathering for local government officials and a few other senior members of the community). Not once but twice, those plans were upended by Imelda Marcos's decision to personally open a new bridge between Cebu and Mactan. On July 2, she announced she would open the bridge on July 3. Suddenly, every provincial governor from the southern Philippines—all the senior officials from Dan's consular district—would be descending on Cebu for their command performance. Since they would be staying overnight, on a day's notice, invitations to our *vin d'honeur* on July 4 were extended to each of them, too. Full steam ahead, the cook and I quadrupled the amount of food the kitchen was producing and ordered more champagne.

Meanwhile, on July 2, in her hometown in Leyte, Imelda gave herself a rollicking birthday party that went on to the wee hours of the morning on July 3. Too tired to be in Mactan that day, Madam suddenly postponed the bridge opening to noon July 4. That commandeered all the *vin d'honeur* guests. We cancelled the July Fourth reception.

The American consul and his wife were not invited to the bridge opening. We were relieved not to sit in the full sun on the bridge. Everyone else waited and waited for Madam to arrive and declare the bridge open, after which she turned right around and went back to the airport. She never set foot in Cebu, the heart of the opposition.

Although we never hosted a Fourth of July reception, we entertained frequently, for many reasons. Peace Corps volunteers (PCVs), among others, found their way to our home any time a group of them was in town. After eating mainly fish and rice in barrios, they welcomed American home cooking. And we enjoyed feeding them. One evening we fed a dozen PCV phys. ed. teachers—men and women, all over six-feet tall. By the middle of the spaghetti dinner they had devoured *all* the pasta and were lining up for seconds and thirds. The kitchen helper ran to the *sari sari* store (the local version of a 7-Eleven) to get more. All told, that small gang went through twenty-four boxes of pasta, gallons of spaghetti sauce, five kilos of salad, and who knows how much ice cream and cases of beer. Thereafter, the cook referred to PCVs as "spaghetti vacuums."

I did most of the detailed planning and management for all our official entertaining. The consulate staff put together lists, issued invitations, and coordinated logistics with me. (Unless it was something small, informal, and for friends only, then I did the needful.) Our kitchen produced the food. Fortunately our cook, Nene, was excellent. She often read my *Gourmet Magazine* before I did, pointing out the recipes we could make with locally available ingredients. More than once, we produced garden buffets for as many as three hundred. Being creative about how we entertained and what we served took effort. It was also fun. By the time we left, I qualified to run a catering business.

Just as often as we entertained, we were invited to events both in Cebu and around the consular district. Glad for every chance to travel, we obliged as often as we could. In northern Mindanao, we helped inaugurate a USAID project: a switch was flipped and, for the first time, electricity was bought to a long string of barrios in northern Mindanao. We were honored guests for the installation of a new president at Silliman University on Negros as well as for the anniversaries of American landings liberating the Philippines in World War II, and countless other events, major and minor, on various islands. Some events required stamina. We stood (I eventually sat) on the steps of the Provincial Capitol in Cebu in the broiling sun while sixty-seven shots were fired—one shot per province, per minute—to honor Philippine Independence Day.

Because we were social in an appearance-conscious society, the Consul's Wife needed to pay more attention to appearance than I usually did. I enjoyed clothes. For years I made many of my own, finding creative ways to use local fabric. Entertaining at home, I practiced my usual informality, being, as the gossip columns put it one day, "the breezy Mrs. Sullivan." Many social events required "something new," thoughtfully chosen for the occasion. Fun in its way, this necessitated an ever-expanding wardrobe.

Then there was my hair. In Jakarta I had decided my long, salt-and-peppering hair made me look too much like my mother. I whacked it off myself and began regularly getting a simple wash-and-wear cut, which I still prefer. In Cebu, just as going to large social events elegantly dressed was *de rigueur*, going to the "parlor" beforehand was a ritual: shampoo, set, fancy blow dry, manicure, pedicure, gossip—especially gossip.

While I expected to attend events, and dress for them, I didn't know that being the Consul's Wife also came with a range of "presumed" responsibilities unique to Cebu. The former Consuls' Wives had chaired the citywide sale of UNICEF cards. Wouldn't I do it, too? I reassembled the committee that had always actually done it. They provided welcomed guidance and sold and distributed the cards. We also hosted a card sale at the Consul's residence. I became the link with UNICEF Manila, managed the income, and sent it to headquarters. This made me the informal resident UNICEF representative. As part of that role I was asked to help staffers who came into town. We once housed one who had had a heart attack and couldn't fly for a week.

Beyond my UNICEF duties, I was also asked if I would serve as the native speaker administrator of the ECFMG exam. Doctors trained outside the United States had to pass that worldwide exam to demonstrate English proficiency before they were admitted to practice in the United States. Since the stakes were high, administering the exam also meant thwarting international cheating.

The American Consul always belonged to Rotary—literally to the senior Rotary club in town, the Cebu Mother Club. Dan joined. I was automatically a "beautiful Rotary Ann," as the wives were routinely called. Rotary, an international social and charitable organization, was all male at that time. We Anns used to laugh, however, that *we* were actually the ones who raised the money and saw that the projects got done.

We supported a groundbreaking malnutrition ward in one hospital. The Mal Ward, run by a renowned local nutritionist who later became Minister of Health, required that a parent stay with each seriously malnourished post-nursing toddler (the age at which malnutrition usually sets in) who was admitted. While they were there, parents would be taught how to prepare healthy food from locally available ingredients to stop diarrhea in order to reverse malnutrition and vitamin A deficiency. Parents learned that bananas, grown in every backyard, were a natural plug (the greener the better because of the pectin content). And also that a small square of coconut provided enough fat for the body to absorb the vitamin A found in the numerous greens that were part of a normal Filipino diet. UNICEF made a movie about the ward and asked me to be the narrator.

Our best project underwrote the cost of drilling wells and supplying pumps that relieved women and children of the burden of carrying bucketsful of river water up a hill. The village women also learned to repair the pumps, giving them "ownership" of pump maintenance so they weren't dependent on men to keep the pumps working. When the pump in the first barrio was turned on, we Anns were there to cheer with the village women.

Each of these Consul Wife activities proved to be welcome opportunities to branch out and learn something new. Better yet, they knit me into the community of active women who did "good works" as well as played together. With them, happy for the occasions, I played bridge again and tried to learn mahjong.

As the home of the Osmena dynasty, leaders of the opposition to President Marcos, Cebu was politically important. Two days after we arrived in the Philippines, before we even got to Cebu, a bomb blast at Manila's Plaza Miranda had seriously injured Senator Sergio Osmena, who barely survived. Dan had been scheduled to call on him as soon as we got to Cebu, which, of course, didn't happen.

Serging, as he was called, recovered slowly. Once he did, dinner at our house was his first social outing. Four well-armed bodyguards followed him into our living room, clearly determined that they would stay there for the evening. I was equally certain that there would not be such a display of guns in my home. In my firmest Consul's Wife voice, I informed the guards that we would keep Serging safe and nothing would happen in our house. I told them to kindly wait at the front gate, and I would have food sent out to them.

They were unhappy. But they left. Inside, the dinner went off smoothly with no harm befalling anyone.

Other times were just as memorable. Soon after martial law was declared in September 1972, Dan had to fly to Manila unexpectedly. The consulate had no secure phone line and he needed to get information to the embassy urgently. Charley, then eight, had buddies sleeping over. The staff went home after supper, leaving the boys and me alone in the house. The night watchman was outside.

At about 9 p.m., the phone rang. The caller identified himself as a colonel in the Philippine constabulary. His name was familiar. "I need to speak to Consul Sullivan," he said.

"I'm sorry, Colonel, he's gone to Manila. He can call you tomorrow when he gets back."

"You're the consul's wife. I need to know now. *You* can tell me then: Does the consul have guns in the house?"

Under martial law, the constabulary was seizing privately held guns all over the country. (They had confiscated an armored car with a bazooka on top from a warlord on another island.)

I knew we had no guns. We never had had guns. (If I felt I needed protection when Dan was gone I kept a nine iron by the bed.) The night watchman's gun had already been turned in (to my vast relief, since it was locally made with a barrel that would shoot in who-knew-what direction).

I also knew I should not answer this question.

"Let me reach the consul in Manila. I'll get back to you. What number should I call, Colonel?"

"You know what number." He slammed down the phone.

I waited a minute, then picked up the phone to call Dan. The line had gone dead. Disconcerting. I checked the boys. Asleep. I went outside to the night watchman. Also asleep. I woke him. "Stay awake,

I'm going next door to use the phone." My neighbors were out. The maids let me make the call. I got through to the Marine Guard at the embassy, and asked them to find Dan and have him call me. In the dark, I went back down through the hedge to our house. I woke the night watchman, again.

I checked. We had a dial tone. I settled in to wait.

At almost 11 p.m., Dan called:

"Phone the colonel. Tell him that, as I have told the general, the consulate has no guns."

I found a number for the constabulary. The colonel was out on duty. "Please have him telephone the American consul's residence as soon as he comes in."

I waited some more. The colonel called eventually. I delivered Dan's message as firmly as I knew how.

"Yes, Mrs. Sullivan. We *know* you have no guns," the colonel said, extremely puzzled.

"Didn't you call me earlier?"

"No, Mrs. Sullivan."

Someone knew I was in the house alone. The colonel was as concerned as I was. He told me the constabulary would go by the house regularly. I woke the night watchman—again—and ordered him to keep his eyes open, literally.

I reported back to Dan. "Call Joe and tell him," he instructed. Joe, the vice consul, was out, the maid said. Because of the curfew imposed with martial law, he would be back by midnight.

"Inday, please have him call me as soon as he comes in," I said. On the stroke of midnight, Joe rang: "I'll come check on you."

"Dan told me to tell you not to go out after midnight on your own. Get a police escort." The consulate didn't have late night passes yet. Joe could be jailed for breaking curfew. He grumbled but agreed to do as "Sir" said.

Exhausted, unnerved, I turned out the lights and crawled into bed under the windows we always kept open to let the cooler night breezes in. About half an hour later, there was a terrible racket. I heard constabulary cars screech to a stop—and Joe. "Wake up." From the upper west side of Manhattan, Joe was endowed with an amazingly colorful vocabulary, all of which he expended on the night watchman and his maternal ancestry more than once at the top of his lungs. Then silence.

A repeat performance roused me from a fitful sleep before six the next morning. A few minutes later, the phone rang. Joe. He was off to a neighboring island to see about an American in jail.

"I came by twice last night to check on things."

It was years before I told Joe my windows had been open, and I had heard it all. He blushed.

There was always something, not always so unnerving. Once, when the vice counsel was otherwise occupied, Dan and I had to juggle two visitors: a "visiting fireman" (an official from Washington, in Cebu to call on various parts of the local government) and a friend from the Admin section in the embassy in Manila, down to check things out. We traded visitors back and forth: I took the admin guy to visit rattan furniture makers (Cebu was famous for them); Dan took the official visitor to the mayor's office. Dan took the admin guy to the consulate for business; I took the official sightseeing.

We continued to trade visitors all day until Dan dispatched the official to the airport and went back to the office. Meanwhile, the admin guy and I went home. "Is it always this crazy?" he mused as we were having a drink. We had barely relaxed when Dan roared in, saying in passing, "Sorry, can't stay for dinner. Just learned I need to catch the last flight to Manila." He grabbed a clean shirt and underclothes and was out the door.

I laughed: "What can possibly happen next?" A deep, rolling rumble headed toward the house. The walls began to sway. Pictures rattled. Earthquake. Dan, in the car, didn't feel it. All in a day's work.

Over our three years in Cebu, people talked to me about all sorts of things, including the backstories and *chismis* that are the bread and butter of Philippine politics. Sometimes, perhaps, they talked because you share information. Other times I'm sure they told me something because they assumed I would pass it on to the American Consul—indirect communication at work.

I heard a lot about land reform. The national government was planning to break up plantations into mandatory four- to five-hectare plots, which would be given to workers, thereby expanding smallholder ownership. In Cebu, however, plantation-sized holdings were infrequent. Cebuanos with limited incomes, such as teachers, and mid-level public servants were buying ten to twenty hectares as retirement investments, farming them for food and extra income in the interim. They were seriously opposed to a nationwide reform.

I heard enough to write a memo. Dan thought that my account of the regional counterpoint was worth passing on to the embassy. He sent it with his own covering memo, but the relevant officers promptly bounced it back. I was a wife, not a university researcher. Had a visiting expert written the same thing, it would have been taken seriously as a regional political distinction. Dan counted to ten then sent it to the Philippine desk at the State Department in Washington. We assume they read it but we never heard back.

In addition to following local issues, in June 1972 we began dealing with our own American political storm: Watergate. As the consul's wife I generally had to be mindful of what I said and did regarding American politics. If asked, for the most part we explained how our system worked (not an easy task in the best of times since it is beyond complicated). We didn't comment on our own views, particularly if we disagreed with an administration's position. Dan and I only spoke to each other, no one else, about what was happening at the White House or on the Hill (hard for me, a would-be political activist).

Even though Nixon was reelected in November, the furor over Watergate and the president himself gained force. So did Filipino puzzlement and concern—as well as my own disgust. Not speaking out grew more and more difficult. I voiced my opinions among a few close friends, American and Filipino. Many Filipinos saw Watergate as politics as usual and didn't understand why Americans were so upset. Our response, on the occasions when one was called for, was that Americans had a hard-to-define but real line for unacceptable lying and cover-up. The president had crossed it. Representing the United States when our country was caught in a political maelstrom was unpleasant and embarrassing.

As with Watergate and later Iran-Contra, what I see happening in the White House in 2018 makes me sick at heart for us all, particularly for our colleagues overseas.

Being the Consul's Wife with this range of obligations (not to mention being the children's mother) kept me more than busy. I enjoyed it. For my own mental balance, I continued knitting my own portable pursuits into my other obligations, the same way as I had in Jakarta.

Painting was one of them. Making art was another way of noticing the world around me: the knobbly feet of women walking down from the mountains or sitting outside Magellan's Cross selling candles; or the peanuts' gallery of small boys watching me sketch, giggling as they realized which one of them I was drawing. Ultimately, I exhibited my paintings in Cebu and Manila. To my great honor, F. Sonil Jose and his wife—I knew them as Frankie and Tessie—mounted a single-artist show of my Philippine work in their gallery, Solidaridad, in Manila. Occasionally, in other people's houses, I still meet some of the work I showed there.

Besides painting, teaching art at the Cebu American School, and literature for the few near-native speakers of English at a local girls school, stretched my imagination and skills. As was my custom, I also explored local products, especially textiles and baskets. The Philippines was richly rewarding in both. Good pieces of hand weaving, when I could find them, were a way of "knowing" upland tribes I didn't have the chance to visit.

I kept on keeping on as the Consul's Wife until our travel orders came. We gave a huge farewell garden party for friends and colleagues, ate our way out of town at *despedidas,* (farewell parties) packed up and moved to the next assignment.

Leaving is always hard. It was especially hard in Cebu. I, we all, look back on our life there with pleasure, grateful for the friendships from that time and rejoicing in the continuing connection. I return now, when I do, as "Tita Margaret."

Moon Glow

One of the joys of our Alexandria condo balcony was moonrise.

In a peek-a-boo moment, the clouds covering the night sky would drift away from the lower half of a pumpkin full moon—a shy young woman tantalizingly shifting her veil. As quickly, the veil would fall over a quarter of what had been revealed, then drop fully, refilling the sky with mellow gray clouds.

The moon had other tricks. The Harvest Moon, fat and golden, rose elegantly from beyond the skyline to glide above our roof, out of view, plating the indigo Potomac in rippling silver.

The most brilliant moon glow was not in Washington, but in Cebu, one gentle tropical night before Christmas. The dowager of a leading political family had invited us to dinner at her villa high on the hills above the city, facing the Bohol Strait. The full moon silvered the water as far as the eye could see.

After a feast (what would a Filipino party be without wonderful food?), a serenade of guitars and glorious voices filled the air with Filipino Christmas Carols. As the evening neared its end, our hostess called for "White Christmas."

"Tita," her senator nephew objected, "that's not Filipino."

"Of course it is," she countered.

"We were living in Tacloban at the time of the Leyte landing," she explained. After the war's privations, she had witnessed McArthur and the American armed forces "returning" to liberate the islands from the Japanese army in October 1944.

"That Christmas," she recounted, suddenly a young woman, alive with memories, "Irving Berlin was there. He sat at our piano and wrote it. It's Filipino."

Never mind that the classic carol was written in 1940. As far as she was concerned, Berlin wrote it in her family home in newly freed Tacloban.

The lyrical dreaming drifted though the balmy night while the moon turned the strait a magical Christmas white.

No More Two-fers, and Yet...

In 1972 (a decade after the publication of *The Feminine Mystique*), I had been a Foreign Service wife, part of a diplomatic team, for sixteen years. As the American Consul's Wife in Cebu, I clearly, unquestionably—not totally unquestioningly—was a two-fer.

Like other wives abroad, I was attentive to the burgeoning women's liberation movement roiling in the States. My friends there were finding new careers or expanding volunteer work into paid professional positions. Women working at *Newsweek*, some of them married, had sued the magazine, demanding to be hired as reporters, a position that until then only men held. These women lived in the United States and could both work and maintain families.

For us, the situation was different. Our Foreign Service husbands served abroad. We "served" with them. How could we be our own professional persons (or just in charge of our own time) when we had to go wherever, whenever our husbands were sent? When we were caught in a two-for-the-price-of-one culture? An increasing number of Foreign Service wives were no longer content to follow the traditional expectations. Many, by no means all, were resentful of "abuses"—real and, more often, perceived—at the hands of the "senior wives" and the system itself. As much as many loved large parts of their lives, they—we—wanted to have the option of careers of their own.

Developing serious, usually unpaid, portable pursuits at each post was my way of partially addressing this dilemma—for me that worked. Nonetheless, I'd already had my Jakarta run-ins over a paid position at the University of Indonesia.

I wasn't alone. Near the end of our time in Jakarta, a strongly credentialed urban planner had confronted bureaucratic roadblocks as she sought professional consulting positions outside the embassy. She was angry (in a way I never was). She had understood before she decided to join her husband that she could work for whomever.

In the Philippines, I enjoyed a twenty-something wife, an interesting person. She had come to Manila with her first-tour husband using her own last name, not her husband's. Skittish about doing the "diplomatic thing," she often hung out with "the wrong people." Her undiplomatic outspokenness could be inappropriate. However, she was as typical of her generation of younger wives as the older, traditional "by the book" wives were of theirs.

American society was changing—we were representative of those changes. What was the State Department to do?

In late 1968, that question was raised at the Secretary of State's Open Forum, a vehicle for bringing substantive issues to the

Secretary's attention. The Under Secretary for Administration initiated a discussion of policies and procedures with a view toward modernizing the Department as a whole. The resulting report, issued in 1970, made scant mention of women, either as employees or as wives. This caused a furor. A group of women in Washington, mainly officers, established the Women's Action Forum. Following discussions, the Forum produced a series of papers about what was needed that were presented to the Department.

In response, on March 22, 1972, the State Department issued the Joint State-AID-USIA Policy on Wives of Foreign Service Employees. The gist: Wives of Foreign Service officers are private individuals, not government employees. As private persons, they are free to follow their own interests, subject to laws of the host country and the US government. Most importantly—best of all—wives were no longer to be graded in the husband's efficiency report.

Effectively, wives were no longer required to do the bidding of more senior wives, and senior wives were not free to require or even ask for the help of lower-ranking wives. Officers were still responsible for representational activities. The practicalities of how these duties would be carried out were not addressed.

The Department also reaffirmed that the tradition of husband-and-wife teams and of wives' participation in the representational activities of a post were major strengths of the Foreign Service. Families abroad, it went on to say, were excellent representatives of American life and values.

Focused on the day-to-day in Cebu, I was unaware the directive was in the offing. The day Dan brought a copy home was a pleasant surprise. I welcomed the new policies, especially no longer being evaluated as part of his work. That aspect of the Foreign Service had always struck me as egregious. Good riddance.

In Cebu, the new policy made little difference. I might have seen myself as a private person. And the Foreign Service might have decided that I, indeed, was (for better and for worse). But Dan's representational duties as an American diplomat didn't change. Neither did our relationship or what I did as part of our team. If I didn't manage the doing of entertaining, who would? It was a two-officer post, the vice consul was a single man; there was no "junior wife" for me to ask to help—and in any case, had there been one, under the new directive she and I were both private people, not to ask or be asked. Much more to the point, in the wider community, the people we lived among certainly did *not* see me as a private person. In that particular fishbowl, I was clearly the Consul's Wife.

Our next post, a direct transfer, was Freetown, Sierra Leone. The name told its own story. In the fifteenth century, Portuguese explorers sailed past a ridge of mountains visible on the West African coast. Whether climatic conditions roared, or the mountains appeared to be lions, is debatable. The Portuguese named the area Sierra Leone (in English, Mountains of Lions). By the eighteenth century, the British had established a colonial settlement on the best-sheltered harbor along that section of the coast. British ships interdicting slave ships in the mid-Atlantic, and returning slaves from Nova Scotia, brought slaves there, freeing them under an enormous cotton tree. Hence Freetown.

We arrived on August 6, 1974, two days before President Nixon resigned. (It's funny, the linkages of dates and places I remember as markers of time.)

During our tour in Freetown, the new policy made minimal difference in my life, in *our* lives. For those two years (we left in June, 1976), Dan was the Deputy Chief of Mission (the ambassador's deputy). When the four-officer post was between ambassadors, he served as the Chargé (acting ambassador). The country was interesting but not important in terms of American foreign policy. The post was nowhere near as demanding as those at larger embassies in strategically vital countries. The embassy wasn't even as demanding as the consulate in Cebu.

Even so, we were part of traditional Foreign Service life. We attended events, assisted at the ambassador's receptions and dinners, and fed contingents of Peace Corps volunteers from all over country when they were in town. (I visited them when they were sick in the Freetown hospital, too). All of this was in addition to our own considerable entertaining. The larger diplomatic round included national days, dinners, wives' coffees, and, sometimes, cultural events. I could have opted out. I didn't—I didn't want to. The friendships we made with people in the diplomatic corps and the international community, and above all, with Sierra Leoneans enriched us. Opting out would have been my loss.

The diplomatic community was quirky. In addition to Great Britain, France, Germany, Italy, and several African countries, China had an embassy in Freetown and a contingent of aid workers around the country. We saw them at functions, where we spoke to each other. Nixon had already gone to China so the process of "opening to China" had begun, but because our countries had no formal diplomatic relations, we couldn't yet go further than limited conversation at events. Dan's counterpart, we learned, was from near where I was born in Shandong. We talked casually about food and mutually regretted we could not know each other better or go to each other's homes to share a meal.

Another unique aspect of Freetown was that it was one of the few capitals anywhere in the world with resident ambassadors from both South *and* North Korea. That made for enormous awkwardness, particularly at large functions when the entire corps was present—or even around town. The North Koreans, dressed in blue wool Mao suits, looking miserable in the equatorial heat, always moved in groups. They avoided any form of contact with Americans, although they obviously knew who we were. If I were pushing my cart through the narrow grocery aisles and they were coming in my direction, they would avert their eyes, back up, and flee.

We didn't have formal contact with the Cubans either, though they were highly visible, and we exchanged greetings. Several of the young men, full of machismo, stared provocatively at our teenage daughter.

The Soviets had a large contingent, living in a compound and keeping to themselves on the far end of the beach. However, their ambassador and Deputy Chief of Mission, along with their wives, went out socially. Once we were at a dinner the French Deputy Chief of Mission and his wife gave for their counterpart couples. The British deputy's wife and I were seated at the same small table as the Russian deputy. The Chinese embassy had recently sponsored an extremely popular visit by their acrobats. So my British friend and I asked the Russian deputy when the Russians would bring the Bolshoi to Freetown. "We would love to see them," one of us chirped. "They would be a smashing success," the other added. He paused, blushed, and finally blurted: "We couldn't. They would defect." To Sierra Leone?

Basically, Freetown was a quiet, small city built on the edge of the hills that surrounded the safest harbor along the west coast of Africa. There was one grocery store, Lebanese owned; expansive wet and dry markets; a good Lebanese restaurant on the shore and a terrible Chinese restaurant in town; a small museum; Fourah Bay College, the oldest and first western-style university in West Africa; a relatively recent hotel, where the Rotary met and foreign visitors stayed; and bones of another hotel going up out by the ocean. The children and I spent afternoons on a wonderful beach.

One of the best ways of catching up on what was going on was to go for a drink at the City Hotel at noon on Saturdays. Dan and I often did. Gathering on the hotel's veranda was a colonial custom well predating Sierra Leone's independence from Britain in 1961. Part of the action in *The Heart of the Matter* (Grahame Green's fictionalized account of his time in Freetown as a British intelligence agent during the war) is set in that hotel. His description of an epic cockroach fight left me glad to drink on the porch, with no desire to go inside the building.

In what could have been a place without much to do, I found plenty. I honed skills that, although not part of the traditional Foreign Service wife's role, added to the American presence in the country. If you used your imagination, small posts offered scope for such things. Larger ones did, too, if you were open to it and there were an officer who would take you up on your ideas. I had put together programs and exhibitions other places. As we were leaving Jakarta, the director of the Bi-National Center advised me to remember I could do so anywhere we were.

It was a useful reminder and I made good use of it. Dan and I moved from post to post with a collection of family pictures going back several generations on both sides. Most of what Sierra Leoneans (and people in other places as well) knew about American life they learned from TV and the movies—think: *Dallas* or westerns. Based on this view of our life, they insisted Americans "don't value families". To combat that idea the United States Information Service (USIS) officer and I put together an exhibit in the USIS library using our pictures to show five generations of American family life—weddings, new babies, children, young adults, family events. That worked well. So another time, the USIS officer contracted with me to help organize an exhibition about the United States for an agricultural fair up-country.

Going to agricultural fairs and haunting the rambling Freetown market, I had seen the wonderful things Sierra Leoneans made for daily use—from baskets and fishnets to beehives and cloth. I itched to know and see more.

There was material for a book. I wanted to write it.

Lisa Larameee, a talented photographer whose husband was there on an international project, had recently arrived. I asked if she might be interested in collaborating on a research project with me with me. She was. We were off.

That project is a story in itself, to tell later, except to say that in the process, it changed how I began to see myself. As the research developed, I had sent a letter about the project to an African art specialist at an American university. I didn't know him, but, based on his publications, I assumed he might be interested. I introduced myself in the letter as a Foreign Service wife living in Sierra Leone and then spelled out what I was doing. This seemed the best way to give myself credibility since Dan's job was the reason I was there.

His response started with a firm admonishment: "Take yourself seriously. You are a writer and a researcher. Don't mention the

Foreign Service. Don't mention that you are a wife. No one will pay attention to that. It doesn't help you." He went on to express both interest and encouragement.

His was a forceful reminder of the evolving world where a woman stood on her own merit, not her husband's position. If I didn't take myself seriously, who else would? Without making reference to my husband and his work, I began introducing myself as a writer and researcher. Occasionally, if it were warranted, I would also say that I was an intercultural communicator and artist.

I owe a great debt to that man I never met. He helped me redefine myself to others, if not myself. The timing was right. Changes were afoot for women, not just in the Foreign Service, but in the wider world. I was hardly alone in pursuing serious endeavors in tandem with being a Foreign Service wife. More and more of us were using our own skills to learn, create, and share. We were fine artists and poets creating new work; anthropologists publishing serious studies; writers authoring numerous guidebooks to cities and countries; doctors working in free clinics; and lawyers finishing degrees and practicing pro bono, British Commonwealth's white wig and all. Indeed, these were only a few of the paths we followed. Many of us would have been driven to do these things under any circumstances. The 1972 Policy on Wives provided us even more fertile ground in which to blossom.

We Hadn't Been There

We transferred home in late June 1976 in time to celebrate the United States' two hundredth birthday on the Fourth of July. The family packed a picnic. We joined thousands on a grassy verge on the Virginia side of the Potomac, sharing food with the strangers sitting around us. Someone's radio broadcast the National Symphony playing the Star Spangled Banner near the Capitol. Everyone stood and sang. As fireworks burst in the air, we "oohed" and "ahhed". On that hillside, we basked in the feeling of connection, of belonging to one nation, of being one people.

By the time our second round of back-to-back overseas tours had ended, the family had lived outside the country for nine years, in three countries, with only three short home leaves. Our oldest child was eleven when we left (he had been not quite three at the beginning of the first tour). This time, the youngest was newly twelve when we returned. The older three had been living in the States at least a year, the eldest one only visiting us for vacations for several years. We were readjusting to being a whole, yet different, family.

Just as the family dynamics had changed, so had the country we had returned to. We moved overseas during the "Summer of Love." In the intervening years, we missed so much: Woodstock; Martin Luther King's assassination; the shooting of Robert Kennedy; Days of Rage; the March on Washington; Kent State; Pentagon Papers; Vietnam Vets Against the War; Watergate's aftermath; *Ms.* magazine; Congressional passage of the Equal Rights Amendment; Title IX; the Saturday Night Massacre; the Paris Peace Accords; *Roe v. Wade*; Nixon's resignation; and who knew what else.

Oh, we knew these events in a distanced, differently experienced real time. Overseas, if something drastic—an assassination or killing, or political outrage—happened at night, we heard in the morning, or later, depending on the time difference where we were and how fast days-late newspapers and magazines traveled.

Other things—a new magazine, a change in education law—slowly seeped into our consciousness, or we weren't aware of them until after we returned home. (Since then, the world has changed. As I write, differences in communication and the electronic media have dramatically altered what, how and when we know things. Everything happens immediately, twenty-four/seven, wherever we are, anywhere in the world. Perhaps it isn't even *real* if it doesn't. Perhaps, or perhaps not, that has modified how we are distanced from events.)

Ultimately, more importantly—what we were *not* a part of, what we missed in that critical, history altering period—was the more personal continual immediacy: The daily impact on a generation of Americans of these events and many others "happening" in their homes via their TVs; on their streets; on their children's college campuses and how they discussed them in conversations around the water cooler or over a cup of coffee. We had no visceral sense of how the national distemper built, how it altered life, and how it didn't alter other, perhaps less obvious, things at all.

When we returned home, we immediately welcomed some of the transformation: Black and women TV newscasters were on local and national air. Washington, DC—finally granted home rule so residents could vote for local offices, more visually integrated—was no longer a sleepy Southern town.

What I felt in the atmosphere for women was just as exciting. There were no more sex-segregated "help wanted" ads in the *Washington Post*. The new advocacy group Wider Opportunities for Women was opening access to employment in occupations often reserved for men. Many of my peers were actively involved in exciting new careers. Women's networking groups were sprouting. Hotly debated, ERA was close to ratification (only to be met with defeat in Virginia the following year). Editors were arguing about how to make language less gendered. "Ms." came into usage.

Other changes were less welcome: Vietnam vets were returning home to be ignored and unappreciated. The war had exacerbated tensions between the generations, in the society and in individual families. The people's trust in government and leaders was splintering.

Reentry shock is never simple. In many ways, it is harder to come back than to adjust to going abroad. That we had returned home before and knew to anticipate the sense of dislocation didn't mitigate the difficulty. We had to relearn America, what it meant to be American, in daily "what's up" life as well as in the existential sense.

We picked up the threads, but not where we left off. For us, in our absence, there were transformational spaces in the American experience that will remain forever blank.

That bicentennial July Fourth on the hillside was a welcome balm during our period of readjustment. America had changed in those nine years.

We hadn't been there.

Curbing the Chicken-Little Virus

Chicken Little was in the woods when an acorn fell on her head. It scared her so much she trembled all over. She shook so hard, half her feathers fell out. "Help! Help!" she cried. "The sky is falling! I must run and tell the king!"

And run to tell the king, Chicken Little did, gathering an equally terrified gaggle trailing wildly in her wake.

When the Ebola epidemic crashed into American consciousness in 2014, you could fit what most of us knew about the disease into the acorn that bonked Chicken Little: It was contagious. Deadly. African.

Maybe some knew that people got it from eating monkeys and bats from the jungle and then spread it through contact with contaminated body fluids. Maybe others knew that, from time to time, it decimated isolated villages in East Africa but otherwise was generally containable.

The initial "bonk" of information was merely that, news of a rapidly spreading, exotic disease in far away countries in Africa many Americans couldn't even find on a map. It received little coverage until August 2, 2014, when the first case of Ebola arrived in the United States in the specter of an infected American doctor, who, wearing white protective gear, was being evacuated from Liberia. After that, too much of what we heard about it echoed Chicken Little:

"Ebola is coming! Ebola is coming!"

Even for those of us who thought we were paying attention, the news that Ebola had jumped across the continent from its usual haunts to three extremely poor West African countries—Sierra Leone, Guinea, and Liberia—came as a jolt. By then it was a raging epidemic.

Because we had lived in Sierra Leone, granted independence nearly forty years earlier, it was one of our family's "countries." News of the epidemic was heartbreaking and personal. Kenema—the location of the isolation hospital in the first news coverage of the epidemic—is five hours down a bumpy, mainly dirt road southeast of the capital, Freetown. The Kenema that appeared on TV looked like the ramshackle place I remember: squat, unpainted tin-roofed buildings; roads muddy from seasonal rains; women in bright wrappers still carrying water from, if not the stand-pipe, then a river further away. In a few weeks the disease had already taken several of the hospital's brave health professionals who'd been caring for the increasing number of Ebola patients.

That isolation hospital was established while we were stationed in Sierra Leone in the 1970s. There had been an outbreak of Lassa fever—an Ebola-related viral hemorrhagic fever that was initially found in the Nigerian town of Lassa not far from Kaduna where we had also lived. Ironically, that Lassa fever outbreak had happened at about our time there. The Centers for Disease Control and Prevention (CDC) had sent a team to study the Sierra Leonean Lassa fever outbreak and, more importantly, to see if they could isolate its virus. Based in Kenema, the CDC scientists drew blood samples, packed them in dry ice, and drove them to Freetown. Flights connecting to the States didn't go daily. The samples needed to be kept cold. So until they could be flown out, they stayed in our second refrigerator. While the disease was concerning, living with live-virus samples in the refrigerator was just one of those things we expected to do.

From the 2014 news reports, it appeared that Sierra Leone's roads were much better than when we had been there, but that there had been little improvement in available medical facilities. When we were there, health care and sanitation were basic at best. Tap water was not potable. Boiling water for drinking and cooking was a daily household chore. It was not easy for local people to come by the fuel that was required for boiling water for long periods of time. Malaria was endemic. So were intestinal parasites. One baby in five died before the age of five, mainly from readily curable diseases like diarrhea and measles.

Freetown's hospitals offered limited services. When a visiting friend required an emergency appendectomy, her excellent London-trained Sierra Leonean surgeon told us to take her home the next morning because, as he said: "You can keep her cleaner than we can in the hospital. She'll be less likely to have post-operative infections at your home than here." Many small towns and villages didn't have hospitals, just simple clinics. Even in cities, people often relied on traditional healers (partly because that was the "medicine" they trusted, partly because hospital clinic hours were limited).

As I followed the TV news reports on the Ebola epidemic, I found myself haunted by people's fearful looks and voices. A man's voice speaking rhythmic Krio still rings in my ears: "I am the last in my family." The pharmacist's assistant at our drugstore in suburban Washington reported: "My folks in Freetown are well. They're petrified and rarely go out. They're afraid to even go to the market, which makes getting food difficult."

When the first stricken evacuee arrived in the States, the tone of reporting here changed. Suddenly Ebola wasn't merely some terrible epidemic ravaging distant countries in Africa. It was *here*. Even when the facts they were reporting about the disease and its transmission were accurate, most newscasters used anxiety-provoking tones and language: "It's here and dangerous. When will it be an epidemic in the United States?" The second case of patient-to-caregiver transmission in Dallas raised the national anxiety level further.

To be clear: Ebola is serious. The exponentially increasing infection rate in Sierra Leone, Liberia, and Guinea were a medical disaster that demanded immediate, focused international action to control. While, ultimately, it was basically contained, it was never totally eradicated. As a nation and as individuals we needed to take it extremely seriously. Its arrival in the United States was worrying, but with wise action, containable.

People only get Ebola from close contact with someone who has active symptoms or things that have been contaminated with the bodily fluids of someone who is actively sick. The incubation period is twenty-one days. Judiciously quarantining people who had traveled in the infected region was sensible. Irrational isolation of those who had been elsewhere on the continent was not. Both happened.

Both then and now I knew that hysterical fear mongering was not the way to contain the epidemic in Africa or stop it from spreading there or here. Yet hysteria was what both the media and, even more, politicians provoked. Conflating Ebola with other world disasters, as many politicians did, kept Americans feeling increasingly off kilter.

In a world where planes fly and people move easily, no one lives in isolation. The world risks pandemics if we do not stay alert to their possibility—to their sudden start in faraway places like Sierra Leone. As I write, the current administration is cutting funding for CDC and the Public Health Service, an act that raises the risk of another "Ebola is coming" moment for which we might not be prepared.

Last time, the Chicken Littles and their ilk squawked way too much. The sky was *not* falling. However, we need to stay alert. The next bonk could be different.

Working Woman

After we returned to the Washington area, I morphed from being a Foreign Service wife abroad into a stay-at-home mom. Eventually, leaving the Foreign Service wife role aside, in a transformation similar to that of many women in the '70s, I became a working woman, fully employed outside of the home.

Writing the phrase "working woman," makes me cringe. It was clear to me then, as it is now, that women have always worked, compensated or not. Traditional homemaking duties are work. Raising children is work—a joy and a privilege, yes, but work, nonetheless. Serious volunteering is work. So is being a Foreign Service wife.

By the time we'd been home for two years, I was more than ready to launch myself into the world of paid employment. We had four children in college or private high school. We needed the money.

Times had changed. Women like me, in our mid-forties with older children and marketable skills, were no longer expected or, in the circles we were a part of in Washington, even assumed to be simply housewives. When people asked, "What are you doing?" they meant what are you doing outside of the home. Opportunities for both government and non-government positions that had been reserved for men had become more accessible.

More than money, I wanted the sense of worth and affirmation that comes with a salary. For all my adult life, I had been expected to volunteer my professional services. I wanted to be paid for what I could do.

As I first adjusted to Stateside living, I easily fell back into my well-established habit of taking on serious, unpaid commitments on top of at-home obligations. In the overseas sense, I was no longer a Foreign Service wife with diplomatic duties. Dan's Stateside job didn't require me to assume that role. I was, however, still linked to the diplomatic world, which is how a unique opportunity found me.

The '72 Policy on Wives, welcome as it was, had unintended consequences. The Association of Foreign Service Women (AAFSW), essentially the wives' organization (although female Foreign Service employees were welcome), had established the Forum on Foreign Service Spouses and Families to study those unforeseen effects.

With the Directive, as the policy was also often called, some Foreign Service wives' expectations shifted, others' did not. Much about the Foreign Service as an organization remained the same. An officer was still responsible for representational activities, even if his wife was not. What did this mean for marriages and families? For the

Department? What were the Service's obligations to families? Who was responsible for maintaining community and support systems in strange and far away places? How would it be done? The differing opinions about all this were intensely held and difficult to reconcile. The Forum had sent the Secretary a report that raised questions and recommended solutions.

While I was in Freetown I corresponded about these issues with a friend who was revamping the Wives Course to make it more useful in the rapidly evolving Foreign Service. When we got back to the States, I got marginally involved with the on-going discussion. Because of Windows on the World, I already knew some of the AAFSW leadership.

At their request, I agreed to edit the AAFSW monthly newsletter for a year, starting in September 1977. As editor I was a member of the Forum. Suddenly, I was the editorial voice in the thick of the discussions about the next steps regarding changes in women's roles in the Foreign Service.

Over the course of the year, two other AAFSW representatives and I met regularly with two successive Director Generals of the Foreign Service. Jointly, we reassessed and rearticulated the Department's policy on the role of family members, as well as delineated the institutional support families needed and how that might best be shaped and implemented.

Based on the Forum's suggestions, that spring the Department established the Family Liaison Office (FLO) in Washington and, at post, Community Liaison Offices (CLOs), staffed by wives (and later husbands) who became State Department employees. Ultimately, these offices offered a range of services: helping to develop and provide information about the post, the country, and its culture; meeting, greeting, and helping new arrivals settle abroad; facilitating employment for the trailing spouse (an increasingly important function); and aiding family members transitioning to the next post or dealing with the shock of returning home. Over time, the Department also negotiated a succession reciprocal bi-lateral work agreements allowing American diplomatic wives to work in that country while the wives of that country's diplomats stationed in the States could work here.

The question of how to deal with representational entertaining, including how much of it was necessary, was not something that the Department could answer satisfactorily. We suggested wives should at least earn social security. (Other countries, such as Japan, paid their diplomatic wives for the work they did.) That, however, would have required legislative action. The idea was dropped. At some posts, ambassadors' wives eventually hired social secretaries (often another wife) to help organize representational functions.

To provide data for these initial discussions, the newsletter undertook a worldwide survey to document the number of hours spouses invested in activities stemming from their mates' connections with a US mission abroad. A small group of us developed the survey instrument. The Department circulated it to every post worldwide. I analyzed the overwhelming response and reported the conclusions.

Unsurprisingly, the results demonstrated a direct correlation between the husband's rank and the un-remunerated hours his spouse devoted on his and the government's behalf. The hours involved were startling—doubly so because we reported them in terms of man-hours and workweeks, in the same way paid work statistics were talked about then.

Being the wife of an ambassador, principal officer, and, to a lesser extent, the heads of sections and of other agencies was more than a full-time job, often involving up to sixty man-hours per workweek of both representational and community-building efforts. (One super-achiever wife of an ambassador reported some eighty-hour workweeks.) The lower the husband's rank, the fewer man-hours their wives invested in representational activities, although many of the wives were heavily involved in community support efforts. If wives were to be truly private persons, new support systems were required.

Several highly visible ambassadorial divorces highlighted a further problem: Wives were not vested in their husband's retirement. These ambassadors' wives, in their late fifties and early sixties, had supported their husbands' careers through long marriages (for the first time, based on the survey results, just how much work that that support involved been clearly documented). When their husbands retired and divorced them, they were left with no employment history, no marketable skills, no health insurance, and, given the acrimony of these particular divorces, no income. The Forum worked with the Department and Congress to change the law so that after ten years of marriage, Foreign Service wives were vested in their husbands' retirement. With their contributions legally recognized, wives were no longer left high and dry.

Foreign Service wives from that time, still coupled or now alone, face another late-life financial problem. Many of us couldn't find employment abroad and even if we did, we didn't earn Social Security there. Depending on when we were employed at home and for how long, for many of us earning enough Social Security quarters to have retirement income of our own has been limited.

Along with editing the newsletter, I wrote a two-part article, "Not for Wives Alone," based on what I had observed overseas and I was learning more broadly about these issues. The article was featured in the *Foreign Service Journal,* the professional magazine for the Service. Its publication allowed the discussion this complex set of issues to reach a wider audience, expanding it to include the Service as a whole.

In that year, major shifts in Foreign Service life solidified. The director general offered effusive thanks to the AAFSW, and those of us, by name, who worked directly with him, for our constructive efforts on behalf of both families and the Service. Being directly involved was, and continues to be, immensely satisfying.

Putting in a voluntary year working on these issues at this level helped me prepare for the next step: employment and a paycheck. I began searching, calling friends, checking the Sunday want ads, sending applications. As is often the case, personal connections got me my first job. In the process of editing the AAFSW newsletter, I had gotten to know the editor of the *Foreign Service Journal* and written several articles for her. She knew that the General Federation of Women's Clubs (GFWC) was looking for a new editor for their monthly national magazine, *Clubwoman,* and recommended me.

The position didn't come with a high salary, but it was a good way to break in. Founded in 1890, GFWC is a federation of over three thousand women's clubs. From an office near Dupont Circle, I worked (by phone) with women across the United States, which provided me a unique opportunity for total immersion in my own country. An editorial assistant and I wrote, designed, and laid out *Clubwoman.* I was not its editorial voice.

About a year after I joined them, the Federation leadership wanted me to write an editorial, in the president's name, that undercut pending Congressional legislation supporting women's work issues. "We didn't have help when we started working. Why do women need it now?" someone on the board asserted in discussing what they wanted the editorial to say. I wrote it. Given my take on women's issues, it was time to look elsewhere for work.

Opportunely, I learned about a great opening. The Asia Society (then a twenty-year-old organization that promoted greater knowledge of Asia in the United States) was opening the Washington Center, their first office outside their New York headquarters. The Center was searching for a program officer to organize lectures and forums on the entire region—Afghanistan to New Zealand, but not China. The Society's China Council, also to be located in the Center, would handle the programming growing out of the recent opening of diplomatic relations with the People's Republic of China.

The position sounded fascinating and up my alley. Never mind that I didn't have the academic qualifications they stipulated—no MA, no PhD in Asian Studies. I applied. My independent projects, connections to the State Department and countries in the region, and, most importantly, my Foreign Service wife time on the ground observing first-hand the history, politics, and culture of parts of the region apparently paid off. I got the job. (By dint of birth, we joked I had actually spent more time in China than the China specialists.)

The Center opened in September 1979 with a staff of five—a small group with an intense mandate. Sharing the office space were two people starting long-range planning for a nationwide festival scheduled for 1985—Aditi—designed to introduce Indian arts and culture to Americans.

Thus, I became a public educator. The Society was well respected both in the United States and Asia. The Washington Center, given its location and audience, would concentrate primarily on foreign affairs and Asia policy. We offered a significant platform for speakers and cache for discussion.

Our audience—government officials (often extremely senior), Hill staffers, academics, journalists, foreign diplomats, business executives, retirees, teachers, and members of various Asian communities—had professional interest in and deep experience of Asia. Because of their knowledge, the follow-up questions and discussion were frequently the most stimulating part of a session. Membership increased as our reputation for solid programming grew.

Every week we hosted three or four sessions, sometimes featuring individual speakers, sometimes panels. Events started at the close of regular office hours, when street parking opened up, and ended with a brief wine-and-cheese reception, which allowed people to network.

The Center staff met weekly to plan programming as far in advance as we could, maintaining balanced coverage of countries, issues, and predictable events. At the same time, I organized quickly when a last-minute opportunity to host a special guest landed on the doorstep: King Sihanouk of Cambodia spoke to a small audience. Ninoy Aquino of the Philippines gave his first speech in the United States at the Center after he had been released from jail and came here in exile.

Our programs provided timely insight on current situations. Coups and crises don't happen in a vacuum. Sudden events required assessment and discussion. Our programs addressed the historical contexts and behind-the-scenes machinations. When President Park

233

Chung-hee was assassinated, we found the specialists to talk about what that meant for Korea and for the United States. After the Russians invaded Afghanistan, we knew just the speaker to help our audience understand those political complexities. As the US president was making plans to visit Asia, we organized a briefing for journalists, with experts who could update them on what they should know before he went.

Among us, we developed a cadre of people with the sources and backup information needed to find speakers, or people who could give us a heads up when a pertinent speaker on a timely topic would be in town.

When the American embassy in Teheran was overrun and its staff taken hostage in November 1979, most Americans knew little about Islam. (Alas they still don't, a different matter.) So, working with the Middle East Institute, the National Committee to Honor the Fourteenth Centennial of Islam, and Johns Hopkins School for Advanced International Studies (SAIS), the Washington Center took the lead in organizing a major conference for a popular audience on modern Islam—a major organizing task to accomplish while continuing the Center's routine two or three programs a week.

The conference would cover the world. More Muslims lived in Asia—think Pakistan, India, China, Malaysia, and Indonesia—than the Middle East. We wanted speakers (women as well as men) from across the Muslim world as well as noted American academics to discuss modernization, education, family, and social change. During six months of intense effort, I contacted potential speakers and wrote my first grant proposal to get travel funds for speakers from abroad. We also put together a package of basic facts about Islam for the conference but which could also be used in schools. Finally, on a perfect June weekend, the kind that usually sends Washingtonians outdoors, over four hundred conference attendees sat riveted for two days learning about Islam in the SAIS auditorium.

A popular book on Islam was much needed. We approached the Syracuse University Press, which decided to publish an edited compilation of the conference papers of our international panel-participants. With two colleagues I helped edit the manuscript, titled, like the conference, *Change and the Muslim World*. A year later, the first book listing my name as a coeditor was published.

Two conversations I had while working on the conference stuck with me. The first one happened early in the planning process. Four of us were discussing potential panelists: the heads of the other two organizations, both distinguished retired ambassadors; a senior woman academic, who was an associate of one of them; and me. Every time one of the others of us suggested a woman academic doing substantive, important work on a topic (say, Muslims in China) as a panelist, one of the ambassadors would comment, "Well, she's good to look at. That helps the panel."

After the third time, I heard myself saying, "Okay, who should we put on the panel for the women to look at?" The other ambassador eyed the one who made the comments and quipped, "What about you?" The offending ambassador reddened. Point taken.

The second conversation provided me a useful insight into Islam. We hoped the wife of the Saudi ambassador might serve on the panel on family issues. A well-educated native of Damascus who dressed in Dior and Givenchy, she was one of the most elegant ladies in Washington. I made an appointment and called on her at her home, staying longer than either of us had anticipated. Being the same age and with children in the same high school grades, we conversed easily. After a while, as the conversation drifted to more personal topics, I inquired how she handled her western approach to independence and dress when she returned to Saudi Arabia, where she wore complete covering and lived a circumscribed life.

The injunction in Islam, she explained, was to be modest. "If I covered myself here in Washington, I would be obvious. That would not be modest. If I dressed this way in Riyadh, I would offend, which is not at all modest. I dress for modesty according to where I am." She was interested in our conference but ultimately declined the invitation to speak. Since then, as I have spent more time in the Muslim world, particularly where women are now covering their heads more than they did when we first lived there, this observation has given me a greater appreciation of why some of them make this decision.

I had been organizing the Washington Center's events full tilt for almost a year when two of the high-ranking women on the Center's advisory board (a Deputy Assistant Secretary of State and a senior academic and leader in the "women in development" movement) pushed the director and the Society to change my title from program associate to associate director. Appropriate titles that reflected women's actual function and status were important, they insisted. Like money, titles provide status and recognition. As associate director, my status would be on par with my male colleagues in other organizations around town, and thus would command more respect for me and for the Society. This would enable me to do my job more effectively. They pushed it. My boss and the Society agreed. I got no raise, but I did have a title that matched my responsibility and visibility.

I'd already experienced why titles matter. Soon after I started at the Society, I'd gone to a forum on Asia at a well-known think tank. While there I made a point of approaching the organization's director and introducing myself as a new colleague. Rather than being equally collegial, he had merely smiled and kissed my hand, as if to say "nice young thing" (never mind I was his age and had as much responsibility).

There was also the Cosmos Club, a prestigious organization, especially in the world of government and foreign affairs. The Asia Society gave the Washington Center's director a membership. Membership was by nomination, open only to men who had distinguished themselves in government and other significant ways. (Pictures of Nobel Prize winners lined an entire wall.) Women could attend events by invitation but entered through the side door, not the front.

A few months after the Center opened, my boss wanted me to set up a small off-the-record dinner and discussion at the Cosmos Club. I did and went—through the side door. Afterward, I commented that if I were the director, I could not become a member of the Cosmos Club because I was a woman. Further, some of the senior women in Washington we might wish to invite to another event should not be expected to enter through the side door. If he wanted to host something there perhaps he should be the one to organize it, not me. Thereafter, while he used the Club for personal lunches, we never hosted a Society event there again. Years later, and after a loud public debate, women were allowed to become members.

Sexism reared its head in other ways. For the most part, people wanting the Center to give them or a visiting dignitary from their country an opportunity to speak came directly to me to plan a program and set the date. However, the all-male representatives from the Korean Embassy *invariably* went first to my boss, who was both male and a senior executive. He always told them that if they wanted to suggest a speaker for the Center they had to come directly to me. They would nod in agreement and come to my office. But the next time they came back, they, again, would go to my boss first—he was both male and senior. When the next director was a woman, things changed: the new, less hidebound Korean embassy representatives came to her.

I'd been at the Asia Society for two years when Dan was due to be reassigned abroad. Suggesting the possibility of promotion, my boss and the Asia Society asked me to stay in Washington. I enjoyed what I was doing and was sorely tempted.

Dan and I faced a dilemma that was becoming increasingly common among Foreign Service families:

He goes to his good transfer, and I stay in my stimulating job: We endure a long-term separation.

He gives up his transfer, and I keep my job: We both stay, perhaps to the detriment of his future.

He takes his transfer, and I give up my job: We both go, to the detriment of my future.

Even though I loved what I was doing, and thought more than twice about staying, I had itchy feet. We both went.

My successor, a talented colleague who had recently joined the Center, went on to become its director. For many years under her leadership, the Washington Center remained the preeminent organization presenting programs for people who followed events in Asia. The quality we established when the Center opened remained. I missed the challenge and the status of that position but had the satisfaction of helping the Center get off to a good start.

Like the old horse and the fire wagon, I answered the clang of the next travel order.

Releasing Assumptions

I only remember bits and pieces. I was five, perhaps six.

However mother showed it, clearly something unusual, something important even, was about to happen. A Jew was coming to dinner.

A Jew? What did I know?

Ours was a protestant missionary family on a college campus in China. Looking back, I can see how in a usually closed missionary community, even though not all of the students or professors who were regularly in and out of the house were Christian, this person was outside the ordinary dinner guest.

In any case, the excitement built over several days. A Jew was coming to dinner. A Jew was coming. A Jew?

The evening came. My sister and I weren't eating with the big people; we had our supper upstairs with Amah. We were to come down and say hello when the guests arrived.

We did. He looked like all the other Chinese I saw every day.

He must have been a descendant of the Chinese Jews who had been there since the seventh century.

Fast forward to the fall of 1976. Gay, barely eighteen, brought Rick home to dinner. Early in her freshman year at a women's junior college in DC, she had met him at a mix-and-mingle the second or third week of school. Hailing from outside Philadelphia, he was a Georgetown grad student working on Capitol Hill. Five years older than Gay, he was bright, ambitious, humorous, and Jewish.

She kept bringing him home.

When we had moved back to the States earlier that summer, I had arrived loaded with arguments about why an eighteen-year-old was too young to move in with a man. (I could imagine that coming.) I had no ammunition against an eighteen-year-old getting married. We didn't have much of a leg to stand on. I'd married young—not *that* young but when I was still in college.

In January, Rick formally asked her father for our daughter's hand. What could we say but yes? The blessing, however, came with a stipulation similar to the one my parents placed: Gay could get married but should continue going to college, a full four years, not just a junior college. Like my parents, we would cover the tuition. Under no circumstances was she to take time out and support him while he got started. He was to see to that. She was to graduate and to do it on time.

I worried she was too young and that their relationship had progressed too fast. I was even more troubled by how much they *didn't* have in common. He'd always lived in Philly. She was a multicultural rolling stone, wistful perhaps for belonging to a single place but without any idea what that meant. Dan and I came from families with similar backgrounds and shared values. Rick's family was close-knit but, nonetheless, quite different from ours. They were second-generation immigrants, business people. Jewish. This was not better or worse, just *different*. It gave me pause.

Our family had lived in and established close, lasting friendships in the Muslim world. We were adopted into a deeply Catholic family in the Philippines. We also had cherished Jewish friends and colleagues. Religion, as such, was not an issue.

In Freetown, one Friday evening, we had invited a devoutly observant Orthodox official visitor to spend the night at our apartment so he could join his colleagues for a dinner at our home and then walk downhill to his hotel the next morning. He accepted. He was travelling across Africa, being careful to never fly on Shabbat and to carry his own kosher meals. Given the limited airline schedules and the off-beat places on his itinerary, the complications of that were staggering.

We made sure he and Dan arrived at our house before sundown. We served salad on glass plates so he could share at least a small portion of our meal. He had refused my candles and wine for Shabbat prayers—his own were kosher. Blessings on him, he took great pains to explain to our children, mainly in their teens, what he was doing and why as he said his prayers.

For all our friendships with people of many faiths, there was so much we didn't yet know about all the differences involved—Judaism, Rick, his family—and needed to understand. As much as we liked Rick and were happy for the couple, we had conflicting feelings about the marriage. (Later, when Dan had a role in Fiddler on the Roof, Tevya's songs about his daughters took on a special meaning.)

Rick laughed heartily when I told him of my first meeting with a Jewish person—the Chinese man from long ago. He hadn't known about the small Jewish community in China that had long since intermarried with the Han Chinese while maintaining their religion. The same story broke the ice with his parents—who were no doubt even un-easier about a Christian daughter-in-law than we were about their son.

I had joined Dan's denomination after he and I married; Episcopalians were within the same larger protestant tradition with Presbyterians or Methodists. We were regular parishioners at our church in Virginia and had found Episcopal or Anglican churches overseas. Gay had been christened and confirmed within that community. I had always assumed our daughter would be married at St. Peter's Church, where we belonged.

Now, sooner than I had anticipated, I'd gotten my first crash course in learning that if you raise your children to be responsible, independent people then you shouldn't be surprised if you have to throw your assumptions for how their lives will be out the window. There is a jolt to it, a gulp—a sense of loss for a day or two, maybe longer. Then you join your daughter in the excitement of planning a wedding. They would wait until after Gay finished junior college— which meant an eighteen-month engagement. Then they would marry that June. She would move to New Jersey and complete college.

Gay made her dress, embellishing it with a bit of lace from her grandmother's wedding gown. Her bouquet would come from her grandmother's rose garden. The wedding and the reception were to be in our garden, not in our church.

Our parish priest and a rabbi would co-officiate. Finding a rabbi who would participate took some effort. It was the late '70s. Interreligious marriages were not always readily accepted. Finally, a close family friend found someone.

The service would incorporate *all* the words of both the traditional Jewish wedding ceremony and the ceremony found in the Book of Common Prayer. Because, as our priest explained to Rick's parents at the rehearsal dinner, "there are words you need to hear at a wedding or it's not a wedding."

"Can we say 'Mozel Tov' at the end?" Rick's mother asked somewhat timidly.

"Of course," the priest roared. "Mozel Tov."

The wedding day was perfect: a Sunday afternoon in late June, leafy green, filled with birdsong. My dad, then past seventy, had spent the morning climbing up long ladders and over railings, putting the finishing touches on a new deck off the back of our house. The reception meal was cooking in our kitchen. Dan walked our daughter out of the porch and to the designated spot. Rick's parents escorted him. Charley sang his last solo as a boy soprano: "Morning Has Broken." (By fall, his voice had dropped.)

They were married under a huppah constructed with a tallit that had belonged to his grandfather, a rabbi. Gay's brothers and Rick's oldest nephew held the poles. The wine glass was on a small Chinese table that had belonged to Gay's Grandmother Sullivan. It was covered with a tablecloth I had made embellished with the Jerusalem cross. Symbols needed to be seen, traditions needed to be kept.

The different services, divided into sections, interlaced with ease. Familiar words were said twice in English—the Book of

Common Prayer, the Jewish liturgy—and then again in Hebrew: "There are words you need to hear." We saw and heard them all.

"Mozel Tov."

Gay and Rick moved first to New Jersey, then to Pennsylvania. Gay was the first of our gang to graduate from college, beating out her brothers, which gave her a particular pleasure. Her in-laws were proud that a woman in their family had a degree, a first for them.

Dan and I went to Singapore and returned three years later. The year after we returned, Gay was pregnant. While she had not yet converted, they had agreed that children would be raised Jewish. Eventually she would convert, because she decided it was right for her, not because she was pushed.

Christian babies are baptized. She knew how that process worked. She only knew vaguely about bris rituals for Jewish baby boys. How would that get organized? She asked her in-laws, who weren't members of a synagogue. Then she raised her concern with me. The thought of two Sullivan women going to synagogues near Philly to inquire how to make a baby Jewish seemed unhinged.

Rick's parents asked around for names and details. If the baby were a boy, they would call a moile to come for a bris on the eighth day after the delivery. For a girl there would be a naming ceremony at the end of the first month.

I had made a lovely dress for Gay's christening, long white dimity, simply tucked with a scalloped hem. Gay asked if her baby could wear it. Gulp. It was for a christening—not something else.

Then I realized whatever the service, we would be giving thanks for a safe delivery and welcoming and blessing the child as much as initiating a new member into a religious community. I got out the dress, washed and pressed it carefully, and gave it to her.

She told her mother-in-law, who did more than gulp. She was vocally uncomfortable with the idea. Gay stuck to her guns. "My mother made this. It wasn't easy for her to let our baby wear this. She gave it to me. We will use it." In case it was a boy, Gay crocheted a quarter-sized blue and white yarmulke.

Samuel Phillip arrived in due course, named after his two paternal great grandfathers, "may they be of blessed memories." He was given the name Samuel in the Jewish tradition of using the first initial of a family member's name. "S" was for Rick's grandfather, who's Hebrew name was Saul. Phillip was Dan's father's name.

I went up to help a few days later and learned the special joy of a grandchild's small head and sweet baby smell snuggled on my neck and shoulder.

On the eighth day, the family, including my mother, Sam's great grandmother, gathered in Gay and Rick's living room. Sam, tiny and still new-baby hamburger pink, was wearing his mother's dress and the little yarmulke Scotch-taped to his head. The moile, son of the chief moile of Philadelphia, drove up in a red Jaguar, and, dripping with turquoise, strode into the living room.

"What a lovely dress the baby's wearing," he said.

"It was his mother's christening dress," I blurted.

"I love tradition," was his reply.

Issue solved; the bris proceeded.

Jewish faith is passed down through the maternal line. Both Gay and Sam formally converted with a ritual bath. As is customary, when Sam was twelve he was bar mitzvahed. By then, his parents were divorced and Gay had reverted to her birth name. At Gay's synagogue the event was the "Sullivan Bar Mitzvah." Gay and I jointly read the prayers that Friday night. In her turn, when Gay was fifty, she was bat mitzvahed with all of us in attendance.

There are many ways to be faithful and many forms of worship. We are a distinctly multi-religious family. In addition to Gay's being Jewish, Dan and I, though not regular church attenders, are Episcopalian. One of Gay's brothers is a Liberal Catholic deacon. The other two are Quakers. As a family, we spent most of their growing-up years in the Muslim world.

We have played with dreidels and lit Hanukkah candles on Christmas Eve and served haroset and matzo with Easter's paschal lamb. Our family sends greetings for Idul Fitri, Devali, and Chinese New Year to friends around the world. We rejoice in their Christmas greetings to us. So it is.

The Gift of a Road

In 1981, after a nearly five-year stay in Washington, Dan's orders came—US refugee coordinator, Singapore and Indonesia. For the first time, we moved with no resident gaggle. The older triumvirate were in college or otherwise on their own. Our youngest was a senior in boarding school. We were still parenting but long distance.

We had lived backwards, in a way, with no independent young adulthood to enjoy being just us: We married as students, and then almost immediately became frenzied parents moving around the world. The Foreign Service shapes a marriage; it brings joy and angst—and its own identity. As a constantly moving, shape-shifting family, we were more dependent on each other than we might have been had we lived in a single place with a continuous wider network. International mobile living can strengthen a basically good marriage—or it can break a less stable one. Most rolling stone couples have times of harmony and of instability. We did.

Although we had thrived as a Foreign Service family, there had been little time left for Dan and me to deepen being *us* as we grew and changed as individuals. We were ready for being *à deux*.

In my final bout of pre-trip shopping, I bought a lovely new set of sheets and a transparent shower curtain. When the extremely young saleswoman suggested I also needed a liner for the curtain "because you can be seen through it if you don't," I inwardly ogled.

We had lots to learn or relearn about adult couple living. It was a delight that we could get up when we pleased on weekends, go out for dinner or stay home as the mood hit, or do things together or separately with only our own schedules and plans to consider.

Dan was assigned to the American embassies in both Singapore and Indonesia. He would be coordinating our government's programs for boat people—who had been fleeing Vietnam en masse since 1979—and Cambodian refugees walking to Thailand to escape the killing fields.

Boat people were winding up on Galang, an island in Indonesia not far south of Singapore where the United Nations High Commission for Refugees and the Indonesian government had established a big refugee camp. Representatives of the United States and other countries worked with the refugees to decide who would be resettled in which countries. Cambodians from camps in Thailand were also brought there for resettlement elsewhere. Singapore had a smaller camp, for refugees in transit to the United States and other places of asylum.

Although Dan was assigned to our embassies in both Singapore and Indonesia, we lived in Singapore. He went to the camp on Galang frequently and spent several days a month in Jakarta.

Dan had gone to Singapore before I did. For the first time—another first—we did not arrive at post together. I agreed to stay at the Asia Society to help my successor and hand over the Washington Center programming. I also got the house ready for tenants, took our middle son to college for his senior year, and ensconced the youngest as a border for his last year in high school.

On the south end of fifty, new sheets and transparent shower curtain in my suitcase, I joined Dan three months later.

Dan had found us a sprawling three-level apartment on the twenty-second floor of a building just off of Orchard Road, a "main drag" for up-to-the-minute, international-goods shopping. Our apartment had a roughly two hundred eighty–degree view of a city peppered with tall cranes (which we came to call Singapore's "national bird") and reverberating jackhammers (the "national anthem"). We had a helper, Ah Lan (a remarkable illiterate woman with a mind like a trap), who came in on weekdays to wash, clean, and do some of the cooking. I did the shopping and "ran" the house.

Throughout our three years, we made time to travel together. We also got involved in community theater, Dan on stage and me behind the scenes. The city had a symphony; Dan sang in their chorus while I was a faithful member of the audience.

Singapore was the perfect place to explore food. Talking about various dishes and the best place to get them was without question the national pastime. Food courts, each with their own specialties, were located all over the island. Saturday mornings often meant a stroll to find a different interesting breakfast.

Even so, no matter how busy we were with life on our own, parenting never stopped. This time it was via letter writing and scheduled phone calls. They called us; it was cheaper to call internationally from the States. Unlike our earlier tours abroad, at least communicating over the phone was doable regularly.

The two younger boys came out for holidays. Since they weren't yet twenty-one, the government still paid for them to travel. We were glad to see them. Then we comfortably sent them on their way when they had to return to school. Having the apartment to ourselves again always felt as good as the hubbub of their arrival. That first June, we went back to the States as the proud parents of Walter, who was graduating from college, and Charley, who was finishing high school.

In Singapore, I had returned to being a Foreign Service wife in a new way: I was no longer a two-fer. The ground rules were different. So was I. Even though Dan belonged to two embassies, he was not on either diplomatic list. We were invited to some embassy and diplomatic functions, but not many, unless there was a refugee connection or it was an informal party for "family," meaning friends and colleagues. We continued our pattern of entertaining because we enjoyed it. I was only loosely connected to the embassy. For the first time, I operated primarily with my own identity.

Before we left Washington, using my Asia Society connections, I had applied for a position as a visiting fellow at Singapore's Institute of Southeast Asian Studies. I had proposed to do research on "modernization" and social change—an amorphous concept, to say the least, one that would take time and luck for me to shape into a viable topic. Since the visiting fellowship involved no money on the Institute's part, only a title and an already existing office space, they accepted me, assuming that because I had worked for the Society I had more academic qualifications than I did. I appreciated the formal status being a Visiting Fellow conveyed and the identity it gave me.

My goal, even before I arrived in the high-rise, rapidly transforming city, was to find a vehicle for studying people, continuity, and change—and that nebulous whatever, modernization. Based on the work I'd done in Sierra Leone, I had a vague idea of how to approach the research. "Mother, how can you write about crafts in Singapore?" Jerry, the budding anthropologist, had asked. We both assumed that making things by hand was no longer pertinent in the growing city. "I'll look for something else to study," I responded.

Singapore—formally, the Republic of Singapore—was not new or strange. We had been in and out the country since 1959; we'd just never lived there. The city-state, a diamond shaped island at the bottom of the Malay Peninsula, a mere degree off the equator, is tiny: thirty-one miles east and west and seventeen miles north to south, at its largest points. A Sumatran prince allegedly established a settlement there centuries ago. After he landed and saw a lion, which he took as a good omen, he called the place Singapura (*Singa*, or lion, *pura*, city). In 1819, Sir Stamford Raffles founded "modern Singapore." It became a trading post and port in the British Straits Settlements. The Japanese (brutally) occupied it, like they did the rest of that part of the world, in 1942. At the end of the war, the British returned. When we were in Kuala Lumpur in 1959, Singapore was granted self-governing status but remained a British Crown Colony. Lee Kwan Yew became the prime minister. The Republic of Singapore—predominantly Chinese, with communities of Malays and Indians—became independent in 1965. By the time we lived there less than twenty years later, Kwan Yew, still the Prime Minister, had transformed it into a modern "world city."

Singapore had been a tropical, British colonial entrepôt of largely low-rise, traditionally Chinese shop-houses (several-story dwellings with the bottom floor open to the street and dedicated to the family businesses) when we had passed through on our way to our first post in Kuala Lumpur in 1959. It had changed little a decade after that when we periodically visited from Jakarta to go shopping or to the hospital. When we moved there in 1981 it was sprouting high-rises like mushrooms after a rain. Singapore had become clean, orderly, organized, and oddly sterile. What was I to research there?

Almost as soon as I walked into our apartment, Dan took me to the balcony, pointed down, and "gave" me Killeney Road—a stretch of tile roofs and the open storefronts of old-fashioned shophouses still rooted in "old Singapore." Our first stroll down Killeney Road revealed a furniture repair shop; a multi-generational family-run hardware store; a noodle factory; and a wonderful traditional coffee shop, Kopi Tiam Killeney Road (*kopi*, the Malay/Hokkien term for coffee; *tiam*, Hokkien/Hakka for shop; and Killeney Road for its location).

The dim space with slowly chunking overhead fans and round, marble-topped tables with café chairs was perfect for stopping for Saturday morning coffee. The proprietor poured the rich, dark liquid back and forth between large brass pitchers and then streamed it with hot milk into big mugs. Served with egg-toast and coconut custard, it was an extremely satisfying breakfast. The coffee shop was also a great place for a cuppa if I were walking past on my own, which I took to doing almost daily. The habitués—older Chinese men, sitting with their mugs, smoking and chatting—slowly began to return my greetings and nod recognition. So did the owners of the various stores. Gradually I was becoming a familiar person, not merely a foreigner bustling past, paying no attention.

As I walked down this road that Dan had located below our balcony, my "something else"—cottage industries, small family businesses that still made things in high-rise Singapore—found me. These businesses were not just on Killeney Road, but tucked all over the otherwise rapidly modernizing city. Others still remained in *kampongs* (a Malay term for the semi-rural villages on the outer fringes of the island). Some families had taken their extremely small making-things business with them into the increasing number of Housing and Development Board (HDB) flats. The government was constructing these mid-rise buildings to replace older traditional dwellings, both as a form of social engineering to mix the ethnic communities and as a form of urban land reform, since the residents owned their own flats. The more I looked, I realized these small making-things family businesses were much less amorphous than I had thought.

The research took form simply enough. After I had been there a short while, someone told the editor of *Silver Kris,* the in-flight magazine for Singapore Airlines, that I was a writer. He invited me to his office for a chat. I explained what I was interested in. It fit with what he was looking for. I left committed to writing a monthly feature: "Made in Singapore."

The assignment gave me an initial format: a short article profiling a single person or family and their traditional making-things business. To the degree I could, I would let them tell their own stories; give them their own voice. The editor also put me in touch with two wonderful young Chinese photographers, Henry Wong and Michael Neo.

The three of us went around town hunting for "making-things-people." We started with the stand-bys, people the Singapore Promotion Board trotted out as symbols of "old" Singapore and "dying trades"—redundant, in their view, in a city rapidly becoming a technological and financial hub.

The articles accumulated. I profiled a barrel maker, a candle maker, a woman who made quilts outside her door in Chinatown, my Killeney Road noodle makers, a little old man who made stools on the five-foot way (Singapore's covered walkways), among others.

I'd been writing articles for about a year when I was asked to give a talk at the National Museum. Choo Campbell, a member of an old Singaporean family who, with her Scots husband, was publisher of Graham Brash, a small local press, heard the talk and invited me out to lunch. "You have the makings of a book. I want to publish it," she said.

The book and the expanded research grew from there. Through the American Chamber of Commerce, I received a small grant to hire University of Singapore anthropology master's degree students to work primarily as translators but also as cultural informants. Four impressive young people, two Chinese speakers, a Malay speaker, and a Tamil speaker, joined our project.

Over the course of a year, Henry, Neo, our young associates, and I went all over the island, ultimately interviewing over a hundred thirty families or individuals who were in the making-things trades.

We interviewed people—mostly Chinese, but also Malay and Indians—working in shop-houses, HDB flats, small industrial parks, and on sidewalks. The more we looked, the more people who fit our criteria there were. As Singaporeans and foreigners heard what we were doing (I was excited about my project and loved to talk about it), they would say: "Do you know about...?"

I was talking with the older generation about their lives and aspirations for themselves and their children. In giving them voice, I had a clear way to see modernization and cultural change extremely personally; indirectly, but through their eyes.

What I found was that these trades were and weren't dying. They came from an earlier time when technologies depended on the hand, the eye, and the person's skill and businesses were family-owned and run with no outsiders. Whether they were dying or not in 1980s Singapore depended on whether they had a market, whether that allowed them to earn a living, whether the next generation was willing to stay in the family's "cottage industry," and whether the parents wanted their young to do something less "dirty"—work in an office.

Many of the older generation had little education or only Chinese language schooling. They were continuing a trade because they knew how, took pride in their ability to do it well—and felt too old to learn more modern skills. Their children, who were in better schools, mostly educated in English (the city-state's common language), and often going on to university, didn't have to be part of the family business.

We were also finding that while Singapore was a modern high-rise city, many traditions of an earlier age were still practiced and thus there was a market for the supporting trades. The Chinese hungry ghosts still walked its streets in late August or early September—or so the offerings left out on the sidewalks ("five-foot way" in local parlance) for them would suggest. Doors of a major hotel had been moved to ensure good *fung shui*; with locally made incense (usually three sticks; uneven numbers were inauspicious) lit daily and left inconspicuously in a small holder near the door. Business there improved. So did the need for incense.

Many of the trades we were finding—all the ritual things made for Chinese funerals, for instance, or the hand-done noodles or Indian flower garlands—were deeply rooted expressions of what made Singaporeans who they were. Mostly, though, within the larger context of a homogenized national identity, these trades reinforced *community* particularity.

The honored departed Chinese required paper houses, cars, and other household goods (even paper computers), and money ("hell notes")—all of which were ceremonially burned to accompany them on their journey. The business of making these expensive, elaborate bamboo-and-paper objects was booming, even though the younger generation buying them for their elders knew little about the rituals.

"They are earning more and want and can afford to honor their parents," one maker reported. "I teach them how."

Heavy wooden caskets were still made in traditional boat-like shapes and closed with six nails. "Which is why my mother never puts six buttons down the front of a dress. Bad luck," a friend explained.

Not everyone was Chinese. For formal occasions, Malay men still wore *songkok*, black velvet hats, which a smiling man from Sumatra made in his Housing and Development Board flat. Malay seamstresses made the special clothing required for the *haj*, the annual Muslim pilgrimage to Mecca. They sold them in Malay markets and Indian stores catering to Muslims.

In the city's "Little India," flower stringers created garlands for Indian household deities while Indian goldsmiths made jewelry for brides' dowries. Spice grinders overwhelmed the air with the smells of sharp red pepper or earthy cumin, both necessary for Indian cooking. Different people made the various *bumbu* (spice) mixtures sold in wet markets for Malay cooking.

With modernization, some trades were failing. Used rubber tires were taking over the business of men who wove bumpers for the sides of boats out of coir (a fiber made of coconut husks). At the same time, business was thriving for the men who sat in a small dark room threading pieces of marinated beef on narrow bamboo sticks for satay shops.

Some businesses evolved. We met a family that made traditional *daching*, a Chinese balance-beam scale—a long blackwood poll that had been hardened so it wouldn't change size. The marks for each kati (Chinese measure of weight equaling about one and a third pounds) were inscribed in lines of dots brass wire embedded into holes made by a hand-thrown drill. The family abandoned that technology when Singapore had changed its standard measurement from *katis* to kilograms. The three brothers and several sons had shifted to manufacturing mechanical-balance scales. They ran their business in the customary family way, as they always had, hiring distant relatives and meeting nightly over dinner to discuss important matters. Their mother, we learned when they invited us to join them one night, was an extremely fine cook.

I kept writing the articles for *Silver Kris,* and sometimes the *Straits Times*, that ultimately became the bulk of the first draft of the book. In the process, I learned to use a computer. I've been linked to one like an umbilical cord ever since: mind to fingers to computer to page. The entire text of the book (as well as feature articles on other subjects I was writing both for Singaporean publications and for the *Far East Economic Review* and the *International Herald Tribune*) was written on an early IBM PC. That meant less, much simpler text-editing and proofreading galleys. Although we weren't aware until it was published, the book was the first in Singapore to be written and edited on a computer.

Despite the fact that we worked with the text in digital form, the layout was not computerized. That part I did in the back room of our apartment the old-fashioned cut-and-paste way, a process that took nearly six months. I was grateful for my earlier experience as a magazine editor and art director—and for the printer who taught me print and layout skills in high school. One of the reasons Choo decided to publish the book was that she knew I could lay it out. More money could go into full four-color printing instead of a layout artist.

Choo decided to title the book *"Can Survive, La" Cottage Industries in High-Rise Singapore.* Each time we asked a tradesman "How's business?" the response was: "Can survive"—they were "making it," whether poorly or extremely well. *La* is a sound marker dropped into Singaporean English, the equivalent of the American "huh" or more recently "like." I settled on the term "cottage industries" because it reflected the interlacing of shop, workplace, family, and home, whether the trade occurred in a shop-house or an HDB flat. By mid-December 1984, the page layout was finished, and I had seen and marked up the first round of the dummy. It was nearly finished.

Simultaneously, not unexpectedly, we received travel orders. At a timing that suited the Department—a most *inconvenient* time for me—we were headed home. We were packing up and closing down a segment of our lives, including my not-quite-completed book. I would review the final set of blue-lines after I got to the States

Publication was scheduled for March. Dan and I made a deal: We would return for the book launch, paying for the tickets ourselves. With mixed feelings, we left friends and colleagues in Singapore and flew home, celebrating our thirtieth wedding anniversary and Christmas with Mother and all our children.

In the hierarchical, up-or-out, "get promoted into the senior Foreign Service or leave the Foreign Service" world, Dan was required to retire on January 1, 1985, after a twenty-nine–year career. Although I knew it was coming, I wasn't ready when it happened.

Respected for his steady judgment, he was the kind of officer the Service needed, but he was not much into playing Department politics. A wife's view, yes. Still.

In those twenty-nine years, I had found my own work-life balance between the demands of his job and the development of my own professional talents (not to mention being a parent) and come into my own. As his adjunct, I may have been the two-fer, but the role sent me to interesting places, where, because I had a roof over my head and food on the table, I was able to feed my own work. I also had the honor to represent my country and my people.

I was not ready to stop being a productive, visible outsider—a happy, life-long rolling stone. I was angry—not at him, but at the Foreign Service. They hadn't seen *his* value, as they should have. *I* felt fired.

Just before Christmas, Dan (and I) walked out of his last post, the American Embassy in Singapore, the same building (which then housed the American Consulate General) that was the first US diplomatic office he had walked into as a Foreign Service officer on for two days briefings on our way to Kuala Lumpur. Our almost thirty years in the Foreign Service was a good run.

That March we returned to Singapore, staying with friends. On the way there, we had stopped in Bangkok. Dan bought me a Burmese ruby ring (my birthstone from one of my home-places) to wear next to my wedding band in honor of our first thirty years and my first book. The day after we arrived in Singapore, Choo called: The books were in her office. I walked back into our friends' apartment, the first copy in my hand, shouting, "There is a book!"— an exclamation I made every few minutes. A new book is not unlike a new baby. It takes longer to gestate but its arrival is met with as much excitement.

"Can Survive, La" was launched in the Palm Court of the Raffles Hotel, one of the grand dames of colonial hotels that dot Southeast Asia. Ghosts of writers like Somerset Maugham who had also launched books there floated around the stairs. The people we had interviewed were our honored guests; each was presented with a copy of the book as a show of thanks. We were as glad to see them as they were to see us. When we had interviewed them, we had not just popped in, asked questions, and left. We had gone back more than once, which like always saying hello to the shopkeepers on Killeney Road, made us people to them.

I can still see the tiny old man who made stools on the sidewalk in Chinatown squatting in one of the hotel's palms, taking it in. Most of our tradespeople had never thought about walking through the door of this hotel. Here they were, stars of the show.

Five years later, Dan and I had the opportunity to go back to Singapore for a month. My goal was to find as many of the people I originally had interviewed as I could to update the book for a second edition. We found perhaps three quarters of them and several we hadn't talked with earlier. The noodle makers were still on Killeney Road. The daughter ran the shop; her father was gone. Kopi Tiam Killeney Road was still there, too, but had been "discovered" in the same way the whole road and its shop-houses had been. Except for the noodle shop, all of them were "tourist-ed" up. As for the small stool maker, we learned he had died the week before we got back to Singapore.

Just before we left in 1984, I had heard about a family of potters who had migrated to Singapore from south China before World War II and ran one of the last traditional dragon kilns on the island. We found them on the return trip. The family had made pots that Singaporean pickle and sauce makers had used for decades. We had featured the condiment makers, along with photographs of their products, in the first edition of *"Can Survive, La."* When I went to talk with the potters and showed them the book, they flipped through its pages, pointing to the pickle and sauce pots, saying, "We made that one…that one…that one too."

Their business was threatened. The kiln was being forced to close because Japanese businessmen wanted to develop the land and the Singaporean government wanted the investment. Though the kiln eventually shut down, our record of it and the family's story, complete with pictures, is in the second edition.

Some of the other businesses had changed with the times. One of the shops that made and sold Chinese funerary paper was now selling carved household gods.

"When did you start carving gods?" I asked. I knew from talking to generations of carvers that carving gods was a hard and slow-learned skill.

"Oh we don't. Family in China makes. Ships here," the shop owner said.

"Household gods in Singapore don't necessarily look the same as ones in China. How do they know how they should look?" I asked.

He whipped out a paper drawing. "Fax."

The *daching* makers were the only business that had completely changed. The youngest son, who had graduated from the National University of Singapore, headed the company, which now manufactured large computerized scales. They had moved from the family shop-house to a factory in an industrial park across town and hired outside-the-family specialists to perform the necessary technical work. Some of their older employees were kept on to repair the balance scales in the old-fashioned way. "They are family. We take care of family," the youngest son explained. The old uncles and elder brothers still had offices (which several of them napped in). They remained part of the company, though they no longer made the decisions. It was not a totally family-run business but had diversified and shifted form: modernization personified.

The second edition of *"Can Survive, La"* added updates showing that small making-things businesses were still alive and well but diminishing. When it was published in 1993, the Singapore Book Publishers Association gave Choo Campbell and her publishing house, Graham Brash, their annual award for the best book on Singapore. Without her belief and persistence, neither edition would have ever happened.

I wonder how many such small making-things businesses we would find now, nearly thirty years later. By the grace of email and Facebook, I am still in touch with Lee Chor Lin, one of the young women who were a vital part of the *"Can Survive, La"* project, and her American husband, Peter. (I had a hand in introducing them, another story altogether.) She went on to head the Singapore History Gallery at the National Museum of Singapore and is now an art historian and museum consultant. In 2017, while I was writing this book, Chor Lin and Peter went into a shop near their house in Singapore to pick up *popiah* skins (extremely thin crepes used to wrap savory fillings) for Chinese New Year. On the wall was a poster the shop-owners had made of a page in *"Can Survive, La"* showing their earlier shop, one of the owners, and *popiah* being made. Peter posted a picture of it on Facebook and tagged me: evidence that at least one of our making-things families still plies their trade.

Other than the *popiah* maker, there might be a few such trade-oriented cottage industries I suspect, but not many. Perhaps some new small "home" industries have emerged with changed technologies, employing computer- and cyber-based skills, like web design, instead of an earlier generations making-things businesses.

Maybe we will know the answer. In one of those quirks of family, John Donaldson, a kissin' cousin in one of those shaggy dog *southern* ways related to someone related on the Love side of her family to Aunt Ruth, is continuing the search. About the age of our youngest son, he lives and teaches in Singapore, and is beginning a new search for "making-things" businesses there. The world works in odd and wonderful ways.

Soul Food: Fifth Course

Singapore, 1982

If you ask about food, you can talk to anyone in Singapore, even the most monosyllabic Chinese businessman. He might whisk you away to his favorite food stall. Ask about *jiaozi* and more often than not, he has no idea where to find them. Most Singaporeans are from rice-growing South China, not the wheat-growing North, where *jiaozi* are commonplace.

Eleven years ago—when we were visiting from Jakarta—there was a shop-house restaurant in old Chinatown. Four of us Round Eyes with Chinese stomachs went there one noon. We kept ordering and ordering, ten dumplings to a plate. The owners and the other patrons stared in disbelief. When we had eaten twelve plates' full, we ordered a thirteenth, which the owner gave us free of charge. We had devoured the day's production.

Dan and I live in Singapore now. Alas, that restaurant is gone. One Saturday, walking down by the river, however, we stumbled on another food stall specializing in *jiaozi*. We've made it a regular Saturday lunch place. The cook is tall with a big, square northern Chinese face. After a few questions, I discover he is from Shandong, not far from Jinan, my hometown. His *jiaozi* are soul food for us all.

Passing I, March 1984

"Winfields," he used to say, "are born with their tongues fastened in the middle and going at both ends." The words of my father, a born storyteller, burbled forth.

Many of his stories and tales about him echo in my head: "Once upon a time, there was a water dwarfy named Nosey who met a dragonfly…" He wrote these fact-based whimsies for his little girls so they could understand freshwater biology.

Then there is the family saga about the Model A: "We were all waiting in the barnyard when Daddy got back with the new Model A—the first car in our part of east Texas," Dad, a kid himself that day, told us time and time again. "They had taught him to drive when he picked it up in Fort Worth. Guess he forgot how to stop it on the way home. He drove into the yard pulling back hard on the wheel and yelling 'whoa Bessie' at the top of his lungs…." Laughter overtook his tongue as he remembered, barely able to get out the rest of the story: "…he drove it into the back of the barn to make it stop."

"Look at this, Margaret. These are ascarid," the always-teaching scientist in him instructed, as he showed me the long, grayish-white intestinal worms. Safely entombed in a glass tube, they were produced a few days earlier by five-year-old me.

Terms like "night soil," which he studied to develop methods of breaking the parasitic cycle that made it such dangerous fertilizer, were dinner conversation—hardly good preparation for "polite" table talk for us children.

"Perhaps you knew my father," I ventured to a new acquaintance as we crossed the Pacific by ship together: "Jerry Winfield."

"Do I know Doc Winfield?" the Colonel bellowed. "Of course, I know the World's Expert in Chinese Shit."

Well after that, his first grandson, also named Jerry, would churn out his own doggerel on the subject with the family's rueful irreverence on such things:

Old Doc Winfield was the world's expert on Chinese shit.
Joe McCarthy wanted to know
How he became privy to a people's inner workings.

Dad laughed at both the story about the Colonel and the doggerel. We didn't tell Mother either of them.

Now the world's expert is unnaturally quiet, the brain tumor devouring his words. He is all Indian-nickel nose and cheekbones, wispy, near-colorless hair, and alive, blue eyes framed by the stark white pillow.

"You going?" he says, as I prepare to leave the hospital room. That many words are still there.

Or another day, he says, "Read," indicating the draft of my book on Singapore, which I had been working on it while I sat with him.

He listens.

"Good," he murmurs. "Just right." His eyes approve. Although neither of us yet knows it, those are to be the last words he is able to say to me—a benediction.

The stubby, freckled hands that never met a tool they didn't want to take home—to Mother's despair, but she didn't understand the imperative to make things, only to repair them—and fingers that loved to move popcorn from bowl to mouth last thing before bed are quieting.

No more organizing the blocks by size so that he and his little girls—now mothers of not-so-little children themselves—could build fanciful cities. No more grabbing a baseball bat, swinging it and running the bases, chewing gum as he goes. I once announced that habitual wad of gum when I said to one of his mother's lady friends, as only a small person does: "My daddy doesn't smoke. He doesn't dip snuff. He CHEWS GUM."

No more guiding the plank through the planer to start a chair. No more drawing intricate, to-scale plans for a table. No more devising bits of metal and mirror into a sunlight filmstrip projector to educate the un-electrified ends of the Third World.

Words lost, his eyes dart and dance and twinkle when number one grandson arrives—the grandson of the objected-to waist-long hair—whose birth made him literally dance when he popped into the hospital room, tongue going at both ends: "It's my first grandson and they named him for me." That grandson has come into the room, locks shorn. "Good," the eyes say in benediction.

Not so when I must leave. The eyes are darkly angry with knowing anguish. With finality. The vision of those eyes flew with me back across the Pacific. The phone call came in July that those eyes were forever closed.

Now, thirty-four years later, I am nine years past the age when he died. Those piercing eyes still sometimes find me in the night. That finality, that loving fierceness, is an ongoing benediction.

Rolling Back

When we first married we had a small bulletin board in the kitchen. There wasn't much on it except an occasional recipe I thought I'd try and, always, a hand-drawn grid of the streets in our immediate Dupont Circle neighborhood. We kept a pushpin stuck at whichever spot we'd left the car parked. We drove infrequently and had to be able to find the car the next time we wanted to take it out. Also on the bulletin board, was a snippet from the paper I'd clipped soon after we married:

> *Now I am mistress of my fate,*
> *If I am tired, the work can wait.*
> *And that's what's so exasperating.*
> *It's waiting.*

Housework was never my thing. Still isn't.

After we had retired and settled in McLean, a cartoon on our bulletin board expressed a different side of domestic life. It showed an aging couple, she waving him out the door, with the tagline: "For better or for worse. Never for lunch." Dan found it somewhere but it gave both of us a good laugh. Neither of us was ready to be at home underfoot of the other in the middle of the day.

With this final move back to the States, Dan and I weren't only dealing with re-entry shock and relearning America, but also starting our new, non-Foreign Service–affiliated, forever-after lives. We were in our fifties—too young to retire—and energetic. We wanted, no needed, to keep working. Partly we needed the money: His retirement income alone wouldn't cover living, parenting, and being active in Washington. I effectively had earned nothing overseas. Finding work seemed critical to adjusting to this new life—particularly, for me, in a climate where people's identities were based on what they did.

I took "never for lunch" seriously. At least one of us needed to get out of the house during the day.

Before we left Singapore, Dan had explored rejoining the State Department as part of a program that re-hired retired Foreign Service officers on a part-time, paid "when actually employed" (WAE) basis. He applied and was accepted. Much of his work involved examining documents requested under the Freedom of Information Act to determine whether they could be released. He also assessed State Department documents for routine declassification. The second summer, a month-long temporary assignment to work on the refugee program took us to Geneva (and thus more of Europe), where he dealt with refugee matters in the US Mission to the United Nations. It was our only "post," albeit temporary, off the equator.

As a WAE, he received a paycheck that more than covered our travelling expenses. He was up and out, keeping current and connected, chewing the fat with colleagues over coffee at the morning break or at lunch in a nearby Korean diner. Ultimately, more than thirty years later and a year after we had moved into the long-term care community that is now home, at eighty-six he permanently re-retired. All told, he spent more than sixty years serving the country.

For me, marrying and having children early had its rewards. By the time I was fifty, I had graduated from the daily, focus-consuming responsibilities that came with that territory. I had a long working-life ahead of me. With Dan out most days I had my own time and space. This made seeking a full-time career easier, and necessary.

Doing what? That wasn't so simple. I had no clear sense of what was next. I didn't—still don't—come with a clear-cut label. Therefore, I was back in the "re-inventing myself" realm, but in a totally different, much more structured environment. I knew one thing: I wasn't going to start all over with an entry-level job.

Want ads for the kinds of upper mid-level positions that interested me, and for which I thought my experience made me well qualified, expected five years of increasingly responsible, continuous employment in the relevant field and often a related academic degree. "Retired Foreign Service Wife" didn't hack it.

I could produce a résumé describing my self-initiated, unremunerated projects, using corporate jargon: *Self-starter with leadership role in upgrading international schools. Designed and implemented major research projects. Significant writing and editing experience: two books and numerous articles.* I also listed the paid positions I had—editor of *Clubwoman*, associate director of the Asia Society Washington Center—giving legitimacy and spice to my "work history."

I could have included the finely honed organizational skills of a Foreign Service wife—event planning, catering, and staff managing—as well as the logistical expertise required to orchestrate nine major international moves for a family of six. None of that was even considered real work.

Filling out the US government applications for civil service positions (there were a number of interesting ones at the Smithsonian) was even more difficult than building a résumé. Those forms required a continuous employment history plus a salary for each position. "Visiting lecturer, University of Indonesia, English Department," was a credible professional position, but the annual salary, $24.76, was not. "Paid at local rate," which I used, didn't serve either.

So it went. With no sequential listing of jobs and most of what I did do a product of self-invention, potential employers apparently did not recognize a developing career pattern. (Why should they have? There wasn't one.) Nor did they see my skills as something that could meet their needs.

By the mid-'80s, Washington was overflowing with well-qualified women. Some had arrived following their spouses there while others had come straight from college and risen through the ranks. Competition was serious.

Then there was age: I was past fifty and had white hair. I came to understand that this, for a woman, was as much if not more of a hurdle as having an unusual résumé that didn't easily translate.

How many résumés with appropriately focused cover letters I mailed out, I couldn't say. Most of them got no response. I got a few calls and one or two interviews, but no immediate offer. I reverted to what I knew best: doing what I could invent.

The old sewing room upstairs became my office. I outfitted it with a desk, computer, three two-drawer file cabinets—one red, one deep blue, and one office gray—book shelves, an old wooden office chair, and a tiny jade plant in the window.

Business cards and stationary completed my transformation. In Washington, having an answer to the question, "What do you do?" and a business card to proffer made one real. That card read "Words"—my business's name. I described myself as a researcher, writer, and editor. As appropriate, I said I was the former associate director of the Asia Society. At parties or meetings I wasn't automatically cut out of the conversation as non-professional women were (maybe still are today). With a professional veneer, I presented myself as self-employed.

The first summer we were home, Aditi opened. The nationwide festival featuring India had been in the early planning stages at the Asia Society when I worked there. The Smithsonian Museum of Natural History hosted the ground-breaking exhibition of remarkable objects paired with people from all parts of India demonstrating their related skills—a benchmark for such exhibitions that I haven't seen duplicated. Simultaneously, the annual Folklife Festival on the National Mall featured a mela (a traditional Indian fair). I volunteered as a docent for the exhibition, working most days and learning about the festival production process along the way.

In 1991, the Indonesian government and the Asia Society jointly organized the Festival of Indonesia. Modeled on the same idea as Aditi, it had major traveling exhibitions and performances, and was a centerpiece at the Folklife Festival. I volunteered as a docent, this time at the Folklife Festival. Again, because I knew many of the organizers, I learned more about such festivals and the issues involved in putting them together.

Meanwhile, I found short-term jobs that paid money: conducting a brief research project for a friend; putting together country reports for an organization; doing the groundwork and producing background papers for a conference; and being a briefer for a group that ran workshops for families of businesspeople going overseas. Later, I had two longer-term positions as communications director on specific projects for companies that contracted with USAID.

My most satisfying projects—the work, ultimately, I am most proud of—weren't remunerative. However, they were rich in meaning and purpose. I found some of these projects; others found me. My, our, earlier life in the Philippines and Indonesia opened those doors. These are the opportunities I still value.

We had been home about a year when a friend's editor son offered me the chance to go to Asia on a trip that a hotel company and a Japanese airline had organized to promote their services. In return, he wanted articles for his publication on doing business in two locations: Japan, totally unknown territory, and Singapore, familiar terrain. My traveling expenses would be covered. I'd get a paycheck at the going rate for each article.

The timing, I realized, was perfect. President Marcos had called an unexpected snap election for February 7, 1986, that coincided with the end of my trip. Cory Aquino, widow of Benigno "Ninoy" Aquino, who had been assassinated as he returned to the Philippines three years earlier, was the challenger. Dan and I had been in Cebu at the beginning of Marcos' martial law dictatorship. I wanted to be in the Philippines at its potential end. Rather than returning to the States from Singapore, the trip's sponsors agreed to let me fly home from Manila. I paid my own way between the two cities.

Close friends in Manila and Cebu (where I wanted to be for the election) offered places to stay. The flight from Singapore to Manila, usually full, was eerily empty. Tensions were high, had been for months. Few political jokes were circulating. (Because Filipinos love political jokes, each time I arrived in Manila I checked on what sort were being told. It was one of my tests about the state of the Philippines.)

Leading citizens and clergy had formed a nationwide watchdog, the National Citizens' Movement for Free Elections (NAMFREL). I talked with the organization's leadership in Manila. I then spent more time with NAMFREL in Cebu, where many of our longtime friends, including senior clergy, were deeply involved in the movement.

The Sunday before the election, the Catholic bishops ordered prayers for a free and fair election to be said at all masses across the country. The clergy wore yellow and white, the Pope's—and also Cory's—colors. Tension mounted further. Fears of violence were real. Election officers weren't sure the ballots would arrive from Manila on time, much less get to polling places safely. Cory, whose battle cry was "Enough is enough," held her next-to-last rally in a field outside Cebu. A small woman, dressed in yellow, she galvanized the enormous crowd.

Then, on February 5, the last night of the campaign, Cory supporters—activists, politicians, community leaders, voters—crammed a square in downtown Cebu. On the stage, local politicians were winding up the crowd.

Suddenly, the lights went out. Pitch black. Deliberate outage? A frisson of fear. Silence.

On the edge of the crowd, a voice began, softly, clearly singing: *Ang bayan kong.* Then another voice joined in, and another, until the air swelled with singing: "Philippines, my country, my homeland..." The song was "Bayang Ko." Its haunting melodies and lyrics had first been sung in defiance of the Spanish nearly a century earlier: "*Ibon mang may laying lumipad kulungin mo at umiiyak?*" (Even the bird is free to fly, cage it and it cries). "*Aking adhika: makita kan sakdal laya* (My aspiration: to see you absolutely free!). Followed by *Ang bayan kong*...over and over for perhaps forty-five minutes. The lights blinked on. The singing ended. Emboldened, geared up to vote, the crowd drifted away.

On election day, February 7, the long lines moved quickly. The ballot was simple, two candidates each for president and vice president. My visiting press ID admitted me to polling places to watch the voting. When the polls closed, I stayed to observe the election officials call out names as they tabulated the results: "Aquino. Aquino. Marcos. Aquino." From all over town, the locked ballot boxes were transported to the provincial capitol, where, the next day, the tallies were to be checked, then sent up to Manila for the Commission on Elections' (COMELEC) nationwide count.

Designated NAMFEL observers reported the precinct-by-precinct results to their headquarters—a big gymnasium—where I joined the large crowds that had gathered. Rumors of trouble were rife. Walky-talkies crackled. Reports circulated that there were difficulties at one polling place. Students rushed to protect voters and ballots. Citizens' groups with motorcycles escorted ballot boxes from rural locations to ensure they weren't snatched or tampered with as they were transported to the capital. They, too, brought rough counts to NAMFREL. One group of cyclists was reported missing—we held our breath, more anxious than ever. Cheers erupted when they finally strutted into the hall. The second day, concern and excitement rose as we waited for provincial and national results. Senator Richard Lugar and other American observers dropped in. Cheers greeted them. We continued waiting.

Cebu was opposition country. By all reports—quick count and provincial tally—Cory handily carried the election there. By the third day, the nationwide NAMFREL count suggested she'd won. COMELEC (the official count) showed Marcos winning. Late in the afternoon of February 9, thirty tabulators from COMELEC-Manila walked out, declaring that the Marcos administration had tampered with the computer results. National uproar, and a constitutional crisis, ensued. The actual results remain unknown.

I had to leave Manila on my pre-booked flight two days later. Something dire was surely going to happen. The air was electric.

On February 22, crowds took to the Manila streets—the People Power Revolution. The military mutinied. Dramatic images were broadcast worldwide. I watched at home in McLean. The American government hustled the Marcoses out of the country into exile in Hawaii. Cory Aquino was sworn in as president.

I wrote an eyewitness report of the election, sharing it widely. Academics and others who followed events in the Philippines professionally encouraged me to go back and continue documenting the reestablishment of democracy as further elections put the new government in place. For an election junkie, the opportunity was too good to pass up. Dan, as always, encouraged me. A small academic grant from the Association of Asian Studies helped finance my work. Honorary academic positions from Johns Hopkins SAIS and San Carlos University in Cebu gave me credibility. Best of all, Marisol Putong and her brother, Joseling Borromeo, invited me to stay in their house on San Jose Street, welcoming me as a member of their family. I am forever grateful.

Three more elections would put the Aquino administration into place: The first election ratified the new constitution. Several months later, in 1987, another election selected a Senate and House. In 1988, all the governors and mayors nationwide were elected. For each of these successive elections, I returned for a month to six weeks, based mostly in Cebu with a few days coming and going in Manila.

Being the former Consul's Wife meant that I was already widely known, had friends, and, through them, connections with others. As I walked around the city dressed in a denim skirt and white blouse, I was often greeted as "Sister," the locals mistaking me for a Catholic nun, who by then were wearing similar clothes rather than habits. I almost blended.

To people who had never been there, the Philippines sounded more dangerous than I found it. When friends in the States asked whether I was afraid to go, I always laughed, saying "I drive on the Beltway," a DC highway that, in my eyes, was more threatening. A few Cebu friends teased loudly that I was actually there with the CIA. They thought that was a good joke. It wasn't. I put a flat stop to that one. The New People's Army and their assassinating "sparrows" were around. I didn't want to be a target.

Each visit, I spoke with a wide range of people, from leading political figures to the ordinary person on the street. (With the help of a couple of San Carlos students, I ran a street survey. When I asked passersby if they would vote, most, glad to do so after a long hiatus, said, "Of course. *It's our right.*") I recorded interviews, kept notes, took pictures, and collected newspaper clippings, election buttons, sample ballots, and even T-shirts. I witnessed the whole range of vote-buying and voter fraud. I even talked with war-lords, whose "men" managed things.

One election night (provincial and city elections, I believe) after the polls were closed and ballots were being tallied in the precinct where I was an observer, every light in the whole school was on. Then, circuits overloaded, the lights blew out. The election officers and observers immediately barred the door with desks so no one could break in and steal the ballots. Safely barricaded, I used my flashlight to illuminate the counting of votes until the lights finally came on again.

When the long-time mayor and old friend *was* defeated, he cried election foul, even though there had been no tampering. If he hadn't done this, he told me, his supporters would have assumed he was dropping out of politics all together. He wasn't planning to run again, but he wanted to stay at the center of the action.

All together, my trips—the last of which I took to cover the election that ensured the smooth transfer of power from Cory to Fidel Ramos—were an education in politics at many levels. Ultimately, I wrote articles for the *Asian Wall Street Journal* and the *Far Eastern Economic Review,* just no book. Before our last move, the raw data went to the University of Michigan for others to use to flesh out their research.

Between trips to cover elections, I parlayed my Asia background into writing articles for various publications, including *The World and I,* a magazine connected to the *Washington Times.* They wanted an article about Indonesian President Suharto and, later, a piece to accompany images of the Philippines taken by photographer Mark Downey.

Simon and Schuster then wanted to use Mark's images for a sixth grade book on the Philippines. They needed a writer. Mark suggested me. We were on. A friend was teaching sixth grade at a school in Washington. Her class became my readers, commenting on each chapter as I wrote it. They asked good questions and were clear if they didn't understand something or wanted to know more. The resulting volume, *The Philippines: Pacific Crossroads*, was their book, too.

The most interesting discussion—not with the students, but with the editor—resulted when I used the word "Austronesian" to describe the people of the Philippines.

"Too long a word for sixth graders," she insisted.

"They've known 'Tyrannosaurus Rex' since they were four. They can learn this one." It stayed. The book went through two editions.

The centennial of both Philippine independence from Spain and the beginning of a complicated relationship with the United States would be 1998. To celebrate those milestones, the Philippine government had begun organizing major events to take place throughout their country. They hoped for parallel events in the United States. The Smithsonian had already decided that the Philippines would be the primary guest country at their annual Folklife Festival on the Mall in Washington, DC, that year.

Any major national festival involves a vision, several years of advance work, many organizations, hundreds of people, funding, and active coordination of multiple entities in two countries. In early 1996, a group of Americans with strong connections to the Philippines, Filipino-American leaders in the DC area, and representatives of the Philippine embassy met to assess the possibilities. They hired me to do a feasibility study and make recommendations. Aditi and the Festival of Indonesia had established a pattern. A Philippine Festival, as we decided to develop it, would be the first set of events in the United States to showcase the Philippines, Filipino-Americans, and the bilateral relationship.

The organizing committee established the Philippine Centennial Foundation as a tax-exempt non-profit to organize the Philippine Festival. The Foundation set up a working board of directors, headed by Washington's Filipino community leader Ramon Paterno, and hired a staff of two. I would be the executive director. Mitzi Pickard, a dynamic Filipino-American activist, would serve as liaison to the Filipino-American community across the United States and run the office. The Philippine Embassy's Minister of Culture, Jocelyn Batoon Garcia (now Philippine ambassador to Norway, Sweden, Denmark, Finland, and Iceland) was our primary government contact and colleague. Two years of what would be exciting, difficult, and ultimately satisfying effort was underway.

My task was to work with museums and cultural institutions in both countries to develop exhibitions and schedule touring performances to take place in the States. I would also raise underwriting funds. This took me around the country to meet with museums with serious interests in Asia, encouraging their curators to develop exhibitions timed for the Festival. We hoped for two or three traveling blockbuster shows as well as local events at museums with good Philippine collections. In developing the Festival, we were working on extremely short lead-time. Most museums schedule major shows well in advance and require funding assurances in tandem with planning.

I also made periodic trips to Manila, with the aim of linking events in the Philippines and the United States. All this required constant collaboration with a multitude of people and organizations on both sides of the "pond." I started the project when communications had to be letters sent by fax. By the second year, some of it could be by rudimentary email.

Fund-raising involved pitching the Festival to corporate leaders and cultural affairs–funding organizations. We needed roughly a million dollars but more would be good. Fund-raising is never easy, even when you have a good project and are excited about it. The Asian financial crisis of 1997 struck at exactly the wrong time. Several American corporations that might have given us large grants backed out. This crimped our style, but not too much.

Mitzi was tireless. In a monumental undertaking, she encouraged and coordinated what would become more than a thousand events and programs that Filipino-Americans (Fil-Ams) would organize to celebrate their presence in the United States. Mitzi organized and managed the Fil-Am day on the Mall as part of the Folklife Festival. She also developed the Festival's national calendar, merging the Fil-Am events with the national exhibitions and touring arts performances.

Two aspects of working in both countries were central to how the Festival evolved. Many American museums had fine collections of Asian art and cultural artifacts. Most of them were from North Asia—China, Japan, and Korea—and South Asia, mainly what is now India. Museums had less from mainland Southeast Asia and Indonesia, which was still considered Asia.

The Philippines, however, was different. Because of the historical linkage between the Philippines and the United States, many museums had major collections of material. But the curators weren't sure how to classify what they had.

Given perceived commonalities with the Pacific Islands, was the Philippines part of Pacific Islander groups or was it actually Asia?

The curators' dilemma was compounded because their collections also included Christian religious art from Philippine churches. They viewed this iconic art as "derivative" of Catholic Spain, so, in many of their views, it wasn't actually Asian either, even though it was deeply embedded in hundreds of years of Philippine culture. Additionally, many of the artisans who made religious icons were Chinese who had migrated to the Philippines, while others were Filipino; both had made their work artistically their own.

The other aspect of this issue was that the objects were more easily labeled "crafts" and "anthropological artifacts" than art in the vaunted, art-for-art sense. I had many interesting discussions trying to overcome these hurdles; sometimes successfully, sometimes not. Those basic questions had little to do with the Philippines or Philippine culture and art. Rather, they hinged on American views of what defined both art and artist, and on what kinds of art and whose art mattered.

The Festival, particularly at the Folklife Festival, intended to feature artisans and performers representing the whole range of traditional and modern Philippine culture. As Filipinos and Fil-Ams heard this, there were vigorous discussions—often outspoken objections—regarding how Filipinos wanted to present themselves: Should they portray themselves solely as lowland mestizos, and therefore as "sophisticated and modern"? Or should they also include tribal cultural groups, mostly from the highlands, which many lowland Filipinos viewed as neither sophisticated nor modern?

These tensions well predated the Festival. They went back to "colonial mentalities," to quote various scholars. They also reflected deeply felt fallout from the 1904 St. Louis World Fair. Filipinos had been brought there to be exhibited, zoo-like, in ways later generations legitimately viewed as demeaning and that generated heated, ongoing, extremely valid discussions about race and imperialism.

The Smithsonian and the Philippine Cultural Center had already done several years of research to determine how best to present the many cultures of the Philippines. Even so, I found myself needing to articulate to both Fil-Ams and parts of the Philippine government the rationale behind the Smithsonian and the Philippine Cultural Center's decision that the Festival would present the range of cultural communities, tribal and mestizo alike. All told, the intention was to present the richness and variety of cultures and peoples that constitute the modern Philippines.

The Festival took shape. In April 1998, Philippine President Fidel Ramos opened the year of nationwide events at a reception at the Smithsonian. President Clinton endorsed it with a proclamation.

Individual museums, like the Field Museum of Natural History in Chicago, featured outstanding exhibitions, using their own collections.

Two blockbuster exhibitions with elegant catalogs moved from major museum to major museum around the country. One, *From the Rainbow's Varied Hue*, organized by the Fowler Museum at UCLA, featured traditional weaving from Mindanao. The other, *At Home and Abroad*, opened at the Asian Art Museum in San Francisco and traveled to other museums in the States, finally closing in Manila. Showing the work of twenty contemporary Philippine artists, the exhibit introduced Filipino modern art to Americans.

Although it didn't travel, *Sheer Realities: Power and Clothing in the 19th Century Philippines*, a collaboration of the Asia Society Gallery in New York and the Metropolitan Museum in Manila, came the closest to addressing the longstanding questions of how Filipinos presented themselves and why. Curator Marian Pastor Roces showed in her displays that the nineteenth-century emergent bourgeoisie used fine clothing, particularly piña (pineapple fiber made into elegantly embroidered dresses and men's shirts), to project the class status they were creating. They rejected all signs of the "primitive;" even though traditional tribal arts, which the exhibition also included and which were remarkably designed and crafted, were anything but.

The first national tour of Ballet Philippines in the United States started in the Kennedy Center. Bayanihan, the Philippine national folk dance company, also toured the States. Filipino-American groups across the country had organized everything from cultural dancing to food festivals to a commemoration of the first landing of Filipinos on American soil in 1587—evidencing a vibrant community and cultural pride.

The centerpiece of the Philippine Festival was Pahiyas: A Philippine Harvest, at the Smithsonian Folklife Festival on the National Mall. During the last week of June and the first week of July 1998, over a million Americans engaged with a hundred artisans and musicians from across the Philippines. And for one amazing day, seven Filipino-American organizations, comprising several hundred people from around the country, performed for huge audiences, setting the place rocking. On July 4, our Independence Day and Philippine-American Friendship Day, fireworks went off behind the Washington Monument, illuminating a bamboo structure shaped like a Philippine chapel that was the heart of Pahiyas.

All told, the Philippine Festival and its multitude of events showing the full range of Philippine and Filipino American culture, and our shared history made everyone proud.

I am not sure what I envisioned when we moved back to the States. Thirty years, no half a century, as a rolling stone doesn't make one easily sedentary. Through good fortune and the luck of friends and colleagues, opportunities to work internationally continued to find me. My, our, earlier mobile life—and what I learned from it—became the vehicle for continuing to do what I loved in creative and constructive ways. I hope my efforts also helped Americans learn more about the wider world into which we are irrevocably knit. I couldn't ask for more.

My First Op-ed

Washington Post, *August 21, 1985*

"How Do I Stop Them Coming?"

Margaret Winfield Sullivan

"What do you call people who use the natural method of family planning?" goes the old bromide.
"Parents."
That bad joke flashed through my mind the other day. In a major policy shift, the Agency for International Development (AID) announced that, effective immediately, it would also fund groups that promote only "natural" family planning (a combination of watching a woman's bodily signals and abstinence) in underdeveloped countries.

The change undercuts the agency's longstanding policy of "informed consent" requiring family planning providers that receive US government funds to offer a range of choices. AID [still] continues to support other programs that make chemical and barrier contraceptive methods—not abortion—available. The move was an administration response to high-level lobbying by "pro-life" groups that claim they cannot "in conscience" meet the informed-consent policy.

My next thought was of a Malaysian Chinese woman I met over twenty-five years ago. She was—as I was—vastly pregnant. She had come to a shed-like free baby clinic in a village outside Kuala Lumpur where I volunteered as a clerk. She had a snively toddler on her hip; two others, not much older, clung to her pants-legs. Her hair was lank. Her skin stretched almost to snapping across her cheekbones. She looked twice my age but, to my surprise, was only two years older: twenty-six. It was her ninth pregnancy. It was my third: a contraceptive failure, thus a surprise, more of timing than ultimate intention.

"How do I stop them coming?" she pleaded, pointing to the belly. She had nearly died delivering the eighth. Doctors had warned her not to have more. Her husband could not stay away.

There was nothing we were permitted to do other than suggest she go to a government hospital in the city to deliver. Out of deference to some people's consciences, the Malayan government regulations at the time drastically restricted the contraceptive information available and who could dispense it.

She adjusted the child on her hip so that one leg pushed less on her belly, and left. I do not know if she lived or died. Fortunately, if they choose to, her by-now grown children have access to contraceptive alternatives.

I thought, too, of a Filipina doctor friend, a devout Catholic woman of conscience. From a socially prominent family, she abandoned a lucrative practice to start a family-planning clinic in a poor section of Cebu, the Philippine's second city. In spite of the teachings of a church that was central to her life, she felt

269

women desperately needed information, choices, so they could be good, healthy mothers to the children they had.

In the beginning, believing it was right, she would only prescribe after consultation with both husband and wife. If a husband demanded she remove his wife's IUD, she removed it. Slowly, however, as she got to know the women and the conditions of their lives, she developed a deep respect for their judgment about themselves. Eventually, if a woman returned the next day and wanted the IUD back, she reinserted it, no questions asked.

Sixteen years ago when we lived on Java, in Indonesia, one of the world's most densely populated places, we worked out a rough rule of thumb to make the population density comprehensible to our own children: Including volcano tops and rice paddies, each Javanese man, woman, and child had about one-third of a football field in which to live, work, and raise enough food to feed themselves. At the rate of population increase at that time, that area would be about halved to a sixth of a football field by now.

Shortly after that, as my husband and I waited for an airplane in East Indonesia, several enlisted men, realizing I spoke Indonesian, approached me.

"Where do you come from?"

"America."

"Is it true that all Americans use family planning?"

"Many do."

"What method do you use?"

I gulped. I knew the words and answered.

The Indonesian government–sponsored education program providing family-planning options had just begun. Its growing acceptance has extended the time for reaching a sixth of a football field per Javanese.

I tell these stories not to suggest that "natural" methods of family planning should not be taught. They may be right for some people. Preliminary World Health Organization studies show that illiterate women can, if well taught (and their husbands are willing) learn to use "natural" methods. However, they question whether the strict abstinence demanded during about half of each monthly cycle can be maintained over the long haul. Certainly in some places, for strong cultural reasons, it would not be. Nor should people's right to act in conscience be questioned.

It is unconscionable that we Americans, who have relatively easy access to a range of contraceptive choices and who proclaim respect for individual choice, through our government permit a few people to force their "conscience" on others. In so doing, we participate in a bad joke that can make people parents more frequently than they might want or can afford to be.

I wrote this op-ed, my first, about six months after we had returned from Singapore and were living back in the McLean house. My father became one of the leaders in the United States Agency for International Development's international family-planning program.

As a result, family-planning programs were among the subjects I paid attention to as we moved from country to country.

We had arrived at our first post in the days of condoms and diaphragms, before the Pill came into active use. In Malaya, for its citizens, information about the most basic contraception, and who could provide it to whom, was limited.

We lived in Indonesia when their government was inaugurating a massive rollout of Keluarga Berencana (which means "family planning.") The phrase was shortened to the spoken "Ka Beh" (KB, the abbreviation), which is also the Javanese word for "all" or "every." The double meaning probably wasn't deliberate since the full name is a literal translation of the English. Even so, the short form must have resonated with the Javanese, who delighted in that sort of word play and, as inhabitants of the most densely populated area of the country, were a primary target of the program.

In many Asian countries, it was assumed that a couple would have a child within the first year of marriage. Likewise, one of the first questions American women were asked was "how many…?" If a young married woman answered that she didn't have children, the promptly asked next question was "Why?" Questions about who was at fault for her childlessness followed. In different cultures, different questions get asked.

KB was focused not on preventing children, but on spacing them and who best delivered that message. Preliminary studies that the program had done demonstrated that the best spokesperson in a village was an older woman, often the midwife, who had children. At one place we went, that person was the governor's wife, mother of fourteen.

We moved on to the Philippines during a time when President Marcos—concerned about the rapidly growing population overwhelming economic growth—promoted family planning, while the Catholic Church fought against it. My doctor acquaintance was a part of Marcos' effort. So, too, was Dr. Juan Flavier, later the Minister of Health. He preached that using precise, culturally correct words was critical to a successful program: When he was introducing an IUD in one province in Luzon, he called it *kawat* (wire), and the program was a great success. In the next province, his workers also introduced the IUD as kawat, but there it was a disaster. In that provincial dialect kawat meant *barbed* wire. Language matters.

We returned to the States at the end of December 1984, after Ronald Reagan's administration had enacted the Mexico City Policy (which some human rights organizations also referred to as the global gag rule). The policy blocked federal funding for non-governmental organizations worldwide that provided abortion counseling or referrals, advocated for decriminalization of abortion, or expanded abortion services. In so doing it also made it much more difficult to fund informed-consent family-planning programs that were focused on sex education and contraception.

In August 1985, the administration complicated things further by authorizing funding for programs that *only* gave information about the rhythm or natural method and didn't also provide education about contraceptives. When *that* decision was announced, I was outraged (both about the impact of the program, and on behalf of my by-then late-father's efforts). I also realized I had lived experience, stories to tell—and a point to make. (A point I keep returning to.)

My fingers hit my computer and churned out words. I printed my piece, carried it to the *Washington Post* office downtown, and shoved it over the transom. On August 21, 1985, my first op-ed was published. It was the prototype that ultimately led to the "Grandmother" blogs I now post intermittently on the *Huffington Post*.

If there had been space in that first piece, I could have also told the story of a Catholic priest friend in Cebu. When the Cardinal ordered all priests to read a denunciation of family planning at every Mass on a certain Sunday, my priest friend forthrightly informed his parishioners: "I have been informed to tell you that you may not go to the family-planning clinic on Gorodo Avenue." He added the street address and repeated the admonition not to go to the clinic several times. In good Filipino indirection, his parishioners knew where to get the help they needed.

Around this time, I had a conversation with Charley while he, Gay, and I were watching *Gun Smoke* on TV one evening in Cebu. During a break in the show, instead of an ad, a nurse in white with a starched cap appeared on the screen. She held up first a condom, then a diaphragm, and then the Pill, introducing each as important to use in order to "space your family." Charley, age nine, watched the announcement bug-eyed, and then turned to me: "What do you use, Mom?" I gulped. Answered. We went back to watching *Gun Smoke*.

In the years since, the Mexico City Policy has been rescinded and reauthorized by various administrations—Democrats rescinding, Republicans reauthorizing. In light of the current administration's draconian executive orders on the subject, I would add to my op-ed that making contraception information less available will result in more, not fewer, abortions—and more unsafely done. Surely, that is not what people of conscience can possibly want.

My father must have been rolling in his grave over the 1984 Mexico City Policy and the rhythm-method aftermath. When I wrote the op-ed, I used my full name—Margaret Winfield Sullivan—in his honor. I proudly republish the op-ed in this book. I am his daughter.

Venice Lamb Redux

Fourteen years after Venice Lamb and I, both extremely pregnant, "danced" on the altar in St. Mary's Pro-Cathedral in Kuala Lumpur before Walter was born, and ten years after the tree house escapade where, extremely pregnant, I helped four-year-old Walter climb down from his perch, we were assigned to Freetown, Sierra Leone. Nearly twenty years after that, when we moved out of our house in McLean into a condo, we needed to find a home for my collection of carefully crafted items Sierra Leoneans had made from plant fibers—baskets, fishnets, a variety of weaving and dyeing, even a dung-covered beehive. Therein hangs a tale of reconnection.

Sierra Leone provided wonderful fodder for my long-standing interest in beautiful things people make to use in their daily lives. The second year we lived there, less obliged as a two-fer, with the older children at boarding school and Dan willing to oversee Charley's activities more, I was free in a way I had never been before to undertake a major project: I decided to seriously study Sierra Leonean creations and the people involved in making them.

In going to several agricultural fairs up country, I'd seen a range of things that never appeared in the Freetown market, and made contacts to come back and visit the people who made them. Sierra Leonean friends knew other locations that I should visit where products were made, and they opened doors. With these rich resources, lots of interviewing and good pictures, there was the possibility of a book. Lisa Laramee, a photographer with a sharp, insightful eye, was willing to be my partner.

During a four-month period in early 1976, I drove the two of us in the family Peugeot over terrible roads all over the country (the same size as South Carolina). I felt safe enough. It was peaceful then, people were friendly. By doing it, I learned how to drive high-point to high-point on rocky roads. I hit over a dozen chickens as they crossed the road (Lisa and I had a number of rueful jokes about why chickens....). I nearly ploughed into two smoke stunned vultures devouring carrion as our car topped the hill and bore down on them. They missed the windshield as they tried to soar up. Car problems—about that, I knew nothing. We were lucky.

I interviewed. Lisa photographed. How many villages we visited, or how many people we talked with, I can no longer say. Meeting many generous people, we saw, felt, watched, and bought. (Buying was the way one paid for a maker's time and shared knowledge.)

We were recording the skilled work of the artisan's hand and eye: practical implements for daily living made beautiful and beautifully using technologies that predated the industrial revolution. Sierra Leone was full of such things and people. I had stopped calling such items "crafts," although I recognized the doers as craftspeople—a term people take seriously. Say "crafts," however, and far too many people think of something done for the pleasure of it, or to keep idle hands busy, like Great Aunt Lucinda's crocheted doilies. "Crafts," the word, carries a "not serious" load—the things we were studying did not fit in that mold.

Each place we visited, we called on the local chief to request permission to talk with his people before we started interviewing and taking pictures. We also presented the appropriate gifts: twelve kola nuts and a box of sugar. Culturally, this was how it should be done. We were demonstrating that even though we were outsiders we knew the proper way of showing respect and deference.

Because I was visibly an American, driving a car with diplomatic plates, there was a secondary reason. With rumors of increasing American aid floating around, I needed to make it clear that Lisa and I were not there in any official capacity (read: no aid would follow). Our purpose was quite the opposite: We wanted them to help us so we could learn from them.

In a rural district where most people were Temne, we planned to talk with basket makers. We stopped first at the district chief's village several miles from where they lived and worked. The chiefs and elders in their regalia assembled to greet us in their official pavilion. Lisa and I had been seated at one end. The Paramount Chief and his Talking Chief took their places at the other. The elders sat on both sides in long lines perpendicular to us.

Speaking to the Talking Chief, I introduced us and extended greetings. An assistant chief, sitting off to the side, translated my English remarks to the Talking Chief into Krio—the lingua franca, derived from a combination of old English and various West African languages, but based on Yoruba (a Nigerian language) construction. The Talking Chief in turn repeated my remarks (or so I assumed) in Temne to the Paramount Chief, a small, elderly, wrinkly-faced man with great bearing.

We presented our gifts, which were passed among the elders who murmured surprised approval. Getting down to business, I explained we had come as women hoping to learn from them about the skills of their community, particularly their well-known *suku blai*.

The Paramount Chief must have understood Krio as well as Temne (but perhaps not English). In any case, he responded via the same circuitous route. "I am glad you have come as women. When things need doing and changing, it is the women who do it." He continued: "In this international year of the woman…"—his remarks clear acknowledgement of the power of women—and of the shortwave radio.

The elders gave their blessing for us to visit the people we wanted to see: men who made *suku blai,* coiled baskets, unique to the Temne, that they used to store all sorts of things. (South Carolina's Gullah people—descended from Sierra Leoneans who were captured, enslaved, and brought to the United States—are also well-known for sweet grass baskets made the same way as *suku blai.*)

We spent several hours at the row of shelters along the highway where these basket-coiling men made and sold their wares. They cooperated willingly as we observed, asked questions, took pictures, and bought baskets.

Everywhere we went, the craftspeople were glad to show us what they did and how they did it. Outsiders had rarely asked or shown much interest. Over time, in various places, we were hiked off into the bush to see the sources of raw materials, such as rattan and traditional and commercial dyestuffs for raffia and palm leaf. When we needed a place to stay overnight, villagers welcomed us.

We spent a weekend in a relatively large village, going there to experience its rhythms and absorb its sounds. We helped women plunge pounding sticks into wooden mortars to husk rice; followed some men beyond the village to tap the palm wine; listened as children bounded down a hill to carry back water; visited the fields the men were clearing; breathed the evening whiff of cooking fires.

While we were there, a young woman's time came for birthing her first child. The old women gathered, sweeping us up with them while they shooed away the men. In the simple clinic, the mother-to-be was seated on the table, her legs spraddled. Her mother stood close behind her, providing a backrest. The rest of us circled around in support. The midwife gently eased out the wet black-capped head as the baby's still slippery body slithered into the world. A girl. Crying lustily. We all clapped. The old women sang in welcome.

In a country where most agriculture was slash-and burn, men's and women's farming tasks were distinct. Men did the rough labor of clearing the bush and hoeing the soil. Women planted the seed—mainly rice that grew in dry fields, but also a mix of corn, beans, and cotton—and tended the fields. Women owned the crops, including the cotton, which they spun (often, but not always, with a drop spindle, which they used while they walked). For the most part, men were the weavers (a specialized skill for which they were paid). Women owned the cloth, which was their wealth.

Near a different small village in Mende country, we sat a while with old women making fishnets. For several days, they had retted the long straight branches of a bush (a plant in the same family as the hibiscus) in a local stream, which allowed the cambium layer to soften into long fibers. Once the fibers were loosened, the women rubbed them on their thighs, twisting them into a strong, rot-resistant string. In an intricate macramé stitch, woven on a continuous frame of narrow bamboo strips, they knotted the string into fishing nets. The women used the nets, tied on a hooped stick, to catch small fish for the family meals.

In a way I had not seen elsewhere, some tools—knives particularly—were different both in shape and the way they used by men and women. Men's knives were normally long and pointed; they cut away from themselves in a thrusting motion. Women used knife blades that were blunter and that had tips that curved scythe-like; they cut toward themselves. In some communities, men (not women) used needles—again pointed tools that were used with a thrusting motion.

Most of the people we talked with weren't full-time craftspeople. Women we met who were highly skilled at making strong rattan baskets for their own use identified themselves as farmers, not basket makers. They sold a few baskets locally, but consciously limited their production. Primarily, they planted and grew the upland rice that fed their families, and then made their baskets in the fallow season.

Foreign buyers for large international chain stores suggested that these women make and sell their baskets in significant numbers. There would have been a good market abroad. (For years, I used mine as a laundry basket.) However, in order for this to work, the women would have had to make enough money off the sale of baskets so they could buy, rather than raise, rice. They didn't have time to make baskets in quantity and also farm. Given the desire of foreign importers to buy low (a penny market) and sell high (a dollar one), this wasn't possible. Additionally, increased production would have depleted the supplies of rattan. In a year or two, the basket-making resources would have been gone.

The economics of the international "craft" trade has stuck with me and continues to give me pause. The major profit should go to the makers, not the importers. For that to happen, importers should pay the maker fairly, and those of us here must be willing to pay the higher price.

While we learned a little about the export-import business, the focus of our research was not things made for export, but rather things made for local use. Or for pleasure: Little boys made cars and trucks out of palm pith, sticking pieces together with "pins" carved out of the harder palm exterior. Their wheels were made from old rubber flip-flops. The one I bought was painted green and had a bench in it.

On one of our longer, more off-the-main-road trips, Lisa and I stayed in a village where men emptied the contents of large, dry calabash (huge round gourds) so that they could be used as containers for palm wine. They slung the cured gourds on their shoulders in woven string carriers (similar to a fishnet), which they also made. Elsewhere, we saw other men fashion small leather amulets that contained Islamic verses, to be worn around the neck for protection. Near the Guinea border, men made beehives—long, woven split-cane containers that were sealed with dung, leaving a small hole at one end, and then wrapped in grass and hung in trees.

Local fabric, both woven and dyed, was everywhere and wonderful. The word *gara*, literally "herb-died indigo," was also the generic term for both tie dyed and resist-dyed cloth, no matter whether herbal or chemical dyes were used. Brightly colored fabric—usually cotton damask sold in pieces somewhere between two and two-and-half yards long, used for wrappers (tied rather than sewn skirts), tops, and head ties—filled the markets. Commercial dyes—bright, clear colors—had been introduced fairly recently. To see the people who worked with these dyes for near mass-production, we went to small home "factories" and asked if we could to come in. Men usually sewed or tied in the patterns, pulling them tight to act as a resist. After the women dyed the cloth and the stitches were removed the pattern showed white.

In addition to commercial dyeing, we also wanted to see traditional indigo dyeing, the purview of women. The friend who took us to see a traditional dyer apologized: In order to see that dyeing process—to go near the pot behind the screen in the dyer's back yard—we would have to pay her. Not much, ten pence, if I remember, more symbolic that serious money. *Gara*, traditional indigo dying that uses leaves and a ground-up stone mordant, was a closely guarded, transactional skill. If we observed without paying, it was believed we might steal the dyer's skill or spoil the dye pot. She used not only indigo, but also kola nuts, another traditional dyestuff. The nuts produced a rich brown dye, which, when combined with the indigo, made a dull dark green. Having paid, I could return to watch her when I wanted and buy some of her work, and I did. I turned some of the gorgeous pieces with designs either etched in a paste resist or tied in and then dyed that I bought into clothes and saved the others.

Over time, we learned through observation and instruction which skills were ordinary and known by nearly everyone in a community (broom making or some baskets); which were specialized and secret, known by only by some (dyeing indigo, for instance) and which were not only secret but connected with magic power and men's and women's secret societies (certain dying for ritual clothing as an example).

These societies wielded both political and religious authority but, deeply secret, were realm of unspoken power and magic—not a sphere, as foreign outsiders, we wanted to even suggest we might try to enter. Woodcarvers, for instance made masks and other objects that were surrounded in ritual as they were made. Although we met some interesting carvers casually (one made me a wonderful walking stick) we deliberately did not get involved with the ritual aspects of their work. Similarly, we avoided blacksmiths. Although they made knife blades and the other tools used in the trades we were researching, their power was truly "magic" and dangerous.

On our only non-driving trip, Lisa and I flew to Bonthe, the main town on Sherbro, a swampy island sticking out into the Atlantic near the southern end of Sierra Leone. I no longer remember what specific making-things process we were planning to see. I do remember what we wanted desperately to avoid. In a highly publicized political case, the Paramount Chief, a senior member in the House of Chiefs (the equivalent of the British House of Lords), was on trial for cannibalism.

The national government wanted to try him for malfeasance—cooking the books and misusing the chieftaincy funds. But they couldn't prove the malfeasance, so they were trying him for cannibalism, which they could prove. To be clear: He wasn't being charged with the "people in a pot for dinner" vision of cartoon cannibalism. Many Sierra Leoneans still held that the force of a person resided in their hearts and livers. To gain additional power, those body parts—particularly those from young boys—were eaten. The chief had consumed these organs, apparently for the extra strength to win an election

I wanted to stay as far away from the whole circus as possible. We almost succeeded—until we got to the airport to get onto the small twelve-seater that would take us back to Freetown. The chief was traveling on the same plane. Recognized at the airport, the Wife of the American Official could not avoid being introduced to the Paramount Chief. I shook hands with a cannibal.

While we couldn't help but be on the fringes of such widespread secret aspects of traditional Sierra Leonean society, we did indeed only focus on the great variety of ordinary things made for daily use. Ultimately, it was the universal admiration of Sierra Leoneans have for people with special skill for making even common things well that gave me the title of the book-to-be: *Fine Hands People*.

Over the three months we traveled, Lisa and I documented detailed information about how things were made. Many of her pictures showed processes step-by-step. I also had a two hundred fifty–piece collection of lovely, or at least interesting, objects made in a specific time frame, complete with the names and locations of their makers—rare provenance for such a collection.

When Dan's new travel orders and our imminent departure for the States forced an end to the project, Lisa and I mounted an exhibition in Dan's and my apartment of her photographs and the objects we had bought that went with them. Our Sierra Leonean and diplomatic friends came to see it and appreciated what we had done.

I didn't really begin writing until we got home. I made a quick trip back to Sierra Leone to check a few details and ask one or two of my informants to read some of the material.

About a year after we got back, with a full outline and half the book written, I began sending the draft to potential publishers. Books on Africa were just coming onto the publishing scene. Since I didn't count as an academic, university presses weren't interested. I did go to New York and meet with several editors who were clearly intrigued. One sent me a particularly nice rejection letter: "…so well written and wonderful pictures. Why didn't you write about the whole of Africa?" I shook my head at his ignorance of what such an enormous project would have entailed in terms of travel, time, and money. Our major effort had been possible because we lived in Sierra Leone, had roofs over our head, food on the table, a car, and husbands who paid the bills.

All of Africa? I stopped writing.

Instead, Lisa and I mounted a show at the Africa-America Institute and then at the Botanical Garden, both in New York. Meanwhile, I used some of the baskets and country-cloth blankets around the house and turned the fishnet into a hanging lamp in the living room. We built shelves in the basement to store the rest.

When we were downsizing into a condo nearly twenty-five years ago, I couldn't just throw all my Sierra Leonean things away. I gathered my courage and called the appropriate anthropologist at the Smithsonian Museum of Natural History to see if she might be interested in what I had. Yes, she would like to come look. After she saw the collection, she decided the museum would like to have it as well as the field notes, a copy of my partially finished draft, and a snapshot-sized set of my partner's black-and-white pictures.

"These are perfect," she said. "Your material complements our Venice Lamb collection of Sierra Leonean weaving. She had been living in Ghana but doing research in Sierra Leone. She put her collection together at about the same time you were gathering yours."

Venice Lamb. My mouth dropped. We were in the same place a second time, doing related work, but our paths never crossed. Nor have they since we, young and pregnant, were partners keeping the altar clean at St. Mary's. Our other "children," produced by the curiosity that drove parallel efforts, are housed together at the Smithsonian. Venice's book is on my shelf, next to the empty space where my stillborn companion "child" might have gone.

In a way, we're dancing together again on the altar.

Wearing My Places

For years, I've worn as many as six, and as few as three, silver bracelets on my left arm. I never—well, rarely—take them off. I talk airport security into letting me keep them on, even though they make the metal detectors bleep. I sleep and shower with them on, listen to them clink as my arm moves while I work, watch them turn black when I am not well (or the swimming pool has too many chemicals) and glow silver when I am in good health. Each has a story; together, they chart my migration through time and around the world.

When I turned fifty, we were living in Singapore and went to Bali for my birthday. How old I felt—half a century. Every time we landed in Bali it was as if the world had shed its worries. Everything was relaxed—the air smelled sweet; the warmth softened our bones. Even now, with the extra hubbub of growth and traffic, it still calms us. On that Big 5-0 Day, we stopped in one of the thousands of silver shops. Dan chose a bracelet, the kind that can be squeezed to expand or contract, and put it on my arm—a daily "Happy Birthday."

I am not sure where or when I got the Indian bracelet with Buddhist symbols—*om mane padme hum*—in silver, copper, and brass. I think it was in a small shop in the United States, not India. Reciting the mantra, making the long slow *Ooom*, is peaceful and comforting, as I have learned from occasional forays into yoga. I bought it because it reminded me of India, especially my Woodstock high school. I wear it for that and for the universal thought.

Another bracelet I got forty years ago, when we took a trip to Mali. We had been flying in a cramped, two-propeller plane when it landed at "the end of the earth"—Timbuktu, where we got off to stretch our legs. Several men in flowing robes came up to us showing their wares as we stood beside the airplane. One was wearing a bracelet made of tight twists of heavy, edge-marked silver "cord" that ended with round knobs. We had a short exchange. He placed it on my arm. Over the years, the fine silver wire that was wound into each of the bracelet's twists has broken off with wear. I still carry the end of the earth on my arm.

I also wear a piece of Burma. Shortly before I left Burma to come home to college, the family took a trip—our last, as it happened, as a nuclear family—to the Kachin State in the northern part of country. We saw the men on Inlay Lake who rowed with their legs, and the women whose long necks had grown to accommodate the stacks of silver necklaces they wore. We even escaped, by about five minutes, an ambush of *dacoits*. A couple of years ago, I went to the shop that a friend who imports fabric and jewelry runs periodically in her DC home. She had a silver-braided bracelet made in the Kachin State. I bought it so I could wear another of one of my many home-places.

My favorite is as nearly as old as I am. When we were five, Sheena Scott and I were flower girls in a wedding on the Cheeloo University campus in Jinan. The bride and groom were Canadians, their names forgotten, although there is a picture of them somewhere. Someone made Sheena and me long dresses (maybe from old white sheets) with gathered outer skirts made of mosquito netting. They were dyed a pale, pale pink. We had pink bows in our hair and carried baskets of pink rose petals. Each of us also wore a silver bracelet, gifts from the bride, etched with Chinese good luck symbols and the characters for "double happiness," appropriate for a wedding. The bracelet, too big for me then, was put away so I wouldn't lose it. I have worn it now for pushing sixty years, a symbol of happy marriage and where I come from.

In ways, my bracelets are a roadmap of place, time, and values. Any Möbius strip is a surface with only one side and only one boundary component. With its two ends hitched together, it has what appears to be a twist that for a short distance looks like an edge. Mine is a silver bracelet. On the "edge," St. Francis' prayer flows in an unbroken stream: "Lord make me an instrument of Thy PEACE…"

Passing II, March 1996

The others had already gone: the granddaughter, the great grandson, the much-beloved son-in-law. They had departed with tender kisses and would return early the next morning in case, indeed, she had another day. The double room was overly bright, filled with the chatter of many televisions, the clatter of nighttime bedpans, and bursts of other conversations echoing up and down the corridor.

The essential Mother was long gone, fading as her sight fuzzed and memory lost form. Her hearing stayed acute and, mostly, so did her smile. Whenever I visited, she had known I was coming before I came in the room. She had heard my voice as I nattered with others in the corridor. The Mother-who-had-been we had already lost and mourned, having let go of her—and she of us—in increments.

Mother had been on her retirement community's skilled nursing floor for over a year. A week earlier, the head nurse had taken me aside. "I think it's time to write more explicit orders so we can honor your mother's wishes," she said. Gently, she helped me with the alternatives and the reasons for them. I hand-wrote the specifics that went beyond "no resuscitation," my directives guided by what I knew she had done with and for Daddy. When she could no longer swallow, no food or water in any form, we, and she, wanted only palliative measures: wet swabs as needed, a bit of oxygen, and a light dose of morphine to keep her comfortable. I re-read what I had written and signed my name, sad at the inevitable, satisfied at making her going as she wished.

She was almost translucent, nearly insubstantial, as pale as the pillows she scarcely dented.

We sat, her two eldest daughter-parents, stroking her arms and lightly squeezing her hands. She squeezed back—barely. Her breathing rattled quietly as she licked her dried-out mouth. We wet her lips with a swab. She sucked it tentatively, like a newborn.

At about 8:30 p.m., the night nurse suggested that Mother be moved to a quiet room. She wheeled the bed down the corridor and around the corner into a dimmed, silent, private space. We trailed behind, sat again, one on each side of the bed, murmuring across her.

The single lamp cast a soft glow that spun her hair silver and spilled down her forehead, lighting part of her nose and one cheekbone, leaving the rest of her face and shallow chest in shadow.

We talked quietly, Next Sister and I, of her garden just hinting at spring—a sheltered sunny spot home to a few snowdrops and the first opening crocus.

We spoke of Mother's garden: the white peonies from *her* mother's garden; the lilac that smelled sweet in the spring; the well-house surrounded with hydrangeas; the honey locust covered in lavender wisteria. We spoke of the spring she so carefully cut back her roses to time their blooming for her granddaughter's wedding bouquet—only to have the roses not cooperate and bloom too soon. We had had to scramble to cull the bouquet from friends' gardens the morning of the wedding.

We murmured on, telling the remembrances that are the commonplace glue of long family life. Mother seemed to hear and follow what we were saying.

As the clock inched past midnight, the shadows of the room seemed to slip closer. Her chest rose and fell, rose and …fell…rose…and fell, slowing each time…until…it…stopped.

We continued to sit, still holding her hands, much gnarled from gardening and cooking and feeding and showing love.

Eventually we stood and silently hugged each other. We were hugged in turn by the nurses who had loved her, too. We turned out the light.

Still silent, depleted, I drove Next Sister through the dark Alexandria streets to my apartment. Orphaned, we were both ready for bed. The jarringly bright March sunshine swept into the uncurtained bedroom, waking me to a new day. I—not aunts, or uncles, cousins or sibs, or parents—was the eldest in our line.

Aceh—Painting the Sky

December 26, 2004, began—I assume—as mornings do in Banda Aceh. The day's first call to prayer was the initial note in what became the polyphonic harmonies of many mosques repeating the call. The sky faded to lighter and lighter shades of lavender tinged with pink, backlighting the still inky roof-scape punctuated with palm fronds. The night quiet and pre-dawn birdsong gradually dimmed as people kick-started their scooters. After prayers, coffee shops filled with men gathering to drink the rich, dark brew and talk. Cooking-smoke invaded the scented tropical air. Abruptly, cool dawn turned to full, hot daylight.

At 6:58 a.m., the morning tranquility shattered. The world tilted. A magnitude 9.3 earthquake rocked Aceh for nearly ten minutes. The undersea mega-tilt—centered shallowly in the sea some thirty miles off the city—lifted parts of Sumatra and sunk others as one major tectonic plate slid under the other. Sumatra moved northward several inches. The world skewed marginally on its axis. Time changed by a fraction of a second. The Acehnese were only aware that the earth rolled and rolled, as walls cracked and crumbled and roofs pancaked.

"We ran outside, afraid," one man told me later. "Then, after it stopped and we finally felt safe to go back in the house, we heard the water coming."

The first of three gigantic waves roared ashore. Walls of water rushed in, demolishing buildings and throwing together debris, cars, trees, and people. A barge housing a huge generator buried six houses after it was deposited three kilometers inland.

People ran for their lives, grabbing floating coconut trunks or whatever else they could, desperate to hold onto something. Those who could, scrambled to second and third floors, even roofs, to get above the water. The courtyard around the main mosque farther inland filled with smashed cars and debris.

"We had just built a good, new two story house," an acquaintance recounted. "Seventy of us ran in our house and up the stairs. We all lived. All seventy of us up there for two days and two nights."

"I don't know why I am alive and the others are not. I had no choice," another person wondered. "Allah's will."

The power of the water sucked children from their mothers' grip. Six weeks later, a young mother still reached for her two small ones who were swept away.

After the earthquake fractured buildings, the tsunami scoured two to three kilometers inland along the west coast of the Aceh

Province on the northern end of Sumatra, Indonesia—the epicenter of the disaster—around the tip and a short distance along the Straits of Malacca. Whole communities were swept away, leaving a hundred seventy thousand people dead and half a million displaced (out of a pre-tsunami population of more than four million) in Indonesia alone. Some three thousand schools were destroyed and two thousand five hundred teachers died. About a thousand civil servants, the backbone of the provincial and local governments, were lost.

The power of the earthquake sent the tsunami waves sweeping up into Thailand and across the Indian Ocean to India and Sri Lanka and ultimately to the coast of Africa, leaving devastation in their wake. News of the destruction in Aceh did not get to the rest of the world for several days.

A week or so later, the phone rang in our condo in Alexandria, Virginia: "Margaret, have I got a deal for you."

That "deal," offered by a friend who was the president of the United States–Indonesia Society (USINDO, a bi-national educational organization), started me on a journey of nineteen trips to Aceh over five and a half years. My friend wanted me to do a needs assessment for USINDO. The goal was to find an education project that would serve as their part of the tsunami rehabilitation effort. Once I found the project, I would coordinate the implementation team.

Not knowing what to expect, two months and a day after the tsunami, on Sunday, February 27, 2005, I flew into Banda Aceh, the capital of Nanggroe Aceh Darussalam (the formal name of the province), with two Indonesian colleagues-to-be. They were from the Sampoerna Foundation, an Indonesian educational foundation already running tent-schools there.

The power of those first impressions remains as if they were happening today, becoming more painful as time passes and other disasters occur.

February 27–March 1, 2005

The plane descends over the mountains at an angle that screens the destruction on the edge of the sea. Given the TV images I'd seen of a constant round of helicopters and planes lumbering in with emergency supplies, the airport is unexpectedly quiet: just a large Turkish airplane on the tarmac and several helicopters parked off to the side. The mixed crowd of passengers—backpack-laden relief workers of many ages and nationalities, Indonesian military, local men and women—climbing down the movable stairs and crossing the tarmac in the morning heat, buzzes with purposeful life. A scrum of baggage handlers hustles suitcases as they're hand-loaded off the plane. Cars jockey to retrieve arrivals.

We drive toward town through quintessential Southeast Asia—jagged mountains serving as a backdrop for the rice harvest. Coconut palms stand sentinel. Ordinary daily life persists. Nearer the city, the bustle and dynamism, almost a frontier boom feeling, catches me by surprise. There is heavy traffic: official sedans, older cars, four-wheel drive vehicles, trucks, all labeled with red crosses, UN logos, and other relief organization signs; motorized *becaks* (a traditional three-wheeled conveyance with a driver pulling a passenger seat); motor scooters traveling like schools of fish, many ridden by young women wearing *hijab* (as Indonesians call the scarf head-covering favored by observant Muslim women) under their helmets. Occasional traffic jams clog roundabouts with only sometimes-working traffic lights.

I expected total devastation. In reality only a portion of Banda Aceh was destroyed. The eastern side away from the sea is a low rising slope, above the reach of the tsunami, although not the massive violence of the earthquake. In this section of the city, with little visual evidence of damage or disaster, I feel as if I have been transplanted to any number of provincial towns in 1960s Indonesia or even 1950s Malaya, where Dan and I began our life in this part of Southeast Asia.

A familiar hubbub: milling people, for the most part clean, healthy, and undamaged. Shop-houses with merchandise spilling onto narrow sidewalks, wide streets, open drains, and bumpy roads. Vendors and shoppers crowding temporary, blue-plastic tarp–roofed market stalls selling fruit, vegetables, hanging slabs of meat, and plucked chickens, their feet sticking up in the air. Fish are notably absent. (Achenese won't eat them for at least six months after the tsunami because sea creatures had fed on bodies.)

We pass a large heap of overturned earth the length of a playing field. "What's that?" I ask. My traveling companion, who's been here before, answers: "A mass grave."

Refugee tents cluster on the grounds of a government building. Laundry hangs neatly along its metal fence—a scene that repeats across the city. Further into town we pass the rubble of a shopping mall that collapsed in the earthquake, its cement slab roof intact—fenced off but otherwise untouched.

In the center of the city, we circle around the main mosque, cleared of the tangle of cars and trees the water dumped there. People mill around its courtyard. Beyond it are damaged shop-houses, standing in some cases, partly smashed in others. As we go further, the decimation increases. Satellite disks, tilted at odd angles, cling to some roofs. In one partial room, a man shoves at broken plaster, trying to make a dent in cleaning things up.

"You need to see, but don't dwell on the destruction or you will be overwhelmed"—the sage words of a young Indonesian anthropologist, who had been coming to Aceh frequently since the tsunami, echo in my head. "Remember, you are there to do something constructive. See through those eyes."

Capturing images with the camera eases what is otherwise overwhelming. Later, the lens's images may provide a sense of immediacy that tells the story. For now, it offers safe distance. Even so, I yo-yo among observing in order to give myself a frame of reference within which to plan; exhilaration about having a skill set that, for once, is useful and lets me be part of the action; and anguish, over vastness of the decimation. I am a voyeur of human tragedy.

We leave the broken buildings of the center city, and drive into the lower, flatter part of the town. Gray desolation and rubble continues as far as the eye can see. If I didn't know that this had been a place that people had lived and worked for hundreds of years, it would be easy to believe that the landscape had always been like this. I can't imagine the feelings of people who knew Aceh before, looking at what remains, searching for landmarks.

"You can see the mosque from *there* now," an Acehnese friend comments later back in Washington as he looks at my pictures. "Before, it was totally blocked by buildings." The tsunami obliterated his village. Like almost everyone, he lost forty or so relatives.

"What do I say?" I'd asked him before I left on the trip, knowing I'd be facing others' unspeakable loss. "Don't ask," he advised. "Wait for people to tell you. You will know what to do."

Over time, I understand that the anguish is too huge. To talk about or express it is to feel overwhelmed in a tsunami of loss. I see its depths in tiny ways—a child's picture on a cell phone; a person confiding about a friend's small son: "Seeing him is hard, ours..." Sometimes, there are simple, shared silences, other times, detailed gushes of recapitulation.

Two months after the disaster, the fever of immediate response has cooled. People have barely begun to come to terms with carrying on and beginning to rebuild. Sundays have reverted to a day when offices are closed and heavy road-clearing equipment stands idle. Many people, mostly young, zoom around on motor scooters doing the same thing we are: looking.

What was stinking mud is dry. The bodies of people and animals have been cleared and buried. Time and sunshine have dissipated the stench of the immediate aftermath. A mask I was told I would need stays in my pocket. Roads shown in early news stories as impassably water- and junk-logged are more or less cleared. We can drive out to the annihilated villages by the sea.

Cement footprints of houses map tightly packed communities that used to be. Unidentifiable debris lies where the sea tossed it. Across the bleakness, the domes of mosques—whose pillars and open walls were better able to withstand the water's rampage—dot the view. Here or there a fragment of wall still stands. Some have freshly painted numbers—house numbers, the date of the tsunami, or "Angga, 11 years, Iwan, 7, Ranul, 5" that proclaim what has been.

Handmade signs and flags mark the bleakness. "*Tanah Milik Mazis Sekeluarga*" (land belonging to the Mazis family) states a plywood sign stuck into the edge of the tile floor of what was a house. Many of the brave flags, usually bearing the red-and-white emblem of Indonesia, or the yellows, greens, and blues of political party banners, indicate ownership. Plain red flags stand vigil where bodies remain buried in the debris. Too many flags still flutter forlornly across the wasteland. At a more basic level, the signs and flags signal affirmation: This is what was. This is what is. Some of us remain.

Recognizing that bad roads and jagged debris are a hazard to tires, several young men have found a compressor and opened a rudimentary *bengkel* (car-repair shop). Other people pile up salvaged rebar or crushed cars to sell as scrap metal.

Beside the road parallel to the sea, the suggestion of a mosque, the former center of what had been a *desa* (a small community), shines white in the sunlight. Survivors gather for a *selamatan*, a ceremonial meal of blessing and cleansing, under a billowing OXFAM flag. Men stand over great black cauldrons, dishing *gulay*, a soupy curry, over rice. A few women sit under a tarp tent nearby.

We stop to talk. The *ketua* (headman)—a large, gentle man in a crisp white traditional collarless shirt, with a short white beard and humor in his eyes—invites us to participate in their selamatan. We chat a few minutes, listening quietly as several of the men speak matter-of-factly of losses—wives, children, grandchildren, houses. Hardly knowing what to do, except to say a few respectful sorrys and thank yous, we continue down the road.

We round a bend. An overturned table lies in the ruins of a house, a plastic folder of family snapshots open on one of the legs. We pull forward a bit and park. While I get out to take pictures, a young couple perched on a motor scooter stops closer to the table. The woman picks up the pictures, looks at them carefully, and lovingly puts them down. I hang back. Still, I'm close enough for the young man to turn to me and say, "*Semua hilang.*" All lost. I nod mutely in acknowledgment. They drive off.

At the end of the road, a mosque still stands—remarkable since it is at the headwater. There, a relief organization has built a feeding station and put up tents. To sell soft drinks to passersby, villagers banged together a *warung* (a food stall) from remnants of wood. The operator's blazing, almost-smiling eyes contradict the enormous loss in his voice. "I am the only one left," he says quietly in Indonesian, voicing what I am beginning to recognize as a mantra.

The next morning, a small Army helicopter flies us down the coast to Calang. The gently rippling ocean is nearly boat-less—fishing boats have not yet been rebuilt. Only a few small cargo ships are headed somewhere or other. The formerly busy water will bustle again, just not yet. Returning, we fly over the land. Each direction is a delineated safety zone. Air traffic is heavy. With long sections of the coast road swept into the sea, all relief supplies to the remaining habitations must be helicoptered in. The clear scrub line part way up the hillsides—trees above, bare red earth and rock below—marks the tsunami's reach and power. Below us are occasional clumps of tents, a stretch of still-traversed road, a long slab sliding into the water.

We circle to land. Calang, once a small, humming city, is another map of house-prints, dotted with clusters of tents and one big, still-standing house. The Indonesian Marines manage the area. We report to their tented headquarters to get permission to visit the tent school next to them. "No Photographs" declares a sign by the commander's desk. "So many people (like you, he implies) come to look and take pictures for their own benefit. So no pictures," he insists.

"Without pictures," I ask, "how do I tell the story and raise funds to help?" We negotiate. I am allowed to take a *few* photos. He is right to discourage voyeurism and intrusion. All tragedies deserve that respect.

At the school, the little boys make faces and funny hand signs in front of the camera. "The teacher needs lipstick," the teacher, speaking in the third person, half observes, half asks. I wear none, so I haven't any in my pocket. My apologetic, wish-I-had-some smile has to suffice.

Wherever we go during these three days, we see unfathomable obliteration. Yet the most immediate, basic relief needs—clean, bottled drinking water; food; rudimentary tent shelters—are finally being met. The first steps toward rehabilitation and reconstruction—crisply clean children back in tent schools, the first temporary housing going up—are underway.

I begin to make calls on officers in the provincial Department of Education. The offices are sparsely furnished. Piles of waterlogged debris are shoved in corners. At least part of the staff is on duty. I express my sorrow. Ask about needs. They suggest rebuilding a high school in one town, a primary school elsewhere. These civil servants, certainly themselves shattered by loss and dislocation, are getting on with doing what must be done.

I am not sure what I had expected of Aceh, "Islam's doorway to Indonesia," particularly as a foreign woman. I had always heard that the province, which an ongoing conflict had shut off to outsiders for years, was religiously conservative compared to the rest of the country. Their Sunni strain of Islam is traditional and pervasive. In many ways it is also open and tolerant, in the best sense of those words. (Or so it was then. Perhaps not so much now, from what I hear.) I'm only expected to dress modestly with loose sleeves and pants—no head covering, although I carry one for the times we visit a mosque.

Islam is at the heart of Acehnese identity; the minarets are testimony to that. I am roused before dawn to the comfort of many calls to prayer reverberating from individual mosques. They are familiar, peaceful, and reassuring, as are the similar calls governing the rhythm of life that continue to mark the day and falling night. The young women, their hijabs carefully color-coordinated with their shirts, wear figure-hugging jeans. Later I will see young couples, the women's heads covered, jitterbugging. Such are the seeming contradictions to an outsider.

On the way to the airport to fly home we make a last stop: a cold call at Syiah Kuala University, the then forty-five-year-old major provincial tertiary educational institution. We hope to talk with the Vice Rector.

Yes, he's here. Yes, he has time to talk. "USINDO would like to work with the university as a partner in what we do," I explain to him, laying out several possibilities.

"We can help you with those," he says. "But what we *need* is a model high school." His eyes light up as he lays out his long-standing dream—or in his phrase *cet langit* (literally "painting the sky")—of a school like the American one his daughters attended when he was getting his PhD in Oregon. "We needed a model senior high school years ago, but there were no funds."

The new community senior high school of his dreams would introduce modern teaching methods that encourage asking questions and analytical thinking instead of rote learning. The school would not simply teach but also be connected to the university's department of education, with the aim of helping to change instruction across Aceh, perhaps all of Indonesia. The school motto would be "Everyone can learn."

I write the proposal for such a school when I get back to Washington. USINDO accepts it and contracts with me to be the project coordinator. The groundwork is laid for the Syiah Kuala

University Lab School, a coeducational senior high school (grades ten to twelve) to be developed as a partnership of the university, USINDO, the Sampoerna Foundation, the private sector, and many individuals, American and Indonesian.

My work begins—a rare gift for a seventy-year-old. The vice rector's dream takes form.

December 26, 2017

Thirteen years and nineteen trips later the ache of loss still remained. The city had been rebuilt. In the first year or two after the tragedy, I would equate houses to mushrooms, clusters popping up seemingly overnight. Otherwise impersonal rows of houses showed visible signs of life: bright-colored paint, built-on additions, laundry, chicken coops, and the occasional satellite disk. Some even sported a birdhouse or a homemade whirligig fashioned to look like one of the big aircraft that brought relief. Over time, shops were rebuilt and reopened. The center of town was renewed and updated: Internet cafes, KFC, Pizza Hut, ATMs, and sidewalks stacked with air conditioners, flat screen TVs, and refrigerators. Every other shop dealt in cell phones—lots of cell phones.

Vegetation sprouted. At first, it was the odd young papaya or coconut volunteer that shot up around house-prints in the midst of the yellow-gray mud sea. Then much of the rubble disappeared beneath deep, lush grass—brilliant green stretching away. Young trees began to appear, some of them living fences surrounding houses that were no more. While much of the landscape was still vacant, it was no longer bleak. Within two years, rain sluiced some of the rice paddies clean; areas that were supposedly doomed to be over-salinated for years to come were producing their first crop.

After two years, Aceh had an exponential explosion of cats. Human babies were also suddenly everywhere. Lurching on still-unsteady toddler feet and dressed up like dolls, they were watched with care and joy. Those babies are now young teens, the first of the post-tsunami generation.

Marriages and wedding plans bracketed my trips. The first of many weddings I attended was that of a young couple in their early twenties. They had met over a year earlier at a farewell party for volunteer teachers who staffed the Sampoerna Foundation's tent-school project. It was love at first sight. The ceremony was held in a village mosque at the end of Idul Fitri.

On another trip, a colleague from the Lab School project—what we called the vice rector's model-school—simply *had* to share his plans to get married. Months earlier, he had told me of his losses, whipping out photos of his house, wife, and two daughters. The only one who remained was a thirteen-year-old son, who was still lost, sad and disturbed.

One day, this colleague urgently asked me to meet him at the dentist's office, where he was getting some dental work done before leaving the country for a while. It was the only time we could meet. When I walked into the office, I could see a new, quiet joy in his face, even though it was puffy and unshaven. "I want you to meet the woman who will be my wife," he said, introducing the lovely, middle-aged, shiny-eyed lady who accompanied him. "She has one son. My wife knew her before and so did I. She was my neighbor. I took my son to see her; he said yes. I want to save her and her son as tsunami survivors. She can save me and my son as survivors, too." The wedding was a year later. Love—and hope—was still alive.

From the beginning, the Lab School belonged to the university and the dreamers there who envisioned it. The university provided the land—no small investment, given that clearly titled land was difficult to come by. We were a small team of facilitators who worked with the university on behalf of the major partners. Pak Ramang Basuki, the Sampoerna Foundation's man on the ground in Aceh, became my resident contact with the university team responsible for the school. Without his steady presence as a calming bridge and go-between, the project would not have gone as smoothly as it did. Tricia Iskandar, USINDO's Jakarta representative, and numerous staffers from the Sampoerna Foundation were also the day-by-day back-stoppers. When Pak Jalal, from the university's engineering department and the vice rector's day-to-day contact with the project, died after the school opened, a hole was opened in our collective heart that remains still.

Working mainly from Washington, thanks to email, I coordinated activities and raised funds, ultimately three million dollars in cash and kind. I commuted to Aceh, making nineteen trips (most of them for four or five weeks) in five years. Unlike many other development projects in Aceh, one of our advantages was that we were a team—university and others alike—for the entire time. We knew each other and shared a vision for what we hoped to achieve.

Before the school plans were drawn, we discussed the ways space impacts learning. Based on this discussion, we decided that the classrooms were to be large, light, and airy. Instead of the traditional locked-up textbook storage rooms, there would be a functional library that would allow students to actually use and take out books. This would encourage reading and independent research. In addition, there would be Internet connectivity throughout the school. We wanted a computer/language lab, science labs, and, at the

293

neighborhood leaders' request, a community center that could be used for adult education after hours. Above all, the buildings had to be earthquake safe—two-storied with multiple exits—so the school could be a neighborhood safe haven should there be another tsunami.

We, especially I, particularly wanted to replace traditional classrooms' small windows, which were placed above students seated height, with large, low windows. It was a big point of contention both with the provincial department of education and with some of the more traditional education professors. They had arguments like "the students will fall out," "they will fight and break them," and—the real truth—"if they can see out they won't pay attention to the teacher."

To which we responded, "In that case, we will just have to have better teachers."

The design team from the university's engineering department translated our ideas into working designs and ultimately into a cluster of lovely buildings that are an elegant simplification of Acehnese traditional architecture. And, yes, lots of low, large windows.

The school opened in July 2007. The one hundred eight first-year students (tenth graders, in American terms) were mainly from the area around the university, a neighborhood that had been particularly devastated by the tsunami. (They had attended some of the poorest middle schools in Banda Aceh.) The day the school opened, they, as respectful young Achenese, touched their foreheads to welcoming hands extended by the principal, the vice principal, each teacher, and me.

Opening the school's doors was the first step of the next phase: running a successful school. The primary responsibility for this endeavor belonged to school community: parents, teachers, the school staff, and the *yayasan* (foundation). The yayasan was formed to legally own the school and manage the school and its finances, thus separating it formally from the university and its budget. Yet, with the university vice rector as its chair, the yayasan was linked to both the school and the university. Complicated and frustrating as it can be, constructing a building is easier than creating and nurturing a successful school. The process had begun.

Instead of following the traditional pattern of students sitting in one room while different teachers come in to teach their subjects, the students moved from classroom to classroom, each room dedicated to a particular subject. Both teachers and students preferred the new "moving class" arrangement. Instead of the pattern followed in most Indonesian schools—memorizing what the book and teacher said—the students slowly learned to ask questions and look for answers. Shifting those deeply ingrained gears wasn't easy. After a long interactive session, one student asked his teacher: "Why can't you just tell us and we'll listen?"

Over the next two years, the school reached a full complement of three hundred students in three grades. In late June 2010, the first class graduated—within a week of our youngest granddaughter's graduation, half a world away. I attended both.

The members of that first class were no longer the kids who had entered. Rather, their heads crowned with mortarboards, they were young men and women embarking on the world. Underneath their graduation robes, the young men wore shirts and ties while the young women wore colored *kain kebaya* to match their stylishly wrapped *hijab*. The top student was the daughter of a night watchman whose previous schooling had been limited at best. She, like the others, went on to university

The graduating class asked me to be their class speaker. *Hebat* (awesome). The vice principal loaned me his wife's academic gown. I also wore the stole we had made for the school dedication three years earlier. Writing my opening remarks in Indonesian was a struggle. Everyone in the room needed to understand my words—proud parents, and like me, grandparents, as well as those of us who had painted the sky to make this day possible.

As graduates received their diplomas, they touched their foreheads to my hand, just as they had when they entered.

Ten years after it opened, over a dozen years after the tsunami that in its own complicated way made it possible for us to *cet langit*, the Lab School continues to wrestle with the issues of what makes good education. It has also come into its own, modeling its creed:

"Everyone can learn."

Yang Bungsu

Indonesian for the last rain of the monsoon, yang bungsu *is also the colloquial term for the last child born in a marriage, particularly if there is a gap of several years between the other children.*

Our children are sent to teach us.

We continue to learn from our four. We wouldn't do without any of them—wouldn't want two of any of them either. I never knew—and still don't know—what would come next.

This was doubly true with our youngest. Charlie (as we spelled his name then) was born his own person. (The others were, too; those are different stories.) The tail that wagged the dog, he had three older sibs to catch up with. When he was still a toddler, he wanted his room painted orange. I painted a chair and a dresser bright pumpkin to mollify him. He insisted on wearing his sister's red dress. I told him it was ok around the house. Not anywhere else.

Everything went into his mouth: the black coloring to add to Kemtone, Windex, wild mushrooms from the woods. It got so that when I called the pediatrician's office about anything—a kid's cold or a bad fall, or to make a routine appointment—the nurse started with: "Hello, Mrs. Sullivan. What has Charlie eaten today?"

The Christmas he was two-and-a-half, all the cousins came to visit. Santa put boxes of golden, jewel-like capsules of bubble bath in all the girls' stockings. (Charlie says that was sexist; all the kids should have gotten them.) In the middle of the afternoon, Charlie came into the room foaming at the mouth. We didn't know whether to laugh or cry. The Poison Center said it wouldn't hurt him but to use Ipecac, just in case. I did. Each time he got sick, I said: "This is what happens when you eat things that aren't food." We never had that problem again.

There was always something, though. A friend and I were nattering on the porch when, with a not quite three-year-old in the house, it became much too quiet. I investigated. Charlie was sitting on the kitchen floor with a big glass mixing bowl and a full dozen of cracked-open eggs—not one in the bowl. One egg on the floor and I might have at least mentally "throttled" him. A whole dozen? What was I to do but laugh—and clean up the icky mess. He wanted to cook. He is now the family baker.

When his sister, Gay, started ballet in Jakarta, then-four-year-old Charlie watched several sessions. After class one afternoon, he approached the dance mistress: "This is first position, this is second," he demonstrated. She was having trouble teaching seven- and eight-year-old girls those positions. "Would you like to dance, Charlie?" Yes, he would and did.

Gay hated it. Dancing was supposed to be *hers* in a life where she was constantly competing with Brothers. Charlie, however, never looked back. He not only studied ballet but also Javanese and Balinese dance. Encouraging a boy to dance was not something I thought I would do. But for him, it seemed right.

When we moved to the Philippines three years later, he asked to be enrolled in the local ballet school. The other boys at the Cebu American School teased him unmercifully. Ballet was not something *boys* did—certainly not in the Philippines. For the only time in my parenting life, I told him that if they kept giving him a hard time he had my permission to slug them. Furthermore, I said I would go tell his Filipina teachers that they either had to stop the boys from harassing him or let him fight. Somehow, giving him permission resolved the issue. A fight never happened. The teasing slowly stopped and Charlie kept dancing.

If Charlie absorbed dance, he inhaled languages. When he was in first grade, still spelling his name "Charlie" like his grandfather had, he came home with an announcement: "Mommy, today we learned 'ie' and 'ey' make the same sound. I am going to spell my name Charley." (He has, now, for forty-eight years.)

He picked up languages as we moved him around the world. When he was twelve, I participated in a conversation with him and two classmates, one Sierra Leonean, the other Irish. Without missing a beat, he spoke to each of us in our own variety of English. He has kept the knack, now speaking at least three languages in addition to English bilingually, plus bits and pieces of others.

Charley collected stories in the same way he soaked up everything else. When they were youngsters and we were entertaining, he and his siblings rarely had dinner with us. However, he was often in the living room at the beginning of the evening. In the Philippines, he had heard from the Borromeo family that had taken him in as "another brother" about the older generations having escaped the Japanese in the hills above Cebu during World War II. Had that happened to other people in Cebu? Charley began asking everyone who came to dinner: "What did you do in the War?"

The Japanese occupation of the Philippines was a painful time many people were reluctant to talk about. As a little boy who didn't understand he shouldn't bring it up, he asked anyway. As a result, he, and we, heard stories of guerilla raids, hiding in caves, and walking for miles in the mountains. Along with reading *The Diary of Anne Frank*, listening to these living histories was his first step toward becoming a historian.

297

In high school back in the States, Charley over-scheduled himself. Along with a full load of classes, he joined choruses and sang solos, played the organ and percussion instruments, and acted in plays. He also continued to dance, studying at the Washington School of Ballet and dancing in the *Nutcracker*—King Rat one year and the Pompous Boy another. He was a strong competitive swimmer, and, because he was big, he played football his last year in high school. In college, he was a history major, a close-harmony singer, and a varsity rower. He also danced several years in the Triangle Show, the student-written-and-produced musical. For one year's show, he danced on pointe, in a blue tutu (imagine *Fantasia*'s dancing hippo).

On my birthday the year after he graduated, Charley thrust books about being gay into my hand. Then he bolted to his grandmother's, where we were all having dinner. His Dad and I weren't surprised, but the fact of it jolted us nonetheless. That night, we didn't want to talk about it except to ask if he was being careful—the AIDS epidemic was in full swing. I was angry for several days, not because he was gay—that was as it was—but because he had preempted *my birthday party* to come out.

It takes time to readjust a preconceived vision of our children's lives. I mourned the dream of grandchildren with his smile and unexpected ways. What was I to do with the Ming Dynasty shard pendant I had tucked away for when he brought home The Lady? "There will be someone, Mom," he said, when I let it all spill out. "Give it to him." I did. (They're no longer together; that's another matter.)

Daughter Gay had her own problems with his gayness. When she was a teen, she had been hazed so unmercifully about her first name (Beach being her middle name didn't help either) that she was threatening to legally change it to Elizabeth, aka Liza. That her brother referred to himself as gay made matters worse. Not only did he dance, he was co-opting her name.

One night, while we were picking Maryland steamed-crabs, she, her brother, and two of his gay friends began talking on and on about the indignities they suffered in high school because of the "anti-gay" views of their classmates. Suddenly she wasn't alone: Her experiences were another side of the same issue. We heard no more about changing her name.

The thirty years since Charley came out have been as educational and full of the unexpected as life with him was when he was a child. He is Charley. All his adult life, Charley has been forthrightly gay, breaking ground in the process. He is one of a few openly gay men to have been a NCAA Division I head coach. After many years of coaching rowing at the top of the men's collegiate club level, he is now first assistant coach at a major women's varsity program.

Gayness is an important piece of Charley. But it's not solely what defines him, just as the sexual preferences of our other sons and our daughter do not define them. Charley has been a high school teacher and the French announcer for swimming events at the Atlanta Olympics. As a Fulbright scholar in Indonesia doing research for his PhD, he returned seriously to Javanese dance. (A picture of him dancing in a central Java city's International Dance Day parade was all over Indonesian papers.) Today he is a blossoming Southeast Asian historian with a special capacity to fit into different societies.

His friends, both gay and straight, continue to expand our horizons. We know he and they have their own hurdles and loneliness (as well as joys and successes). Like many parents (but not all) we would have supported same-sex marriage anyway, even if our son weren't gay. After more than sixty years, we know marriage is a good way to live. We believe in such publicly, legally acknowledged commitment for everyone who wants and is willing to work at it.

What we want for Charley, married or not—what we want for each of our children and for everyone's, gay or straight—is a joyous, productive life.

Each of our children, not just Charley, is unique. Each has strengths and foibles, ups and downs—and much to teach us.

Sex and Contraception

"Smile Your Mother Chose Life"
 The yellow bumper sticker made me smile. Not because of its pro-life message, but because of how it related to my own story. I've always known that my Christian missionary parents conceived me in love. When the time was right, they made the mindful decision to stop using contraception and have a baby. It was a decision, a choice—to quote the bumper sticker literally—made with premeditation and joy. With a smile.
 For my parents, birth control was integral to a deeply moral, religious worldview that included ones individual responsibility for conceiving life. It was a principle they lived and modeled.

 Times were hard in 1931, the Depression deep. Soon after their June marriage, my parents traveled to the Margaret Sanger clinic in Chicago to obtain contraceptives, then still controversial and not widely used. Much in love, they wanted an active sex life, but it wasn't a responsible time for them to have babies. Dad was a doctoral candidate; mother had a low-paying job at the YWCA.
 At the clinic, as my father delighted in recounting, they were asked how many condoms they'd used. The honeymooners blushingly tried to count how many times they'd made love since the wedding. What they came up with, Dad never told. "Two," was what the clinic wanted to hear—as in "two condoms each time."
 In 1932, after Dad earned his degree, he and Mother were sent to China as Presbyterian missionaries. Before going, they had written a booklet on marriage, sex, and birth control for other young missionaries. Their blueprint for a faithful marriage was joyful, loving, responsible sex and parenting. In a wider moral and religious context, they taught by example. They learned from those around them, whatever their faiths, and respected all people, even those with whom they disagreed.
 Unlike many Americans during the Depression, they had work and an income—not a lot, but enough. They decided it was time. I arrived the following July. My next sister, equally planned, arrived two years later. Our third sister—intended as the first of another pair—was on the way in 1940 when Mother, Next Sister, and I were evacuated in anticipation of World War II. Our brother was the delayed, much-wanted post-war child.
 Physicality and, as we got older, responsible sex were part of unembarrassed family conversation. Sex, they counseled, was the ultimate expression of intimacy. It was also endowed with the awesome capacity of creating life. Their advice was simple: Wait

ideally until marriage, to explore it. Use contraception to avoid unplanned pregnancy. (If we were to have had these conversations a generation later, no doubt there would have been a shift beyond heterosexual sex to include the use of condoms to prevent AIDS and STDs.)

In 1954, when I was engaged to Dan, my parents gave us Van de Velde's *Ideal Marriage* (the sex manual before Masters and Johnson and *The Joy of Sex*). Mother and I went to her gynecologist so I could be fitted with, and get a prescription for, a diaphragm. (We lived in Virginia, not Connecticut, where contraception was illegal until *Griswold v. Connecticut* in 1965.) Sixty-four years later, we have four children and three young adult grandchildren, raised with the same moral framework our parents provided us.

Dan and I learned that, in the heat of the moment, sound lessons don't always lead to sound practice. Our children, the products of our exuberance, we joke, arrived pre-Pill. We were fortunate to be stably married, able to handle the unexpected. Not everyone is.

Life has no easy, one-size-fits-all solutions. My grandmotherly wisdom is that there are several vital components to assuring that unwanted babies are few and that the decision to have a safe, legal abortion is rare: postponement of sex; accurate, responsible sex education; and ensuring, as well as insuring, access to a full range of contraception methods. I'm grateful for *Griswold*, *Roe v. Wade*, and Planned Parenthood. I welcomed the ObamaCare requirement that all health insurance policies should cover contraceptives, no matter the employer's religious views. Using contraception should be a personal decision, not one that an employer makes.

Therein lies the rub. The Supreme Court ruled otherwise. Our current leadership's political definitions of "religious liberty" do not resemble the inclusive pluralism the Founders envisioned. Rather, they increasingly connote exclusive primacy of aspects of Christianity and the groups that espouse them. The few are at liberty to impose their vision of religious morality on us all. They enact laws that allow the government and employers to make intrusive decisions in the most private, deeply personal aspects of our lives.

Fundamentally, although they would say otherwise, these groups and politicians do not respect Americans' multiple religious beliefs. Nor, apparently, do they trust us to make responsible, moral decisions for ourselves. Access to contraception should be available through health insurance, no matter whom you work for.

That is why, seeing the yellow bumper sticker, I smile and cite our family's hardly unique, but religiously based conviction:

Choose when to create life.

Remembering Another Unforgettable Day

In mid-September 2011, Americans focused on the tenth anniversary of 9/11. At Ground Zero, the Pentagon, and in a field in Pennsylvania, we paid tribute to those who died that Tuesday in 2001. We honored the soldiers and wept for the civilians killed in Iraq and Afghanistan in the decade since. We analyzed the knotty impact of that morning "that changed history," and its aftermath.

I found myself also remembering—yet again, as I always will—another world-shattering day: Pearl Harbor. December 7, 2011, was the seventieth anniversary of that "date that will live in infamy."

I was seven-and-a-half that boring afternoon, sitting on the floor at my grandmother's feet in the Methodist parsonage in Magnolia, Mississippi. Sunday dinner was over, the dishes washed. The New York Philharmonic played softly on the round-topped wooden radio. Abruptly, an announcer interrupted. In an early morning (Hawaii time) sneak attack, Japanese planes bombed ships in Pearl Harbor and strafed civilians in Honolulu. Ultimately, we learned that a substantial portion of the US Pacific fleet was sunk or damaged and over three thousand people were killed or wounded. In that moment, we could only listen in stunned, uncertain silence, straining to learn more.

That December Sunday in 1941, along with Mummy and my two younger sisters, I became a refugee. Having already left a China at war, we were living with my paternal grandparents. Feeling like an outsider in a world where I did not yet feel at home, I had been waiting. Pearl Harbor determined for what. We would not go back to Daddy. For years, he would not come home to us.

On December 8, the United States declared war. New places came into our vocabularies and onto school maps: Normandy. The Ardennes. Guadalcanal. Iwo Jima. Hiroshima. We got news from the radio or the paper. The black-and-white newsreels screened before the Saturday afternoon movies only gave us a glimpse of what was happening. Paperboys ran through the neighborhood hollering "extra" for major events like President Roosevelt's death and V-E Day. Bells rang for V-J Day.

I had trouble balancing my experience of a real Japanese person—the "friendly enemy" Japanese soldier in Jinan who liked children—with the ubiquitous propaganda caricatures of "buck-teethed, slant-eyed Japs" shown in the support-our-troops-to-defeat-the-enemy posters.

As I grew up, I knew friends and colleagues, or their parents, who had witnessed the Rape of Nanjing, or suffered internment in camps in the Philippines and China. Others we met had endured the awfulness of the Bataan Death March, or hidden out in the jungle for the duration, moving from place to place to avoid the Japanese soldiers. Making real friends with Japanese people was a slow, difficult process. I had to overcome that other dark shadow of the atrocities of war.

Even later, in northern Virginia, we had a dear, California-born Japanese–American neighbor who had spent much of the war in a camp, interned by our own government. We now have neighbors in our Home who grew up that way. This is a part of our national life we cannot be proud of.

Pearl Harbor was only the beginning of an ongoing lesson on balancing uncomfortable contradictions. As an adult, I've lived and worked in extremely different countries and cultures around the "Muslim world." I see two sides of this coin. Close Foreign Service friends were hostages in Tehran. Having been a part of American embassies, our reaction to the bombing of our embassy in Nairobi by al-Qaeda and the Egyptian Islamic Jihad was visceral. My experience in post-tsunami Aceh allowed me to witness the resilience and tenacity of survivors grounded in deep Islamic faith.

All these experiences led me to appreciate the complexities of judging individuals and groups; to recognize the impossibilities of valid generalizations. I still grapple with the critical distinction between abhorring evil acts and casually lumping together all of a particular group of people as embodying that evil. I am profoundly troubled for my own country when some among us incite hatred against a spectrum of widely differing communities and beliefs as if they were a single, nefarious entity.

For those of us with an active memory of them, Pearl Harbor and World War II—like 9/11—were the pivotal events that defined us and framed our lives. Collectively and individually, we experienced fear and vulnerability as well as resolve and shared sacrifice. We knew bravery and loss.

I remember—as I always will—that sparkling September 2001 morning: the smell of my cup of fresh-brewed coffee, the clear view of Washington from our sixteenth floor balcony—the concussion that shook the building even before the blast reached us. Black smoke suddenly billowed skyward from what turned out to be the Pentagon a few miles north. When we turned on the TV, we saw the fearful images from Ground Zero. A hollow feeling filled me during the surreally glorious blue days that followed.

As I remember 9/11, I am carried back to that also never-to-be-forgotten, sepia-toned Sunday afternoon in my grandmother's living room. I grieve and ponder these days that live in infamy.

Soul Food: Sixth Course

Alexandria, Virginia, Now

At over eighty, I still need an occasional *jiaozi* fix. But I have to think twice. I started life with a cast-iron stomach, impervious to the distresses of eating almost anything, almost anywhere. Over time, I easily developed a cultural omnivore's delight in tastes, especially for noodles and bread—spaghetti, mee, hot biscuits, naan, bao. Above all, I loved *jiaozi*.

Maybe fifteen years ago, I noticed that food wasn't always sitting well. My gut wasn't as happy as it should have been. After doing some reading, I stopped eating wheat.

I don't have celiac disease. Wheat won't kill me. It just sometimes leaves me uncomfortable. Physically, I feel better when I am mainly gluten-free. That means no pasta or chewy hand-pulled Chinese noodles—and, worst of all, no wheat dough–wrapped *jiaozi*.

It also usually means no soy sauce since most kinds contain wheat. However, I have discovered that Whole Paycheck (oops, Whole Foods) carries one brand with no wheat. So with that and rice most of my Chinese—or Indian or Indonesian—hungers are met. I don't starve and usually don't even miss things.

Most of the time. ...

There is an occasional six-year-old in me that will not be denied. *Jiaozi*, anyone?

WHAT IS IT ABOUT SHOES?

"A Negro mother wept in the street Sunday morning in front of a Baptist Church in Birmingham. In her hand she held a shoe, one shoe, from the foot of her dead child. We hold that shoe with her. Every one of us in the white South holds that small shoe in his hand."
—Eugene C. Patterson, September 16, 1963
Editorial editor, *Atlanta Constitution*

These powerful words, this perfect metaphor, embodied so aptly the loss, grief, and sense of community obligation that were the aftermath of the bombing of the Baptist Church in Birmingham. The event became a turning point in the civil rights movement. Widely disseminated coming on fifty years ago, this statement was again frequently cited when Eugene Paterson died in 2013. At eighty-nine, the Pulitzer Prize–winning writer thought that editorial was the best thing he had ever written. Time has not muted the power of the loss or of his language.

Shoes are personal. They take on the shape of the wearers' feet uniquely embodying them, their presence, and their absence. My mind still sees the bunion bump on my mother's soft black leather dress shoes even though she and the shoes are long gone.

Photographic images by themselves speak volumes, haunting us long after they appear or disappear: a small, well-worn flip-flop next to a napalmed shack in Vietnam; a sneaker tossed to the side of the road by an accident; shoes floating in the backwash of Katrina, or in a bombed-out house in Gaza; empty boots standing with a rifle and hat marshaled for a regimental memorial. These images carry infinite sorrow.

We never saw such likenesses from the Sandy Hook school shooting. Though we imagined them and felt the deep pain that visited the homes of those children when, unexpectedly, a single little shoe was found in the back of a closet or under the couch. We hold those shoes in our hands as well.

The absence of shoes can be just as powerful as their presence. I'm thinking particularly of a news clip of a small boy walking without shoes in the snow in a refugee camp on the border of Syria. The video close-ups of the awe-inspiring bare-footed Ethiopian runners in the New York marathon also replay in my mind. And who doesn't cringe at the derision voiced by some men who expect to keep their wives "barefoot and pregnant?"

Going barefoot can also be fun. Don't you remember the childhood joy of wriggling toes in the mud or dancing on the grass? Kicking off my shoes was a release from a winter of sturdy soles and boots. (One of the trials of aging is the imperative of wearing flat "old lady" shoes to walk stably. They remind me too much of the wide Buster Browns of my youth.)

When I hosted my first party as the Consul's Wife in Cebu, the initial guests caught me barefoot. With no time to get my shoes on, that's how I remained the entire afternoon. The society page columnists had a field day. "The breezy Mrs. Sullivan without her shoes on…" they gushed in their columns the next day, their tone more snide than admiring. Never wearing shoes at my own parties became my signature.

Flagrant extravagance with shoes is quite the opposite. Imelda Marcos' collection of three thousand pairs of shoes was so over the top that it became fodder for late night TV humor. (It still is, all these decades later.) A year after the Marcoses were ousted, the lowest floor of Malacañang Palace, the president's residence, was opened to the public. Lines of Filipinos (many of them unable to afford anything but cheap rubber flip-flops) filed in, more interested in seeing the shoes than anything else.

In much of Asia, everyone removes shoes at the doors of homes, as well as before entering temples, pagodas, and mosques. Keeping dust or mud from dirtying the interior is only part of the reason. Footwear also carries the pollution of the outer world into the inner ritually clean one. Leaving shoes outside is an expression of respect and worship. I can still see a corridor in a Singapore Housing Development Board flat: a jumble of flip-flops, children's sneakers, men's scuffed black loafers, a pair of stylish high-heeled white sandals, all evoking the family living behind the door. (Indonesians visiting the States came to dinner in our condo the other night. Their first question as they looked around was where to leave their shoes. "No need. It's not our custom," I responded.)

One of the visions of survival and renewal I remember from post-tsunami Banda Aceh was seeing simple shoes lined up outside a recently erected tent school. Those children's lives were getting back to "normal." Such richly textured meanings, these shoes!

My own most heart-stopping photograph comes from that same time. Driving through the upper parts of Banda Aceh we passed signs of earthquake damage. Nearer the ocean, evidence of the tsunami became increasingly overwhelming: broken buildings, then heaps of rubble until there was nothing but lifeless mud as far as the eye could see. I finished taking pictures. As I climbed back into our jeep, I looked down.

There in the dry, gray residue were two, small mud-caked sneakers. One red. One blue. I snapped the most powerful embodiment of anguish I ever hope to photograph: two empty shoes.

Genus Americanus

"I'm as American as you are."

Her voice was as blunt as her words. It was 1997. My new acquaintance was a second-generation Filipina-American community leader and Civil Rights activist. About my age, she had been born in Seattle not far from where we were meeting. It was the same district where she had always lived and where she was raising her children. Her life had a continuity that I, an international rolling stone, had never known.

Her parents had arrived in Seattle during the early twentieth century, when the Philippines was still an American colony. In the States, Filipinos did backbreaking farm work and labored in canneries or loaded ships in Hawaii and along the West Coast. My new acquaintance's long-time concentration, professionally and as an activist, was the history of Filipinos in America. She focused on the unsung contributions they had made as well as the discrimination, violence, and "invisibility" they had endured, collectively and individually. The latter, no doubt, had shaped her life.

We were in her office to talk about the Philippine Centennial that would take place in 1998. I was helping organize the nationwide Philippine Festival that would honor the Philippines' centenary of independence from Spain and the hundred-year relationship between our two countries.

She had never been to her parents' homeland. I'd lived there for three years and kept in touch since. She saw me (or so I assumed) as visibly WASP. She must have heard that the Centennial's sole emphasis was the Philippines. Or maybe she felt, as I discussed the Festival, that I was ignoring Filipinos' (or Pinoys as Fil-Ams often call themselves) significance in America. Consequently, she may have felt that the Festival was going to make Fil-Ams invisible yet again. She was understandably prickly.

"In some ways, you're *more* American than I am," I countered, as I sometimes did, still do, when faced with such a statement. "I wasn't born in this country." What I meant was that I am not as connected to a place, as she is, in my American identity.

Tension lifted, a bit. The rest of our long, more amicable conversation focused on the activities we hoped would make Americans aware of both the Philippines and Pinoys. Over the next year, I held many meetings with her and others. Her need to say that she was as American as I was—to have our equality as Americans and as citizens clearly acknowledged, in our conversation and in the Centennial itself—stuck.

The other morning I slowly drifted awake to familiar, soft, distinctly Mississippi voices. They were real—the sound I had lived among when I was seven—not a dream. Then I heard names—Chow, Wong—familiar, from my even younger childhood in China. The voices were talking about comfort food—Chinese, with a southern twist, cooked to remember childhood tastes—their mothers' cooking. I cook and eat like that at times, for the same reason. Somehow, voices make people and their stories real, even people we have never met and never will.

Slowly I came to full consciousness. NPR's Morning Edition starts our days. That morning they were speaking with the descendants of Chinese immigrants in the Mississippi Delta. The Delta isn't just black and white. Chinese, the NPR piece reported, began coming there from Guangdong (as Canton is called now) shortly after the Civil War. They came first to pick cotton. As more of their compatriots arrived in the mid-'30s, they became merchants, opening and running grocery stores in the small, largely black towns where they lived. Sometimes there were several in a block. (My grandparents were further south when we lived with them in 1942, and to my knowledge knew nothing of this community.)

Most of those stores are closed now, boarded up on emptying streets. Only a few remain. "Business is slow," a more Chinese, less-Mississippi voice recounted: "People leaving."

The current senior American-born generation, men and women roughly my age, seventies, maybe eighties, grew up in those shops, helping behind the counter as soon as they could make change. "We were in-between the blacks and the whites," a voice named Wong explained. Isolated from both blacks and whites, they gathered regularly for their own parties, creating their own sense of community.

As with most small town folk, the Delta Chinese worked hard, sent their kids to college, and watched them—the second and third generations—move away. Those early merchants' children may have spoken Chinese when they were small. But it was mostly gone now, transformed to pure, soft Mississippi when they started school and learned English. One of the women laughed about the disconnect between her Mississippi speech and her Chinese face. Her college daughter's friends called it "identity theft."

I heard them start their Chinese comfort-food dinner with what could have been a blessing from my childhood, in what sounded like my Methodist preacher grandfather's voice: "Let us pray. Father in heaven…"

With that invocation, my morning began with the reassurance of familiar voices and thoughts of Chinese soul food.

"We work hard and take care of our selves," my blond, blue-eyed friend with an Anglo-Saxon family name said, echoing, in her own way, the children of Chinese grocery store owners. A daughter of high plains farm country and of Depression-generation parents who worked multiple jobs to keep a roof over her head and food on the table, she graduated from the same high school as her mother. She earned her own pocket money by the time she was twelve and worked her way through high school and college. As a divorced single mother, she kept working to educate her own children, rearing them to be generous, honorable, and upright. Ultimately, she moved to a big Eastern city with better opportunities.

Though she lives in an urban environment, her heart, the essential who-she-is, remains deeply rooted in the rugged beauty of her hometown and the plains and mountains around it. She values family, friendship, self-reliance, "standards," and those who "love our flag and our country."

We see politics through different lenses, she and I, often uncomfortably so. Some of what she says makes me cringe. No doubt I have the same effect on her. Especially when we disagree, as we always will on some things, I have much to learn from her. She knows a piece of our common world I do not, in a way I never had the opportunity to.

Then, on Facebook, she posts a picture of an opening rose, an early spring crocus or late fall leaf, or of a much-loved grandson diving into the pool to start his race. She comments about the need for civil talk and understanding. Our differences shrink. Friendship abides. So does fundamental disagreement.

"Like being in a Third World country," our new neighbor observed about the next-door grocery store in suburban Virginia. Having recently moved from somewhere outside New York City, she was struggling to adjust. While her body and belongings had moved, her spirit was still hovering, not yet settled in. Moving even a short distance is a kind of culture shock.

In her old community, everything had been familiar. Even the big, upscale Japanese-owned and -managed shopping center that attracted the area's swank Asian community—definitely not "Third World."

Our grocery store, a Giant, is ordinary. It's larger than some, with aisles often blocked with specials. Global items are mixed easily with more, to us, usual foodstuff: pupusas in the chilled food near the eggs and cottage cheese; pomelo, prickly-pear, and plantains with fruit; masa as well as cornmeal. An enormous range of hot sauces.

Reflecting our neighborhood, its customers are as varied as the food it sells. On any given day I might see a small brown woman, her profile, walking pre-Colombian art; a wrinkled grandmother examining each apple before adding a few to her cart; suburban government workers—black, brown, and white—dashing in, grabbing supper, dashing out; a harried couple with small, black-eyed, black-haired, pink-cheeked children, a *depatta* around the mother's neck and head and a *salwaar kamis* showing beneath her coat.

Many of the women—young, old, and in between—wear hijabs. In bright or subdued colors, they are wrapped, stretched, and draped to cover heads and frame faces. Occasionally, a woman wears complete *niqab,* black fabric flowing from head to toe, revealing only her eyes. If I greet any of these women and the men who accompany them with "*As-salaam-Alaikum*," they are likely to respond, "Have a good one" after "*Wa-Alaikum Salaam*." There will be a recognizing smile as we pass again in the next aisle.

Another day, a smartly dressed young woman, perhaps straight from an office, explains to an older man in his language what's in the box he's holding. Nearby, young Spanish-speaking men, headed home from a construction site, fill their basket with beer and chips in preparation for Saturday night *footbol*—what we call soccer. A young distinctively Ethiopian man—straight, tall, and russet—pushes his cart down the aisle. A tiny Lebanese woman, puzzled about yogurt in plastic tubs, not fresh-made, asks which is best.

I run into a neighbor, originally from somewhere in the Southwest, who jokes that they don't feed us enough at the Home so "here we are, shopping." Working the checkout is a big Irish face—Harold. As we wait in his line, the woman behind me and I chat about cooking black-eyed peas for New Years. She's from "Carolina," and does them about like I do—with a ham hock, onions, and a hot pepper. Our Giant: the increasingly multiple visage of America.

Where are Yarrow Mamout's bones? Several years ago the *Washington Post* reported on a small archeological dig in a backyard in Georgetown that was hoping to find the remains of a freed slave—a turn-of-the-nineteenth-century celebrity who lived an unusually well documented life. Captured as a teenager in what is now Guinea on the west coast of Africa, he was a Muslim who could read and write Arabic and speak English. Records show he had been sold into slavery in Annapolis around 1752. Some forty-four years later, he gained his freedom and purchased a home in Georgetown, where, reportedly, in his backyard, he prayed in the direction of Mecca. It was thought that he was buried there when he died in 1823. His bones, however, were not found.

As a free man, Yarrow Mamout was well enough known that Charles Willson Peale painted his portrait. That picture of him, one of the first African-American portraits ever made, hangs in the Philadelphia Museum of Art. He is depicted as butterscotch, with piercing eyes, a beaked nose, and sharp cheekbones. A Fulani, his face resembles his distant tribal kinsmen, who we sometimes saw herding cattle through our backyard in Nigeria and near the Guinea border in Sierra Leone.

Yarrow Mamout was certainly not the only Muslim among the thousands of enslaved people transported from Africa. Nor would he have been the first. He is, however, one of the few we know much about. We need to remember that Islam, its practice and its people, are not new to this place or our collective life.

Chatty folk in motels and neighborhood restaurants are one of the treats of driving cross-country.

"Are you from around here?" I asked our breakfast waiter. He had the face of an Indonesian friend but sounded and moved like pure California. His name was David. "My mother brought me here when I was eight, eleven years ago," he told us as we continued to chat. "Santa Barbara's home. I'm full-blooded Mexican. Yes, I'm a dreamer," I heard the latter piece of information with worry for the Deferred Action for Childhood Arrivals (DACA) program's future. Later, as he served the eggs, he said, "I'm studying hotel management at Santa Barbara City College and working to help support my mother. She made me learn Spanish as well as good English. Speaking both should help with business. I pay taxes."

"Of course we take Discover. This is America." Our waitress at the Roadkill Café in Seligmann, Arizona, practically danced over to the cashier's desk in her skinny jeans, her sun-weathered face smiling and gray pigtail bouncing.

"My son-in-law tries to make tortilla," volunteered the graying server in the breakfast room in our Gallup, New Mexico, hotel. "Men don't usually. His fingers aren't good for turning them so he uses a…" She pantomimed a pancake turner, a look of disdain on her face about her son-in-law's uncured fingers. "I'm teaching my granddaughter to make them, though—and how to make fry-bread, too. I put lard in the tortilla even though lots of folks don't. I don't put it in the fry-bread, though—enough grease in the pan. I should have taught my daughter when she was younger." Someone needed something; she moved on.

At a Lao-Thai restaurant in Amarillo, Texas, a heavyset white woman—maybe in her late fifties, her neck in a brace—paused at our table as she and her even more heavyset husband were leaving. "They give you a lot of food," she observed. "We used to come here when there was a different owner; it wasn't so good then. Now that I can eat food again—broke my neck in a car accident—we came back and fell in love with it again. I won't have to cook for three days," indicating the leftovers her husband was carrying in a plastic container as she followed him out the door. (Who knew there was a Lao Thai community there, much less with a restaurant serving as good a green curry as any place?)

"Amarillo's all right," the young woman working the front desk said, responding to an observation I made about the city as I walked past her as we returned from dinner. "I came back with my mother when I was about three," she continued, not saying from where. Well into her night duty, she had been sitting at the desk slumped over and exhausted. She perked up as she realized I was genuinely interested in what she had to say. "I'm trying to go back to school, but I have a nine-year-old and a three-year-old. So I'm working two jobs. My sister is the only family I have. She takes care of the three-year-old when I can't."

"Anything else?" The perky blue-eyed waitress put the banana pudding and beignets on the table in a Cajun café on the outer edge of Tulsa, Oklahoma. She eyed my not quite finished fried oyster po'boy and her watch. "Nearly three. I'm looking forward to some oysters myself." Mine were fat, encrusted in cornmeal, scrumptious and, as we learned from the chef, direct from the Gulf. "I miss N'Orleans," our waitress told us. "I grew up there. I left for Vegas and made costumes for drag queens. I'd studied design and dressmaking in N'Orleans and wanted to see places. I'm here now because my mother is, and so I can have my three-year-old full time. I'm still sewing for a couple of my regulars, saving money to get us back home. I stuff my cash in a liquor bottle, so I can't get it unless I break the bottle."

"We want a real American," the Lab School principal in Aceh wrote to me in an email, obviously wanting me to "fix things." The "problem" was that the Fulbright program was sending a young black man, fresh out of university, to teach English at the school for the year.

"He *is* a real American," I banged out in the return message. "Americans find saying he isn't offensive. He will be a good teacher." He proved to be.

Working across cultures, I'm not normally that blunt, or I at least try not to be. I try to listen more. I wanted to head off trouble—for the school and for the teacher, if I could. The principal's comment was disrespectful, if not totally unsurprising. My guess is that it had never crossed her mind that I would react as I did. Racism and color prejudices exist in many forms around the world. I had met it before. We all make assumptions.

Do these verbal *Genus americanus* picture postcards—these images of only a few of the many "I"s that form the "We" of "We the People"—jell in anyway? Maybe.

We are a people of seeming contradictions: Chinese faces speaking Mississippi English; a formerly enslaved Muslim, painted by a famous artist, well before the Civil War.

Ours is a nation, not of land or bloodlines, but of an amazingly imaginative set of principles: We are equally endowed with basic rights—life, liberty, and the pursuit of happiness. We are all equally due respect and human dignity—and expected to be respectful in return. We are free to speak. And free to worship—or not. We live in a nation of laws, informed by a free press.

In theory, we embody these principles, and in doing so, we are united. Far too often, however, we do not embody them. We apply them when we want, to whom we want. Divided we fall.

When the Lab School principal made her request, she triggered a truly sore point: the idea that there are *real* Americans, which is to say some of us are not real. Even if we may not openly articulate this idea, far too many of us actually think that way. She simply had absorbed beliefs about us from what she heard and given them voice.

How can any person or group say, imply, or think that while some of us are real Americans, the rest of us are *not* real? I'm equally disturbed when, in the corollary, politicians and others gather those who agree with them, and then declare, "The American people have spoken" all the while excluding the rest of us who think in other ways. Aren't we also the American people?

As a nation and people, we are wrestling with these issues again—still. Have we ever not dealt with them? There is so much work to do, so much to learn about each other, from each other. So many stories to be told, listened to, heard, acknowledged. Despite our often-cited diversity, despite our polarization, there is—or should be—so much that binds us together.

My Pinoy friend's assertion that she is just as much American as I am rings accurately, yet also painfully, in my ear. Painfully because she has reason to assume she may not be seen that way.

It echoes in my sense of self, in my sense of being American. Given how I have lived and what I look like, I am both an outsider looking in *and* an insider looking out. She is indeed as American as I am, as we all should be: *Genus americanus*, from many, one.

313

Red Bottle, Yellow Rain

The wedding was special. The early September weekend in 2003 was balmy. The groom had grown into a handsomely elongated version of the blond, knobby-kneed two-year-old we first knew long ago and half a world away. His bride glowed with graceful Indonesian beauty. The groom's mother pushed his father down the aisle in a wheel chair. We all rejoiced.

A group of us who gathered to witness and celebrate that weekend in the Berkshires had become good friends in Jakarta nearly forty years earlier. Being together in that place at that time, exploring its specialness was only part of our bond. We also had been part of a "small town" community doing ordinary, wherever things, and this had bonded us just as deeply. I sat with the groom's mother one night as we nursed him through one of those improbably high, anxiety-making childhood fevers. Another of us had been our youngest son's nursery school teacher; he is forever hers. I was in a painting group and worked on school issues with others.

All of us had moved on, but kept in touch. There was always a bed in the groom's family's apartment in New York if fun or work took us there. We heard about each other's children as they grew and went forth into the world.

The groom had returned to Indonesia as an adult, a second generation to work on family planning issues. There he met the bride.

The wedding date was already "saved" when we received word that the groom's father was deathly ill, attacked by a flesh-eating bacteria. We sent love and did what we could do from a distance through those long weeks, glad for each update. Finally, he was recovering—minus his legs, but recovering.

We gathered. After the service we went to a field by a brook to party with music, a dance floor, and scrumptious food. The groom's father, wheelchair-bound, regretted he couldn't dance at his son's wedding. We solved that, he and I, as I whirled his chair around the dance floor, both of us laughing and crying.

Two years later, the bride and groom were back in Indonesia when their child was due. The custom, particularly for a first baby, is to have a seventh month *selamatan* (ceremonial meal) to ensure a safe delivery and healthy child. The mother-to-be is wrapped in seven batik cloths and bathed with water from seven sources by seven older women with healthy children, including the grandmothers-to-be. The groom's mother was in New York and couldn't get there. I would be in Jakarta for the project I was working on. "Please stand in for me," she and the couple asked. The familial sense of connection we had begun years before in Jakarta continued as I poured water over the mother-to-be and the next generation in the womb.

The morning before the wedding, our small group, except the groom's parents, had gone on a hike. We packed a picnic: baguettes, some cheese, a bit of fruit, a bottle of wine. Enjoying the last of summer and the first hint of fall in the Berkshires, we took the time to catch up. We retold stories, laughed, and talked about our children and grandchildren and what we were doing. Even more, we shared our thoughts about where our lives and the world were going next.

With time to kill on our way back to the B and B to dress for the wedding, Dan and I stopped to stroll in a small artsy New England town. A glassblower's shop ached to be walked into. There we met not only the artisan but also the red bottle: glowing ruby glass, a thick triangular base, with three sides undulating up to a slightly off-center round neck. "Take me home," it said. We did.

The bottle assumed a place on the windowsill by my desk. It joined a "big blue marble" (a glass globe) I had received as a thank-you for leading a workshop; my mother's glass paperweight with a red undersea garden in it; and, from my China childhood, her small clear glass obelisk incised with a pagoda. There was also a duck made of two flat stones (one large, one small) that my middle son had glued together at day camp the summer he was nine and we were home on leave from Jakarta. The glass pieces sat on two small wooden stools made by a little old man I had interviewed while I was exploring cottage industries in Singapore.

In the same way that I can't remember when I didn't tell or write down stories, I also can't remember when I didn't make art. I usually credit my mother. Even though she couldn't even draw a stick figure, she knew how to encourage us. She provided paper and pencil in church to keep a wiggle worm quiet during the sermon, which started me observing my surroundings. The choir was perfect for cartooning, particularly a dome-headed round man in the front row. I've long since forgotten his name, but I can still see and draw the shiny dome.

In Kaduna, I became a painter, first for fun and then seriously, carrying art-making with me from place to place. I used my vision of shapes, colors, and patterns to communicate my way of observing the world. (Stories begin that way too—it's all about paying attention.)

Many of the paintings I made there have lives of their own, hanging in a dining room in Cebu, a guest room in Texas, and many other places. Never a neat painter, over time my "painty" pants and the basement floor in our McLean house had turned into Jackson

Pollack derivatives. My painting lapsed when we moved to the condo, which had no space where I could leave a mess.

I missed making art. Soon after the wedding and almost ten years after we moved into the condo, I found a new tool—a digital camera. I delighted in the opportunity it gave to explore the world around me in new ways. The view from my office (and the rest of the condo) changed endlessly as seasons cycled and recycled. Washington spread before me, sunlit and rain drenched, canopied by an ever-varied sky. The city turned into a sea of lights at night. So began an almost daily discipline of looking and image-making, of exploring the play of light and shadow as they shift over time.

As the years have passed, the red bottle has taken on an almost impish personality in the art I make. Sometimes it leaps into a center-stage, full-face portrait as light plays on its rippled surface. Occasionally it pops into the edge of a wider view. Or, unexpectedly, it turns up, reflecting or refracting on a surface across the room, or doubled in the windowpane.

A friend imagined her cherished collection of cranberry glass in those images and shared a picture. One of my favorite captures—an early summer morning as the sunrise rosied the edge of the sky and caught the side of the red bottle, enhancing its tones—stayed in my old office, blown up and framed, a gift to the new residents when we made one last move.

The red bottle and its compatriots found another windowsill to sit on in our new home. If I look just to the left of the computer I am writing on, their colors glow, change, and reflect individually and together. The discipline of observing and image making continues.

We hadn't been in this not-yet familiar space long when, one night, rain pelted our window. Raindrops got caught in the window screen. The streetlights eleven stories below turned the drops yellow. All this danced around and through the reflection of the red bottle on the windowpane.

My hands were unsteady as I held the camera. The image came out as yellow squiggles with just a suggestion of the deep red bottle. The window screen crosshatched the unfocused blue and white lights from cars coming up the road.

I enlarged the shot, mounted it on a canvas I painted eggplant, and named the piece "Red Bottle, Yellow Rain." Neither a photograph nor a painting, but a combination of both, the work was my first entry in a resident art show at our new home.

When friends in Michigan asked for art donations for an auction that would support an exchange program, I donated that picture. A teacher, I'm told, purchased the image, which now hangs in her classroom, sometimes serving as a writing prompt for her third to fifth grade students. Apparently the squiggles and suggestions of objects generate an ongoing discussion about what the students see in it. "Red Bottle, Yellow Rain" is on its own journey, stimulating imaginations and memories.

Meanwhile, as the days shorten and lengthen and the light retreats from and reenters our space, the red bottle changes shades, reflecting light around the room. Other times, sun, the overarching sky and clouds beyond the skyline blaze or soothe, catching my eye and striking my imagination. The camera resides near the computer keyboard, handy when I spot a moment to capture and play with. The red bottle, however it appears in my work, evokes dear friends from one place and time who gathered in another, joining our lives again while we could, at a wedding in the Berkshires.

All this art making, this catching of memory happens as it happens—as I glimpse it: a random notion; an unexpected smell; a glance at a treasured object; a special light in the sky that triggers haphazard memories, tying together past and present, linking fragments from my mobile life. Noticing such moments is not only a way of making art, but also a way of living.

Tacloban and Multilayered Memories

Tacloban—one of many low-lying, central Philippine towns that in 2013 monster typhoon Haiyan turned into matchsticks and heaps of rubble, leaving residents desperate, homeless, thirsty and hungry—lives differently in my mind than it exists today. In my memory, the town sprawls along a white, sandy beach that curls around the end of a bay where waves lap and a few coconut trees stand gracefully. Planes from the nearby airport occasionally appear in the sky. The beach was the perfect place to unwind on a hot October afternoon with our friend Tony Benedicto and his "Regal Friend," as he always referred to the bottle of Chivas that accompanied us.

Tony chaired the committee organizing the annual commemoration of the Leyte Landing. (The October 20, 1944, event was one of the last big Pacific theater engagements of World War II.) Each of the three years Dan was the American consul in Cebu, he and I were among the officials invited to the formal commemorations. We were also Tony's guests, staying in his family's welcoming home with its shaded courtyard. In those days, the city was bustling and extremely pleasant.

The American ambassador was always the invited honoree; we were supporting actors. Somehow, all three years, something intervened—plane trouble one year, a typhoon another—so the ambassador didn't arrive. By default, Dan became the impromptu official representative of the United States. One time he was suddenly tapped to lay the wreath at the memorial. The last time required more of Dan. Just as we sat down to lunch, we heard that the ambassador's plane had returned to Manila to avoid the storm. Tony turned and said, "Danny, you're the speaker."

"Honored guests, residents of Tacloban," Dan began. "It is a privilege to be here today as we commemorate the twenty-ninth anniversary of the Leyte Landing. I feel like I have a special connection with that event. The first time I was in the Philippines I was eleven. In late November 1940, our family, like many Americans around Asia, was being evacuated on one of three large passenger ships sent for the purpose. In our case, we were sailing on the *SS Washington* from Shanghai. The ship stopped in Manila to pick up others being sent home on the eve of World War II. As the ship sailed out of Manila Bay, we passed Corregidor just after dark. Every light was on. Searchlights lit the sky. Airplanes circled overhead. The wives and children of the American forces stationed there were also being evacuated on our ship. Their men were saying good-bye to their families. Many of them never saw each other again. Today's commemoration honors the redemption of the pledge those men and General McArthur made to the Philippines and Filipinos: 'I shall return.'"

Dan sat.

In the fall of 2013, American troops returned to Tacloban, this time ferrying in Philippine troops armed with water and food for the typhoon-stricken residents of that once lovely tropical town.

Packing winds equivalent to a class five hurricane, Haiyan was labeled the century's biggest typhoon, (which literally means "big wind"). Newscasts began predicting its course toward the central Philippines a week before it made landfall.

As news of Haiyan's approach spread, concern heightened. One of the sisters in our Cebu "family" began posting preparations on Facebook. Her posts about Friday morning's aftermath in Cebu reported trees downed and lights off, with family and friends shaken but safe and organizing food and other necessities for others in need. That afternoon, long before Tacloban's destruction was covered in the international news media, she posted a small note from her friend describing it.

Pictures began appearing on the web, then in the news. As with images from the tsunami in Fukushima, Japan, or the earthquake in Haiti, or hurricane Katrina in New Orleans, I was heartsick, plummeted back into Banda Aceh. My nineteen post-tsunami trips there in five years had given me a hands-on understanding of disaster and of the relief and rehabilitation process. At least I could be useful in Aceh.

This time, all I could do was feel hollow. Half a world away, I joined in the concern that the stages of relief were much too slow. I anguished with people pleading for water and food.

I also knew—at least hoped—that help was on the way. As urgent as the needs were, assistance was being organized. The local logistics were beyond difficult. Even so, trucks were being found, roads were being cleared, aid would be delivered to remote places—never fast enough, but it would get done. I sent funds to the major, well-practiced relief organizations on the scene and encouraged others to do the same.

I saw hope in a picture from Tacloban that showed clean clothes on a fence—a struggle for a semblance of normality in the midst of chaos. Meanwhile, Bea Joy Sagales, born the day following the typhoon and named for a grandmother who perished in the storm, was the face of the future. Out of disaster, once again there were reminders of the human spirit's power to endure and renew.

Our Many Santas

"Santa just is white..." Megyn Kelly, Fox News

When I was a child, we believed in Santa. We hung stockings on Christmas Eve and by Christmas morning they were full. I have a visceral nine-year-old's memory of the anticipation, anxiety, and excitement that kept me wide-eyed and listening late into the night. Muffled noises in the living room. Was that Santa? I must have slept because I still feel my eyes popping open pre-dawn on Christmas. Had he actually come? Before daylight, my sisters and I were bouncing near the bedroom door waiting to be called in to the tree to see what he had left.

I don't remember being taken to sit on his knee or even thinking much about what he looked like. We all had a general idea: white beard; red suit and hat trimmed with fur; huge, black belt around an enormous middle; an overflowing bag on his back; and a limited vocabulary—"Ho, ho, ho!" He came in the night, down the chimney (but if he was as fat as everyone said he was, how did he do that?). He filled the stockings, finished his cookies and milk, and, reindeer and all, went on to the next house. But what did he do about houses like ours that didn't have a fireplace? Clearly he came in somehow. Did Santa know that year that I was in Missouri, not Mississippi or China?

After I grew up and started raising a family of my own overseas, I became truly aware that there are as many ways of keeping Christmas and incorporating Santa as there are families who keep these traditions. But you don't have to live elsewhere to become aware of this. Just look around at the wondrous range of faces, names, languages, and customs all over the United States. Whether we were in the Philippines, Indonesia, Nigeria, or Malaysia, or home again in Virginia, Dan and I perpetuated Christmas magic for our own children and grandchildren.

Back to Santa. We don't actually even know his real name. He operates under a number of aliases: Old Saint Nick. Father Christmas. Pere Noel. Kris Kringle. Santa Claus. Whatever his name, or how and whenever he comes to children, we certainly don't actually see him. No one did when I was a child in Missouri or even earlier in China. We only saw evidence that he'd been there.

Santa is far too busy making his lists and checking them twice. So, if he goes to lots of places and talks to lots of children, he needs helpers to embody him. For several years, one of our sons, well endowed with bodily presence, including twinkling eyes and his own white hair and beard, was the official Santa Claus every Christmas season for the Ann Arbor Symphony. In that mid-Western polyglot American university town, he gave kids the gift of being greeted in their own languages: English, French, Spanish, Italian, Thai, Vietnamese, Chinese. Of course, Santa has to know all the languages children speak.

More than language is important. Our communities have become more complex, with a rich variety of customs and ways of celebrating Christmas. Not just December 25. On December 6, American children with German or Dutch heritages still put out their shoes for Saint Nicholas, who leaves small gifts in them. If he talks with them after that, Santa needs to ask what they got in their shoes. Spanish speaking kids anticipate El Dia de los Reyes, Three Kings, on January 6. Santa needs to anticipate that as well.

As our Santa-son recounts, several years ago a small Chinese-Hawaiian–American boy, maybe six, climbed on our son's lap, worried that he didn't have a chimney. "So how do you come to me?" the boy asked. "In the rice cooker" Santa responded. The answer satisfied the boy that year.

He came back the next year older and with a serious question: "Why a rice cooker?" "Oh," said our nimble St. Nick, "a chimney is for heating and cooking. So is a rice cooker." The little boy and his mother, who beamed at the answer, understood this cultural parallel and its magic. For that boy, Santa was his. Since then, his family has "adopted" our son as their family Santa. Every year they take a family picture with him. They even have their own cultural addition to the tradition: Ninjas protect Santa. Inclusivity is much more suitable to the season than a highly codified, one-size-fits-only-some.

The truth of actually sighting the *real* Santa is a different matter. Take "Santa's" older brother Jerry. The Christmas he was four, we were living in Kuala Lumpur. An American friend and I heard that Robinson's, the British-owned department store, had a Santa Claus for children to visit. Perfect, we thought, our boys are the right age to go see Santa for the first time, let's go do it. We took them—both prancing with excitement.

The store was decked out for Christmas with colored balls, red paper garlands, and fake snowflakes—for us a dislocating "where-are-we?" experience, in what was otherwise a Malay and Chinese city with a smattering of Indians. Following the thoroughly British "This Way to Father Christmas" sign, we herded the boys up the escalator (a rare treat in itself) to the second floor.

There he was: a tall, skinny, ashy chocolate Tamil in a moth-eaten costume and scraggly fake beard. My friend and I blanched—Santa Claus? The boys were delighted. Santa, as we Americans called him, was like the other people they lived among and saw on the street. They each sat on his knee and told him what they wanted.

Like children in many places, Jerry went home satisfied that his wishes had been heard. On Christmas Eve, he and his younger sister hung their stockings, leaving milk and cookies by our makeshift tree created with bamboo branches and hung with lightweight ornaments. Not entirely happily, they went to bed so Santa could come. Christmas morning the stockings were full and there were presents for everyone—Santa had heard.

Perhaps three months later, Jerry and I were out for a late afternoon walk around the neighborhood when we passed a Hershey-colored Sikh, his long white hair and beard undone, bathing himself at the standpipe of a house under construction.

Jerry could barely contain himself. "Oh, Mommy, look," he said, pointing. "There's Santa. Santa lives here. I see him."

On Christmas Eve most of our children and all our grandchildren gather if we can. There are no little children anymore, but we still keep the traditions alive. The same stockings that have been carried around the world or made especially for grandchildren are laid out on the table. According to our family custom, each of us fills in as Santa's helpers, sneaking presents into stockings that are opened before breakfast Christmas morning. For us, Santa has many faces and comes in many guises.

And Megyn, if you need your Santa to be white, fine. That's what you need. Others of us see him other ways. They all work. So: "Merry Christmas to all and to all, a Good Night."

DOWN-SIZING

Tabo's Foreign Service Blocks

The big basket filled with wooden Playskool blocks and similar playthings lived in our condo's front hall closet for twenty years. When small children visited, its contents were spilled over the floor and turned into all sorts of buildings and towns.

The block basket started fifty-seven years ago when number one son, Jerry, received them as a first birthday gift from his Grandfather Jerry, my father. Dad had played blocks with my sister and me, but our blocks were left behind when we were evacuated from China.

With this gift to Jerry, Dad handed down the tradition. The new blocks started their Foreign Service journey in February 1959 when we flew to our first post with Jerry, then nearing three, and his infant sister, Gay. Walter joined the family there and discovered the blocks as he began to crawl.

The blocks traveled on to Kaduna, then back to our first house in Vienna, Virginia, where Charley entered the ranks of the block builders. Along the way more blocks and a miniature red and blue wooden train were added to the basket. (The train's engine, about two inches long, ultimately became a Christmas ornament.) The basket and its contents moved to McLean, then Jakarta, Cebu, Freetown, then home again.

Over time, even more things were added: wooden train tracks and a bigger train—Christmas presents—several wooden tops and some plastic squares that hooked together.

The basket accompanied us to Singapore, even though we were empty nesters. When friends' children came by, we pulled out the blocks from under the stairs. When we returned to the States for good, the blocks, too, returned to McLean. In time, grandchildren Sam, Rebecca, and Grace built with them.

The blocks moved with us again to Alexandria. Over the years, too many visiting children to count have played with the blocks in the basket.

Today the blocks go on a new journey. We're driving them into Washington for a cheerful toddler to enjoy. Monday they get packed for shipping to Vietnam, embarking on another family's Foreign Service journey.

Some things get sent onward joyfully. Even so, letting go causes its own hollow pit in the stomach, a momentary sense of loss.

Enjoy building, Tabo.

From One Jerry to Another

My dressing table, once my father Jerry Winfield's writing table, moves to our son, Jerry, in Texas this week. When he was born, my father bound into my hospital room to look at him, a bundle with dark hair in a crib. "That's my grandson and he's named after me," he exclaimed.

I don't know when or where my folks got the graceful oak table with its interesting grain and curved legs and braces. I clearly remember Mother sitting at it, when it was Dad's writing table, over thirty years ago. Dad was lying in their bedroom, his voluble words lost, dying slowly. She was dealing with family bills and records for the first time since she and Dad were separated during World War II.

While she searched through the papers, she went on and on about how he had done a terrible job of organizing things. In reality, he was meticulous. It was all there, clearly organized and labeled—not the way she would have done it, perhaps, but in good order just the same.

We had rarely if ever seen her display anger, but those weeks she seemed overwhelmed with it. She was furious at Dad's impending death—for her, it was easier to be mad at him for his paperwork.

Before I used Dad's writing desk as my dressing table, I had a dressing table that came from Dan's Michigan family. Also made of oak, that table had a marble top and two drawers. My mother-in-law had used it as her vanity before it came to me when we broke up their household.

Perhaps twenty-five years ago, Dan's cousin Bud came to visit. For some reason, as he was about to leave, he was in our bedroom. "Oh," he exclaimed when he saw it, "Bobo's telephone table." Bobo was his and Dan's Grandmother Sullivan. "She used to let me play with the string and rubber bands and other things in the drawers when I was little. I haven't seen it for years. I didn't even know where it was. I loved that table."

It fit in the back of Bud's car and went back to Michigan.

By then, Mother was breaking up her household. Dad's writing table came to take the place of Bobo's table. Thursday it goes to Texas, and our son Jerry's home office—from one Jerry to the other.

Heart-Stopping Files

Sometimes you come across something heart-stopping in a long-unopened box. "What should we do with these unused legal file folders?" Dan called from the other room. He had found them under his desk.

"Would you use them?" I asked.

"Not sure."

"Put them on a shelf in my office for the time being."

"Oh," he said, turning a few over and looking closer. "These were your Dad's. See this label: 'Research on High Temperature Composting in China.' They have to be his."

I had grown up on dinner conversation about composting and how to stop the cycle of intestinal parasites. As a child, I knew such startling statistics as: If you laid all the liver fluke in all the intestines of all the Chinese (at that time) end to end they would go to the moon and back eight and a half times.

The headings seemed right.

A little while later, Dan gently placed his hands on my shoulders. "Those aren't his *old* folders. They are the folders for the trip he never took back to China. See: 'Recent Developments on Composting in the US and other Parts of World,' 'Characteristics of Sanitary Systems in China 1940s and Now.'"

In the mid-'80s Dad had a grant to go back to Cheeloo, his old university (although it had a new name), to redo his research. He wanted to learn how the composting system in use, which was largely based on his earlier research, was doing and what positive changes had been made. He was excited about spending six months in Jinan on the same campus on which he and Mother had lived and Harriet and I had been born. Mother wasn't excited about it. She was going because he wanted to.

Instead, he developed a brain tumor. One of the last things he said to me while he could still speak was how much he wanted to return. Part of his heart, of his self was there. He regretted not being able to go.

Now the residue was on my shelf. What to do with a last regret?

My heart was empty with the rarely recurring enormity of loss.

The Dutch Clock

After nearly fifty years striking the hours in our various houses, the Dutch wall clock was silent. Dan had raised the weight for the last time.

We met it, or it met us, in Kitty Naier's antique shop in Surabaya a year or so after we had gone to Indonesia. We were visiting old friends—and found a new one.

The works and face were eighteenth-century Dutch: elegant Roman numerals and curlicue brass hands encircled by a gilded plaster wreath and Greek nymphs, topped by a face that displayed the phases of the moon. The case was an Indonesian wood. Termites must have done their handiwork on the original along the way.

We loaded it, well wrapped to protect it against the bumpy roads, into the back of the Jeep Wagoneer and drove back to Jakarta. The clock needed a bit of looking at so we took it to Mr. Tan's shop downtown. "Oh," he said. "I know that clock. I sold it to Miss Kitty." Full circle.

We hung the clock on our dining room wall in Jakarta. It kept good time for being two hundred years old. It moved with us to the Philippines, where it again hung on the dining room wall. When we were going to Sierra Leone, the clock came to DC in our airfreight and stayed with my parents until we returned two years later. Then it went to our house down the street until it revisited Mother and Dad when we went to Singapore. In 1985 it came home to us again.

The clock had been on our wall ever since, keeping the time, ticking in the quiet of night, telling us with its count of the hour that it was time for lunch. It would shock dinner guests with a full-throated whirring strike of nine or ten, momentarily bringing a lull in the conversation. Later, it would reassure the wakeful that there were several more hours to sleep.

When it was time to move out of our condo, our long-time clock caretaker—who several years back did the only major repair the clock had ever needed—came to pack up our trusted timepiece. First he removed the weight and the pendulum. Then he carefully tied the chain, so it wouldn't slip off its sprockets, and bagged the chains, tucking them down inside the cover to hold them in place.

For two weeks, the Dutch clock hung quietly on the wall until we gently wrapped it in an old duvet and placed it in the back of Jerry and Phillipa's van for its ride to Texas.

When next it struck, the clock would be hanging on their wall in McKinney. Like so much in life, the clock moved on to another generation. Round and round in the circle game.

Last Move?

April 15, 2015

Yesterday, it poured.

Appropriately, the final images I took from our condo windows—the last of at least a five-year discipline of near daily picture making of our view—were taken while the packers stowed the final winnowing of a lifetime's accumulation into boxes for today's move.

A moment's night wakefulness had shown the light-dotted city splayed around us—one of those memories best held close in the mind rather than captured by camera like a pinned butterfly. A morning deluge had filled the window with raindrops, dulling the gray view across the river. By late afternoon a gentler spring rain showcased the increasingly lettuce-green landscape. The weather was appropriate on a day for which I had mixed feelings at best.

Deciding to move was not simple.

Twenty years ago, the impetus for leaving a house came when shoveling snow off a driveway the length of two football fields and pruning a hundred fifty azaleas seemed excessive. The thought of living high above it all beckoned. When we walked through a sixteenth-floor front door and saw a window with a direct view of the Capitol, DC glittering white and the Potomac circling through the foreground, it felt right.

Ultimately, so did this last move. After months of vacillating between "I don't want to give up the view and my balcony of orchids," and "what happens when one or both of us can't manage?" we finally made the decision to leave our condo. We are active but slowing, more than that is inevitable. Downsizing now is simpler (well, it has been anything but simple) than it will be later. We will be living independently in the new retirement community confident that caregiving will be available when we need it.

So it's done. In theory, the rolling stones have made one last move and come to rest. Well, maybe. Wanderlust doesn't pack up well at all.

Different high-in-the-sky windows have different views to photograph. The same red bottle on the windowsill will dance in and out of the frame.

The guardian of the new front door—the miniature Nigerian house post—is in its place. The mover had set it in the corner. It fit. We had landed in the right space.

Bits from earlier fragments have gone on their own journeys. For us, a new fragment begins.

Walking Sticks by the Door

As I get older and stride less easily on uneven ground, walking sticks have become an addiction. I don't use one all the time. When the way is long or rough or the ice is slick or old bones ache, it's good to have one at hand.

Years ago, when we took short hikes along the Appalachian Trail, I'd pick up a stick by the side of the path, then leave it for someone else to find when we were done. As we traveled, canes found me or I found them. My accumulation lives by the front door in a tall brown dragon jar that joined us in the Philippines.

The round handled bentwood walking stick comes from the weekend we spent high in the Alps above Grindelwald. Visualize rich yellow wood, with delicately incised edelweiss up the stick, and a sharp steel tip. That summer weekend thirty-some years ago I was neither young nor old, but still, for me, nimble. Even so, it seemed like a good idea to get a walking stick from a tourist shop before Dan and I hiked one of the narrow paths about halfway up the Eiger, below the snow line and above the tree line.

That cane *was* a good idea. A mile or so along, the path crossed the grubby brown end of a glacier no more that fifteen- or twenty-feet wide. Until then, even though we were crossing a steep slope of grass and bush, the walk was exhilarating. The cane moved easily with me, and I was doing well.

I had made it part way down the single-board walkway across the glacier, with Dan already on the other side ahead of me, when I froze. As I looked to my side—shades of a mountainside in India—there was nothing, even ankle high, between me and the deep valley below. I could neither go forward nor back. The German briskly walking toward me was completely disgusted as he side-stepped onto the glacier and brushed past me.

Petrified, I gripped the cane's handle and pushed the point into the ice. I stood there until I gathered the courage to inch forward. One foot... the other foot...one...the other. Eventually, I exhaled. How triumphant I felt when I got off the glacier and back onto the dirt path! We wended our way back into town for a celebratory cheese fondue. Even now, here, on icy winter days that cane is helpful on our sloping driveway.

Another cane—perhaps my favorite—joined me when we visited friends in Ulan Bator, Mongolia, nearly twenty years ago. As we drove into the interior, we stopped at a reserve for miniature Mongolian ponies. The land was bumpy with tufts of grass. It clearly looked like rough walking. "By any chance, do you have a stick I could use to walk with?" What a silly question for me to ask; there were no trees in sight.

The manager of the reserve disappeared briefly. He returned with a red baton, adorned with pink, blue, green, yellow, and gold designs on three sides and roughly shattered at one end—a broken rib, one of many that had supported the roof of a *ger*, the portable round tent of the nomadic Mongolians. He also came armed with a big machete, which he used to carefully shorten the rib to match my height, rounding the top of it to fit easily in my hand.

That stick took me across Mongolia, down into the Gobi, and back to the States. Later it accompanied me to Italy for a wedding, drawing all sorts of comments from every one who saw it, never mind our lack of common language. It's quite a fashion statement, and a sturdy one at that.

My "immortal" cane echoes something else altogether. In 2002, we were in China on a tourist boat going down the Yangtze. It was the last such boat to go through the Three Gorges before the cofferdam forever blocked the river, and later, the Three Gorges Dam turned the upper Yangtze into a lake. One after another, the old villages clinging to the sides of the gorge would be submerged. The boat stopped at small towns where villagers were selling old bits and pieces they otherwise would leave behind: fragments of carving, architectural odds and ends, old dishes, traditional furniture, jewelry—well-worn remnants of their lives.

At one stop, I spotted the cane. Completely covered in thin brass, the multiple variations of the character for "long life" were incised up the length of it. The handle was an elegant head of one of the eight immortals, legendary figures whose powers can bestow life or destroy evil. "Take me home," it said. After a bit of dickering, I walked up the gangway using my elegant walking stick.

When we got to Shanghai and packed to fly home, the walking stick wouldn't fit into a suitcase, even crosswise. I decided to play old lady and use it as a cane to get on the plane. We were early, among the first to go through security.

"Do you know what you have?" the Chinese official asked, picking up my cane and pulling it apart as it emerged from the x-ray machine. Suddenly he was wielding an ugly square-sided pig sticker. I shrieked. The thought had never crossed my mind. Instead of confiscating it, he said: "You still have time. Take it back to the airlines counter and check it through." I show it to people occasionally but that one stays in the jar, handsome and dangerous.

Other canes live in the jar, too. I intend to keep on keeping on for a while. The sticks and I will walk together.

Uppity Women

"Only uppity women make history"

On June 4, 1919, Congress proposed the Nineteenth Amendment giving women the right to vote. On June 7, 2016, ninety-seven years and three days later, the first woman became the nominee for president of either major party. Whether or not you liked Hillary Clinton—who wore suffragette white that June night—her nomination was a major milestone.

On August 18, 1920, Tennessee became the final state to ratify that amendment prohibiting United States citizens from being denied the right to vote on the basis of their sex. The evenly split vote would have failed had not Harry Burn, a young state representative, planning to vote nay, received a note from his mother, Phoebe Ensminger Burn. It read in part: "Hurrah, and vote for suffrage! Don't keep them in doubt." He hastily changed his vote to aye.

The next day he explained: "I know that a mother's advice is always safest for her boy to follow, and my mother wanted me to vote for ratification."

In that moment, thanks to an "uppity" woman who raised a thoughtful son, American women gained the right to vote. In 2016, some one hundred forty-four years since the first woman—Victoria Woodhull—ran for the office, another "uppity woman" raised by a strong mother broke through a longstanding barrier and ran for the highest office in the land.

Achieving near universal suffrage in the United States has been an on-going struggle. It took activists many years to make sure women—as well as African–Americans, Native Americans, and Asians—were allowed to vote. Our gains have been achieved step by often-painful step. For the oldest of us, the bloody violence and political struggles of a half-century ago are vivid memories: the March on Washington, August 28, 1963; the Civil Rights Act, July 2, 1964; the Voting Rights Act, August 6, 1965.

These struggles were part of a larger civil and voting rights continuum. Hilary was nominated only weeks before the hundred sixty-eighth anniversary of the Seneca Falls Convention of 1848. That Convention was the first gathering on this continent aimed at gaining social, civil, and moral rights for women.

Surprisingly, the convention's formidable leaders—Susan B. Anthony, Elizabeth Cady Stanton, and Lucretia Mott—debated fiercely whether the suffrage resolution should be included in their closing document. Many, including Lucretia Mott, urged removing it. However, Frederick Douglass, who also attended, argued eloquently for it. The suffrage resolution was retained.

States began passing laws allowing women to vote. The constitutional amendment, however, took seventy-two more years. Susan B. Anthony and Elizabeth Cady Stanton, who drafted the amendment, first introduced it unsuccessfully in 1878. In 1916, suffragist Alice Paul, a determined Quaker suffused with teachings of equality and non-violence, and her well-connected women friends began a campaign of non-violent civil disobedience in Washington to force the issue on President Wilson and a reluctant Democratic party.

Over the next three years, they were hit by crowds, abused by the police, jailed, beaten to unconsciousness, and force-fed during their hunger strikes. The news of their treatment struck the conscience of the nation. In 1919, after being called into special session to address the issue, Congress passed the amendment and submitted it to the states for ratification. It became law within a year.

In exercising the right to vote, we make it real. We learn by example and then by doing about the empowerment of debating, of disagreeing, of making our choice, of casting our ballot, of accepting the result, even when we lose. In 1920, my mother's mother was already voting age. She voted until the end of her life, always cancelling her husband's vote. As I sat on my grandparent's porch as a child listening to the adults talk politics, I inhaled my responsibility to participate in elections.

My mother voted as soon as she was old enough. She told her mother she was going to vote for Norman Thomas, a pacifist socialist who ran for president six times. Her mother responded: "That's fine, Louise. Let's just not tell your father." When Mother was seventy-one, she and her friends, wearing suffragist white, marched in the parade down DC's Constitution Avenue, celebrating the sixtieth anniversary of women's suffrage.

I was old enough to vote 1956. However, we were living in the District of Columbia and DC residents didn't have the right to vote—wouldn't for another five years. Instead, I pushed a baby carriage around Dupont Circle with an Adlai Stevenson bumper sticker on it—as near to voting as I could get that year.

In 1957, we moved across the river to Virginia. I was determined to vote and went to register. Virginia was in the middle of massive resistance—the effort to obstruct the effects of *Brown vs. the Board of Education*. Registration requirements had been changed to inhibit Negros from becoming voters.

I was handed a blank piece of paper. The registrar instructed me to provide the necessary information. She didn't tell me what the information was. I knew what to write because I had known to ask a voting official, a family friend, ahead of time. The blank-paper practice was soon stopped. (So was the poll tax.) But my *registration* from that day is still valid; all I have had to do as we moved around Fairfax County was change my address.

Our daughter and her brothers started working elections when they were kids. A neighbor, a solid Democrat, enlisted them to pass out flyers. "Inculcate them early," was her motto. As an adult, Gay shifted political gears. She was still active, but she switched parties (not literally, we don't register by parties in Virginia). When I heard she'd voted for Oliver North for the US Senate, I almost stopped asking her to dinner. She has since done a one-eighty, supporting progressive candidates, handing out flyers, and hosting phone banks.

In 2012, my granddaughter began voting. She texted to tell me that she had voted against the North Carolina constitutional amendment banning gay marriage. I welcomed her to the legion of those of us who lose while voting for what we believe is right.

Until five years ago, I had been the chief election officer of my precinct in northern Virginia for thirty years. We election officers worked together across parties, taking pride in a fair and honest vote. With our role came a ringside seat to the diversity of proud citizens exercising their right: first-time voters; new Americans; wouldn't-miss-it reliables; parents modeling responsible citizenship.

I keep seeing a particular voter in my mind's eye: Small, stooped, with bright eyes shining out from a crinkled tobacco-leaf face, she was wearing her Sunday-go-meeting—well, Tuesday-go-to-vote—dress and hat. Leaning on her grandson, she moved slowly across the room. She stated her name for the election officer then entered the booth to cast her ballot. As the chief election officer, I offered: "We could have brought the ballot to you in the car."

"No, thank you, Ma'am. I come to vote under my own steam," she said with a satisfied smile. Still supported by her grandson, and proudly wearing her "I Voted" sticker, she walked out just as slowly as she had walked in. This determined elderly black lady epitomized the dignified majesty of voting at the heart of our elective democracy.

We weren't given the right to vote—or to run for office. We stand on the shoulders of the many uppity women and men. In 2016, whether you liked her or not, voted for her or not, Hillary Clinton took a step for our daughters, granddaughters, and great-granddaughters—and for our sons, grandsons, and great grandsons. An uppity woman was the US presidential candidate of a major political party. Even though she lost, others will follow. The "pink wave" of women running for all levels of office in 2018 is setting a record.

'Tain't "uppity" anymore.

Yellow Dust

"The yellow dust of China gets in your eyes," my mother always said. I left China when I was small; in a way it never left me. I feel a sense of recognition among Chinese, Asians in general, that they don't necessarily feel with me. At our house, we eat off of Qing Dynasty plates. Small pieces of Chinese art, including a hand-painted scroll with my *mingzi* (name) in Chinese characters on it—a childhood gift—hang by our bed. The camel-train rug by my desk, a carved stool from my childhood under the glass coffee table—each is a piece, but only a piece, of me.

For years, due to post-World War II politics and the lack of diplomatic recognition and tension between the People's Republic of China and the United States, the nearest we could get to China was Hong Kong. Once diplomatic relations were established in 1979, the lure to go back was an increasingly curious niggle. But we didn't get back—not until 1994.

Our first trip was to Shanghai. Dan had lived there until he was eleven; the city was truly his hometown. More tied to place than I am, he ached to return. The timing was right. I had a working trip to the region; one ticket across the Pacific was paid for. I could take a week's leave to go there with Dan. Friends assigned to the American Consulate General in Shanghai invited us to stay with them.

We had another reason to go, beyond simply returning. Dan's father, head of the economics department at St. John's University, had completed his doctoral dissertation on the 1920s labor movement in Shanghai (the beginning of the communist party). He hadn't been able to get it to the University of Michigan before he was interned in a Japanese prison camp in 1943. Rather than take it into the camp and risk having it confiscated, he buried it, wrapped in oilskin, somewhere under their house. He was never able to return and retrieve it. Our friends in the consulate had connections. If ever there were a chance to find the dissertation, this was it.

Dan and I—plus his brother Don, who joined us when he heard what we were up to—were on a filial mission the Chinese understood and respected. The university, no longer St. John's but rather the East China Institute of Political Science and Law, welcomed us. They gave us a tour of the campus. The chapel where Dan, at six, had first sung in a choir was no longer there. The rest he recognized. They took us to the Sullivans' house, which looked the same, but had been converted into a clinic. The brothers roamed their old rooms.

Our university guide had floorboards in the front hall pried up and found a ladder so that we could go down. With the clinic staff

333

watching, we explored underneath the house. We knew it was hidden safely, we just didn't know where. Dan and Don dug here, tapped there, and poked elsewhere. The search was futile. We thanked our hosts profusely and left. It wasn't until we mulled things over again on the way out of Shanghai that we realized we had been looking in the wrong place: It was probably bricked into the back wall of the house. There was no going back.

In a profound sense, Dan and Don were home again. As we drove around the city, Dan could still name the streets from his childhood solo travels. He always knew what would be next: "…when we turn left at the next intersection, on our right will be …" It was always there. He stores maps in his head.

A group of their fathers' students, by then elderly and well established in their fields—some of them leading academics—hosted a dinner to honor their old professor's children. We also found Dan's aunt and uncle's church, which was still a worshiping congregation. A few of the elder congregants fondly remembered their former pastor, "Brother Anderson." We talked our way into the former Shanghai American School on what had been Avenue Petain in the French Concession. It's now an off-limits military communications facility. Even so, we were allowed in and escorted to visit Dan's classrooms.

With free enterprise resurfacing, street markets were selling all sorts of things were being sold. Among the mounds of Mao's *Little Red Book* and chipped ceramics, we spotted a tourist map of Shanghai, printed in the early '30s, with the street names in English, as Dan knew them. Framed, it hangs on our bedroom wall.

All together, it was an extremely satisfying trip.

Our last trip, over a decade ago, took us on a small group guided tour that started in Beijing and then went out to the Great Wall, over to Xian and the terracotta warriors and then on to Chongqing (Chungking, as my father knew it during the war). We also went on a tourist ship down the Yangzi—the trip where I got that pig-sticker cane, when the dam was about to be completed. We cruised through the gorges, past trails cut high in the cliffs for the coolies as they hauled boats up the river. We glimpsed old towns and perched pagodas and saw vertical fields that had been farmed for generations as well as markers for where the water would rise. The scene stood under the shadow of new high-rise cities that were housing people displaced by the rising river. At the end of the gorges, we stopped to see the bulk of the dam that was already completed and admire the model of the complete hydraulic system it housed.

I wondered what my father would have thought of the dam. During World War II, because his Chinese was good and he was a scientist, he had traveled with a US geological survey team behind the Japanese lines down this river. They were looking for the best site for a dam to be built after the war—a dam that would control the disastrous downstream floods, divert water to drought-stricken Shandong, and provide electricity to a huge section of the country. Less thought, apparently, was given to the silt buildup behind the dam and other potential ecological difficulties. How it will all play out is still unknown.

We sailed on down the river to Shanghai and flew out of China for what was no doubt the last time.

Altogether we returned to our shared "homeland" three times. For me, however, the middle trip, in 1999, short as it was, remains the highlight. We had been in the Philippines for the last of the exhibitions I had worked on for the Philippine Centennial. Dear friends were living in Mongolia, where the husband was the American ambassador. It was a country we had never thought of visiting. Their invitation was too good of an opportunity to miss.

We were supposed to go in through Beijing, taking the embassy's liquor order for the Fourth of July reception in on the train with us. The United States had just bombed the Chinese embassy in Belgrade—not an opportune time to be in Beijing, even briefly. We flew to Ulan Bator, Mongolia's capital, from Korea, instead.

For two weeks we strolled around Ulan Bator and drove around the country—out beyond Gengis Khan's birthplace, across the grasslands inhabited by nomadic herdsmen. Then we flew to the Gobi desert, staying in a *ger* and exploring sand dunes, finding odd bits of dinosaur bones. Our drive back to Ulan Bator was in the pitch dark and driving rain. We left the city by train.

Before we evacuated from China in 1940, Dad had promised that our next trip back to the States would start on the Trans-Siberian Railway. That "next" trip never happened. This train, a southern extension of the Trans-Siberian, came from Russia, went across Mongolia, picked up passengers in Ulan Bator, and terminated in Beijing—for us, a thirty-two–hour trip starting one morning and arriving at nearly noon the next day. It was as near as I would get to Dad's promise.

The tracks in China and those across Mongolia to Russia are different gauges, one wider than the other. About midnight, before we left Mongolia to enter China (at the Outer Mongolia border), the train pulled into a long, brightly lit shed. In succession, each car was disconnected, put on a lift and jacked up so that one set of wheels could be rolled out and another rolled in. After the wheels were switched, the car was lowered and reconnected to the rest.

That finished, the train steamed into China, stopping at another station, where immigration officials boarded. The customs officer looked at Dan's passport: born in China. Then mine: born in China.

He looked at us again and began speaking, not in the halting English he had begun with, but in Chinese. I didn't know the words he was using, but I *understood* what he was asking. The meaning was clear. As I answered his questions, out of my mouth came complete Chinese sentences, a child's sentences, but sentences nonetheless: "*Shao haizi* (small child)," I said, letting him know how young I had been when I was last there. I went on to explain that I was a Shandong person and Dan was a Shanghai person.

He smiled and bowed, welcoming these venerable white-haired (at least my hair was white, Dan's was barely salt-and-pepper) people to their childhood home. The word must have spread. Never mind that relations between our two countries were severely strained. Every official on the train stopped by to greet the returning elders.

The next morning we rolled steadily toward Beijing, playing tag with stretches of the Great Wall, traveling through the North China countryside. The colors were right: dull grays, dusty greens. The gray-tiled villages had more trucks than I remembered. There were still a few of the old wooden carts with resounding squeals—I could see them through the window and hear them in my mind. The roads were lined with tall poplars. The fields were *gaoliang* and wheat, as northern Chinese fields should be. It was the China of my memory. I had been welcomed and "placed" where I began.

Although my father regretted not returning to Jinan to complete what was, for him, unfinished business, I don't need to go back. The train ride through "my" countryside was enough.

If I make another long trip across the Pacific, it will be to Southeast Asia, where my adult- rather than child-self, has been invested. That is where I have unfinished business: I need one more visit with Filipino friends, the children of our "family" who now have near-grown children of their own. I need to roam the streets of Singapore and look for the few cottage industries that may still be there. I would like to visit the Lab School in Aceh, for a few days.

For me, returning to Jinan is no longer necessary. That place lives forever—in my memory, my stomach, and my heart. In my mother's yellow dust.

Afterward

I had one more place to visit. Only I didn't know it.

As this book was nearing completion—with place, time, memory, mobility, and meaning rattling around full tilt in my mind—Dan and I were driving from California to Virginia with Charley. Part way across, we realized that one route to our next destination took us through Springfield, Missouri.

Springfield: where my grandparents' house, the house of my childhood, was, on Market Street.

Suddenly, I had to *see* it, to know it still existed.

The white, two-storied house was clear in my mind: A porch with swings and rocking chairs completely crossed the front. Downstairs and up, a long hall ran from front to back, two high-ceilinged rooms on each side. The only running water—cold, from a pump on the back porch—was at the kitchen sink. Our Saturday night baths were in a tin tub filled with water heated on the stove. Food chilled in an icebox. The iceman chipped bits of ice for us to suck on hot summer mornings. At night, we squatted over chamber pots. Mostly, we used the three-holer outhouse. (The nearly-as-big-as-me white rooster from next door chased me into it, twice, one morning.) Sometimes I carried in wood for the living room stove. The yard, with an arbor of concord grapes that attracted bees, and Granddad's huge vegetable garden surrounded the house. Alley cats and chickens lived in the barn where he parked the car.

The house dominated that single "Ellis family" block of Market Street.

We set that day's course so we would travel from Texas, across Oklahoma, into Missouri—I-40 to I-44—and reached the city limits in the late afternoon. I remembered Market Street and roughly where the house had been, but not the house number. We found Fassnight Park, with its big swimming pool, which we used to walk to on summer afternoons. Once Charley drove into the park, without even having to think, I was oriented: "Take that way out...now right…now left…. This is the block…"

Yes.

There it was: 1075 South Market. A classic, foursquare farmhouse built in 1884 that had originally belonged to my great-grandparents Ellis.

The house glistened white with crisp black shutters. A columned brick porch had replaced the wooden one. It was barely wider than the front door—no sitting there to tell stories and talk politics.

The front walk, fragmented by roots of the over-arching maple, was unchanged. "I remember going up that walk holding Great Granddaddy Park's hand," Jerry commented when he saw the picture. That was 1961, the last time we were there; Jerry was five. When my youngest sister (a baby in that house) saw the pictures, which I emailed to Australia, she too remembered that walk.

A carport off what had been the back porch, and a driveway to the street, had been added. No more driving in down the alley with the day lilies (next-door-Gretchen and I smoked the dry stalks in late Julys). The barn and out buildings had no doubt been demolished, although we couldn't see out back. I imagined the steep kitchen steps, which I fell down one morning as I raced to breakfast, were still at the end of the hall upstairs.

One of the maple trees Granddaddy nailed the fireworks to was a level stump in the lawn. The other, surely over a hundred years old, stood firmly upright, shading the yard. Granddaddy's garden had been turned into an overbearingly close red-brick house. No more corn or tomatoes or lilacs.

The "Ellis family block," where life had centered when I was an elementary-schooler, remained familiar but altered. Across the street and down a bit, what had been Uncle Charlie and Aunt Ruth's home with its Uncle Sam mailbox out front, had been turned into two-story apartments.

The other houses weren't much changed: The house Granddaddy Parks lost in the Depression was opposite the big farmhouse. Aunt Nancy and Uncle Pierce's place (across from Ruth and Charlie's at the far end of the block) had been fenced and labeled a bird sanctuary, its deep porch barely visible through a thicket of shrubs and saplings, Beyond the new red house, Uncle Hershel and Aunt Lucy's house was as small as when they built it. The Scharff's bungalow between Nancy and Pierce's and the big house (where Gretchen and Kathy's tree house had stood) was now home to a pleasant young grandfather, who, curious about strange folk taking pictures of the farmhouse, stopped to talk.

It was so *right* to be in this neighborhood—to see the house, as near a childhood American home as I have. Solid. Well kept. Clearly loved. *There, that's enough.*

We drove on.

The unchanged concrete front walk stays with me, as unforeseen, important details do. In its own binding-life-together way, it's comparable to my Chinese rug with the camel train and city wall. I walked up that walk from China and into a new American life at six. As a teenager, I dashed up it from Mamaroneck for summer vacations. I went up it after I flew alone from Burma, bound for college and adulthood. From Virginia, I brought my new husband up it to visit my grandparents. Coming back from Malaya and heading to Nigeria, I walked it again with my own family, turning it into a fragment of our five-year-old son's life.

Soon after that visit coming back from Malaya, Granddaddy died, and Grandmother moved to Mother and Daddy's. The house and its front walk left the family.

After half a century, countless miles, and many places, I walked up the walk again, knocked on the door and waited a bit as I breathed in just being there. When I got no answer, I walked away.

In the non-linear way life evolves, that walk links together many isolated fragments of my mobile life. In it and in that house, the "bones" of memory remain.

Acknowledgments

The fragments of each journey are built on the succession of those from whom we come, the partner who joins us, and those who follow. This is for my particular people with deep love and gratitude for their company along my way:

George Freeman and Harriet Preston Keller Winfield
Charles Wilson and Lida Love Ellis Parks
Gerald Freeman and Lida Louise Parks Winfield
Harriet Winfield Warfield, Nancy Winfield Cogan, Ted Winfield

Daniel Peyton Sullivan
Gerald Winfield Sullivan and Phillipa Vinten
Gay Beach Sullivan
Walter Hjelt Sullivan and Traci Hjelt Sullivan
Charles Parks Sullivan

Samuel Phillip Abrams
Rebecca Lipscomb Sullivan
Grace Bennett Sullivan

"Helping out" comes with the family territory: My siblings confirmed, corrected, or argued with the details of my memory. My children read and commented in light of their professional and personal experiences. An ace speller proofread parts of the manuscript, asking "Is this what you meant to say?" and best of all, partnered with me on the adventure of the book and of life.

My Wooster college roommate, Lee Collins, and I marked our seventy-fifth birthdays by taking a week's seminar together at the Iowa Writers Summer Workshop; ultimately we shared four such workshops over as many years. Those weeks of deep immersion in writing started some of these essays. Thanks to seminar leaders Hugh Ferrer, Carol Spindel, Jim McKean, and Tim Bascom for their thoughtful comments and encouragement. Special love to Lee for the idea, for the chance to be "roomies" again, and for being a willing, thoughtful reader.

Inspiration comes from many sources. The *Washington Post* articles by Candace Wheeler on Yarrow Mamout were published the summer of 2015. Melissa Block's story "The Legacy of the Mississippi Delta Chinese," was broadcast on NPR's Weekend Edition on March 18, 2017.

Melissa Chianta's skillful copyediting, and her knowing when to send it back and say, in effect, "not baked yet" were critically important. The mistakes, the mis-remembrances, the run-on sentences, the fragments of thought that have made their way through to the end are mine.

Without the faith of colleagues, who mentored and offered me a chance to do something worthwhile, the substance of this book would not have happened. My everlasting gratitude is owed to many, many people. I must thank Shirley Newhall, Evelyn Colbert, Irene Tinker, John Forbes, Mitzi Pickard, Lisa Laramee, and the entire Borromeo clan, Marisol and Joseling in particular. I also give a special tip of the hat to Susie Borromeo Milne, who became my Visayan- and Tagalog-language informant, and to Jerry Stryker, a Foreign Service elder who checked the Chinese spelling. Sharon Ewing and Kjirsten Johnson Blander generously donated sharp eyes and red pencils at critical junctures. Many people helped with fact-checking: Ellen Gregory; Ambassador Evan Ralph Garcia of the Philippines; and Marian Pastor Rocca.

A profound thanks goes to American taxpayers, who paid to send us where we went as their representatives, thus giving me tales to tell and ideas to share. I hope we earned our keep.

A special thank you to Dan, by name not just fleeting reference: friend, lover, father of our children, companion, teammate, enabler— your gentle huffles in the night signal that all is well. With this book published, you can stop asking: "How's it going?"

Above all, I must thank Susan Gardner both as a person and as my publisher.

Susan and I first met when I asked her to write a piece for the AAFSW newsletter I was editing, forty some-odd years ago. Our friendship deepened as the newsletter developed and circulated a survey of Foreign Service wives around the world, asking how much time at post wives invested in the business of the Foreign Service. Susan was one of the dedicated team that carried out that survey. We both moved on, then back again, picking up our threads of connection. Long friendships are a special gift.

My essays, articles, and "Grandmother" blog posts would have remained fragments if Susan had not seen the possibility of something whole and encouraged me onward, using her special gifts to help shape the manuscript Whether it is what she (or I) expected is a different matter. I offer my profound gratitude, therefore, to Susan, Devon Ross, and Red Mountain Press for their faith in this project and for giving it life. Without them we could not say: "There is a book."

Fragments From A Mobile Life is set in Garamond, named for the sixteenth century Parisian printer and engraver, Claude Garamond.